CANADIAN UNIVERSITIES
IN CHINA'S TRANSFORMATION

Canadian Universities in China's Transformation

An Untold Story

Edited by
RUTH HAYHOE, JULIA PAN,
AND QIANG ZHA

McGill-Queen's University Press
Montreal & Kingston · London · Chicago

© McGill-Queen's University Press 2016

ISBN 978-0-7735-4729-2 (cloth)
ISBN 978-0-7735-4730-8 (paper)
ISBN 978-0-7735-9918-5 (ePDF)
ISBN 978-0-7735-9919-2 (ePUB)

Legal deposit second quarter 2016
Bibliothèque nationale du Québec

Printed in Canada on acid-free paper that is 100% ancient forest free (100% post-consumer recycled), processed chlorine free

This book has been published with the help of a grant from the Canadian Federation for the Humanities and Social Sciences, through the Awards to Scholarly Publications Program, using funds provided by the Social Sciences and Humanities Research Council of Canada.

McGill-Queen's University Press acknowledges the support of the Canada Council for the Arts for our publishing program. We also acknowledge the financial support of the Government of Canada through the Canada Book Fund for our publishing activities.

Library and Archives Canada Cataloguing in Publication

Canadian universities in China's transformation: an untold story /
edited by Ruth Hayhoe, Julia Pan, and Qiang Zha.

Includes bibliographical references and index.
Issued in print and electronic formats.
ISBN 978-0-7735-4729-2 (cloth). – ISBN 978-0-7735-4730-8 (paper). – ISBN 978-0-7735-9918-5 (PDF). – ISBN 978-0-7735-9919-2 (ePUB)

1. Educational exchanges – Canada. 2. Educational exchanges – China. 3. Universities and colleges – Economic aspects – China. 4. Universities and colleges – Social aspects – China. 5. Canada – Relations – China. 6. China – Relations – Canada. 7. China–Economic conditions – 20th century. 8. China – Social conditions – 20th century. I. Hayhoe, Ruth, author, editor II. Pan, Julia Nai-Rong, 1955–, author, editor III. Zha, Qiang, 1965–, author, editor

LB2286.C3C35 2016   370.116'2   C2016-901410-X
                                  C2016-901411-8

This book was typeset by Marquis Interscript in 10.5/13 Baskerville.

Contents

Tables and Figures ix

Note on Chinese and Western Name Order xi

Abbreviations xiii

1 Transforming Canada-China Educational Cooperation: Significant Legacies and Future Challenges 3
Ruth Hayhoe, Julia Pan, and Qiang Zha

PART ONE THE POLITICAL AND SOCIO-CULTURAL CONTEXT OF CHANGE

2 Canada-China Relations and the Evolving Role of Universities: Toward Partnerships 2.0 35
Paul Evans

3 University Linkages Past and Future: As Seen from a Diplomatic Perspective 54
Fred Bild

PART TWO MANAGEMENT EDUCATION AND CHINA'S ECONOMIC TRANSFORMATION

4 Transforming Canada-China Educational Cooperation: Legacies and Future Challenges in Management Education 79
Rolf Mirus

5 The Impact of Cross-Cultural Experience on Academic
  Leadership from Individual and Process Perspectives   102
  Xi Youmin, Zhang Xiaojun, Zhang Xiaofeng, Ni Jie, and Li Huaizu

6 The Case Study Legacy of Ivey's Early Linkages in China   125
  Paul W. Beamish

PART THREE   COLLABORATION IN ENGINEERING
AND ENVIRONMENT

7 Canada-China Collaboration in Engineering Education
  and Its Societal Influences   141
  Li Chongan, Lü Shunjing, and Yao Ling

8 Impacts of Canada-China Environmental Research   167
  Jing M. Chen, Joseph Whitney, and Julia Pan

9 Society, Economy, and Environment: Minorities in the
  Collaboration between China and Canada   190
  Jan W. Walls

PART FOUR   EDUCATION AND EQUITY

10 The Educational Dimension of China's Transformation: From the
   Perspective of the Canada-China University Linkage Projects   211
   Qiang Zha and Ruth Hayhoe

11 Nurturing a Leadership Cohort for Chinese Faculties
   of Education   230
   Qiang Haiyan and Wang Jiayi

12 Sino-Canadian Legal Partnerships in Law and Education:
   Genesis, Groundwork, and Growth   254
   Guy Lefebvre, Marie-Claude Rigaud, and Elizabeth Steyn

13 Gender and Development in CIDA's Programs: A Reflection
   on the *Doing* of Feminist Collaboration   275
   Ping-chun Hsiung

14 Closing the Circle: Reflections on Past and Future Partnerships across the Disciplines   297
Ruth Hayhoe and Christy Hayhoe

References   311

Contributors   329

Index   339

Tables and Figures

TABLES

5.1 Results from the study of academic leadership change 112

7.1 Engineering university linkages and CCULP engineering projects 143

FIGURES

5.1 The research design for studying the influence of overseas experience on academic leadership 109

5.2 The process of academic leadership improvement 118

5.3a Improvement of academic leadership in the early stage of the CIDA program 122

5.3b Improvement of academic leadership in the later stage of the CIDA program 123

6.1 Approaches to foreign market entry 127

8.1 Distribution of three core sites (red) and two auxiliary sites (green) for the project entitled "Confronting Global Warming: Enhancing China's Capacity for Carbon Sequestration" 182

Note on Chinese and Western Name Order

Chinese name order puts the surname before given names, and we have preserved that order for all Chinese contributors to this volume who live in China. For those living in Canada, we have followed Western name order, putting the given name before the surname.

Abbreviations

AACSB	Association to Advance Collegiate Schools of Business
ABC	Agriculture Bank of China
AMI	Asian Management Institute
APFC	Asia Pacific Foundation of Canada
AUCC	Association of Universities and Colleges of Canada
BLOU	Bethune-Laval Oncology Unit
BNU	Beijing Normal University
BUAA	Beihang University of Aeronautics and Astronautics
CAE	Chinese Academy of Engineering
CAS	Chinese Academy of Sciences
CASS	Chinese Academy of Social Sciences
CCBC	Canada China Business Council
CCHEP	Canada-China Higher-Education Program
CCICED	China Council for International Cooperation on Environment and Development
CCLTTC	Canada-China Language Training and Testing Centre
CCMEP	Canada-China Management Education Program
CCP	Chinese Communist Party
CCUIPP	Canada-China University-Industry Partnership Program
CCULP	Canada-China University Linkage Program
CDGDC	China Academic Degrees and Graduate Education Development Centre
CEIBS	China Europe International Business School
CFDMAS	Canadian Federation of Deans of Management and Administrative Studies
CHSUBC	Centre for Human Settlements, University of British Columbia

CIDA	Canadian International Development Agency
CIN	Central Institute for Nationalities
CMCC	China Management Case-Sharing Centre
CNMESC	China National MBA Education Supervisory Committee
CPC	Communist Party of China
CS	carbon sequestration
CSC	China Scholarship Council
CTP	China Teaching Project
CUN	Central University for Nationalities
CUPL	China University of Political Science and Law
DEA	Department of External Affairs, later DFAIT, and still later DFATD
DFID	Department for International Development
DSS	Decision Support System
DST	decision support tool
DTM	digital terrain model
ECNU	East China Normal University
ECUPL	East China University of Political Science and Law
EMBA	executive MBA
EPGEP	Consolidation of the Management Training Project: Educational Policy Implementation and Gender Equity in Human-Resource Development, abbreviated as the Educational Policy and Gender Equity Program
ÉRI	UdeM's School of Industrial Relations
FRQSC	Fonds de recherche du Québec
FRSC	Fellow of the Royal Society of Canada
GAD	Gender and Development
GCIRC	International Consultative Research Group on Rapeseed
GFG	Grain for Green
GIS	Geographic Information System
GRASS	Geographical Resource Analysis Support System
GTP	Global Teaching Project
HEC	École des Hautes Études Commerciales de Montréal
HRD	Human Research Development
HAU	Huazhong Agricultural University
HUST	Huazhong University of Science and Technology
IA	integrated assessments
IBJ	Ivey Business Journal
ICBC	Industrial and Commercial Bank of China

ICDS	Institutional Cooperation and Development Support Division of CIDA
IDRC	International Development Research Centre
IGSNRR	Institute of Geographical Sciences and Natural Resources Research
ILEAD	Institute of Leadership & Education Advanced Development
INSGR	Institute of Geography (now the IGSNRR)
IP	Ivey Publishing
IR	investigative research
JCTDP	Joint Case Training Development Project
JV	Joint Ventures
LJU	Lanzhou Jiaotong University
LLM	Master of Laws
LRI	Lanzhou Railway Institute
LRT	light rail transit
LU	Laurentian University
MOE	Ministry of Education
MOFERT	Ministry of Foreign Economic Relations and Trade, now the Ministry of Commerce
MOFTEC	Chinese Ministry of Foreign Trade and Economic Cooperation
MOU	Memorandum of Understanding
MRPC	Mustard Research and Promotion Consortium
NAEA	National Academy of Education Administration
NBUMS	Norman Bethune University of Medical Sciences
NENU	Northeast Normal University
NFU	Nanjing Forestry University
NIES	National Institute of Education Science
NNU	Nanjing Normal University
NPC	National People's Congress
NSERC	Natural Sciences and Engineering Research Council
NWNU	Northwest Normal University
ODA	official development assistance
OECD	Organization for Economic Cooperation and Development
OISE	Ontario Institute for Studies in Education
PRC	People's Republic of China
QR	qualitative research
RBC	Royal Bank of Canada

RS	Remote Sensing
RU	Renmin University
SAWF	Shaanxi Association for Women and Family
SCNU	South China Normal University
SEdC	State Education Commission
SEMGIS I	Soil Erosion Management Geographical Information System
SEMGIS II	GIS-Based Erosion Management Outreach Program
SEU	Southeast University
SFU	Simon Fraser University
SHO	Sexual Harassment Office
SNU	Shaanxi Normal University
SOE	state-owned enterprise
SoM	School of Management
SPC	Supreme People's Court
SSHRC	Social Sciences and Humanities Research Council of Canada
SUES	Shanghai University of Engineering Science
SULCP	Special University Linkage Consolidation Program
SWIT	Southwest Institute of Technology
SWNU	Southwest Normal University
SWUST	Southwest University of Science and Technology
TUNS	Technical University of Nova Scotia
TYP	Transitional Year Program
U of A	University of Alberta
UBC	University of British Columbia
UdeM	Université de Montréal
UM	University of Manitoba
UNDP	United Nations Development Program
UNISA	University of South Africa
UQAM	Université du Québec à Montréal
USST	University of Shanghai for Science and Technology
USTB	University of Science and Technology Beijing
UT	University of Toronto
UTSC	University of Toronto Scarborough
UWO	University of Western Ontario, now Western University
WUST	Wuhan University of Science and Technology
Xiada	Xiamen University
XJTU	Xi'an Jiaotong University

CANADIAN UNIVERSITIES
IN CHINA'S TRANSFORMATION

1

Transforming Canada-China Educational Cooperation: Significant Legacies and Future Challenges

RUTH HAYHOE, JULIA PAN, AND QIANG ZHA

A MOMENT TO BE REMEMBERED

On 9 May 2014, a group of about 200 scholars, educators, community leaders, and government officials from both Canada and China gathered in the magnificent assembly hall of Tsinghua University's iconic main building in Beijing for the opening of a conference that had been in the planning for more than two years.[1] Present were leading figures from universities in Canada and China across nine major disciplines – agriculture, earth and ocean sciences, environmental science, medicine, engineering, management, law, education, and minority studies – together with senior representatives of China's Ministry of Education, the Canadian Embassy in Beijing, the Department of Foreign Affairs, Trade and Development Canada, and the Asia Pacific Foundation of Canada. The purpose of this gathering was to reflect on the legacy of Canadian development assistance for China's universities in the first two decades after the Cultural Revolution, and the modality of university linkages that had been intended to foster a multiplication of contacts at the thinking level. How far had they contributed to China's remarkable transformation, and what had been the impact on the development of Canadian universities? What lessons could be drawn for the very different circumstances of collaboration in the twenty-first century?

Two days of dynamic keynote presentations, with lively plenary debate and discussion, were complemented by seven concurrent sessions focusing on contemporary collaboration between scholars in China and Canada. The conference ended in a memorable reception hosted by

Ambassador Guy St. Jacques in his official residence at the Canadian Embassy.[2] This volume, which includes twelve of the keynote lectures as chapters, is an effort to share with readers in Canada and China the rich deliberations and profound insights that gave this conference national significance.[3] In this opening chapter, we set the stage by giving an overview of the research project that gave birth to the conference and the project's preliminary findings.

BACKGROUND TO THE STUDY

On the occasion of the fortieth anniversary of the restoration of Canada-China diplomatic relations in 2010, we were struck by a sense that Canadian universities had played a key role in the early years of China's opening up to the world, but were now somewhat lagging behind their counterparts in countries such as the USA, UK, Australia, and various European nations. With a typical Canadian tendency to self-effacement, the major programs of collaboration with universities in China had been largely forgotten, and it seemed that no one had made an effort to investigate their long-term contributions. We decided to apply to the Social Sciences and Humanities Research Council of Canada (SSHRC) for a modest grant that would enable us to interview key participants in these projects in both Canada and China, and ask about their experiences and their assessments of the long-term outcomes of the projects. We also collected as many relevant documents as we could find.

Three major national-level programs were examined in the broader context of a period of development collaboration between Canada and China that was initiated under the terms of the General Agreement on Development Cooperation, signed by the two countries in 1983.[4] The Canada-China Management Education Program (CCMEP) linked eight major national universities on both sides, expanding to draw in other universities into a series of mini-networks in China and Canada. This program operated from 1983 to 1996, funded with Can$39.7 million from the Canadian International Development Agency (CIDA) (Canadian International Development Agency 1992, 8; 1995, 9). The Canada-China University Linkage Program (CCULP) included a wide range of universities, both national and local, in both countries. It embraced projects in medicine, nursing, agriculture, engineering, urban infrastructure, environment, education, and minority cultures, and ran from 1988 to 1995, funded with Can$19 million from CIDA (Canadian International Development Agency 1995a, 10). The Special University Linkage

Consolidation Program (SULCP) provided ongoing funding for the consolidation of eleven CCULP projects, with a budget of Can$10 million, and ran from 1996 to 2001 (Tunney 2001, 4).

In addition to these three programs, which attracted $68.7 million in total, there was a wide range of other projects in human-resource development involving diverse partners, including community colleges, businesses, and a range of non-governmental organizations (O'Brien 2000). A total of about $250 million was expended by CIDA on higher education between 1981 and 2001 (Jackson 2003, 43). After the Tiananmen tragedy of 1989, there was a period of reconsideration in the relationship, and a new country development program was adopted in 1994, which sought to integrate collaboration around three broad areas: economic cooperation; environmental sustainability; and human rights, democratic development, and good governance. Universities played a key role in all these areas.[5]

A unique aspect of the first decade of these programs was the fact that Canada was the only Western country to engage with Chinese universities in its development aid at a major programmatic level at that time.[6] The other significant actor was the World Bank, which was persuaded by the Chinese to abandon its usual focus on basic education in the loans it offered, and to provide eleven major loans to Chinese universities that added up to over US$1.1 billion (Hayhoe 1989, 162). This funding was largely targeted at rebuilding China's teaching and research infrastructure, with a small percentage given to support university scholars in study abroad, as well as visiting experts from the Organization for Economic Cooperation and Development (OECD) countries. Given that CIDA focused on human-resources development, and described its goal as "the multiplication of contacts at the thinking level," these two approaches were complementary to each other (O'Brien 2000, 41).

Between July 2011 and the autumn of 2012, we carried out about sixty-five interviews at universities in different regions of Canada and China. It soon became evident that there was considerable interest in having the stories of these programs told. However, it was also clear that we were not competent to assess outcomes across such a diverse range of knowledge areas. Thus the necessity of bringing leading figures in each discipline to our Tsinghua conference – and how honoured we were that they came! Most of these senior scholars consented not only to a keynote presentation, but also to the preparation of a chapter for this volume. For our part, we provided such background literature on the programs as we could find, mounting this information on the conference website.[7]

We also developed a set of key research questions and theoretical perspectives that could help to frame their work.

FRAMING THE RESEARCH QUESTIONS

We have drawn upon the higher-education literature in identifying frameworks for interpreting the preliminary research findings presented in this chapter. We had no intention, however, of imposing these frameworks on the authors in this volume, who represent diverse disciplinary fields. We simply asked them to keep in mind the four broad research questions, which are elaborated at the end of this section.

Dependency theory has had a longstanding influence in the higher education research literature due to its focus on understanding and seeking to mitigate the inequitable development between centres and peripheries in terms of both higher institution and nation. This conceptual framework emerged from critical reflection on dilemmas of postcolonial and other developing societies in the 1960s and 1970s, as they struggled to establish themselves in the polarized context of the Cold War, and saw universities as crucially important for the formation of capable leaders and for research that could strengthen the nation. Among many others, Philip Altbach (2006) led the way in research that explored the factors that kept universities in developing nations in a peripheral position: "brain drain" problems, inadequate libraries, scarcity of research funding, issues of language, and access to publication networks. In spite of these difficulties and barriers, effective strategies were identified and exemplified in the successful development of universities in some developing contexts.

With the end of the Cold War, things began to change. Universities in East Asia have attracted attention for the ways in which they broke out of a dependent mode fairly early (Altbach and Selvaratnam 1989) and asserted new patterns in terms of the interaction between basic and applied knowledge and the role of the "development state" (Cummings 2010). Mainland China was a relative latecomer in this movement, with Japan, Korea, and Taiwan having moved forward much earlier. Probably few scholars could have anticipated China's rapid and dramatic economic rise; our question is, how far have the university linkage partnerships nurtured by CIDA contributed to this, in the view of those who participated in them? The fact that these partnerships spanned a crucial period of global change, before and after the end of the Cold War in 1991, may also be significant.

The second body of theory that is relevant to this study is that of human capital and the knowledge economy. The end of the Cold War spawned a new era of economic globalization, including forms of economic integration undreamt of in the Cold War period. This has led to an intense focus on ways in which countries around the world can benefit from participation in an increasingly globalized world system. A new importance has been placed on universities as knowledge institutions, since they are seen as crucial to national success in competing in the global knowledge economy. As early as 1993, China led the way in setting forward goals for its top universities to strive for world-class standing in research and innovation, and in providing resources under the aegis of Projects 21/1 and 98/5 (Zha 2011b). Many other nations developed parallel projects in the years that followed. By the early twenty-first century, global ranking systems for universities were developed, with Shanghai and London leading the way, and many nations around the world joining the competition (Marginson and Wende 2007).

Clearly the literature on the global knowledge economy is foundational to this volume, yet we wish also to balance it with consideration from a third area of literature, that of the global knowledge society, and criteria that go beyond economic indicators of success in evaluating university linkages. In his *Theory of Communicative Action*, Juergen Habermas sketched out the contours of a "jagged profile of modernity" dominated by instrumental technical rationality, and called for the redemption of modernity through the revitalization of the cultural life-world in a conscious rationalization of the moral-practical and aesthetic practical spheres (Habermas 1984, 1987). This idea was extended to dialogue across civilizations in the suggestion that Chinese scholars might respond to the Western metaphor of redemption with a call for the humanization of modernity, rooted in Confucian philosophical sensibilities (Hayhoe 2000). Fruitful understanding could then be nurtured through university partnerships that nested scientific technical collaboration in a jointly developed moral and cultural framework.

This volume thus also addresses the question of how university linkages have facilitated mutual learning around such major issues for humanity as the environment, health, social cohesion, cultural vitality, and spiritual fulfillment. Equity has further been a persistent theme in the design of collaborative projects, including gender equity, the participation of minorities, representative geographical participation, and environmental justice. Recent literature introducing the concept of "path dependence" suggests strong tendencies for the persistence of diverse institutional patterns, rooted in distinctive histories and civilizations, which may resist the sweeping pressures for homogenization coming from economic globalization (Krucken 2003). We are thus interested in some of the unique configurations that have emerged from this interaction between Chinese and Canadian universities.

A fourth body of theory that is relevant to this volume is derived from the literature on university partnerships across nations and regions that has been built up over many years, as projects of collaboration have been monitored and evaluated (King 1990, 2009). This literature yields a practical framework of evaluation that goes beyond issues of short-term effectiveness in knowledge transfer and application, and looks at conditions that lead to longer-term sustainable collaboration, capable of drawing in other social institutions on both sides in efforts to address major issues of human well-being. King (2009) stresses the importance of adequate time periods in linkages supporting African universities and emphasizes the importance of an enabling environment that can sustain fundamental research, as opposed to short-term problem-solving projects.

This point was born out in an evaluation of the CIDA-supported university linkages carried out in 2001, which identified the following factors as crucial to their success: ten to fifteen years of organized cooperation; high levels of partnership; trust and respect; continuity of leadership and effective leadership succession; the creation of an organizational vehicle through which skills or knowledge were applied or extended; and close service ties to local and provincial governments (Jackson et al. 2003). Another study commissioned by CIDA provided an overview of the history of CIDA's China involvement, and noted how the assessment of the first phase of linkages had culminated in a re-thinking, following the setback of the 1989 Tiananmen events. It concluded that the focus on human resources that shaped the linkages had proven its value, and that the program should go forward in ways that fit with the three main foci adopted in CIDA's 1994 China Country Development Policy Framework: supporting economic linkages and partnerships; promoting environmentally sustainable development in China; and increasing China's capacity to improve governance, respect human rights, and foster democratic development (Wilson 2001).

We thus asked the authors of each chapter to reflect on the long-term consequences and contributions of the linkages they examined in highly diverse knowledge areas in relation to four key questions. Firstly, in what ways did universities, acting in partnership, contribute to China's economic revitalization and rapid transformation? Secondly, how far did university partnerships foster the spawning of new ideas that would address crucial issues of humane and democratic governance, social justice, and environmental sustainability arising in the train of rapid economic and technological change? Thirdly, what organizational or contextual features of the linkages were important in enabling them to be effective and what serious hindrances arose? Fourthly, what lessons for current and future collaboration between Canadian and Chinese universities may be drawn from past experience?

RESEARCH METHODOLOGY

The purpose of our study was to build a comprehensive and multifaceted understanding of the outcomes of past Canada-China university linkages as a basis for identifying present synergies and future possibilities. We began with a small-scale research project supported by SSHRC, as noted earlier, which developed into a larger collaborative project in which we invited senior scholars involved in the leadership of projects across many disciplines to prepare chapters for this volume. Each determined his or her own research methods, as appropriate to the themes being dealt with. Some chapters address the broader context of the evolution of Canada-China diplomatic relations, while many take up specific knowledge areas, drawing on personal experience, documentation, and survey or interview material. With chapters from scholars in both countries, the reader can see how university linkages were perceived and experienced from each side.

The main source of information for the preliminary analysis presented in this introductory chapter comes from open-ended interviews with about sixty-five participants of past projects in both China and Canada, including academics, institutional leaders, government officials, and those involved in the facilitation of projects.[8] We hope this will prepare the reader for the more systematic, focused, and in-depth analyses that appear in subsequent chapters. Our interviews gave some insights into factors that may have contributed in significant ways to China's economic transformation, though we are not able to provide measurable indicators of this relationship. We also obtained interesting insights into the ways in which collaboration spawned new thinking in relation to important issues of equity, justice, and sustainability. We further received some sense of the kinds of synergy that made it possible for some projects to blossom into forms of collaboration that have modelled a genuine mutuality between universities on both sides, as well as overflowing into the wider society.

We have divided our analysis of the interview data into three sections, following the chronological development of the linkages and projects. First, we look at interview findings from those involved in management education, since the CCMEP began earliest and enjoyed the largest budget over its two phases of operation.9 Next, we turn to a wide array of linkages organized under the CCULP and SULCP, running from 1988 to 2001, and covering the areas of education, engineering, medicine, and agriculture. Finally, we discuss two major culminating projects arising out of the re-thinking of the early 1990s in the areas of environment and good governance. Perspectives from interviewees in China are presented first, followed by views expressed by Canadian partners and participants, whom we interviewed subsequent to the interviews in China. It was not always possible to match partners on each side of specific projects, but we tried to listen carefully and make such connections when possible.

CCMEP AND MANAGEMENT EDUCATION

Generally speaking, we encountered great warmth and enthusiasm as we sat down with scholars in various Chinese universities and went through our interview questions. Most spoke about how this program had been an opportunity for institution building through a sustained relationship with a Canadian university, where faculty were given training opportunities, new courses were developed, collaborative research was initiated, and new educational models were encountered – from pedagogical reforms in the classroom to ideas about university management, which affected governmental styles of management through their graduates.

We begin with some views from the officials who put the whole relationship in context, and then go on to report views from scholars in two of the key universities on the Chinese side of the network. Management was organized as a large-scale network project in two phases, the first beginning in 1983, the same year as the signing of the General Agreement on Development Cooperation between Canada and China. Three senior education officials from China's Ministry of Education (MOE), two already retired, gave retrospective views on this. They noted the strong consensus on the Chinese side that management education was a matter of crucial need, with 300,000 enterprises operating in conditions of an increasingly market-oriented economy, and no one capable of training their managers. Academics in the field were largely engineers or Marxist economists who had been trained under Soviet patterns of macro-economic planning and had no relevant teaching material nor the capability to deal with the rapidly changing circumstances in China's economic environment.

In this situation, the MOE saw the importance of giving high priority to management education. One of the vice ministers took responsibility for selecting eight leading Chinese universities to enter into partnership with corresponding universities in Canada; not surprisingly, there was much jockeying over the negotiation of these partnerships. After the lead partnerships were established, each Chinese and each Canadian university later chose two additional allied institutions to join forces with, resulting in eight mini-networks, with five or six institutions in each. The original purpose of the program was to develop courses to train managers in China by first sending teachers to obtain their MBAs in Canada, and then having these teachers start new MBA programs upon their return. In retrospect, they realized that sending young scholars for MBAs in Canada was not an appropriate way of preparing academic staff to develop such programs. The program's strategy therefore changed to sending experienced faculty members to engage in research and course development abroad. The key achievement, by 1988, was the unveiling of China's very first MBA programs in five of the eight partner universities. This involved the development of a complete set of Chinese-language course materials, the designing of case-study methods of research using Chinese as well as Canadian cases, and the formation of a new cadre of young faculty.

The officials we interviewed commented on a number of aspects of this long-lasting program. One was the scale – they noted that they had approached both Australian and American development organizations for assistance at that early period, but the Americans replied that it was not possible for them to help, and the Australians were only able to offer a set of support activities with a very low budget. By comparison, they felt that Canada was a kind of "saviour" to China in this critical period of its economic development. They also noted how cordial and collaborative the relationships with Canadian officials in CIDA and other government offices were. While other countries looked down on them, they felt that Canadians were open and helpful, as well as being respectful. There was no political colour to their negotiations with Canada, they noted; rather, everything was dealt with in a practical way.

Scholars at Tsinghua and Xiamen, two of the five universities that were core partners and launched early MBA programs, gave us their perspectives on the CCMEP project. A Tsinghua scholar noted the desperate need for a scientific approach to management at the time. He described how engineering universities such as Tsinghua and Shanghai Jiaotong saw this need most clearly, since most of the managers of enterprises had been trained as engineers, but had no idea how to apply that training to management. This Tsinghua scholar was one of the first to go to the University of Western Ontario (UWO). During his year in Canada, he felt that he learned a kind of thinking and a knowledge structure that were appropriate for the establishment of Tsinghua's MBA program. He was involved in developing case studies at UWO's Ivey School of Business, and later collaborated with Ivey professors in Beijing to create Chinese cases that are now used to train people from all parts of China at Tsinghua. Paul Beamish provides more information on this collaboration in chapter 6.

A second Tsinghua scholar noted that over thirty members of Tsinghua University's School of Economics and Management were trained in Canada, and since Tsinghua was an MBA leader in China, its influence was widespread. He compared his experience of cooperation with a major American university, and noted how the fact that CCMEP was negotiated at the national level meant that it led to collaboration across the country, and was not limited to the two universities. He also emphasized the need for China to rethink its model of development in ways that would take the environment more seriously into account. His vision was of a move away from focusing on megacities, steel, and cars, and toward an approach that would connect urban people to rural areas. He viewed research on this kind of issue as only possible within the spacious time frame modelled by this type of long-term cooperation with Canada.

Xiamen University (Xiada) on China's southeast coast was paired with Dalhousie University in Halifax. Our interviews with two scholars at Xiada gave us another angle on the impact of the CIDA-supported management education project. Xiada also saw itself as a pioneer in developing an early MBA, recruiting students beginning in 1988 to a jointly developed Chinese-Canadian program. Fully half of the fifty faculty members at Xiada's Management College have spent time in Canada, with both the dean of the college and one of the university vice-presidents being returnees. Most recently, the dean led a group from Xiada to a conference on the development and use of case studies at Concordia University in Montreal, with participation from the US, the UK, France, and Hong Kong. Many of the Chinese cases presented at this conference had been developed cooperatively with Dalhousie. The other area of great importance developed through this project was public administration, considering that a complete change in perspective was being demanded by the market economy, and there was great need for a totally different approach to educating public servants.

The other scholar interviewed in Xiamen gave insights into the impact of this partnership on accounting and auditing standards at the national level in China, a crucial area in terms of China's capacity to participate in global business and financial transactions. This scholar got an MBA from Dalhousie and a PhD from Xiada, rising to head the Department of Accounting and then serving as dean of Xiada's Management College. He subsequently set up one of China's largest accounting firms. As a result of his leadership in these areas, he was appointed vice-president of the China National Accounting Institute in Xiamen. The institute was established in 2003 as one of three national institutions responsible for setting and implementing accounting and auditing standards for the nation, the other two being in Beijing and Shanghai. At the Xiamen Institute, 30,000 masters of professional accounting students from all parts of the country are trained every year.

This scholar is also a member of a small and highly influential committee for national auditing standards, and serves as adviser for a parallel committee on national accounting standards. He noted that his participation in the Xiada-Dalhousie partnership in the early 1980s was fundamental to his personal career as well as to crucially important national developments in accounting and auditing. He expressed a strong interest in cooperating with Canada to launch similar projects of development through partnerships with universities in other developing countries. His institute is already heavily engaged in support projects for underdeveloped hinterland regions in China, and he sees the possibility of extending this kind of work to the international arena.

The feedback from these scholars at Tsinghua and Xiamen Universities focused on benefits to the university and contributions to the nation at a time of rapid and dramatic change. There were also downsides, however, with the most serious resulting from the events of June 1989, and the strained relations between Canada and China in the subsequent years. The Tsinghua professors noted that ten of the eleven young scholars sent to Canada before 1989 for MBA degrees stayed permanently in Canada, leaving a great sense of loss at Tsinghua. The Xiada professors noted similarly that the five doctoral students they sent to Dalhousie for one year of joint doctoral training also failed to return. Subsequently, arrangements were changed so that mature scholars went to Canada for shorter periods, with a smaller number ending up doing doctoral programs. The fact that CCMEP began earlier than CCULP meant that it was more severely affected by the problem of brain drain.

At the national level, MOE officials we interviewed noted that this had been a very difficult time, and that some top government officials had suggested terminating all the aid projects with Canada, although the

MOE took the position that they must continue. One official noted how their relations with senior personnel at CIDA continued to be warm, despite problems and disagreements at the top level, and commented that he found CIDA officials to be sincere, hardworking, and genuinely committed to supporting Chinese universities.

A second downside noted by the Tsinghua and Xiada scholars was the somewhat dictatorial stance of some project leaders in Canadian universities, who controlled budgets tightly and did not always include their Chinese partners in financial planning and decision-making. An example given by one scholar at Xiada related to the publication of the Chinese-language textbooks created for China's first MBA. The Chinese side wanted to have a reputable national publisher, while the Canadian project director insisted on going with a low-status provincial publisher in order to get them done at a cheap price. They felt that he did not understand the Chinese environment, and this stance undermined the influence of their work in China.

On the Canadian side, we were able to interview the scholar who had the earliest involvement in organizing CCMEP, while serving as dean of management at York University, and who was later invited to set up a national CCMEP office in Montreal for the second phase of the project. He noted the remarkable speed with which the Chinese developed management programs, going from zero to over 300 MBA programs in operation by the end of the second program cycle. The diffusion of models throughout the higher education system was also remarkable. He further noted how many of the returnees quickly rose to positions of leadership as department heads, deans, and vice-presidents in their universities, and how many had a significant influence on management practices, a point that is emphasized in chapter 5 of this volume. As for the Canadian universities, he felt that this project was of crucial value to their management schools in learning how to manage international projects and develop lasting international linkages. Both of the schools with which he was associated went from being very Canada-focused to collaborating with universities in Thailand, Russia, Ukraine, and various African countries.

The other Canadians we interviewed were at the University of British Columbia (UBC)'s Sauder School, which was paired with the Management School of Shanghai Jiaotong University, and at the University of Alberta (U of A)'s School of Business, which was paired with Xi'an Jiaotong University (XJTU) under CCMEP. One of those at UBC had been a doctoral student from Shanghai who stayed to develop his career in Canada. He felt that the most crucial contribution for the Chinese side was in the area of faculty development. In the early years of the program, faculty development occurred mainly through course development and academic upgrading; now, in the aftermath of the program, there is considerable collaborative research between partnered universities, which facilitates Chinese faculty in getting articles published in international journals. Other Sauder faculty members spoke about UBC's International MBA that was operated from Shanghai Jiaotong, and the opportunities for UBC students to participate in four-week summer programs in Shanghai. Overall, however, there was a sense that more could have been done to build on the early collaboration in the years after the CIDA funding ended.

A senior management professor who led the Alberta Business School's collaboration with XJTU over a twenty-year period noted the significant number of leaders of highly prestigious management schools and transnational institutions, such as Xi'an Jiaotong-Liverpool University in Suzhou, who emerged from the project. The fact that XJTU was recognized as China's top management school for three years in a row, from 2005 to 2007, demonstrated how well its leaders had used their opportunities for collaboration in selecting areas of focus relevant to China's needs, as well as the quality of the collaboration they experienced with Alberta (Mirus and Wegner 2002; Mirus, chapter 4 of this volume).

It is now more than thirty years since a group of Canadian management deans visited China in 1982 and gained support from CIDA for the first phase of CCMEP. Most of the partnerships were funded for two phases of five years each, while some continued through participating in new programs of supported collaboration. One of these new programs was the Canada-China Higher-Education Program (CCHEP), and another was the Canada-China University-Industry Partnership Program (CCUIPP), a $5 million program running from 1996 to 2001, which was managed by the Canadian Association of Graduate Management Schools. The latter program supported collaboration between management schools and major industrial sectors in the areas of power (Hydro-Québec and China's State Power Central Company), telecommunications (Nortel and China Telecom), and financial services (KPMG and the Bank of China). It is extremely difficult to evaluate the impact of these long-lasting linkages on China's dramatic economic transformation over these years, from a developing society in transition to a manufacturing powerhouse and the world's second largest economy. The economic trajectory is clear, but how much can be attributed to these early experiences of cooperation in management education will probably never be fully known.

From the Canadian interviews, it is clear that one of the great satisfactions of these projects lay in the speed and effectiveness with which reforms were carried out. There was certainly what King (2009) has called an "enabling environment" on the Chinese side, which was crucial to success. How far was the transformation mutual? It seems that only recently has the Canadian side realized how much they benefitted from these opportunities and how important it is to build further upon them in the current period.

Finally, how much evidence is there of a dialogue that goes beyond issues of economic effectiveness to broader questions of human well-being and global justice? The two remarks we found most striking from this perspective were those of the Tsinghua management professor who called for a fundamental rethinking of the interconnection between urban and rural development, and the Xiamen accounting professor who proposed the idea of joint Canada-China cooperation in support of developing countries that are struggling to function effectively in a global economic and financial environment.

UNIVERSITY PARTNERSHIPS IN EDUCATION, ENGINEERING, MEDICINE, AND AGRICULTURE UNDER CCULP/SULCP

While CCMEP had its own national coordinating body during its second phase, the CCULP and SULCP were coordinated through the international office of the Association of Universities and Colleges of Canada (AUCC) on the Canadian side. The CCULP supported thirty-one university partnerships across a wide range of knowledge areas, with multiple partners on both sides in some cases. In the SULCP, the eleven partnerships considered to be most effective were selected through a competitive process for a further period of five years. From the perspective of officials at China's MOE,[10] who coordinated the projects on the Chinese side, this was a truly collaborative relationship – projects were jointly designed and jointly implemented, managed, and evaluated. There was a joint steering committee that met every year, alternately in Canada and China, which included scholars as well as officials in discussing the various problems that arose. MOE officials noted how they felt respected and treated on equal terms, something that was quite unusual at the time.

On the Canadian side, we learned from those involved in the early decision-making that the student exchange program with China, negotiated shortly after the restoration of diplomatic relations in the early 1970s, had resulted in very positive people-to-people relations in Ottawa, which may have influenced the decision to keep CIDA's development work focused on education. A senior CIDA official, who had a long-term involvement with the China program, further noted that it made sense for CIDA, which as a medium-sized organization could not compete with the kinds of infrastructural projects being supported by World Bank loans, to focus on human resources, and to aim for "the multiplication of contacts at the thinking level." Feedback from participants in four of these projects – education, engineering, health, and agriculture – should give an indication of how far this oft-quoted CIDA aim can be detected in what actually transpired.

Education

We begin with the field of education. One interviewee had been vice-president of Beijing Normal University (BNU), which housed the Canada-China language training centre for almost a decade, providing English and French language preparation for scholars and graduate students nationwide who went to Canada under the projects. In addition, he served as project director for Canada-China Joint Doctoral Programs in Education, a CCULP project that linked seven Chinese normal universities in all regions of the country to the Ontario Institute for Studies in Education (OISE) at the University of Toronto (UT). He noted how this project was extremely important for education in a situation where educational theory had been dominated for decades by the pedagogical views of the Russian theorist Ivan Kairov as well as by those of the nineteenth-century German philosopher Johann Herbart. Educational scholarship in China was greatly in need of new ideas and perspectives at the time.

He felt that the project had nurtured a generation of students who became leaders in the field, and who were spread throughout the country, since he had ensured that all normal universities that had doctoral programs at the time should be included in the project. However, he believed that outcomes might have been even better if there had been more exchange and dialogue. In terms of sustainability of collaborative relations, he described the need for an organization at the university level that could give long-term continuity to changing forms and themes of partnership. He had developed such a centre with a high-profile US partner somewhat later, and regretted the fact that cooperation with the Canadian partner was not sustained after CIDA funding came to an end.

We held interviews with six educators who participated in the project, three as doctoral students and three as visiting scholars, in six institutions in different geographical regions; these interviews give some insights into the outcomes. In total, the project had sent twenty-two young scholars to Canada: ten as doctoral students and twelve in visiting-scholar roles. Twenty had returned to China, and fifteen continued to be active in educational leadership, teaching, and research, including one who served as a university president, two vice-presidents, four deans, and a number of department heads.

One influential dean noted how intercultural understanding was a key dimension of the project, and stressed the importance of educational scholars on each side understanding how problems in education were viewed and analyzed. The gap between the language and thought worlds of the two cultures was so great that it had inspired him to find ways of communicating core educational values and perspectives from the Chinese tradition on a global stage by promoting publications about Chinese education in English.[11] The second major impact the project had had on his scholarship was in the arena of teaching. He was deeply impressed by the detailed course outlines he saw at OISE, and has established a practice at his institution whereby all faculty members are expected to update their course outlines every year and make them available publicly, and all doctoral students are required to develop and defend one course in their specialist field before graduation.

Another scholar articulated her strong sense of how timely this experience had been. She had wanted to develop her doctoral research in a feminist framework, yet found Chinese literature on feminism non-existent at the time. Her period of study in Canada thus opened up this world of scholarship and she was, in turn, able to assist Canadian scholars and activists in preparing for the UN's Fourth World Congress on Women, held in Beijing in 1995. She also found a fully developed field of research on multiculturalism in Canada, which stimulated her to work in this area upon her return to China. "In a period of rapid social change, gender problems are particularly notable, while when things settle down, this is no longer the case," she commented. For her, timing was crucial. Now, more than fifteen years later, she described the quality and status of gender studies in China as high, giving women in leadership in Chinese universities a scholarly basis to support their work.

A third scholar was vice-president of China's National Institute of Education Science (NIES) at the time of our interview. His research focused on classroom environments, and on his return from Canada he had set up China's first research institute for educational experimentation, as well as organizing a related national association and a number of experimental schools. The ideas nurtured in these projects were seminal to national curricular reform initiated in 2001, in which his standing in the NIES gave him a strong leadership role.

Another area crucial to China's educational development was moral education. As China moved rapidly to a market economy, its old-style ideological political education became more and more dysfunctional, and a new approach to ethics and moral education was needed. A fourth scholar highlighted how the research project he was involved in enabled principals and teachers to learn how to analyze their decisions from moral, environmental, economic, and political perspectives. They developed ideas for dealing with the conflict between moral and environmental concerns, and with the brash pursuit of economic benefit that was engulfing China's rapidly changing society. This training subsequently had some impact on both policy and curricula for moral education. A more detailed analysis of these various areas of educational collaboration and their outcomes can be found in chapters 10 and 11 of this volume.

While this educational project had a wide-ranging impact throughout the country, in areas including minority and bilingual education, moral education, and gender in education and curriculum, no genuine institutional partnership survived the end of the twelve years of collaboration. This was regretted by the first Chinese project director, as noted above, and seemed to reflect the issue of continuity in leadership, which is raised in the partnership literature. Leadership of the second phase of the project under the SULCP shifted from BNU to Shaanxi Normal University (SNU) in Xi'an. Shortly after the project concluded, two dynamic leaders from SNU were able to move to Shanghai and Guangzhou due to the more open environment for the mobility of university faculty, facilitated by the market economy. Thus there was no ongoing institutional partnership between the faculties of education of either BNU or SNU with OISE or with UBC's Faculty of Education.

Although there was no ongoing institutional linkage, there were many spin-off projects, which continue to the present day. One of the most striking of these is the development of hundreds of English-language immersion schools, adapted from the French-immersion model in Ontario, and integrated into public / elementary school environments in Guangdong, Beijing, and Xi'an (Qiang and Kang 2011). The second Chinese project director, whom we also interviewed, identified a reason for the long-lasting impact of this project in different sectors of education; according to her, it lay in the focus on basic research in areas of common concern (see Qiang and Wang, chapter 11 of this volume). By contrast, her experience of collaboration in development work with other Western countries had been highly practical and responsive only to current problems. The importance of collaboration in basic research, one of the points raised in King's research on university partnerships with African countries (King 2009), found clear agreement in the perception of this Chinese project leader.

Engineering

In the field of engineering, one significant CCULP project was led by a visionary institutional vice-president who subsequently rose to be vice-governor of his northwestern province, and then vice-chairman of a national democratic party. His retrospective view of the project was thus extremely broad. The focus of the project was on computer applications, on the surface a rather specialized area, yet our interviewee felt that the social impact of the project had been very broad. This scholar had prepared in detail for the interview, and emphasized that the project had involved new knowledge, new technology, new ways of teaching, new ways of thinking, and new approaches to the use of technology. Within his institution, the Lanzhou Railway Institute (LRI), teaching content and methods, as well as classroom organization, were transformed by the project. The fact that five institutional leaders from the LRI spent periods of time at the Ryerson Institute of Technology, as well as visiting other Canadian universities, led to considerable changes in institutional management. Examples of these changes included open access to library stacks and the use of computers to manage library resources.

Of even greater consequence, this scholar believed, was the influence on national and provincial government ministries, which had to face institutional leaders who were far more demanding and proactive than in the past as a direct result of the project, and which found themselves employing graduates with new engineering and management skills. Specifically, the project's focus on the use of technology led to much closer relations between universities and enterprises, and to a transformation of railway system management through the introduction of new computer technology. Since civil engineering, mechanical engineering, industrial control systems, electronic communication, and railway systems are all dependent on computer science and technology, it was impossible to measure the full extent of the project's influence. Social influences were also notable, particularly in the area of gender and leadership. CIDA's demand for full participation of women in the project meant that five of the ten researchers who spent time at Ryerson were women, and a project-initiated training seminar for women technical workers resulted in a book of proceedings that garnered considerable attention. Chapter 7 of this volume gives profound insights into a range of partnerships in engineering, which had significant social and economic impacts.

On the Ryerson side of the project, although the specific institutional linkage was not maintained, this early experience of international collaboration has left its mark. Ryerson was upgraded from a technical institute to full university status in 1993, and its international programs are now both innovative and extensive, including significant current research collaboration with Chinese institutions. One high-profile project that recently won a major grant from the National Natural Sciences Foundation of China is a digital media lab operated in cooperation with the Beijing University of Posts and Telecommunications.

Medicine and Health

In the area of medicine, Université Laval in Quebec City had a long-lasting partnership with the Norman Bethune University of Medical Sciences (NBUMS), located in the northeastern city of Changchun; the NBUMS now forms the medical school of Jilin University after a major merger. This partnership was supported through both the CCULP and the SULCP. The focus of the partnership was on treatment for cancer, and the senior surgeon whom we interviewed in Changchun noted how cancer had originally been dealt with in a highly sectoral way in China, with treatment divided among many different specialists. Through this project, a Bethune-Laval Oncology Unit was established, which became a national model for holistic cancer management and prevention under the SULCP. Our interviewee was involved in every phase of the project's development, and as a young medical professional he felt that it enabled him and his colleagues to develop a much broader perspective than would have been possible without the opportunities of the project.

Many of those working with him in the early years of the project have now relocated elsewhere, some in the south of China, and he sees these movements as a positive factor that has contributed to the national influence of the model developed for oncology treatment. Of the ten core people in his unit, seven are returnees from this collaboration with Laval. Even though CIDA funding ended in 2001, they continue to have a flourishing relationship with Laval. Both undergraduate and masters students are sent there for periods of study, and Laval professors are invited to lecture and participate in collaborative research. Some of the wider offshoots of this focused medical cooperation include a sister-city relationship between Changchun and Quebec City, and a French-language capacity at NBUMS that is often helpful at international conferences and in receiving Francophone visitors to the university or city. Finally, our interviewee described a strong sense of confidence and competence that is present when he and his colleagues participate in international colloquia in their area around the world.

On the Laval side, we were able to meet with three generations of surgical leaders: the founding director of the project, formerly head of surgery and a legendary figure in China; his successor; and the current head of the surgery department. Leadership continuity was clearly an important factor in the longevity of this collaboration. Another factor we found striking was the fact that Laval itself had been in the process of creating an integrated oncology unit at the time of its efforts to establish the Bethune-Laval Oncology Unit in Changchun. This brought genuine stimulus to the collaboration for both sides, as conditions for cancer treatment in China at the time were so problematic that the need for a totally new approach was even more evident.

Agriculture

One of the highest profile CCULP/SULCP projects was in agriculture, leading to the dramatic commercial success of canola oil as a health-enhancing edible oil. Jackson (2003, 45) noted that the project was credited with enabling low-income Chinese farmers to plant three million hectares of new rapeseed varieties, increasing the value of their yield by 1,500 yuan per hectare. Of all the university-linkage projects, this one clearly had the most direct impact on poverty alleviation. On the Canadian side, one of the participating scholars noted that canola has surpassed wheat as a cash crop in Canada.

This cooperation arose out a joint interest in the potential of this particular plant. A distinguished scientist at the University of Manitoba (UM) had done pioneering early research on rapeseed, and an outstanding scientist at the Huazhong Agricultural University (HAU) had done similar research quite independently during the decade of China's Cultural Revolution. After two phases of CIDA-supported collaboration between the universities, the Departments of Plant Science and Food Science at UM continue in active research collaboration with partner departments at HAU, and collaboration has spread to involve numerous other agricultural institutions in both China and Canada.

On the Chinese side, the scholars we interviewed noted the impact of the project on the university's leadership, with both the president and vice-president being returnees from Canada in the mid-1990s, and with significant honours having been won by several other returnees. The university includes two members of the prestigious Chinese Academy of Sciences (CAS), one being the pioneer in rapeseed research, four national key labs, and ten national research centres. On the Canadian side, one senior researcher who joined UM toward the end of the project noted that he was able to attract excellent doctoral students and visiting researchers through this project with China, and also get connected to "a beautiful network of collaboration" with colleagues in his area of plant pathology in several agricultural universities in China (see chapter 14, 300–2, for more detail on this project).

Downsides and Upsides in Collaboration

These four CCULP/SULCP projects in education, engineering, health, and agriculture were not without downsides, of course. Although they started some years later than the CCMEP partnerships, they were still affected by the aftermath of the events of June 1989, losing a number of the younger scholars sent for degree study in the early years. There were also some concerns about the need for Canadian models to be carefully adapted to the Chinese environment, and the tendency for Canadian project managers to have such an intense commitment to projects that they could not see beyond short-term setbacks associated with the non-return of visiting students.

On the positive side, the projects included a strong sense of family relations between project members on both sides, set in the context of a national framework of cooperation between the two countries. A number of our interviewees noted how this familial sense differed from later cooperation with American and Japanese universities, where there was a greater focus on immediate pragmatic goals to be fulfilled, and less of a sense of working together in a context of mutual learning. Most unique of all, and mentioned by most of the interviewees, was the sense of a critical period of social transition for China, when Canada was open and ready to engage in wide-scale cooperation around areas of crucial importance for China. As far as we know, Canada was the only Western country to make higher education a core focus of its development aid to China in this crucial early period. The emphasis was on human resources, the multiplication of people-to-people contacts in areas of importance to the modernization drive, complementing the major infrastructural improvements in Chinese universities facilitated by loans from the World Bank over the same period (Hayhoe 1989, 157–90).

CULMINATING LINKAGES IN PRIORITY AREAS

CIDA officials in Ottawa explained to us that it was always intended that the linkage projects they supported should become self-sustaining, and also that the China program was expected to evolve in response to changing circumstances on both sides. We have mentioned the reframing effort of the mid-1990s, with CIDA's new China Country Development Policy Framework of 1994 highlighting the decision to focus on the three broad areas of environment, governance, and economic cooperation. In this final part of the discussion of our preliminary findings, we will look at two culminating projects in the areas of environment and good governance.

Environment

UT was linked with the Institute of Geographic Science and Natural Resources Research (IGSNRR) of the CAS under both the CCULP and the SULCP for collaborative research in the area of soil erosion management through geographic information systems (GIS). The earliest cooperation between these institutions had been funded by Canada's International Development Research Centre (IDRC) in Guangdong Province. The CCULP/SULCP projects developed out of that cooperation, and looked at land-use management and soil and water conservation issues in Shanxi Province and Inner Mongolia, seeking to integrate bio-physical and socio-economic factors. The social dimensions of the linkage involved a strong education and training element, including workshops for women, and were intended to ensure that farmers were motivated to adopt the new techniques developed. Close cooperation with government bureaus at the provincial level in both regions was also important. The great benefit of this for UT was the opportunity for graduate students to have extended field experience in China and opportunities for faculty to work with scholars at the CAS, which was already far more advanced in the use of GIS systems than UT at the time.

While the CCULP/SULCP projects had relatively modest budgets, the opportunity arose for UT to compete for a larger-scale third project that built upon the earlier linkage work and ran from 2002 to 2006. It was entitled "Confronting Global Warming: Enhancing China's Capacity for Carbon Sequestration," and the linkage was expanded to include three other Canadian institutions and seven Chinese institutions. The project was led on the Canadian side by a Canada Research Chair who had just come to UT from the Canada Centre for Remote Sensing in Ottawa, where he had been responsible for building Canada's capacity for monitoring vegetation by satellite. This major project, with a budget of $2.3 million, made it possible to test models he had been developing in the Canadian context in temperate and subtropical forests in China, terrain very different from that of Canada. As a result, the model is now used globally.

The overall purpose of the project was to produce research outcomes that would enable China to develop a scientific system for accumulating data that would substantiate its commitment to the Kyoto Climate Change Accord. This was clearly a project of national significance on both sides, and in 2010 the lead Canadian scholar was invited to sit on a panel under China's Ministry of Science and Technology that decides how 300 million Chinese yuan is distributed for global climate-change research in China each year.

This project has also been closely connected to the work of the China Council for International Cooperation on Environment and Development (CCICED), which was established in 1992 and received Can$20 million from CIDA for the first three five-year phases of its operation. The Council is chaired by a Chinese vice-premier, and brings together international and Chinese experts on environmental issues, as well as coordinating the work of task forces on environmental concerns in different sectors. Council members have the opportunity to present related reports to the Chinese premier with concrete action-oriented policy recommendations on a regular basis. While this is a national-level body with broad global connections, there has been a link to the university level in that the Canadian Secretariat is housed at Simon Fraser University (SFU), and has worked closely with the Chinese secretariat located in the State Environmental Protection Administration in Beijing. More on this sustained collaboration in environmental research and policy can be found in chapter 8 of this volume.

Law and Good Governance

None of the CCULP/SULCP projects had focused specifically on law and good governance, possibly due to the sensitivity of these areas in the early years of collaboration. However, the $4 million project developed to support China's National Judges College in 1997 reflected a strong interest on the Canadian side in strengthening the rule of law in China. The tender was won by the Faculty of Law, Université de Montréal (UdeM), and although the project was not a university linkage per se, it provided the opportunity for UdeM to build significant and ongoing linkages with the China University of Political Science and Law (CUPL) as well as with other Chinese institutions. Over a period of four years, two cohorts of judges were trained, with each spending one year in Canada and one year in China under the project. There were two joint seminars each year in which a group of Canadian judges and legal scholars met for a week with a large number of Chinese counterparts, including judges, law specialists, and legal scholars, to discuss legal themes that had been decided by joint negotiation. These seminars were held in different regions of the country and used lively methods of communication such as mock trials.

UdeM benefitted greatly from this project, as the dean of law who organized it moved on to become vice-rector international of the university and subsequently provost. As dean, he had observed how faculty members were invigorated by the presence of the young Chinese judges in training, and decided to launch some exchanges. He started with organizing a four-to-five-week summer seminar in Beijing for law students from Montreal, which was followed by a summer program in Montreal for Chinese students to learn about Western legal systems. This has been followed in turn by a master's degree in international business law oriented to Chinese students. As vice-rector international, he went on to negotiate with the China Scholarship Council (CSC) to fund thirty PhD students to come to the university each year, concentrating in the discipline areas they chose.

Meanwhile the current dean of law, who was also involved in with the National Judges College project, has developed close cooperation with both the CUPL in Beijing and the East China University of Political Science and Law (ECUPL) in Shanghai. The cooperation includes exchanges of masters and PhD students both ways, research projects, faculty visits between countries, and the joint organization of conferences in constitutional and administrative law and international economic law in Beijing and Montreal. There are also active programs to publish scholarship in books and journals that they sponsor in Canada and China.

On the basis of this strong bilateral program, Montreal is now beginning to see itself as a bridge between law students in the two emerging countries of China and Brazil, since a large number of graduate students funded by the Brazilian government are coming to Montreal, and connecting there with their Chinese counterparts. A further visionary effort funded by the MOE focuses on global governance and the international legal order, and UdeM's Law Faculty is currently partnering with CUPL, Wuhan University, and a US law school to bid for this project.

While the balance of benefit in the earlier linkages was weighted toward the Chinese side, the way in which UdeM has moved forward on the basis of its CIDA-supported opportunity to train judges illustrates a remarkable shift that is underway. The former dean and vice-rector who built so effectively on this project noted in our interview how much Canadian universities now have to learn from their Chinese counterparts, and how important it is to engage in active dialogue with Chinese peers, with critical thinking, values, and ethics at the heart of the discourse. A more detailed account of this ongoing collaboration can be found in chapter 12 of this volume.

PRELIMINARY LESSONS FROM PAST LINKAGES

If we return to the theoretical frameworks sketched out at the beginning of this chapter, there can be no doubt that China has moved from a peripheral position in the world economy in the early 1980s to a central position, and the speed at which this has been achieved is stunning. In terms of path dependence, it is also clear that China has done this on its own terms, while making effective use of the support provided through such external funders as the World Bank, CIDA, and many other agencies. A recent volume on China's move to mass higher education, profiling twelve universities in different parts of the country that represent different knowledge areas, demonstrates how epistemological and institutional aspects of China's scholarly heritage have shaped this process (Hayhoe, Li, Lin, and Zha 2011). Meanwhile, China's universities have been assigned the role of key partners with universities, school boards, schools, and NGOs around the world in the creation of Confucius Institutes intended to foster cross-cultural dialogue and understanding (Hayhoe and Liu 2010; Kwan 2013).

For more specific reflection on lessons from the legacy of Canada-China cooperation, the partnership literature is probably most helpful. The first point emphasized by both King (2009) and Jackson (2003) is the need for a lengthy time frame, so that partners on both sides can develop a real understanding of one another. This was a unique feature of the linkage projects described above, with time frames between five and fifteen years. While not all of them continued after CIDA funding came to an end, some blossomed into continuing collaboration and widening circles of engagement.

A second point noted was the importance of collaborative research at a basic level around issues of common concern on both sides. Much of the current collaboration is commercially motivated, as institutions on both sides look for the revenue generated by students, programs, and even institutions moving across borders, and fail to take up the challenge of seeking long-term and stable funding for the advancement of knowledge and mutual understanding (Zha 2012). The cases of collaboration in the priority areas of environment, law, and good governance that culminated from the CIDA-supported linkages provide a model in this regard. Everyone would recognize these areas of development as crucial both to China's future well-being and to its emerging role in global governance. What could be more important or satisfying themes for Canadian universities to engage in long-term research cooperation? Another area that was highlighted by our conversation with scholars and leaders at Laval was that of health and social policy in China. No matter how much progress is possible in the most advanced treatment of diseases such as cancer and heart problems, if this treatment is not available to the majority of Chinese due to a failure to develop an effective healthcare system, to what avail are all the scientific efforts?

A global knowledge economy that focuses entirely on competition in the areas of instrumental-technical rationality and fails to address fundamental human needs is clearly unsustainable. There is a whole range of areas around health provision, balancing excellence with equity in education, environmental protection, and protection of cultural diversity, which are rooted in the deep regions of what Habermas has called the cultural life world. These need to be addressed through efforts to connect the moral and spiritual heritage of Confucianism and Daoism on the Chinese side with Judaeo-Christian values and indeed the broader values of multiculturalism on the Canadian side. This could be the wellspring of a shared vision for the future that could be developed by scholars and leaders in Chinese and Canadian universities. Under the current global neo-liberal environment, modernity is in even more urgent need of redemption or humanization than when Habermas first coined the phrase in the early 1980s, and short-term commercially motivated collaboration will not suffice. This may be the most important lesson to be learned from the legacy of past collaboration between Canadian and Chinese universities.

To drive this point home, we would like to close this preliminary reflection on past collaboration with a quote from a young scholar of higher education in China, deeply concerned about the crisis facing Chinese universities today: "The reputation of a university does not depend on how many books and articles its faculty have published, but on how it guides every member in taking up their social responsibility through what they publish and the way in which it formulates moral standards and develops its mission, guiding ideas and approach to education. Unfortunately, few contemporary Chinese universities have this kind of tradition, perhaps due to the disruptions in their history over the 20th century" (Xun 2012, 244).

Are Canadian university scholars ready to join hands with Chinese scholars such as this one and develop linkages that respond to the real human, social, and environmental needs universities should be concerned about in both countries? It may be there are now more practical resources on the Chinese side than the Canadian side for such efforts, but first there needs to be a vision. "Where there is no vision, the people perish" (*Proverbs* 29:18). Or, in Confucian terms, "The master focuses on what is fundamental, and the way grows once the foundation is established" (君子务本, 本立而道生, *Analects* 1:2).

OVERVIEW OF THE BOOK

This book has been organized into four major sections, which will take the reader on a journey through major experiences of collaboration between Canada and China across the disciplines. In part 1, which lays out the political and socio-cultural context of change, we are privileged to hear first from a leading scholar on Canada-Asian diplomatic relations.

Professor Paul Evans provides an illuminating historical overview of the role of universities in the relation between the two countries, as well as presenting a compelling vision for current and future collaboration in chapter 2. Chapter 3 follows with a moving personal reflection from Ambassador Fred Bild, who served in Beijing from 1990 to 1994, and gives astute insights into unfolding relations between Canada and China, as well as a carefully researched account of Quebec's unique approach. Part 2 moves from the political to the economic dimension, with three chapters that elaborate on the two phases of the CCMEP. Professor Rolf Mirus of the U of A leads off in chapter 4, with a thoughtful analysis of the ways in which this program contributed to economic and social change on both sides. Chapter 5 then turns to a Chinese perspective, with President Xi Youmin of Xi'an Jiaotong-Liverpool University and associates examining the process and stages of cross-cultural learning and their impact on leadership in the Chinese context. Chapter 6 by Paul W. Beamish, a leading professor of management at UWO's Ivey School, gives a fascinating account of how case studies took off in the Chinese context, deepening understanding between the two sides.

In part 3, we turn to engineering and the environment, two important dimensions in the collaboration supported by CIDA. First we hear from a senior Chinese academic and political leader in chapter 7, as Professor Li Chongan, former vice-governor of Gansu Province and vice-chairman of the China Democratic League, presents a detailed account of engineering linkages across eleven universities on each side, which had striking social impacts in addition to their scientific contributions. Environmental research impacts are then presented in chapter 8 by Professor Jing M. Chen and his associates at UT, with an interesting chronology that moves from issues of soil erosion through sustainable water management to carbon sequestration in face of global warming. Chapter 9 by Professor Jan W. Walls, noted sinologist at SFU, approaches the environment from a socio-cultural perspective, detailing the learning that arose from sustained cooperation with minority communities in different regions of China who were seeking to preserve their unique cultural identity and natural environments while dealing responsibly with the economic challenges of modernization.

Part 4 moves to the theme of education and equity. In chapter 10, Qiang Zha and Ruth Hayhoe provide an overview of the educational dimension of China's transformation, and show how three CCULP/SULCP projects involving universities spread across both countries contributed to educational innovation. Chapter 11 gives a perspective from

China on one of these projects, with Qiang Haiyan, a senior scholar of comparative education at South China Normal University (SCNU) and Wang Jiayi, director of the Gansu Provincial Department of Education, providing a deep-level analysis of long-term outcomes from their unique perspectives as alumni of the project. Chapter 12 turns to the arena of legal education, as UdeM's Dean of Law Guy Lefebvre and his associates unfold the story of a project for the training of judges that has expanded into a network of cooperation in legal education that is benefitting students and scholars on both sides. Gender equity was a central dimension in CIDA's policies, as is evident in many chapters. Chapter 13 by UT Sociology Professor Ping-chun Hsiung focuses on how this policy was experienced in the doing of feminist collaboration. Chapter 14 then closes the circle with a summary of presentations by high-level scientists in marine and earth sciences, agriculture, and medicine who honoured us by participating in the conference but were not able to write chapters for this volume. It also draws together the major threads of argument, highlighting core dimensions of the legacy of this remarkable series of university linkages and their lessons for the current time.

In bringing this chapter to a close, we recollect a vivid moment in the research project that has led to this book. We were interviewing a senior education official in Beijing who had served as director of the MOE's Department of International Exchange over much of the period of the CIDA-sponsored university linkages. He shared many insights with us in a candid way, gradually becoming more and more animated as he recollected some of the crises that had been overcome and highlights that had been celebrated. Suddenly, he jumped up from his seat, saying, "There has to be a book about this, it was such an important time for China!" We hope he will be satisfied with the efforts of all those who have contributed to this retrospective and reflective account, and we hope it will inspire a new generation of scholars in both Canada and China who are working together under very different circumstances.

NOTES

1 Special thanks are due to Professor Shi Jinghuan, executive dean of Tsinghua's Institute of Education and Professor Wang Xiaoyang, director of the Higher Education Research Institute, who so graciously hosted this event at Tsinghua, and supported us in every phase of its planning and preparation. Tsinghua University was a partner with University of Western

Ontario under the Canada-China Management Education Program (1983–96) and Professor Chen Zhangwu of Tsinghua's School of Economics and Management chaired the conference session on collaboration in management education.

2 We are truly grateful to Dr Sarah Taylor, deputy head of mission at the Canadian Embassy in Beijing, who visited us in Toronto in March 2014 to discuss plans for the conference and took an active part in our deliberations as well as speaking at the closing ceremony.

3 The Powerpoints for keynote presentations, many of which were compellingly illustrated, can be found on the conference website under Keynote Speakers on the Canadian side and on the Chinese side: http://www.oise.utoronto.ca/cidec/Research/conference_2014.html.

4 This document can be viewed on-line at www.treaty-accord.gc.ca/text-texte.aspx?id=101079.

5 We are immensely grateful to Mr Kent Smith, a recently retired CIDA official, who held senior positions in CIDA's China program in both Ottawa and Beijing over many years, for providing us with significant help and documentation for a clearer understanding of CIDA's education programs.

6 O'Brien (2000, 86–7) notes that the USA, Germany, Japan, and Europe all established management training centres in China in the 1980s, but these were small-scale efforts at particular sites, not necessarily universities, and somewhat limited in scope (see also Hayhoe 1989, 146–51). Other programs, such as that of the French at Wuhan University and the Germans at Tongji University, fell under the category of cultural diplomacy rather than development aid (Hayhoe 1989, 140–4).

7 http://www.oise.utoronto.ca/cidec/Research/conference_2014.html.

8 Due to the ethical requirements of our research protocol we are not able to identify the interviewees by name.

9 Phase I had a budget of $12.1 million and the budget of Phase II was $27.6 million.

10 Between 1985 and 1998, China's Ministry of Education (MOE) was called the State Education Commission, but we have used MOE throughout this chapter for the sake of simplicity.

11 This scholar played a crucial role in developing *Frontiers of Education in China* from a journal of translations into a peer-reviewed journal that presents educational scholarship from and about China in a form that is accessible to the international community.

PART ONE

The Political and Socio-Cultural Context of Change

2

Canada-China Relations and the Evolving Role of Universities: Toward Partnerships 2.0

PAUL EVANS

INTRODUCTION

In the sweep of almost a century and a half of Canada-China relations, universities have been a comparatively minor player on an expanding and now busy stage. In a relationship dominated by missionaries, migrants, and heroic individuals in the period before the Communist victory and political leaders, diplomats, and business people since then, the role of higher education is only starting to be recognized as a principal driver of connections between the two countries. Current efforts to market Canadian educational services are only one part of a much bigger story.

The role and significance of universities are increasing because of activities on campuses in both countries, but also because of partnerships, exchanges, and activities linking them. Rather than seeing universities solely as independent players with their own agendas, they need to be understood as a part of a larger effort led by national governments to cement a bilateral relationship that traverses two nations with very different histories, cultures, values, and political, social, and economic systems. From a Canadian perspective, cultivating university interest in China has been a central part of a broader strategy of engagement. While the Canadian government now plays a comparatively less-important role in shaping what the higher-educational sector does, academic activities have always been part of a larger political and diplomatic agenda in more than forty years of building a bilateral relationship. Here academic relations with China are unique. University collaborations are both the product of an engagement strategy and possibly its most durable and effective agent.

My aim is first to outline the thinking that lay behind the creation of the state-sponsored exchanges that began in 1970 and took on a new dimension with the large-scale programs funded by the federal government, principally the Canadian International Development Agency (CIDA), in the 1980s and 1990s. Government policies laid the foundation for these relationships to grow to the point where they now have a life of their own and involve almost every institution of higher learning in Canada and many in China. I will introduce the idea of "Partnerships 2.0" to frame the contemporary period in which the number of participating institutions, the levels of faculty and student exchange, the range of collaborative programs for teaching and research, the sources of funding, and the issues being faced have all shifted in substantial ways. Bilateral collaborations are a central node in a web of connections that show enormous potential and also raise a new set of challenges and questions.

HISTORICAL EVOLUTION

The university story begins with the missionaries, Canadian and otherwise, who helped establish institutions of higher learning in several parts of China in the late Imperial and Republican eras as part of their broader evangelical efforts. Very few if any of the missionaries studied China at Canadian universities before setting forth. Their era of building educational projects based on personal and church connections slowed with the war with Japan and ended with the creation of the People's Republic of China (PRC) in 1949 and the outbreak of the Korean War. For the next twenty years there were occasional private visits by Canadian educators like Claude Bissell, but virtually no two-way flow of students or bilateral programming.[1] A few universities in Canada invested modestly in Chinese studies, with programs in language, the humanities, and social sciences like those at the University of Toronto (UT), McGill University, and the University of British Columbia (UBC). Returned missionaries and missionary offspring, the "mish-kids," provided much of the expertise in the halls of the academy and diplomacy. Canada's first three ambassadors to the PRC were born in China of missionary parents.

A new era began with the establishment of diplomatic relations in 1970. Universities and other non-governmental organizations became part of a governmental agenda for building a bilateral relationship. The foundation of this agenda was a strategy of engagement that has had three dimensions: economic, geo-strategic, and moral. Starting with Trudeau, successive governments have calculated that engagement is preferable to Cold War containment, isolation, or confrontation; that Canada has both an opportunity and a comparative advantage in assisting China's development and bringing China into the international system; and that opening China economically would eventually induce political liberalization.

The distinctive feature of Canadian-style engagement was that it was not only expected to produce commercial advantages and diplomatic leverage but also to promote a value-driven agenda for changing China's domestic institutions or, in a more modest framing, influencing Chinese behaviour. While leavened by a search for mutual learning and understanding, most Canadians have held the idea that values including human rights and democracy are universals to which China should aspire and adapt.[2]

Universities were hard-wired in from the beginning. In building the infrastructure for engagement, an early priority was the creation of a bilateral agreement on scholarly cooperation. Signed by Prime Minister Trudeau and Premier Zhou Enlai in 1973, it put in place a mechanism for organizing and overseeing the selection of a small number of students and faculty to spend periods of time either studying or doing research in the other country.[3] The Canadian Embassy created a new position, the equivalent of a sinologist-in-residence, for an academic seconded for a period of time to assist with reporting and managing cultural and educational affairs. Before its termination in 2003, several of the dozen or so professors who held the position went on to play major administrative roles at universities across the country after they returned home.[4] The program strengthened and symbolized a unique connection between professors and diplomats not replicated in any other Canadian embassy. For twenty-five years, officials from the formerly named Department of External Affairs (DEA) not only worked with China specialists, but made special efforts to groom and consult them, including providing occasional funding for university appointments.

The DEA played an anchor role in incubating and managing academic contacts, working directly in some instances with individual professors and institutions, and coordinating with and encouraging other federal agencies and departments as well as provincial governments to provide various kinds of support. Because education is a matter of provincial jurisdiction, Canada does not have a federal ministry or organ responsible for coordinating and promoting international collaborations. Yet successive governments have had an interest in not just assisting but guiding educational and other non-governmental connections with China as part of an engagement policy. The DEA was the instrument for setting the institutional framework and tone.

In two detailed reports, the first published in 1986 and the second in 1996, Martin Singer has provided a very useful chronicle and assessment of Canadian academic relations with China in the twenty-five years after the establishment of diplomatic relations.[5] He breaks his history into four periods. I will add two more.

1970 to 1979

In addition to establishing the scholar and student exchange and the sinologist-in-residence programs, Ottawa worked with Beijing in creating a series of small-scale scientific and technical exchanges beginning in 1974 in fields including geology, oceanography, remote sensing, metallurgy, coal mining, railways, ports, agriculture, forestry, and fisheries. In July 1974, a first delegation of Canadian university presidents visited China, followed by a reciprocal visit of Chinese higher-educational officials in October 1975. A few students and faculty arranged private visits, but there were very limited opportunities for research or formal degree study. In a closed China, these early bilateral efforts opened a small window but not a door.

1979 to 1983

In June 1979, a bilateral agreement on academic exchanges was put in place that included a visiting-scholars program intended to bring mid-career Chinese academics to Canada for two years of non-degree studies, mainly in engineering and medicine, and to encourage new linkage agreements for the exchange of degree students and research scholars as organized by universities and colleges in both countries. According to Singer's estimate, about 400 Chinese academics visited Canada between 1970 and 1978 and more than 2,000 more in the next five years. Between 1970 and 1983, at least 600 Canadian academics visited China. Between 1970 and 1983, perhaps as many as 400 Canadian students visited China for academic purposes, about half of them in the formal Canada-China Student Exchange. By 1983, twenty-four Canadian universities had or were negotiating bilateral exchanges with Chinese counterparts. Universities across the country made a raft of appointments in Chinese studies, and several new centres for Chinese studies or research were established. The first centres for Canadian studies in China took root. Deng's Open Door policies and economic reforms increased China's need for outside expertise and technology, and were changing the landscape for international collaborations and exchanges.

1983 to 1989

The decision by the government of Canada to create a bilateral aid program opened a new chapter. Universities were a principal focus. Both the decision and the implementation were the product of close collaboration between CIDA and the DEA, conceived under the Liberal government and operationalized by a Progressive Conservative government that embraced a similar engagement strategy. The objective of the China program was to match Canadian capabilities to China's long-term development needs. In March 1982, the president of CIDA, Marcel Massé, outlined two distinctive features of the new program. The first was what he famously called the "multiplication of contacts at the thinking level." He stated, "Multiplication of contacts, that is how we should spend not only our money but also our administrative resources, multiplying them in a large number of fields, high technology preferably, but also methods of doing things, training trainers. We should help multiplying contacts in terms of the universities, but also maybe a number of small projects." Second, in training the trainers to develop new technologies, he argued that, "We can create the contacts, the understanding. We can create the contacts in terms of training trainers at levels where you have to deal with attitudes and values and where our people who are training will gain as much as they are giving." He also made the case that these could be more valuable to the Canadian economy in the long run than large-scale commercial contracts.[6] The bigger aim, as Fred Bild notes in chapter 3 of this volume, was not just benefiting Canada commercially but building a market economy in China.

For a little more than a decade, CIDA provided major financial support for several linkage projects focused on universities. The four main ones, which started shortly after 1983, were: (i) the Canada-China Language and Cultural Program ($23.5 million over ten years); (ii) the Canada-China Human Development Training Program ($30 million over twelve years); (iii) the Canada-China Management Education Project ($39.7 million over twelve years; see chapters 4, 5, and 6 of this volume); and (iv) the Canada-China University Linkage Program (CCULP) ($19 million over eight years; see chapter 1 and others in this volume).

In addition to the CIDA funding, the International Development Research Centre (IDRC) developed a program with the State Science and Technology Commission that over eight years contributed about $35 million to 145 China-based, China-related projects. Both the Social Sciences and Humanities Research Council (SSHRC) and the Natural Sciences and Engineering Research Council (NSERC) established special programs with Chinese institutions. Four Canadian provinces – Quebec, Alberta, Saskatchewan, and Ontario – established educational exchange arrangements with Chinese counterparts.

In quantitative terms, the results were formidable. Forty-five universities in Canada, thirty Chinese provinces, municipalities, and autonomous regions, and 659 institutions across China were involved in CIDA-sponsored activities alone. Consonant with China's economic reform agenda, Chinese students could apply directly to Canadian institutions. Enrolment surged. By 1986, China was the principal source of international graduate students in Canada. By 1989, there were more than 200 university linkages, about half of which received IDRC or CIDA funding.

1990 to 1995

Unlike the events in Tahrir Square a generation later, the events in and around Tiananmen Square in June 1989 did not bring down a regime. They did, however, change the chemistry of the Canada-China relationship. Shock, anger, and a sense of betrayal were palpable. Political reform would not follow lockstep with the economic reforms begun a decade earlier. The Mulroney government expressed horror and outrage in describing what Foreign Minister Joe Clark called a "tragedy of global proportions." Ottawa put in place a package of targeted economic sanctions, deferred high-level exchanges, and delayed approval of three new CIDA-funded projects. But rather than reverse the broader strategy of engagement, it made an adjustment. "A poorer and more isolated China," stated Clark in August 1989, "is not in the broad interest of the Chinese people."[7]

The impact on the university sector was significant. Logistically, it proved difficult in the short term to continue with business as usual as officials and organizers assessed the fall-out. Though most of the professors and staff active in exchanges continued to believe in the value of their projects, a few lost faith that they were making a difference. The federal government's decision to adjust immigration policy to give a fast path to citizenship for all Chinese students in Canada at the time of the Tiananmen event, about 10,000 in total, exacerbated the concerns of Chinese administrators already concerned about the "non-return" problem. Three provinces – Alberta, Saskatchewan, and Ontario – suspended or let lapse their educational exchange programs.

CIDA began a rethinking of its approach. In part this reflected the view that the phase of major investment in university linkages had already reached a point of diminishing returns. It also reflected a new political reality in Canada and demands by politicians and the public that the terms of engagement be altered. Almost immediately, CIDA began to emphasize the need for more in-China activities and short-term non-degree study programs in Canada. It began a longer-term shift away from universities as the principal vehicle for meeting its human-resource development objectives. This was made clear in its 1994 Country Development Policy Framework which emphasized a somewhat different set of priorities: economic cooperation, environmental sustainability, human rights, democratic development, and good governance. University-to-university linkages were almost all concluded by 1995 and replaced by projects that had "multi-stakeholder" results and support, and a wider array of executing agencies.

Individual universities and university-based activities continued to get support from CIDA throughout the 1990s. Reflective of the new approach, the largest and longest running project in the history of the bilateral program was launched in 1992, the China Council for International Cooperation on Environment and Development (CCICED). In addition, CIDA provided bridging support for programs that were continued by other means.

1995 to 2006

CIDA support for university-centred programs continued, though on a restricted scale. The Special University Linkage Consolidation Program (SULCP) that succeeded the CCULP ran until 2001. It eventually supported eleven projects involving twenty-five Canadian and 200 Chinese universities, teaching hospitals, and schools. CIDA also provided funding for a variety of partnership arrangements in which universities played central roles, such as training programs for judges and lawyers related to its good governance and human rights foci. Others supported by the bilateral program or its regional program included a decade of workshop activity focused on Canada-China collaboration on regional security issues and institution building. Other CIDA-funded regional projects, such as the seven years of work on managing potential conflicts in the South China Sea, involved significant Chinese participation.

During this period, both the SSHRC and the NSERC of Canada altered and reduced funding for their China programs, concentrating on individual projects focused increasingly on research. The IDRC maintained an abiding focus on China, providing more than $52 million since 1981 for support of 240 activities.

By the time that prime minister Paul Martin and Chinese President Hu Jintao announced the strategic partnership between the two countries in September 2005, the role of Ottawa as funder, cheerleader, and leader in shaping and promoting academic activities was diminishing. This was not because of lessened interest in these activities but rather the calculation that they were well-launched. Chinese studies at Canadian universities were flourishing, the number of exchanges and collaborations multiplying, and the flow of Chinese students continuing to grow.

The coming to power of the Harper government in 2006 produced a significant shift in the whole approach to China. In its first three years of "cool politics, warm economics," it focused on trying to expand commercial relations with China while cooling the political relationship as part of its principled foreign policy defined by a credo of freedom, democracy, human rights, and the rule of law. In a significant policy shift in late 2009, words like "friendship," "engagement," and "strategic partnership" reappeared in speeches by the prime minister and his senior ministers. But engagement, Conservative-style, rested on different foundations that combined anti-communism, a belief in a smaller role for government, and a belief that the role of government is to facilitate transactions rather than build and lead relationships.

In practice this meant advocating human rights and democratic values while doing little by way of new programming in or with China to encourage them. It narrowed the focus of the bilateral program to environmental sustainability and human rights. It insisted that Canadian funds not support Chinese government officials or Party members. It terminated the aid program, effective March 2014, while finding alternative sponsorship for the CCICED with Environment Canada but not creating an alternative instrument for supporting other bilateral initiatives of strategic importance. China continued to remain eligible for CIDA support for humanitarian assistance and partnerships administered through international institutions such as the UN and the World Bank.

In the roughly thirty years of the bilateral program, CIDA contributed almost $250 million for activities focused on higher education.[8] CIDA was only one strand, albeit the best-resourced, in spinning a web of connections and activities focused on university linkages and partnerships. Several of the essays in this volume evaluate the results of the major projects that in the 1980s and 1990s held centre stage. Their accomplishments, legacies, and lessons are important. They helped establish personal and institutional networks, provided institutional memory, stimulated interest inside universities in both countries, and generated research and teaching of mutual benefit. In some instances they generated ideas that clicked, sparking policy and commercial impact in both countries. And there is little question that they improved the lives of those who participated in them and those who benefited from their results in areas including agricultural protection and public health.

Marcel Massé's aspiration to multiply contacts at the thinking level was amply achieved. But have they contributed to the objective of fundamentally changing China or influencing Chinese behaviour? There is little debate in China or elsewhere that the efforts of Canadians and those of academics from many other countries have played instrumental roles in facilitating economic and social change in China, though only as one part of a complex blend of factors. As revealed in several of the chapters in this volume, the individuals who led the many programs of exchange prided themselves on not being imperialistic in outlook or expectations. They frequently use phrases like "mutual learning," "two-way understanding," and "trust," and point to both personal and institutional experiences that transformed their own research and teaching agendas and, to some extent, those of their home institutions. Almost all of them saw China advancing and changing, though not on a path to becoming more like the West but rather in adapting ideas and knowledge to its specific circumstances. Big ambitions for steering China in the direction of freedom, democracy, human rights, and the rule of law have at best produced a zigzag effect with partial and indeterminate results.

The real value of university exchanges seems to have lain elsewhere. Universities are the point of intersection for building knowledge, deepening understanding, negotiating differences, and finding commonalities. Linkages and joint programming are part of their terrain, but even more fundamental is the teaching and critical thinking that takes place within them. Many questions remain to be answered. How has exposure to Canadian institutions affected the views of those Chinese students and professors who remained in Canada or have returned home? How have they affected the Canadian participants? Have these interactions spawned common or shared new ideas related to humane and democratic governance, social justice, or environmental sustainability?

CONTEMPORARY SETTING

China is no longer "over there"; it is an integral part of campus life across the country. It is the domain of a much larger group of students and professors than those who are China specialists. Gone are the days when

Professor X was *the* "China person" or *the* "China scholar" known across campus. Great individuals still exist and still are needed. But the era of great individuals has passed. In Canada, it is the institutions, the universities themselves, sometimes in cooperation with the federal and provincial governments, which are the key drivers.

The activities of universities are larger, more intricate, more vibrant, and more multi-layered than its diplomat architects of the 1970s could have foretold in an era of a closed China and a sometimes complacent Canadian university scene. They include many hundreds, probably thousands, of faculty visits in each direction every year, dozens of jointly organized workshops and conferences, about 100,000 Chinese students enrolled in Canadian institutions, around 3,890 Canadian students in Chinese institutions, exchanges, experiential learning opportunities, collaborative teaching and supervision, summer institutes, centres of Chinese studies across Canada, centres for Canadian studies in China, Confucius Institutes (on some campuses), and alumni networks. A large number of universities now offer courses on China as part of their permanent curriculum. Several teach the Chinese language, and some have extensive course offerings in the humanities and social sciences focused on Chinese studies. Several have China strategies as part of their international programming. Professors at most institutions have constructed a bewildering number of collaborations in research and teaching with partners in China.

Universities in the two countries are partnering with each other for a diverse set of purposes, by multiple means, and on an increasing scale. They are collaborating with Chinese partners other than universities, including research institutes, government ministries, Party schools, NGOs, and corporate entities. Sources of funding have diversified, with the majority of support, financial and entrepreneurial, for two-way movements of students as well as faculty and bilateral collaborations coming from Chinese rather than Canadian sources. The Chinese sources include international student fees paid privately, scholarships provided by the Chinese government, especially the China Scholarship Council (CSC), support from local and provincial governments, and private and corporate gifts. Governments continue to play significant roles. Doors that they have opened are not guaranteed to stay open. On the Chinese side, ministries in Beijing fund scholarships, exchanges, and visits. On the Canadian side, Ottawa plays a continuing role in providing the infrastructure for interactions, including providing information, continuing to support a small bilateral exchange program, issuing visas, and helping Canadian universities with recruitment and the marketing of Canadian educational services. Ottawa does provide a small amount of support for special collaborations, especially in science and technology. But the vast proportion of energy, funding, and dynamism comes from the institutions themselves.

Three broad forces shape the dynamics of university-centred exchanges and activities. First, the societal roles played by universities in both countries are changing rapidly. In Canada, the defining feature is a growing emphasis on research, an increasing amount of it connected to commercialization, direct economic benefit, and policy-related matters. Almost all remain public institutions, independently governed but funded heavily by provincial governments and, indirectly, from the federal government through support for research and scholarships. In China, the quest is for creating world-class universities, incubating research, and attracting international and internationally trained talent in an era of staggering expansion. As noted in one recent study, in 1978 Chinese universities enrolled about 860,000 students; in 1990 about two million; in 2000 about six million; and in 2013 about thirty million. In 2000 there were about half as many students enrolled in Chinese universities as in American universities. Fourteen years later, the number of Chinese students studying at Chinese universities is twice as large. That number is expected to double again within twenty years.[9]

Second, China is now a central component of the international strategies of most Canadian institutions of higher learning. Some of this focuses on marketing Canadian educational services and recruiting qualified Chinese students. Increasingly, it focuses on partnering with Chinese universities for purposes of increasing the global competitiveness and quality of our own institutions. Some professors and administrators are drawn to China for reasons of ethnic heritage, intellectual and cultural curiosity, and the fact that China is the object of their study. Far more are now drawn because it is a significant part of their professional interest. To be successful in their professional fields, in doing the most important research and teaching possible, partnerships with China are increasingly seen not as a luxury but a necessity. Building relationships is now essential for serious research and teaching about China and work with Chinese partners. The aim of building capacity in Chinese institutions remains significant but is no longer the principal or dominant aim. Rather, the aim is two-way partnerships. In less than a generation, university linkages have shifted from training and helping Chinese to solve their problems to working with them for mutual advantage, something described as "collaboration on equal footing." In fields like medicine and public health, Chinese institutions may be twenty years behind, but the trend line is impressive.

Third, significant asymmetries and differences remain in the scale and organization of the university sector, governance systems, and surrounding political structures. Individual institutions in both countries are fiercely competitive. One of the major differences is that the Chinese government is far more directive and strategic in setting priorities and organizing around them. Decision-making and priority-setting is far more decentralized in Canada. Only a few institutions have campus-wide China strategies, deep collaboration between universities is rare even in the same city or province, and at the federal level the constitutional division of powers plus the Conservative aversion to national strategies of any sort makes for a largely uncoordinated scene. In many areas, China's political and academic leaders know better where they want to go, and have clearer strategies and priorities than their Canadian counterparts.

CASE EXAMPLE: THE UNIVERSITY OF BRITISH COLUMBIA (UBC)

UBC may be distinctive in the length, scale, depth, and breadth of its China connections, the city in which it is located with enormous links to greater China, and its geographic location as a port on the Pacific. Yet the scope and nature of its current interactions with China are far from unique. They give us some clues as to what is happening and what comes next on a national scale.

Compare 1986 and 2011. The information collected in the 1986 study by Martin Singer indicates that between 1970 and 1983, UBC annually hosted roughly ten visiting scholars from China, six graduate students, about the same number of privately sponsored undergraduates, and one visiting delegation. It negotiated exchange agreements with five Chinese partners, and on average seven or eight faculty members travelled to China each year.

Twenty-five years later, about 3,000 students from the PRC are currently enrolled in undergraduate programs at the university, with a further 600 in graduate programs, and more than 100 in post-doctoral positions; scores of Chinese professors visit each year for short or longer term stays; UBC faculty, senior administration, and staff make several hundred visits to China each year; and the university has Memorandums of Understanding (MoUs) with fifty different institutions and functioning partnerships in more than ninety locations.

In 2010 and 2011, UBC conducted campus-wide surveys to assess the breadth and nature of the Asian activities of its professors.[10] Commissioned by a "China Strategy Working Group" composed of twelve faculty members from units across campus who met for a year to produce a report for senior administration, the surveys were complemented by interviews with several members of faculty and staff.[11] The key findings paint an interesting picture:

- 425 professors completed the survey and self-identified as having "a significant professional interest" in Asia. About half of them identified China as their principal interest, roughly three quarters focused on the mainland, and about a quarter noted exclusive or additional attention to Hong Kong and Taiwan.
- The largest number of professors interested in China is in the Faculty of Arts but with significant numbers in forestry and wood science, engineering and applied sciences, education, medicine, and nursing. In total, there were respondents from more than fifty different departments, schools, and units.
- More than sixty faculty members focus on China as their principal field of study, the large majority concentrated in the Faculty of Arts.
- About one third identified teaching and training as their principal interest in China. More than two thirds indicated they were teaching students from China. Less than a quarter were engaged in teaching UBC students about China. Slightly more were engaged in teaching or training professionals from China and a slightly higher number yet (about 25 per cent) involved in teaching or training Chinese in China.
- More than three quarters identified research about China as a principal interest.
- About two thirds identified having research collaborations with individuals in China and about 40 per cent were involved in formal institutional partnerships with Chinese universities. More than a third identified having collaborations with industry, government ministries and research institutes, and non-governmental organizations. The total number of different partnering institutions was more than ninety.
- Most of the research projects and collaborations are centred in the social sciences and humanities. But the biggest funding is in the areas of medicine, public health, engineering, applied sciences, and

business. One project based in the Faculty of Medicine ($100 million over ten years) is about equal to the sum of annual research support in all of the social sciences and humanities combined.
- The funding for scholarships and exchange funds provided as part of the Canada-China scholarly exchange program is considerably less than 1 per cent of the total. Funds provided by the national granting councils were difficult to calculate but probably comprise about an additional 15–20 per cent.

The working group made several recommendations including: the creation of a China Council to support, catalyze, and coordinate university-wide activities;[12] establishment of a representative office in Beijing; re-design of the Centre for Chinese Research and Institute of Asian Research; support for new faculty appointments to fill gaps and imbalances in course offerings especially in key policy areas including environment, energy, natural resources, public health, and public policy; exploration of ways to generate new forms of teaching and research collaborations with Chinese partners; assessment of ways to get more UBC students to China for exchange programs, summer institutes and experiential learning opportunities; expanded recruitment of top students, especially at the graduate and post-doctoral levels; and work to resolve the complicated ethical, moral, and value-based problems inherent in the deeper interaction of different intellectual and political systems.

The experience of UBC and other institutions in Canada indicates that we are now in a different era in which the defining characteristics are: a far more diverse set of academic champions; more diverse constellations of partners on both sides, including universities but not restricted to them; diversified sources of funding; cross-campus coordination as part of "whole of university" arrangements; collaborations with multi-university consortia; prospects for representative offices in China or, more ambitiously, permanent facilities for offering courses, facilitating research, or giving degrees or certificates.

Four areas are especially important in constructing a next generation of what might be called Partnerships 2.0.

Student Recruitment and Exchange

Increasing effort is needed to connect student activity, especially at the graduate and post-doctoral levels, to collaborative teaching and research programs. The aim is to facilitate long-term collaborations through mechanisms including 1+3+1 undergraduate collaborations, and 1+2 joint degree graduate programs directly connected to faculty-led research activity. More resources will be needed for improving student satisfaction and tracking and connecting to individuals after graduation. Joint appointments between Canadian and Chinese universities are being considered and pilot programs on dual doctoral programs soon to be launched. Whether or not Canadian universities establish campuses in China, the contribution they can make to China is through returned and transnational graduates working in both Canada and China as well as helping with the innovation agendas in both countries.

Chinese Studies

Almost every China specialist has active and ongoing collaborations with scholars and institutions in China or is involved in international networks in which China is a focus or has Chinese participants. China is no longer a place studied from its periphery and by telescopes. Rather than an exotic thing apart, it is an integral part of a global conversation. When graduate students are working on a specific field, like the history of China, they can no longer miss out on the global perspective or close collaboration with Chinese counterparts. The new scholarship is producing dramatic advances in our knowledge of China.[13] That said, universities are only one of the places where the new knowledge is being generated. News agencies, media, private research firms, and government agencies are producing kinds of analysis and information that may well have more reach and impact than what universities are producing alone. The best universities in the world are generating innovative programs for helping China scholars better engage policy and applied issues and serve as hubs and partners with other knowledge generators.

Multi-Sectoral Collaborations

While independent, curiosity-based research remains central to the academic mission, China specialists are being called to work as part of interdisciplinary teams and on problem-based topics including population health, environmental protection, and the provision of social services. These collaborations are necessary but difficult, even within individual institutions. In many parts of the university including forestry, medicine and public health, engineering, and education, partnerships are already more complex than simple university-to-university linkages. Some of the most successful are tri- or multi-sectoral arrangements that involve universities and other kinds of institutions including think tanks, government ministries, NGOs, and the private sector. One example is a project at UBC on regional security issues in East Asia co-hosted by UBC and a research institute in Shanghai, involving academics from four Canadian and five Chinese institutions, including participation of officials from the two foreign ministries, and funded by a private Canadian corporation.

Navigating Value and Institutional Differences

These are becoming more numerous and more important as the level of interaction increases. Academic values, norms, and practices are not identical and occasionally collide. Growing trade, investment, human flows, and academic exchanges have punctured the national boundaries separating contrasting value systems. Never before has the Chinese state been more active in attempting to increase China's soft power and projecting Chinese values overseas, including through Chinese language media and surveillance, especially of individuals of Chinese descent, and state-controlled programs like the Confucius Institutes. Several Canadian universities have had intense internal debates, and occasionally public ones, about the Confucius Institutes as well as matters of academic freedom, openness of expression, and research ethics related to issues like consent. It is going to be an ongoing challenge demanding sensitivity and open dialogue to manage these matters and to underwrite sustained and deeper partnerships.

This will become even more challenging if, as other essays in this volume argue, the next frontier in Chinese higher education is deeper collaboration in the humanities and liberal arts. So far as education is about educating the whole person and inculcating an approach that combines curiosity, critical thinking, reflective and sceptical thought, and a capacity for life-long learning, there is a more complicated era ahead. Mutual learning will be essential but not easy as is being seen in other Asian experiments, including the new collaboration in the humanities between the National University of Singapore and Yale University.

CONCLUSION

Most of these challenges will need to be met by the universities themselves, alone or working together. But they will also need support from actors beyond the university, especially federal and provincial governments. In part this is because the Chinese state continues to be the driving force in setting the pace and direction of Chinese educational policy and providing the funding for most of the major initiatives, even as private educational institutions are emerging in China and new foreign campuses and joint ventures are springing up in several parts of the country. In part it is also because all of Canada's G-7 and G-20 partners have national programs and national strategies for expanding academic relations with China.

On the Canadian side, in the absence of a national educational ministry in Ottawa, funding for strategic initiatives, showcase projects, and policy-related collaborations remain essential. The conclusion of the bilateral aid program without provision for alternative funding is a serious handicap. There is no need to reprise the linkage projects of the past. What is needed is matching funds for a small number of strategic initiatives, show case projects, and policy-related collaborations. Contrary to the transactional view of a strictly limited and diminishing role for government in the Canada-China relationship, governments still have the capacity to structure incentives, coordinate, convene and, perhaps again, inspire. At the same time, hundreds of educational institutions from countries other than Canada are also competing to build their own linkages, often with substantial governmental encouragement and funding.

The emerging challenge confronting Canadian academic relations with China and the engagement philosophy which they reflect may be the rise of negative views of China in the general public. Canadians see China as big and getting bigger, two thirds of them feeling that within a decade Chinese power will surpass that of the United States. At the same time they are growing increasingly anxious about Chinese business practices, environment, food and product safety standards, defence modernization, and human rights.[14]

Learning to live with global China is proving more complex than living with China of the Maoist period. Getting China right will depend in large part on the expertise, understanding, and relentless interactions that have no better home than universities. Whether Partnerships 2.0 can unfold at the speed and at the scale they are needed depends on whether they can communicate their role and achievements in a context where publics are increasingly anxious. "Nothing in international cooperation is more precious," writes Fred Bild in chapter 3 of this volume, "than sustained contacts in all of fields of learning and research" (58). Even if this is correct, Partnerships 2.0 will be judged by whether they are seen to produce a larger societal and global good consonant with an evolving strategy of engagement.

NOTES

1 On the Bissell visit, see Macdonald (2010).
2 For the history of the role of educational exchanges as part of the governmental agenda and, later, the rising tide of non-governmental interactions, see Evans (2014).
3 The professorial exchange was launched in 1974, soon terminated, and then resumed in 1977, initially with a heavy emphasis on sending Canadian language teachers to China.
4 The memoir of one of them who later became vice-president international at the University of Alberta, Professor Brian Evans, contains a colourful account of the roles and frustrations of the position. See Evans (2012, 113–85).
5 See Singer (1986, 1996).
6 CIDA files, quoted by Frolic (1996) in his paper presented at the Canadian Political Science Association. Frolic draws heavily on a paper presented by Maybee (1985) at the Conference on Canada-China Relations, in Montebello, Quebec.
7 As quoted in Evans (2014, 40–2).
8 A figure quoted by Qiang Zha (2011, 101).
9 Abrami, Kirby, and McFarlan 2014.
10 The 2011 census compiles results from the 2010 and 2011 surveys. The results, including a map of the locations where UBC faculty have partners, can be found at http://www.iar.ubc.ca/LinkClick.aspx?fileticket=59Kcv2HjUZw per cent3d&tabid=618.
11 The working group addressed four sets of issues: (1) what could be done to promote excellence in research, teaching, and experiential learning in Chinese studies, already a core foundation of UBC's international reputation and identity; (2) what could be done to facilitate next-generation linkages and exchanges with partners in China and expand two-way flows of faculty and students; (3) what could be done to advance UBC's role as global educator and contributor of public goods for its provincial, national, and global communities; and (4) what could be the design of a new administrative infrastructure for UBC in China and on campus better to stimulate, advocate, and assist China-related activities? The final report, "A Next-Generation China Strategy for the University of British Columbia," was submitted to the vice-president research and international on 11 May 2012.
12 Information about the Council is available at www.chinacouncil.ubc.ca.

13 For a recent survey of the state of Chinese studies in Canada, see Manning (2012). While decrying the atomization of scholarship, she chronicles the rise in the number of China specialists and their contributions.

14 See the series of annual national opinion polls produced by the Asia Pacific Foundation of Canada, especially that of June 2014. The results are available at https://www.asiapacific.ca/surveys/national-opinion-polls/2014-national-opinion-poll-canadian-views-asia.

3

University Linkages Past and Future: As Seen from a Diplomatic Perspective

FRED BILD

INTRODUCTION

My appointment to Beijing in 1990 did not come at the best of times. The Chinese economy was in the doldrums, with export activity sharply down, and investments at a standstill. In foreign relations, attitudes varied from guarded to downright hostile. What made these impressions patently obvious was the fact that hotels were virtually empty of foreign guests. Visits from Canadian business people were extremely rare, and the same was the case for most Western offices in Beijing or Shanghai. Judging from the billboards exhorting citizens to beware of foreign influence, one got the feeling that confidence in the future, which had been the hallmark of previous years, was shaky. And yet, when it came to discussing the road ahead for our own, now twenty-year-old relationship, the tone was friendly and optimistic.

After the much-heralded moment in 1970 of the diplomatic opening of China to most of the world, a moment in which the People's Republic of China (PRC) constantly recognized the key role played by Canada, the strength of our ties grew apace. Trade missions, several high-level missions, the Canada-China scholars' exchange program (1974), the designation of China as an eligible recipient of Canadian development assistance (1981), and finally, two years later, the bilateral agreement to establish a Canadian International Development Agency (CIDA) program in China, were all positive steps toward a progressively closer relationship (Evans and Frolic 1991). As the pace of China's reforms resumed, so did our business relations and gradually our political relations. References to Bai Qiu En, the illustrious Norman Bethune, became less frequent; more varied references were made to Canadian cooperation with China in many sectors. What was not so often referred to, yet more thoroughly appreciated, I believe, was the ongoing Canada-China partnership in development cooperation.

PARTNERSHIP TYPES

Throughout my diplomatic career, I had convinced myself that the links established through cultural, academic, and development cooperation were more long-lasting, compared to those following economic partnerships and exchanges. I still believe this, although during the ultra-rapid phase of China's renewed economic take-off in the mid-1990s, one was tempted to invert the above comparison. Joint ventures in industry were booming, foreign banks and insurance companies were setting themselves up for the long-term in China, and the break-neck speed at which the economy was growing seemed to predict a truly sustainable future for our economic relations. And yet, by no means have all those endeavours been long-lasting. Some of the major Canadian companies involved have entirely disappeared. Huge projects, like the Three Gorges Dam, which involved several important Montreal engineering firms, turned out to be disappointing. More importantly, the institutional memories embedded in private enterprises are even less sustainable than those in the public sector.

At the Tsinghua University conference on which this book is based, there was some discussion about the flaws in the Canadian constitutional system, which suffers from the absence of a national authority or coordinating body in the field of education. As a result, whatever linkages we create through our academic exchanges tend to be deprived of a structural memory. This is a fair criticism and does hamper, over time, the sustainability of the links created. Yet the universities do continue to exist and some of them do have viable institutional memories. To a certain extent, they can fill the gap. What they do not do very easily is to create groupings among their brother and sister universities to plan future projects of cooperation (Cao and Poy 2011). Today, as China is moving swiftly into becoming as much of an exporter as an importer of education, and is eager to have many links world-wide, this is even more important to bear in mind and should be of concern to everyone connected with international exchanges in this rapidly globalizing world.

Nevertheless, in spite of the foregoing, I maintain that the human resources developed under the various linkage programs, the training they provided, and the new approaches to social problems they fostered, have not only left serious indelible marks in the minds of all participants, they have also created deeper understanding of the other's culture and habits of thinking and created a positive receptivity and understanding for products, both material and cultural, of each other's milieu. To the extent that each particular experience was not too specialized, it will have been applied in multifarious situations. Whether these new applications will continue to be renewed or adapted is a harder question, and here is where the existence of a central body could be valuable. I think a thorough re-evaluation of the Canada-China University Linkage Program (CCULP) and other linkage programs might yield answers to what sort of organism is required.

In my view, however, what should never be lost sight of is that training in a different milieu, planning and conducting research with people from a different culture, and solving problems by adapting new learning, are experiences of life-long benefit and create links that are treasured along with relations that go beyond just friendship. If contact is regularly renewed and varied through different sorts of common endeavours, it can lead to a meeting of minds that can be called intimacy. That is why any nation that wishes to carry on an enduring relationship with China must devote resources to regularly renewing its old linkages and establishing the necessary institutions. In the absence of federal or provincial governments inclined to tackle this endeavour, Canadian universities are best placed to do so, if only they can set aside their internecine competition.

EARLY PITFALLS

These conclusions are based on admittedly intermittent observations over the last forty-five years. I think they will be justified, however, by the accounts I give further on in this chapter of the linkage programs I have surveyed in Quebec. First, I should return to the beginning of my assignment in China in 1990.

It was a bright, warm October day when my wife and I landed at the Beijing airport to be greeted by the Foreign Ministry's chief of protocol and his retinue of officials. Unbeknown to me, there were five returning Chinese students on the same flight, on their way home from one or two years of study in Canada. I found this out a few days later when a member of the Chinese People's Association for Friendship with Foreign Countries pointed out to me, more in sorrow than in anger, what a pitiful small return this was, considering the large number of Chinese students in Canada at that time. As I went through my various diplomatic courtesy calls on ministers and other senior officials in the weeks that followed, the same lament was reiterated: "China and Canada have become close friends in recent years; we have developed mutually beneficial exchanges, especially in the field of higher education where China is in great need of being able to advance its economic reforms. But how can we continue these exchanges if the Canadian Government deliberately discourages Chinese students from returning to their homeland to make use of what they've learned?"

SANCTIONS

At first, I interpreted this obviously orchestrated complaint as being a barely disguised way of bringing up the sanctions that had been imposed on China by many Western countries. Indeed, the previous year, at the G-7 meeting in Paris, I had accompanied Prime Minister Mulroney and Foreign Minister Joe Clark, in my previous capacity of assistant deputy minister of foreign affairs, and personally witnessed how they worked out with President Bush Sr, Margaret Thatcher, and François Mitterrand the sanctions each country would put into effect in reaction to the recent Tiananmen tragedy. In the case of Canada these had already been spelled out two weeks earlier:

(i) Reorient our programs to favour people-to-people relations
(ii) Reorient CIDA programs away from the coercive arms of the PRC government
(iii) Keep senior official contacts to a minimum[1]

This meant that I could now, a full sixteen months later, minimize the extent of our so-called sanctions. Our trade relations were hardly affected, and our development cooperation programs even less so. An important $19 million umbrella arrangement (later to be known as the CCULP), under which were funded linkages between Canadian and Chinese universities and colleges, was spared and in fact went forward with renewed energy.

In the months to come, as I reflected on this first experience of my Beijing assignment, it brought home to me a number of factors germane to the theme of this volume. Nowhere was the challenge of modernizing China greater than in the field of education, especially in the area of the social sciences. The speed with which market mechanisms were being introduced into the economy entailed social and institutional transformations with which Chinese universities could not hope to keep up, nor could the resources for them be imported in sufficient numbers. The best recourse would be to send students and teachers abroad to acquire the requisite skills. As of the early 1990s, this did not yet seem to be an approach the Chinese government was prepared to embrace wholeheartedly. Little did I realize, even when I left China four years later, that it would soon become obvious that this was indeed the policy being adopted, and obviously with great success.[2] The numbers of Chinese students and researchers now abroad or returning to take up high-level posts in China is ample evidence thereof.

Need I have wondered at the anxiety demonstrated on this question in my early encounters? Particularly as an even greater shadow now loomed over government policies as a whole: the sudden decline in trade and economic exchanges was threatening the whole of *Gaige Kaifang*, the reform and opening campaign of Deng Xiaoping. The question on leaders' minds seemed to be: would the industrialized world actually end up putting a halt to China's modernization? Practically everyone I met in these first weeks was at pains to convince me of two incontrovertible facts:

(i) China is too big and too well connected to be isolated.
(ii) China is resolved never to abandon Gaige Kaifang.

With the benefit of hindsight, it has now been clear for some time that those concerns and resolves were real and well-founded.

TRUE FRIENDSHIP AND USEFUL CONTACTS

What became even more obvious to me in these early days of my sojourn was the fundamental role played by Canadian and Chinese university linkages in maintaining a steady flow of exchanges, data, and contacts in support of useful bilateral projects as well as a continual conversation on how to apprehend the future in a constructive way. As the discussions in this volume will prove, nothing in international cooperation is more precious than sustained contacts in all fields of learning and research. The Chinese side has been consistently faithful to this belief. Unfortunately, I cannot say the same for all the Canadian governments that have been in charge of this supremely important relationship.

The rest of this chapter will be devoted to showing examples in which I have had the privilege of seeing for myself either spectacular results or opportunities lost. I shall not limit myself to university linkages, but will also touch on other projects which such linkages have influenced (either by design or by accident). The vast majority of people who have been involved in cooperative projects in China have, of course, voiced some frustrations. I think that is the nature of the beast. Teaching, studying, or doing research into subjects that entail many actors and are meant to change the future will inevitably give rise to some friction and disagreements. How could it be otherwise? By and large, though, an even greater number of people express satisfaction, a sense of achievement, and genuine personal enrichment. Where they have reservations, or even serious criticisms, is often in the area of failures in institutional memories, the lack of sustained contacts, and as a result, not being able to achieve the full benefits of that which had been set in train. Achievements, it would seem, have mostly been remarkable where faculties, institutes, departments, or schools have been able to maintain constant contact at both senior and intermediate levels to consult about the unforeseen just as much as about future endeavours. Where project funding has been logically programmed and not subjected to fits and starts, results have been more predictable. Where there have been many different sorts of participants involved (such as provincial, national, and local governments; NGOs; and private enterprises), outcomes have been directly in proportion to the effectiveness of the coordinating agency.

LAVAL AND NORMAN BETHUNE

One of the best examples of success in applying the above criteria is the partnership that grew up between Université Laval and the Norman Bethune University of Medical Sciences (NBUMS) located in Changchun, Jilin Province.[3] The outcomes of this Quebec initiative illustrate well the scope and depth derived from an energetic, imaginative, and devoted team effort over decades. Perhaps the initial spark for this relationship can be attributed to the illustrious name of this northeastern medical university, since that may well account for one of their young surgeons (Liu Guojin) being sent in the 1980s to do a two-year post-doctoral fellowship at the thoracic surgery division of the Université Laval. Liu managed to interest members of the Laval faculty as well as the president of NBUMS to have a small group of Laval surgeons visit Changchun. A few months later, in 1989, Dr Jean Couture, then director of Laval's surgery department, led a team of surgeons on their first visit to China.

These first contacts were remarkable for the spontaneous mutual realization that their respective concerns made for a perfect match, and that their needs and capacities could give way to a cooperative project that might yield rapid results and long-term development. Processes such as tumour registries and a general integrated approach to cancer treatment were seen as promising areas of cooperation. And indeed they were. More fundamentally, both teams developed a strong sense of mutual respect. Dr Couture attributed the highest importance to this factor.

CCULP funding from CIDA lasted for five years, until 1995. In that period, some twenty-five doctors and technicians of different sorts came to Quebec City for training periods that varied from four to eighteen months. Most of these people participated in the creation of the Bethune-Laval Oncology Unit (BLOU), which I had the privilege of visiting when it was still in its infancy. When Changchun hosted the international conference on cancer in 1993, a first for China, it was clear to all the Chinese and Canadian specialists present that they were witnessing the emergence of a new model for cancer care and treatment that would spread throughout the medical sphere in China. Indeed, several BLOU units were instituted thereafter in Jilin Province and their methods promulgated throughout the country. The Laval participants consider that the impact of their project went much further afield than they had anticipated. The project influenced profoundly not only the student body and faculty of Norman Bethune University, but also local governments, other hospitals, local industry, and the public. In Canada, it helped make universities more aware of the realities of joint projects of this sort in China, and how to ensure that such projects fit into the local context.

What impressed me in the exercise I have just now completed is the realization that a specific results-oriented approach, such as the Laval-Bethune enterprise, could more easily give rise to secondary, though overarching, consequences than those that were spelled out in the initial agreement. The long-term impacts on the practice of medicine – and oncological treatment in particular – were, of course, always in the participants' minds. Less obvious benefits, however, such as environmental concerns, human resources development, and ancillary social policies, did not seem to come up frequently in discussions or planning sessions. I never did fully appreciate why so many agencies had to be involved in overseeing, coordinating, and reporting on activities, but I assumed it was necessary to ensure that maximum benefit would emerge from the funds invested.

CIDA renewed the financial support under the Special University Linkage Consolidation Program (SULCP) to 2001, with results that justified the "consolidation" label. By that time Dr Liu had become the director of the Oncology Department, and a tumour registry had been established and linked to other cancer-treatment and research centres.

Quebec hospitals began corresponding with their Jilin counterparts, and established "miniature BLOUs." All of this had given rise to a general trend of information exchange and media attention. The flow of documentation and translations became constant, especially between major centres like Beijing, Shanghai, and Tianjin, which together had a total population of fifty-six million. Perhaps even more important than the institutional development and proliferation was the general acceptance in practice of the emphasis to be placed on early consultation and diagnosis.

The best evidence of the seriousness with which the Jilin cancer treatment community pursued its outreach and PR task can be found in the fact that they enlisted the help of Dashan (Mark Rowswell), the best-known and beloved Canadian in China. Thanks to the instant recognition and popularity he enjoys in all parts of this vast country, his TV appearances in support of anti-cancer campaigns are always effective. Be they posters about how to detect early signs of cancer, or televised appeals about the danger of tobacco consumption, his pro bono work in these areas has invariably had highly useful fallout.[4]

From my own perspective, the most rewarding feature of these more than twenty years of bilateral cooperation in the medical field lies in the mutual rewards and the respect the various participants have developed. I found it particularly pleasing that the Chinese side has given Canada credit on two counts. The first was that after the atrocious harm the Cultural Revolution had done to medical services throughout the country, Canada had helped China repair the damage and develop a modern approach to cancer treatment and prevention. The second great challenge in this relationship was to keep the project on track after the serious political fallout of the Tiananmen crackdown. With assiduous insistence on both sides, Laval folks managed to convince CIDA to keep all of it not only alive, but to speed it up. On the Chinese side, Jilin partners confronted an even greater obstacle: how to persuade Beijing authorities to allow additional trainees to travel to Quebec in the face of fears that they might be encouraged by those wily Canadians not to return. Their assurances worked and the project encountered neither major obstacles nor retardation. The success of the Laval-NBUMS cooperation is perhaps one of the most spectacular, if only for its sustainability and long-term results, but luckily there are others equally inspiring.[5]

CLEAR PLANNING

Efforts by specific individuals and devotion by whole teams of participants, as in the example cited above, are quite clearly an important part of the equation, but one must not overlook an even more basic requirement: the foundations of these exchanges were realistic and sound. When the CIDA China project was negotiated in 1982–83, the understanding on the Canadian side was that the immediate objective of the project could not be to forge markets for Canadian products, but rather to assist in the launching of China's development of a free market economy – that is, to help the PRC implement its program of reforms. This was a strategic approach rather than a narrower one of short-term commercial returns. The basic emphases therefore were to be in managerial and technical training, energy conservation, improvement of agricultural technology, and the fostering of human and institutional contacts.[6] These objectives did not emerge simply from a bilateral negotiation between CIDA and the Chinese Ministry of Economic Relations and Trade (MOFERT); they also received support from a number of government departments in Ottawa, as well as from provincial governments, universities, NGOs, and significant private stakeholders.

These objectives may not always have been uppermost in the minds of project managers, but they were subjected to periodic reviews by CIDA headquarters, as well as the Department of External Affairs (DEA, later DFAIT, and still later DFATD). Among the development cooperation groups in Canada, CIDA, International Development Research Centre (IDRC), and many NGOs, the crackdown at Tiananmen also gave rise to anxiety and concern about the future. What would become of government-to-government relations? Would the new guidelines on CIDA programs lead to a slowdown in activity? How badly would future budgets be cut? Without ministerial visits, how could one count on repeated declarations of continued collaboration? On our side too there were worries about what would happen to China's programs of economic reform and the impact any slowdown could have on existing Canada-China activities. Luckily, the worst fears did not materialize.

COOPERATING ON HUMAN RIGHTS?

The Chinese economy did indeed slow down for a time, but ongoing projects were hardly affected. In fact, the new focus on people-to-people relations proved salutary for many programs. CCULP orientations were in fact tailor-made for multiplying linkages at levels of society below those of senior officials. Since we had had no meaningful contacts between the military or other bodies of state control, there was no diminution in the overall level of our joint activities. Even more significant was the newly awakened Canadian emphasis on human rights. While there was little inclination among collaborators on either side to get involved in acrimonious debates on the subject, the recurring themes of good governance and institutional modernization lent themselves well to open and frank dialogues on how programs could be oriented to encourage advances in these fields. A rather civilized dialogue thus grew up around these questions. Democratic governance, human rights, social justice, and equality before the law are examples of the subjects that flowed quite naturally from any discussion of the social consequences of rapid economic growth and social transformation. Eventually, this would lead to the program of training judges at the Université de Montréal (UdeM) described in chapter 12 of this volume and in several programs of managerial training. In passing, I might say that what I have been able to conclude from these various exchanges is that those that made more lasting impressions on the participants were those that happened in the context of wider questions, be they institutional (such as how to fashion business management courses so as to attract more female students), structural (such as how to ensure more equal access to a new medical clinic), or related to particular community development questions (such as how to ensure genuine worker representation on the board of a village enterprise).[7] These turned out to be the discussions more frequently referred to in later meetings or in following projects.

Donors, we were told by headquarters, like to see results. Where one is dealing with ethereal subjects like equitable growth, environmental sustainability, and good governance, quantifiable achievements are usually hard to come by. People in the field often say they can see them, but what they mostly mean is that they can feel changes in attitude and habits, not the kind of evidence that their far-removed masters will readily accept. Progress in matters of poverty reduction, health benefits, and school enrolment can of course be quantified, but only many months or perhaps years later. For my part, aid workers' reports of conversations were often more revealing than those much-delayed and laboured-over official reports. I can well remember, for example, one of my CIDA staff telling me that in a chat with a Chinese partner working on a student technician exchange project, the latter had opened an unprompted discussion on how institutional restructuring of education would inevitably lead to fundamental changes in political governance. Quite apart from the fact that such a subject would have been considered far too sensitive only a few years earlier, it was proof to my staff worker that the collaboration he and others had established was paying off. I dare say this sort of "evidence" occurred regularly, but could not be adduced. Nonetheless, these sorts of results describe the meeting of minds and transcultural adaptation of ideas that are the very purpose of linkages in the field of higher learning.

In a more empirical and systematic fashion, results were described in CIDA's twenty-year review of its China program and of the university linkages in particular. I learned of it some years after my departure from China and was extremely pleased by its conclusions. There were, of course, some shortcomings; how could there not be? The conclusions were nonetheless very clear about the value of higher-level educational cooperation and the long-term impact it can produce; given the right sort of structural conditions and dedicated leadership and participants the effects are felt not only on national policies, but tend to promote further contacts and relations of a mutually beneficial kind (Wilson 2001). The review thus makes a strong argument for furthering the most valuable of the linkages through continued cooperation not necessarily of donor-recipient type. Several of the exchanges established at the outset through Canadian funding have in fact been converted into bilateral give-and-take arrangements (such as the twenty-five or more Canadian study centres originally established through Canadian funding and book donations, now counting over forty-five, all of them financed entirely through Chinese sources).

I am aware that this recital of my own experiences and the lessons to be derived from them may give the impression that the practice of traditional forms of diplomacy, or their more modern adaptations, covers the entire field of country-to-country interactions. That would be a vast exaggeration. Yet one must not neglect to note that the traditional form of diplomacy has given way these days to a multi-varied professional practice where questions of development cooperation rate just as highly as those of political relations; where, in fact all activities abroad that involve government participation lead the local Canadian missions to provide assistance in some form or other. Such involvement, moreover, will range from peripheral and preliminary advice to headquarters about the wisdom or feasibility of a proposed project, all the way to hands-on participation in planning and execution. For example, I found helping in the design and financing of a minor water purification project in a Xinjiang village more satisfying than adding several pages of recommendations to a billion-dollar World Bank project on cereal storage and transportation facilities. There was no question, of course, which one was likely to have more impact in the longer term, but for the participant in the field, direct human impact and short-term implementation are far more satisfying.

Many professional practitioners in the field of development cooperation have over time made comparisons between their own philosophies of international cooperation and those that drive the governmental actors (Henders and Young 2012). In today's cosmopolitan world, non-state actors are far more numerous than official representatives. In most cases they have more latitude in behaviour, as well as in the views they express. This disparity is bound to grow as globalization progresses. One should not, however, assume that state functionaries always whistle the same tune. Only within governments with a particularly strict control of the "official message" is the homogenous discourse effectively enforced. Nor should one conclude that where one side sticks to the officially authorized version (what the French call *langue de bois*) and the other feels free to speak his / her mind, no worthwhile interaction is possible. On the contrary, that sort of apparently unequal dialogue can be an additional path toward better mutual comprehension. This would appear to hold true at the state-to-state level as much as at less-official levels, and explains why sometimes even highly constrained discourse can lead to surprising results (Bild 2007).

Nor should one jump to the conclusion that in the bad old days of the Cold War, when for all practical purposes only strictly official contacts existed between the two antagonists, there was no possibility of unofficial communication.[8] What makes for a more relaxed environment in today's and tomorrow's interactions is their vast diversity and the instantaneity and exponential growth of media available for all communication needs. Some might argue that the latter phenomena render closeness of contact less important, perhaps even more difficult. The members of the Université Laval surgical cancer unit would, however, maintain that the length of time it took for the lessons learned from their teamwork with the Bethune Hospital to be distributed and absorbed by all concerned has vastly improved and done nothing to diminish the value of the personal linkages and intimacy that created the preceding joint lessons.[9]

SOFT POWER

Much has been published in recent years about the modern version of propagandistic, cultural outreach of powerful state realities. In the present context, the more fashionable description of these activities comes under the heading "Soft Power" and is often cited in the context of globalization. No nation of any importance today casts this "new-fangled" concept aside; certainly not China, which is in the process of fundamentally rethinking its old-fashioned notions of propaganda. Indeed the PRC is making full use of the Internet to disseminate vast amounts of information about itself, to occupy a major place on this global network, and to furnish it with well-fleshed out opinion-forming articles.

It should be obvious to any rational observer that in this new international environment, where countries are competing more than ever for market opportunities, access to resources, and most of all to the results of cutting edge research, nothing is more essential than joint endeavours and other forms of cooperation. The fact that the Canadian government some time ago decided that the former university linkage programs no longer suited its purposes merits closer examination beyond the vituperative criticism that has so far been levelled at it, but I do not think it will serve the more constructive objective of how and by what it can be replaced. Our government has given a low priority to this major development in inter-state relations. Its approach seems to be: "What practical purpose can be served through unfocused diffusion of all the non-economic attributes of Canadian reality?"[10]

As Professor Qiang Zha has pointed out (Zha 2011a), some Canadian universities have not succumbed to throwing up their hands and agonizing at the downgrading of the old linkages; instead they have fashioned new arrangements. As we see in all aspects of international relations today, transformative changes are underway in how to adjust operations to the realities of this post-modern world. Following the example of their more enterprising counterparts in China, universities have taken up the challenge and negotiated bilateral arrangements with Chinese institutions for regular exchanges and joint research projects.

TRAINING JUDGES

Funding for that sort of autonomous joint venture is more readily available in the natural sciences than in the social sciences, but even in the latter, determined attempts for support from provinces, think-tanks, or NGOs can produce the means to continue old partnerships or create new ones. In the case of UdeM, the highly successful four-year CIDA-funded collaboration its Law faculty established with the National Magistrates College of China for the training of judges has now been transferred to the Supreme Court of Canada, where, one hopes, longer-term resources will be more easily accessible. The UdeM has recovered from the loss of its Chinese juridical apprentices by forging new programs in Beijing for its own law students and by hosting Chinese students in Montreal for its summer law school sessions. (More discussion on this topic occurs later in this chapter. See Lefebvre, Rigaud, and Steyn in chapter 12 of this volume.)

INDUSTRIAL RELATIONS

Equally interesting, though on a smaller scale, is the UdeM's School of Industrial Relations (ÉRI). As Canada's foremost institution in this field, ÉRI has found a ready demand in China for expertise in human resources management and labour legislation. In 2011, the school established agreements with the School of Labour and Human Resources at Renmin University and, the following year, a similar agreement with the School of Labour Economics at the Capital University of Economics and Business (Beijing). The agreements provide for regular student and faculty exchanges, as well as joint research projects. In order for the agreements to become rapidly effective, the ÉRI has organized a summer school in English for Chinese students in the final year of their baccalaureate and for those studying for master's degrees. Courses offered are in topics such as international aspects of health and safety at work, human resources training and development, international human resources management, and labour negotiations.

The Quebec students who benefited from the counterpart summer courses in Beijing were able to follow a course (in English) on the economic implications of labour in China. As of 2013, internships are also available in selected multinational enterprises and two post doctoral students are at present working at the ÉRI and at the university's International Research Centre on Globalization and Labour. The interest on the Chinese side appears largely due to the urgent need felt in China for fundamental changes in the entire field of workers' rights and the autonomy of unions.[11]

CARDIOLOGY

In an entirely different context, international university collaboration can be much more commercial and self-financing. The Montreal Heart Institute, for example, the leading cardiology hospital in Canada and one of the largest cardiology institutes in the world, is also the largest centre for preventive medicine research in Quebec. Affiliated with UdeM, the institute has for several years engaged in viable commercial relations with corresponding institutes for joint research projects often financed by pharmaceutical companies or other medical service organizations. Their findings are published under peer review and cover a wide range of cardiological concerns. It is an esteemed organization, recognized for its high degree of scientific rigour and its world-wide range of collaborators. Its links with Chinese research institutes have not only widened the relevance of its findings, but have also given those of its personnel involved in planning and elaborating new projects a much wider perspective in the methodologies and applications of their results.[12]

TRANSPORTATION

In the field of transport technology we discover a slew of entirely different sorts of engagement. Since the early 1990s, the faculty at UdeM has included a geographer, Claude Comtois, who is a specialist in all questions of transport. He has studied in Hong Kong and done research on the mainland as well. He is familiar with every deep-water port, and most others, in East Asia, as well as with river traffic throughout China. Early in the CCULP era, he was invited to Shanghai to help out with methodologies for analyzing data related to the development of a light rail transit (LRT) network. While there, Comtois met many experts who were involved in local and country-wide transport. They appreciated his approach and the know-how he brought to bear on the problems at hand. He soon found himself training trainers and increasing needed linkages among Chinese universities. He was able to get repeated grants in the 1989–95 and 1996–2001 CCULP phases. Through the fortuitous timing of Montreal's sister-city relationship with Shanghai, he was able to get both mayors committed to the success of the LRT studies. This translated itself into partnerships with both the public and private sectors and into very privileged access to all transportation-related data in China.

Throughout this collaboration, extremely useful synergies of outlook were established, as well as links that are still eminently operational today. Public- and private-sector participants recognized that it was essential to success that both sectors work together. They agreed that the development of environmentally friendly logistics could not be left to the private sector alone. In a recent meeting in Shanghai, it became quite clear that the methods (such as technical indicators, performance controls, and various types of software) developed during the days of CIDA-sponsored cooperation were being applied and were proving their worth. The study extended to the governance of port cities, how to compare urban with rural transport needs, and studies of best practices. Similar links were established with the Chinese Ministry of Railways (four million full-time employees at the time) in a bid to reform the entire structure and its administration.

Other studies flowing from these were funded under a separate CIDA program which included more institutions in China and Canada. Links were created with the Université du Québec à Montréal (UQAM), McGill University, Concordia University, the University of British Columbia (UBC), and the University of Victoria. In China, these links were extended to the provinces of Gansu and Guangzhou, in order to create a vast network of research centres to tackle the truly long-term problem of China's future railway network. At the same time, this pluralistic collaboration helped the Canadian participants become more familiar with the challenges of China's process of privatization and how best to train large groups of technicians to bring themselves up-to-date on state-of-the-art rail-linked software. Very valuable data became easily accessible to Canadians on Chinese maritime transport and terminal capacities. Several of the participants in these studies regret the fact that the ready access to data they had through their extensive contacts of long ago will likely die when those contacts disappear. To them the cancellation of these programs, or their downgrading, represents the height of bad management, since it is wasting the most valuable fruits of the initial investment.

ARCTIC RESEARCH

One of the many surprises that arose from this survey of people who had been closely involved in Canada-China joint studies was that, despite their unanimous and deeply felt disappointment at the present fate of CIDA programs and the curtailment of cooperative programs with China, they are still hopeful that viable alternative sources of funding might be discovered. One suggestion was that since China is manifesting a serious interest in arctic affairs, they might be willing to set up a joint umbrella organization for arctic research, which could even include native, environmental, and transport studies.[13]

BRAIN DRAIN

As we pursue this examination of achievements and sorely missed programs, I am struck by the fact that not much attention seems to be paid to a practice I've called "brain raiding," the counterpart of what in Canada is a north-south brain drain. This was, of course, the not-entirely unfair accusation Chinese officials levelled at us in the aftermath of 4 June 1989, as mentioned earlier in this chapter. Here, however, I raise it in a more general sense. Ever since I can remember, there has been an argument current in Canada about how to provide our economy with the necessary inputs. It is essentially about the bad habits we acquired as a colonial dependency, when in exchange for our raw material exports, we imported our industrial machinery and brains from abroad. In my tender youth I had the privilege of working for a time in the personnel department of a major Montreal telecommunications firm. Much of our time was devoted to recruiting technicians and graduate engineers in the UK, and most of the company's hardware was imported from the US. I learned that this was not an isolated practice, but a fair representation of what my sophomoric cynicism then called general Canadian parsimony. Canadian industry saved itself the expense of training its young technicians, while the country avoided the expense of producing the numbers of engineers required. At the same time, Canadian industry also saved itself from having to invest in the production of machinery by importing much of it from the US. In exchange, we exported our raw materials with little if any value added.

Some people would say that, in fact, very little has changed. That would be unfair, since Canadian engineering schools have over the years become far more productive and our instrumentation capacities have grown, but some of the old habits remain. A report by *Engineers Canada*[14] informs me that in 2011 Canada produced fewer than 12,000 engineers, and that at this rate by 2020 there will be a gap of some 80,000 engineers. Meanwhile China claims to be producing over 600,000 engineers per year.[15] While quality comparisons of these graduates may reduce the ratio, the trend may well see us importing more and more Chinese technical and engineering talent in years to come. Would we not be better advised to import the students and hire them *sur place*?

China's leaders seemed to have been spared from struggling over these conundrums in their striving to modernize their educational system. As they emerged from the Great Proletarian Cultural Revolution, they found that their backwardness in the natural sciences was dire compared to other countries; in the social sciences it was even worse; and in more modern fields, like management and entrepreneurial skills, it was almost nonexistent (Purvis 1991). It was clear that if China was to participate in open free markets, it needed to train a whole generation of managers and technicians. It also soon became apparent that these gaps could not be filled by relying only on internal bootstrap measures. Even by opening the door to private institutions of higher learning and founding additional state-run schools and colleges, the catch-up rate would be too slow.

Thus was formed the decision to let young people seek educational opportunities abroad. This whole-hearted three-pronged approach soon paid off.

On the other hand, in the whole period since 1983, Canada has been doing well in the field of training Chinese foreign students in our colleges and universities; indeed, in the year 2000, China's share of PhDs in Canada reached 25 per cent (Zha 2011a). Must we therefore conclude that an important portion of the funds we have invested in high-level training of Chinese is nothing more than self-serving? The argument could well be made, but it is really quite an old debate, which has never been settled. How can one prevent a professional who has acquired first-world skills from selling his labour in a higher-paying country?

In some ways the Canada-China model could be held up as the answer. Yet China is in many respects an exception in this field, since its vast modernization program produced a demand for skilled people far in excess of what its own institutions of higher learning could produce. In the last two decades of breakneck rapid growth, it was able to count on the students it sent abroad to return to well-paying positions and contribute to the furthering of the development process. The developed partner, Canada, while continuing to broaden and deepen its trade with China, seems no longer to be the great attraction for technology transfers or joint research projects. With some notable exceptions, China's essential interest in Canada now appears confined to raw materials and energy. The reasoning, one assumes, is: "Why not just encourage Canada to continue foremost as a provider of primary materials, while China becomes the supplier of brains and technology?"

THE YEARS AHEAD

If the above imagined quote does indeed reflect today's official thinking, it should not be surprising; after all, was that not the strategy of Canada's major trading partners past and present? What makes it different in the present circumstances is that this time we are not dealing with a friendly, though formidable, hegemon with whom we are quite intimate, nor with an erstwhile colonial master, but rather with a rising star which is still far from its apogee. Its array of future prowess is still unclear. Its directions are still debatable. The closeness of the long-term relationship is as yet not discernible. Nor is this a country of similar political and cultural traditions. Yet what is clear is that Canada will have to develop a strategy in the face of this new phenomenon. It shall have to be a strategy not based simply, as in the past, on shared history and assumptions about shared values, but on expectations of being able to work together in developing means of coping with the formidable challenges that the world is to face in this new century.

Since the end of the Second World War and before China's surprising rise, only two other countries had risen from the ashes to become major economic powers: Germany and Japan. The former threw its lot resolutely in with the European Union (EU) and, while serving as a potentially strong backer of the EU's current challenges of economic restructuring, is far from emerging as a major political force. Japan, on the other hand, after having played a significant part in China's modernization, is now struggling with the shaping of its future role in East Asia. Neither of these nations is a model for what we can expect in the rise of China. In the early 1990s, as I was witnessing the remarkable economic take-off of China from my post in Beijing, I was reminded of a similar experience in the early 1960s, when the Japanese economy was starting to raise the average citizen's standard of living and to hoist the economy to a level where twenty years later it would be buying up large vineyards in France and vast pieces of real estate in Manhattan. Much of this was a result of a burgeoning surplus of exports, grounded in the advantage of a highly disciplined and underpaid work force. It was also, however, a result of determined efforts in high-tech research, development, and innovation.

Many articles and several books have since been written about the need for Canada to renew its policies of engagement with China. The more fully reasoned ones underline the mainstays of our strategies throughout the years: fostering *balanced economic exchanges*; encouraging China's membership in *multilateral institutions* and respecting their norms; and increasing *cooperative educational, research, and cultural* activities for the mutual benefit of our respective populations and the solidity of their friendship. There is one consideration that is not stressed enough, however, in most of these generally germane proposals. It has to do with the future trajectories of China's rise. Most observers agree that while China's heretofore staggering economic growth is beginning to slow down, it is far from the end of its rise, and the latter will certainly continue its trend toward modernization (Shambaugh 2013). Even if the models and structures of some of China's new modernity will not inevitably follow those we are familiar with, what is becoming fairly clear is that the long path ahead will lead China into scientific, technological, and even social transformations that will have important repercussions for the rest of the world. Some of its advances in technology may well give rise to more evolved and more practical means of tackling future challenges such as new epidemic diseases, environmental problems, and institutional practices and management. (I can't forget how quickly Japanese car makers transited from zero sales in North America to teaching Detroit how to make more economical and practical vehicles.)

China's rise is of a different magnitude and length than that of its immediate predecessors. It will inevitably reinvent key aspects of dealing with contemporary problems. Canada would do itself an unforgivable disservice if it failed to be associated with the research and development leading to some of these advances. These thoughts do not reflect merely unalloyed optimism. They flow from recognition of size and mass. We have already witnessed many instances in which the consequences of a local Chinese catastrophe have made themselves felt around the world, not to mention such pandemic repercussions as the SARS and the swine and bird flu outbreaks. In a country that produces 50 per cent of the world's pork meat, it is not surprising that genetic recombination of such viruses should originate there, particularly in densely populated cities; the international effects are, moreover, hastened by the pace of globalization and the scale of intercontinental travel. When the Beijing Genomics Institute (located in Shenzhen) manages to sequence the genome to help decipher the roots of Alzheimer's or schizophrenia, do we wish to see Canadians involved in the research or will we just wait until we have sold enough oil to be able to buy the results?[16]

Canadian firms have, it is true, been active over the years in working together with their Chinese counterparts in developing, building, and engineering all sorts of advanced projects. These include hydroelectric dams, grain handling and storage facilities, long bridges, tall buildings, and complicated railway networks. In some instances, such associations have had more long-lasting social effects (Jackson et al. 2001). Generally, however, they have not created the continuing close associations that come from linkages formed in together devising approaches to major problems, such as has been accomplished through past inter-institutional cooperation. Some university linkages have no doubt fallen short of expectations; by and large, however, they have proven themselves even more effective than some of the best of the other development cooperation projects. As the dean of law of UdeM, Guy Lefebvre, explained to me, "Without the various by-products resulting from the initial linkage with China's National Judges College, we would never have developed the close institutional relationship, nor the other very promising ties with China University College, or Shanghai's East China University of Political Science and Law." He underlined that none of this would have happened had the institutions involved not achieved the close working rapport and continuity of contact that they did. Nor could they have worked out the reciprocal studies programs or those for Chinese and Canadian business executives, that are all now marching forward and bound to blossom in the next few years beyond the university's wildest expectations[17] (see chapter 12 of this volume for further detail).

Thus, as China enters this far more critical phase of its development, it is through true and long-lasting partnerships that Canadians can further their own interests and those of the world's future, in general. The above are strategic concerns. Canadians have traditionally sought to balance their lack of weight compared to the great powers not by playing them off against each other, but by helping them build a modern international architecture for meaningful communication and for reducing harmful rivalry. Now is the time to put to work our long experience on the world stage to fashion for Canada a new constructive role. It starts not by simply imitating our old and trusted friends, but rather by reinforcing the trust and amity we have earned over the last forty-five years with China.

As Edward T. Jackson has so clearly demonstrated (Jackson 2003), with the right approach and proper funding, the successful results of university linkages have many types of multiplier effects, and these derive largely from the advantages inherent in teaching and research activities themselves. The intergenerational make-up and multidisciplinary features of most development projects, combined with the influence scholars often have in government circles, can strengthen institutions and produce policy changes that generate further development over larger regions and time. I believe the Quebec examples I have briefly described above show that the permanent nature of the institutions, and the durable memory they have, lead also to positive mutual modernization phenomena that often result in unexpectedly enhanced and different productive projects.

Canadian and Chinese institutions are facing quite different growth and development trajectories, if for no other reason than that their capacity requirements are on such different scales. Yet, the global issues they confront are similar. It would be a shame if, simply for lack of official encouragement, the habits of collaboration we have established over the years were allowed to fade away.

NOTES

1 Joe Clark, "China and Canada: The Months Ahead," Ministerial Statement on 30 June 1989.
2 "Time to take a proactive approach in the global hunt for rare skills," *China Daily*, 15 July 2013.
3 The views and summaries in this section are based on interviews with four surgeons involved at different stages in the cooperative project between Université Laval and the Norman Bethune University of Medical Sciences, Drs Jean Couture, Yvan Douville, Jean Deschênes and Jean Deslauriers, between 1993 and 2013.
4 See the "Conclusions in Evaluation" report prepared by France P. Belleau, Chief of Oncology Unit at Hôpital du Saint-Sacrement, 1995.
5 See the *Globe and Mail* article, 11 June 2005.
6 See CIDA China Country Program Review, 2007.
7 Based on discussions with provincial officials in charge of organizing village governance reform, in Henan Province, 1994.
8 For frank and outspoken conversations, see the 1974 discussions with Zhou Enlai at Geneva in Chester Ronning's memoir (Ronning 1974, 235–9). For my own part, I remember vividly an encounter with a senior Foreign Ministry official, shortly after my accreditation in 1979 to the Socialist Republic of Vietnam, who informed me that he had been able as a young Viet Cong soldier during the worst part of the war to form a very positive picture of the Canadian people through three separate visits he had made to several Canadian cities. Everyone he met, he told me, had said how much they deplored the USA's support of the Vietnamese traitors in the South. It turned out that his visits had been fundraising tours he had made to Toronto, Montreal, and Vancouver, sponsored by various Canadian church groups.
9 My interviews with Drs Deschênes, Deslauriers, and Douville at Université Laval, Quebec, 18 July 2013.
10 See speech by Rt. Hon. Joe Clark at Lecture at the Centre for International Governance Innovation (CIGI), 28 May 2013.
11 The above is based in its entirety on an interview I had on 18 December 2013 with Jean Charest, director of the School of Industrial Relations.
12 This information is based on an interview I had with Dominique Johnson, director of research at the Montreal Heart Institute, December 2013.
13 Much of the foregoing is based on discussions with Professor Claude Comtois at the Université de Montréal, who is a foremost expert on transportation problems in China and has led major research projects in this area, thanks to funding under CCULP and SULCP.

14 www.engineerscanada.ca is the website of the national organization of the twelve provincial and territorial regulating bodies that oversee the practice of engineering throughout the country. It also has a site providing useful information to engineers abroad seeking immigration opportunities in Canada. The site is prepared under the guidance of the Canadian immigration authorities.
15 See www.bloomberg.com.
16 See the article by Christina Larson in the MIT *Technology Review*, 11 February 2013.
17 Interview with Guy Lefebvre, dean of law, Université de Montréal, 9 January 2014. Part II: Management Education and China's Economic Transformation.

PART TWO

Management Education and China's Economic Transformation

4

Transforming Canada-China Educational Cooperation: Legacies and Future Challenges in Management Education

ROLF MIRUS[1]

INTRODUCTION

The objective of this chapter is twofold. Firstly, it presents a description of the operations of the university partnerships formed under the Canada-China Management Education Program (CCMEP) of the Canadian International Development Agency (CIDA) in the 1980s and 1990s. This description relies heavily on the experience of those at the University of Alberta (U of A). Secondly, this chapter has the task of evaluating the impact of the partnerships along four dimensions, namely the extent to which the university linkages: (i) contributed to China's rapid transformation; (ii) fostered ideas that addressed humane and democratic governance, social justice, and environmental sustainability, that is, issues that resulted in the wake of rapid economic and technological change; (iii) contained features that made them effective or presented challenges; and (iv) resulted in lessons for future collaborations between Canadian and Chinese universities. A brief historical perspective follows to set the stage.

Western-style universities in China in the first half of the twentieth century were an outgrowth of colleges established by Christian missionaries in the late nineteenth century, and were greatly influenced by the American model. After 1949, Soviet/Russian influence was paramount for a decade before the Chinese educational system was thrown into chaos by Maoist experiments and the subsequent Cultural Revolution, when universities were forced to put politics ahead of learning. In a sense, therefore, the 1982 start of China's cooperation with Canada in management education represented a reformation or a reorientation rather than a transformation.

In the late 1970s, Deng Xiaoping's "First Liberation of Thought" led to pragmatic economic reforms that initiated dramatic change in China. Others who contributed to the political acceptability of management education were Hu Yaobang and, a few years later, Zhao Ziyang. As management education has a significant social sciences orientation (in addition to the "art" of management), and the social sciences had been severely criticized during the Cultural Revolution, there was some delay before the field gained political acceptability. It was initially embedded in polytechnic and engineering institutions under the title Management Engineering. Hayhoe relates a conversation with academic leaders at Tongji University, who in the early 1960s saw the need for managers with an economic focus and set up a specialization called Construction and Industrial Economics. But they "found no understanding or support in the outside political climate for this initiative" (Hayhoe 1986, 10). At that time, the political focus was on training technical experts, not managers, and the new specialization at Tongji University was closed down.

In the wake of the reforms initiated by Deng Xiaoping under the heading of "The Four Transformations," China emphasized the delivery of economic goods to the people. This task required a group of elite administrators to implement the new policies effectively; hence an awareness emerged at institutions of higher education of the need to train new cadres with technocratic skills. The cadre recruitment system was reformed between 1982 and 1987 (Zheng 2014, 26), and in this way the opening for a renewed cooperation with Western models was created.

Canada's relationship with China prior to these changes was a special one: grain was supplied during periods of need, and there was no direct colonial history. The Minister of External Affairs visited China in 1981 and a planning mission followed in 1982. In the spirit of mutual respect, CIDA signed a Memorandum of Understanding (MOU) with China's State Education Commission (SEdC) with the purpose of strengthening management education programs at eight of China's "key" universities.

The objectives of the MOU were to assist in the training of "teachers who will master the knowledge of modern management science, strengthen their teaching and research capabilities, and promote through cooperation both friendship and mutual understanding between the universities of Canada and China" (Ryan 1987, 1). The underlying notion was to achieve a multiplier impact with limited resources by "training the trainers."

In October 1982, the formerly named Ministry of Foreign Economic Relations and Trade (MOFERT), now the Ministry of Commerce, sent a delegation of twenty-three Chinese university administrators to Canada to discuss the nature of the prospective cooperation with their Canadian counterparts. A conference hosted in Ottawa by the Association of Universities and Colleges of Canada (AUCC) in November of that year led to negotiations between prospective partner universities regarding the specific components of the institutional linkages. In the case of the University of Alberta (U of A), a delegation from Xi'an Jiaotong University (XJTU) led by Dean and Vice-President Wang Yingluo came to Edmonton and concluded a draft cooperation agreement with Dean Roger S. Smith of Business. This agreement was subsequently finalized in the spring of 1983, when three professors from the U of A and the University of Saskatchewan visited Xi'an.

While the planned activities differed among the linkages, the Canadian Treasury Board granted approval for the funding of seven linkages in September 1983, and for an eighth linkage in August 1984. Once funding was approved, the activities commenced. The budget for the five-year initiative was set at roughly $12 million, and oversight in Canada rested with CIDA's Institutional Cooperation and Development Support Division (ICDS). The Chinese partner institutions provided substantial in-kind contributions in the form of housing for visitors, food services, local transportation, medical services, and general hospitality.

GETTING ACQUAINTED: THE CANADA-CHINA MANAGEMENT EDUCATION PROGRAM (CCMEP) PHASE I (1983–1988)

Background

Given the substantial cultural and developmental differences between Canada and China at the time, Phase I of the cooperation can be characterized as a period of getting acquainted and building trust between the partners. This included institutional agreements with eight "key" universities in China. The components of the agreements were:

- graduate degrees (MBA, MSc, and PhD) for junior faculty
- visiting scholarships for senior faculty
- course delivery in China for the purpose of supporting new local MBA programs
- research in China by visiting Canadian faculty
- provision of books, equipment, materials, and expertise for management education

Little is known or documented regarding the state of development of management education in China at the time the linkages became operational. A visit during the second year of Phase I revealed that the library of the School of Management at XJTU contained only a handful of English management books and no periodicals. Other schools may have had different initial conditions, but as a technical university in the then military-industrial complex of China, XJTU had a strong set of professors, junior staff, and students who were very well trained in quantitative skills. At the same time, Canadian observers noted a lack of capability with respect to teaching and research in marketing, finance, international business and the psychology- and sociology-based areas of management education. In addition, the infrastructure, such as classrooms, libraries, office space, housing, and guesthouse facilities, was very basic.

The original linkages in the CIDA program were as follows:

1 Huazhong University of Science and Technology and the University of Toronto (UT)
2 Tsinghua University and the University of Western Ontario (UWO)
3 Shanghai Jiaotong University and the University of British Columbia (UBC)
4 Xi'an Jiaotong University and the University of Alberta (U of A)
5 Tianjin University and both Concordia University and the École des Hautes Études Commerciales de Montréal (HEC Montréal) of the Université du Québec à Montréal (UQAM)
6 Renmin University and McGill University
7 Nankai University and York University[2]
8 Xiamen University and Dalhousie University

Nankai, Renmin, and Xiamen were comprehensive universities, while the other Chinese participants were science- and technology-focused institutions. As a result of their different strengths, locations, and specializations, the activities undertaken by the linkages differed in their details. Furthermore, some Canadian partners did not offer PhD programs, and therefore excluded support for PhD programs in Canada from their work plans. In addition, some linkages settled on in-China teacher training programs, while others decided on specialized courses or lectures by Canadian faculty in China. Different agreements and different input activities therefore led to differences in outputs from the linkages.

Several of the participating Canadian institutions also worked in partnership with other schools in their regions to support the CCMEP activities, for example by hosting Chinese academics or providing teachers. As a result, employees from the management schools of the Universities of Calgary, Saskatchewan, Regina, Manitoba, Carleton, Waterloo, Queen's, Université de Sherbrooke, and others have also gained Chinese experience over the course of the CCMEP.

In sum, as the CIDA-commissioned evaluation report of Phase I of the CCMEP put it in 1987, "The goals, then, are human resources development and institutional development of Chinese universities in management education" (Ryan 1987, 1). The results, of course, were much more than that, but we will return to this point later.

The Operations of the CCMEP I and the Division of Responsibilities

The linkages operated under the administrative guidance of project coordinators appointed by the deans, with initial budgets for four years, beginning in August 1983. In the case of the U of A–XJTU linkage, the agreement specified placing nine MBA students, five PhD students, and seven visiting scholars at Canadian universities. Additionally, starting in 1984, at least six visits of six-week duration by Canadian faculty to China were to be undertaken to transfer MBA-equivalent courses. These activities were supported by library material and computer shipments also funded by CIDA.

Communication with China was in English and by telex, and the Canadian coordinators maintained communication for the purpose of sharing experiences by means of occasional meetings hosted by various partner schools. Administrative oversight by CIDA's Institutional Cooperation Division (including Peter Hoffmann and Elizabeth Racicot) was relatively loose. Alternating visits of coordinators from both countries took place for the purpose of assessing results and planning future activities. The more formal organizational structure of Phase II of the project is described in a later section, as it was a result of learning and adapting from Phase I.

The process of selecting appropriate students and scholars in China was a Chinese responsibility and the Canadian partners were not involved, except to stipulate that a threshold capability of English be met by degree candidates coming to Canada. To this end, CIDA had funded the Canada-China Language Training and Testing Centre (CCLTTC) in Beijing. Later, perhaps when it was realized how many Chinese students might have to be trained at Canadian expense, the provision of English language instruction became a Chinese responsibility.

The first MBA courses delivered by Canadian faculty in China were translated paragraph by paragraph by local language experts. Most of the latter had never been outside of China. In the case of the U of A–XJTU linkage, prior to Canadian course delivery in Xi'an, a Canadian language expert would prepare the Chinese students for the idiomatic and specialized phrases, as well as the "Canadian sounds" that they were likely to encounter in the classroom. According to Chinese students, considerable socialization and bridging of the then large cultural gap was achieved by the pioneering work of these language teachers.

As China had been managing its state-owned production facilities by a combination of engineering and Communist Party principles of operation, there was particular interest in subjects such as marketing, finance, accounting, international business, economics, sociology, and psychology. These fields were relatively unknown and under-serviced, so Canadian professors visiting China focused on them. The Chinese partners shared their new knowledge with affiliated institutions (for example, Chongqing- and Chengdu-based universities were partners of XJTU), so that CIDA's concept of "training the trainers" resulted in a deep and wide range for the relatively small sum of $1.2 million per linkage.

Phase I was a crucial start-up period that facilitated trust, established friendships, and helped to identify future joint tasks. To our knowledge, no detailed account of the activities of all the linkages for the entire period is publicly available. The activities were diverse, with successes and complications, and insights from this phase gave rise to changes in Phase II which, as a result, is much better documented.[3] The suggestion by Jeff Nankivell, a senior and experienced representative of Canada's Department of Foreign Affairs Trade and Development,[4] that experience plus knowledge plus understanding lead to innovation in the field of development, would apply here: the experience and knowledge gained in Phase I, in conjunction with a better understanding between participants from the two countries, created the conditions for the successful and innovative transfer of management education in Phase II.

WORKING TOGETHER: THE CCMEP PHASE II (1988–1994) AND THE CANADA-CHINA HIGHER-EDUCATION PROGRAM (CCHEP, 1997–2001)

Phase II Experience and Accomplishments

The experience of Phase I, along with emerging needs, led to modifications in the second phase of the CCMEP cooperation. There was also some realignment of partnerships. For example, the Tsinghua-Western linkage expanded to include Dalian University and the Nanjing Institute of Technology (Southeast University) in China and the University of Waterloo in Canada. Additions to the project included a joint national PhD program with an in-Canada component, and a national executive development program involving McMaster University with Tsinghua and Fudan universities. In addition, some Phase I activities continued during Phase II. Due to the length of doctoral study, there was some overlap in doctoral programs between the two program phases. Naturally, several lessons were learned from the first phase, some of which were discussed at a joint conference at Shanghai Jiaotong in May 1986.

For example, of the eight MBA recipients trained by the U of A, only one had returned to China, and only until he found a way to obtain another exit visa. This was not a problem unique to the U of A–XJTU linkage. The two-year MBA program in Canada led to social and cultural adaptation, awareness of job opportunities, and expectations of a better quality of life. Exit visas were difficult to obtain then, so graduates, who held the view that another chance for further study or work abroad would not come for a long time, found ways to extend their stay in Canada. The Canadian government did not actively discourage this behaviour, and the universities did not have jurisdiction over the students once their degrees had been granted. Although representing a breach of their commitments, the awardees' choices could not be prevented by the host universities. Non-returnees argued that a later return would still serve China's goals, since more training and practical experience would be acquired in the meantime.

This issue of non-returnees led to increased focus on the MBA programs in China in Phase II. For example, three classes graduated in the late 1980s and early 1990s from the joint U of A–XJTU MBA program – approximately seventy-five degree holders in total – after instruction by Canadian professors in the summer months and subsequent complementary courses taught by Chinese professors. Many of these graduates became junior instructors, passing on their knowledge.[5]

The need for more research-skills development in future academic staff led to a joint national PhD program in Phase II, with a significant in-China component that would limit stays in Canada to one year. Nationally selected students in China, supervised by recognized Canadian professors during students' visits to Canada, would obtain their PhD degrees at centres located at XJTU and Nankai. Candidates were identified by Shanghai Jiaotong, Huazhong University of Science and Technology, XJTU, and Tianjin University, with initial course delivery by

Canadian academics at the Chinese centres. The upheaval of 1989 potentially exacerbated the non-return of candidates. As a result, the in-Canada portion of the joint PhD program did not take place, and instead many candidates finished their degree programs in China after exposure to PhD-level courses taught by visiting Canadian professors. In this context, it should be noted that in the summer of 1992 Université Laval and Wuhan University joined the CCMEP Phase II efforts to stimulate research.

The technology transfer regarding executive education provides a separate topic of inquiry. Here we merely observe that XJTU started executive training in Shaanxi and Henan provinces with E-MBA programs right after Phase I as a direct result of perceived demand and the knowledge gained from the cooperation with Canada. Considerable consulting opportunities resulted for the academic staff of the management schools involved in these programs. Such consulting activities had a positive feedback effect on the teaching and research activities of the faculty.

A joint national conference was held by the participating schools in Xi'an in 1990, highlighting many of the research collaborations to date and featuring Nobel Prize laureate Herbert Simon as a keynote speaker. Simon's keynote address was a major signal of the quality of aspirations held by the CCMEP for its research endeavours. The Annual Report 1992/3 of the National Coordinating Office (CFDMAS 1993, 162–8) consequently lists 181 academic research publications from the CCMEP, many of them with both Canadian and Chinese authors, and mostly in English, with Paul Beamish, Luke Chan, Myron Gordon, Michael Gibbins, and Cecil Dipchand as the prolific Canadian senior authors.

By the end of March 1993, 2,562 students had completed 103 different courses and a total of 162 courses overall. Executive training had reached 1,256 participants in forty-four courses, and PhD training had been extended to 339 graduate students in twenty seminars. Undergraduate courses had been given as additional preparation to 131 students. These accomplishments required the equivalent of roughly fifteen person-years of full-time teaching. To this direct teaching and research productivity must be added the numerous textbooks and even more numerous case studies that some of the linkage partnerships created for future generations of students and instructors, both in Canada and in China. Beamish highlights the crucial role played by the Ivey School with respect to these activities in chapter 6 of this volume.[6]

Yet these impressive contributions still hide the gradual shift of focus in Phase II from MBA training to PhD supervision and executive education. These activities obviously required much more intensive personal interactions. The above-mentioned "production statistics" also do not take into account the students who audited courses, nor the many consulting and speaking activities of visiting Canadian teachers. The accomplishments of the CCMEP were appropriately celebrated by a national conference in Vancouver in 1994, including significant participants from both countries.

Phase II Organizational Structure

The administrative arrangements for the execution of Phase II were between the Canadian Federation of Deans of Management and Administrative Studies (CFDMAS) and the various linkage universities and their domestic partners. As the structure and nature of the administrative setup illustrate the complexity of the management education transfer, a brief overview follows. It was an extremely ambitious undertaking, unique in CIDA's history and unique in scope for Canadian schools of management, resulting in a network of roughly fifty Canadian and Chinese institutions. In addition, these linkages weathered the storm of the June 1989 events in China.

After CIDA had executed a country focus contribution agreement with the CFDMAS in early 1988, the CFDMAS established the National Coordinating Office (NCO) for the Canadian linkage partners at McGill University, led by Dean Wallace Crowston and his staff. Under this umbrella, a university in Canada would work with its Chinese partner university to carry out a series of integrated activities, which were jointly proposed. On the Chinese side the formerly named State Education Commission (SEdC), now the Ministry of Education (MOE), would select appropriate partners from the set of the top twenty universities. On the other hand, CIDA's arrangements under the bilateral assistance envelope were with the formerly named Ministry of Foreign Economic Relations and Trade (MOFERT).

As with Phase I, the negotiations between the lead partners in Canada and China involved in-kind contributions on both sides, including hospitality, housing, faculty and staff time, physical infrastructure, and local transportation in China. Similarly, infrastructure, library access, postage, staff time, communications, and supplies were the in-kind contributions of Canadian partners.

An accounting framework with detailed unit costs of the various activities, inflation escalators, and overhead allocations was developed to structure the CIDA financial contribution. A reporting framework was also developed, with annual work-plans, quarterly progress and financial reports, annual reviews, and a final report, all delivered to the NCO at McGill University, and then passed on from the CFDMAS to CIDA.

Needless to say, the structure and execution of Phase II represented a new high point of complexity in institutional cooperation across Canada and with China. In hindsight, even former participants are amazed that it worked as well as it did!

The financial contribution by CIDA varied according to the linkages' operational plans, with a separate budget for the NCO. For example, the budget for the U of A–XJTU linkage under Phase II was $2,179,669 (in current dollars) for 1988–92, and we believe this amount to have been typical for all linkages. The costs of administration in Canada were shared between associated universities and the lead school, and the overall administrative costs, net of overhead, was 23.4 per cent of the budget in the case of the U of A. These figures do not include the in-kind contributions of the partner schools.

CIDA continued cooperating with China under the umbrella of the Canada-China Higher-Education Program (CCHEP) in 1997–2001, which shifted the emphasis to new areas of concern in China: poverty alleviation, the environment, and the role of women in Chinese society. Only a few of the original eight Canadian management schools continued their linkage activities in the CCHEP. But for XJTU, the CCHEP introduced the field of environmental economics and opened up a new research and policy dimension for Chinese management academics. The CCHEP supported the visit to Alberta of a delegation of women entrepreneurs from the state-owned enterprise (SOE) and non-SOE sectors. Former Lieutenant Governor of Alberta Lois Hole graciously hosted the delegates in her Edmonton home.

The foregoing descriptions not only outline the breadth and geographical reach of the CCMEP and the major boost management education in China received from the Canadian knowledge transfer, but they also imply that participating Canadian scholars learned much about modern China, its economic trajectory, and themselves from their assignments. We therefore turn briefly to the impressions of some of the first Canadian instructors in Xi'an.

TEACHING AND WORKING IN CHINA: A CANADIAN PERSPECTIVE FROM PHASE I[7]

Chinese educators had realized that their economy was moving from a production and output orientation to a system that was more sensitive to market forces, especially in the export sector. Therefore, managerial training requirements had to change. The West offered a curriculum based on the disciplines of mathematics, economics, and behavioural sciences, stressing the functional areas of finance, marketing, accounting, human resources, and production. The MBA curriculum stressed the student's development of problem-solving and decision-making skills.

At that time, two pedagogies were used in Canada, in combinations that varied between business schools. Today, these pedagogies are generally blended at most schools. The case-study method, most strongly represented in Canada by the Ivey School, exposes students to a business situation, followed by a class discussion of alternative solutions, and attempts to infer generally valid principles for future applications. The second approach starts with the general theoretical and empirical concepts of the disciplines in the first part of an MBA program, and then applies them to business problems in the second part of the program, after interactions between teacher and students and discussions among students. Both approaches require student input and presentations in the classroom.

In the mid-1980s and early 1990s, Chinese pedagogy, business environment, and cultural norms were dramatically different from those in Canada, causing the transfer of a Western-style MBA curriculum into a Chinese context to be a problematic undertaking. One of the implicit assumptions of the CIDA-funded cooperation had been that management education, linked to Canadian strengths such as agriculture, forestry, and energy resources, would be easily transferable and non-problematic in terms of culture and ideology (Hayhoe 1984, 223). Yet several Canadian MBA instructors, when reflecting on their experience in Phase I, explained why they believed this assumption to have been misplaced. Their perceptions are briefly summarized below.

The MBA model as transferred did not allow for the dual decision-making structure of Chinese enterprises that includes a significant role for the Party secretary. Furthermore, Chinese finance and distribution infrastructure was at a substantially lower level of development than North American infrastructure. Therefore, the Chinese institutional environment into which the Western MBA degrees were transferred differed in major ways from what Canadian teachers were accustomed to and prepared for. These differences, coupled with the then-prevailing Chinese pedagogy of one-way communication and learning by memorization, meant that Canadian instructors faced significant barriers to the education transfer. The challenge was magnified by the fact that Chinese

MBA students did not have work experience. They had lived on campus as undergraduates, and were then selected for graduate programs, while continuing to live on campus. MBA students in Canada by contrast had at least two to three years of work experience before their admission to the program, and therefore brought an understanding of organizations and their structure to the classroom.

An additional complexity in the attempt to transfer MBA programs to China via in-China instruction derived from the difference in social norms. Since the Chinese perception of an individual cannot be separated from his/her relationships, this behavioural standard had repercussions for a Chinese MBA's motivation and goals. Where a Canadian MBA will be aggressive, innovative, questioning of existing ways, and financially rewarded accordingly, the interests of the state or the group played a stronger role in the motivation of Chinese MBA students. Contrary to what common sense had suggested, transferring the science in management (that is, the quantitative skills) turned into a potentially greater problem than transferring the art in management (that is, the people skills) because the cultural conditions underlying the science were less obvious. To illustrate, the Canadian professors teaching macroeconomics and organizational analysis found the students adept at handling models and doing calculations, but their questions revealed that the philosophy underlying the application of the models had not been understood. The lack of knowledge of how other societies functioned prevented it. By contrast, this was less of a problem in courses like microeconomics and individual behaviour where the instructors could reduce the cultural context and personalize the material. As our instructors learned these subtle differences from their teaching experiences, they became Canada's first new "China hands," a new generation of Canadian management educators with actual experience in China, who were capable of sharing these insights with their students in Canada.

The CCMEP-linkage program therefore helped fill a glaring void that had developed at Canadian schools of management, namely a lack of knowledge and understanding of the emergence of China, its culture, business practices, hierarchies, problems, and needs. Canadian teachers were also humbled; they felt that their Western content may have had little relevance for the Chinese students they taught. Hindsight suggested that a description of our system with emphasis on why in Canada we do what we do would have better served the students' needs. Relating their experience also made clear to Chinese educators the benefit of training managers with prior work experience. Thus, valuable lessons were learned by both sides of the cooperation from MBA teaching in Phase I. And the Chinese partners were quick to act on these and other insights.

THE LEGACY OF THE MANAGEMENT EDUCATION PROJECTS IN CHINA

Assessing, let alone attempting to measure, the legacy of the transfer of management education to China is an inherently difficult task. Even the meaning of "legacy" in this context presents a challenge. Using "sustainable impact" as our definition of "legacy" still leaves several dimensions to "impact" and no widely accepted methodologies available for ascertaining them. Recourse is therefore to a limited set of objective indicators, as well as interview responses of Chinese participants from the U of A–XJTU linkage. They are suggestive of a lasting – as opposed to transitory – impact resulting from the cooperation. Of the approximately sixty junior visiting scholars and a much smaller number of senior professors and administrators who had participated in the U of A–XJTU linkage, twenty-four were interviewed by the author on the occasion of a visit in 2008.

The working philosophy of the administrators of the U of A–XJTU linkage had been that the Canadian side, within the constraints of the budget and the available human resources, would provide course content and the rationale for the approach, materials, and program processes, somewhat analogous to the menu in a restaurant; the Chinese side would choose what they deemed the most appropriate offering. We assume that this process was followed in the other linkages as well; they were headed by some of Canada's best academics in management education.

The new generation of Chinese management graduates with the "Canadian connection" can be found in leading positions all over China. The U of A linkage can point to many participants who have become respected Chinese leaders, including: the former (and first) dean of Beijing University's executive MBA program and current dean of the Chongqing Graduate School of Business; the president of Everbright Bank in Hong Kong (and founding head of the Royal Bank of Canada's office in China); the president of XJTU-Liverpool University in Suzhou, as well as one of its vice-presidents; the dean of NW-Polytechnic University's Business Program; the dean of the Management Program in Urumqi (Xinjiang); the dean of the Finance Program at Jiangxi University of Finance and Economics; the vice-president of the Science and Technology University (Xi'an); the vice-president of the Petroleum University (Xi'an);

and the dean at Chongqing University's Management School. The resource constraints of this book did not allow for a more general account of the impact of alumni for all linkages, so this snapshot from one linkage must suffice, yet it should be suggestive of the CCMEP's overall reach. It is very likely that an even more impressive list could be compiled by a full survey.

The Chinese partners at XJTU accepted the research challenge readily and with strong results: they were chosen by the Ministry of Higher Education as China's best management school for three years running (2005–07). While there may have been a Canadian impetus, it was the Chinese partner university's strong leadership and the dedication of the staff members that adapted the Canadian educational technology to the local needs.

The views of former Dean and XJTU Vice-President Dr Wang Yingluo carry weight inasmuch as he is also a member of the Chinese Academy of Social Sciences (CASS). He believes that the high rankings of the MBA program and XJTU's Management School are attributable to the Canadian support and the extra state government funding that the national ranking then bestowed on the top schools. In an earlier conversation (11 June 2002), he reflected on CIDA's contribution along several lines. First, as regards the governance structure of XJTU's School of Management, it was built on the model of the U of A's School of Business, with five departments, four of which at the time were headed by academics who had been students or scholars in Canada. Former Dean Wang felt that the stress they assigned to transparency and efficiency in decision-making was influenced by the Canadian experience. As regards staff training, it was his assessment that the early exposure to Canadian models helped XJTU to prepare for the changes that were happening in China at that time. XJTU's management academics were thus ready to take on consulting contracts for emerging businesses and government units.

The second contribution, according to Dean Wang, was a strong impact on curriculum building, both in the MBA and the PhD programs. For example, an elective on gender issues was incorporated into the undergraduate program for the first time and offered to the entire university. Textbooks in English were introduced due to CIDA funding, enabling students to look at business practices in the West, and spreading the new practical knowledge beyond the teaching staff. A text on international business and finance was published by XJTU Press, co-authored by the Canadian linkage coordinator and his colleague Edy Wong. It was written on-site, with a Chinese version added by a team of junior faculty from XJTU. In this way, a wider audience was reached and a team of young teachers was mentored.

Naturally, the Canadian partner universities brought their emphasis on research to China. Research productivity became the most important criterion for promotion at the Chinese partner universities. Teaching was evaluated as well, with teaching evaluations by students gradually introduced, although, according to Dean Wang, the research productivity of staff became the key criterion for promotion to the rank of associate professor. The Natural Sciences Foundation of China expressed its confidence in the quality of research achieved at XJTU by selecting the Management School as its partner in the administration of block grants for management science and management education projects. This pilot practice streamlined the process of reviewing lengthy individual applications and allowed XJTU to find Chinese partners in areas where its own expertise was thin.

Dean Wang noted that the Canadian cooperation program had an additional impact in the initiation of an alumni network. With a thirty-year history of management graduates, the Chinese partner universities have become adept at building relationships with their graduates. The CIDA contribution is perhaps not so clearly visible in this context, but the Canadian schools' practices of fund-raising activities and, as mentioned above, executive education programs for the business community, were adopted by and transferred to the Chinese partner universities. They were implemented speedily due to China's relationship-based culture and strong work ethic. As a result, there is now a significant XJTU-alumni network in Shenzhen and Shanghai.

Other Chinese participants in the CCMEP provided the following selected but typical comments regarding the impact of the linkage cooperation during interviews:

- "Many of us got funding from the National Science Foundation after we came back from Canada."
- "We learned how to write empirical papers and how to publish in international journals."
- "After visiting Canada I have changed my teaching style to encourage students' participation in class."
- "More than 30,000 copies of my book on research methodology have been sold, and the book was the result of my Canada visit."
- "The joint program had a great impact on my life and career. I am in business now."

- "I think the cooperation with Canada influenced the teaching style and the research at our Management School, for example the standardization of teaching and the development of new research fields including environmental protection and the industrial-ecological system."
- "For my research especially the stay in Canada has given me more vision, and I can look at it with an international perspective; for my teaching I learned advanced methods from case studies."

The comment regarding an international perspective gained from the cooperation with Canada is particularly germane. It was this dimension that was missing and is still in need of improvement in China. To this author an experience from 1990 comes to mind: beautiful Chinese silk ties were available in stalls and stores at the equivalent of $2 apiece, yet they were not selling to Westerners because the designs were out of touch with current international fashion. It required knowledge of the outside world, in this case a joint venture with a luxury designer from Italy, to sell the same silk ties with a different pattern at $20 apiece.

It has to be mentioned again in this context that the initial management education cooperation included the CCLTTC in Beijing. The latter provided many early outgoing Chinese scholars with a "crash course" in English, and a test result that would determine the applicant's suitability for a stay in Canada. The CCLTTC's preparation of visitors and the Canadian language trainers' work at the various linkages were key contributions to the successful transfer of Canadian management education to China. Their activities bridged the period until China's own efforts at accelerated language training became effective.

As regards the contribution of equipment and materials, under Phase II alone CIDA funded purchases and transfer worth $1.75 million. These acquisitions enabled the partner universities to use the research and communications tools, including bibliographies, databases, fax communication, local area networks, and computer labs that were the standard in North America at the time. The speedy catch-up was facilitated by the aptitude and eventual enthusiasm for technology at the partner universities, although occasionally obstructed by rules of a traditionally hierarchical administration. The case of a fax machine transferred to China comes to mind: when the Canadian partner came for a visit and wanted to use it, it was found stowed away in its original packaging, because permission to operate it had been withheld by the central administration.

THE LEGACY OF THE MANAGEMENT EDUCATION PROJECTS IN CANADA

While the foregoing may have created the impression that the CCMEP represented uni-directional assistance in the implementation of China's reforms, there were also lasting impacts in Canada from the CCMEP. Interviews with Canadian linkage coordinators Victor Murray and Geoffrey Bonnycastle (1993, 5) distinguished three strands of such benefits, namely the impact on management education in Canada, the impact on understanding China, and the impact on the climate for Canadian-Chinese trade. Moreover, Canadian skill in managing complex international development projects received a boost.

With respect to management education, many case studies were written by CCMEP faculty and the internationalization of the curricula and teaching at the partner schools were strengthened significantly. In particular, the joint venture literature was pushed forward by CCMEP participants, with the materials finding audiences in Canada as much as in China. Generations of Canadian graduate students have developed research proposals and produced results involving aspects of business in and with China, and some have received international acclaim.

Graduate programs in Canada have admitted many Chinese students as a result of the early connections of senior Canadian faculty visiting China. Since the 1979 inception of the U of A's program in business, 149 PhDs have been granted. Of these, thirty-three were to Chinese students. Resource constraints make it impossible to list the papers these students have written and published with their advisers, but it is reasonable to assume that other Canadian doctoral programs have had similar results. In short, the Canada-China cooperation in management education has brought access to a valuable source of graduate students.

Canada's understanding of China and China's understanding of Canada have received a major impetus from the CCMEP and other CIDA programs with China. Executive education programs brought Canadian business practitioners into the loop here in Canada. Given China's rapid growth and the market opportunities for Canadian business, the linkage operations provided timely consulting expertise in Canada, and increased people-to-people contacts for mutual benefit and the bridging of cultures. The executive MBA program of the U of A annually takes its students to Beijing and Shanghai. In return, the U of A hosts Chinese officials from the Chinese Academy of Government and the Shanghai Administrative Institute for tailored executive programs. Recently, U of

A students include Xi'an in their itinerary, extending the relationship with XJTU and obtaining company visits through XJTU's network.

Finally, the numerous visiting scholars, Chinese students, and administrators have interacted with Canadians in untold ways, fostering an understanding of and appreciation for Chinese history and culture. As this review is to a considerable extent a personal memoir, the visit of Professors Li Huaizu and Wang Yingluo to my sons' school must be mentioned. In Alberta, the curriculum in grade six included China. In 1991, the personal appearance of two engaging Chinese professors, who addressed the students in English, was an extraordinarily memorable event in the lives of these young students.

The goodwill created by the thousands of interactions from the CCMEP planted the seed of many more collaborations. Most of these were not anticipated or even explicitly considered by the CCMEP. A few of these offshoots from the Alberta experience are described in broad outline below.

SELECTED INNOVATION SPIN-OFFS FROM THE CCMEP: THE CASE OF THE U OF A

Several aspects of the CCMEP and its successor program, the CCHEP, convey the complexity, impact, and legacy of just one of the eight cooperative programs. Since there were eight partnerships that were supported by CIDA in Canada, the coordination of programming and the design of budgets for universities with diverse accounting systems and different specializations represented a considerable challenge for CIDA's administrators. The relationships with Ottawa across time zones from Halifax to Vancouver presented communications issues within Canada. Furthermore, cost allocations had to be made across different expenditure categories: from visiting scholars and graduate students in Canada to teachers, teaching assistants, and language specialists in China, not to mention charges for the shipment of books, fax machines, and computing equipment. The division of overheads within universities also required time-consuming negotiations.

The CCMEP strained CIDA's resources to such an extent that an administrative layer had to be inserted between CIDA and the Canadian universities, and the National Coordinating Office at McGill University, headed by Dean Wally Crowston and his staff, came into being. The complexity of a human resources development program led to the introduction of Results-based Management, which forced the management schools to focus on the link between their activities with Chinese partners and the specific outcomes and ultimate impact in the partner country. Reporting along these lines represented an innovation for the participating schools in Canada. It focused attention from the short-term activities, like curricula and staffing of courses, to the longer-term effects in China. This CIDA-imposed focus on the long term proved beneficial for the strategic planning activities of participating management schools.

The CIDA process of budgeting involved a high degree of transparency, and this process had to be shared with the partner university in China when activities were planned. Therefore, an open financial book was the basis for the joint activities. One cannot help but believe that this example of a transparent accounting system will have spread to other institutions as well.

There was heavy emphasis on creativity and quality control in the design of the PhD programs, with a nudge away from voluminous to shorter three-publishable-essays types of theses. The emphasis on modern business-research methodology, work with empirical data, and the collaborative approach of students and teachers from both countries, represented important innovative steps in the development of China's management education. It also opened eyes to dual-degree programs.

Similarly, the collaboration between universities in China and Canada enabled an innovative experiment in a tripartite cooperation between a Chinese bank employing XJTU (and other) business graduates, the Canadian partner school, and a major Canadian bank. In finance and banking, China's development had seriously lagged behind that of the outside world in the 1980s and early 1990s. In certain ways the lag still exists, but a small step with great results for those involved was cobbled together between the U of A, the Industrial and Commercial Bank of China (ICBC), and the Royal Bank of Canada (RBC). It involved fast-tracked junior-VP staff from the head office of ICBC coming to Canada for up to a year of finance courses at the U of A, combined with an internship in various departments of the RBC's head office in Toronto. This program allowed academic exposure to be supplemented by actual Canadian work experience. It led to several editions of a textbook on commercial banking by one of the trainees, a significant spin-off from the CCMEP. Negotiating an MOU between a state-owned bank, a Canadian corporation, and a business school in the early 1990s represented a learning experience for all partners. The program required intensive commitment by all partners, which explains why it was limited to a small number of trainees. Yet, when one looks at the subsequent careers of the four trainees, one can see a high impact for all, and the two banks involved benefitted significantly as well. The current RBC Group's office in Beijing is a direct outcome of this CCMEP-spinoff.

As has already been mentioned, XJTU's implementation of a system of evaluating teaching by means of surveying students was a transfer of the U of A's approach. As a feedback mechanism for self-improvement of instructors, it is now firmly established, and not only at XJTU.

Finally, mention must be made of the technology transfer with respect to editing and publishing a refereed academic journal. With CIDA's financial support, the *Journal of Chinese Management Issues* was created by a joint U of A–XJTU editorship and a binational editorial board. For China's management academics, blind review of submitted manuscripts was an innovation; rejection of manuscripts on the basis of detailed critiques was not the practice, and academic writing in English was also a new experience. The substantial editorial work necessary on the English manuscripts then led to cessation of the effort. Yet its initial issue – volume 1, issue 1, Fall 1995 – today represents a milestone in CIDA-supported technology transfer in academic publishing.

CONCLUDING EVALUATION: LEGACIES AND FUTURE CHALLENGES

For the Canadian teachers, graduate students, and administrative staff involved in the cooperation, the exposure to the discipline, studiousness, patience, curiosity, respect, gracious hospitality, and especially the loyalty of the Chinese participants, was an eye-opening experience.[8] Across Canada, a group of China-wise academics resulted from the CCMEP, with research and collaborative ventures still ongoing. Among current business PhD registrations at the U of A, twenty out of sixty-six are Chinese.

The long-standing contacts and the trust established by the CCMEP enabled just last year the establishment of a master's in financial management degree offered jointly by XJTU and the U of A in Shenzhen. With its in-Canada component, this degree is the first offshore dual degree program of the U of A's School of Business. Currently, a joint undergraduate degree program with two years in each country is being explored by the two partners. Other linkages have also established a presence or collaborations in and with China, and it can be said that without the foundation of trust built by the CCMEP, these ventures would not have happened. A lasting network of CCMEP alumni now exists in China as well. The CCMEP's joint conferences led to closer contacts between Chinese universities and ongoing research collaborations.

Looking back then, the CCMEP represents a fine example of a "win-win" experience in international cooperation between universities. Returning to the four evaluation dimensions listed in the introduction, the foregoing review has shown that the transfer of management education through the CIDA-funded university partnerships of the CCMEP made an essential and lasting contribution to China's economic revitalization and rapid transformation. Without the tools of modern management techniques, the phenomenal economic growth in China could not have been accomplished. The Canadian linkages were the first partnerships in management education.

The CCMEP also contributed significantly to the educational and institutional infrastructure in China to address the emerging issues of humane and democratic governance, social justice, and environmental sustainability. This was particularly evident in the focus of the CCHEP which, based on the relationships and trust established by the CCMEP, introduced courses on gender issues in business, women entrepreneurship, and environmental economics. In this way, new ideas were injected into the curriculum of Chinese management schools.

There were four organizational and contextual features of the linkages that enabled them to be effective. The collaboration was characterized by *equity* and *equality* of the partners, with budgets being transparent, and administrative visits shared evenly. The partner universities also maintained a high degree of *autonomy*. For example, XJTU selected particular activities from the menu offered by the U of A. The friendships that still exist between staff members from the partner schools are testimony to the *solidarity* the cooperation created. And last but not least, the program was one of active *participation* by both partners, a participation that is still being built on today.

A future challenge for all higher education in China, not just for the business fields, is moving away from overly heavy emphasis on the quantity of research for promotion and hiring decisions, as well as on the rankings of universities. The focus on quantity of research output is a disease that China seems to have imported from Canada and the West in general. This focus gave rise to unethical practices, as reflected in a "market for research papers" with prices of up to $25,000 for a "commissioned" journal publication.[9]

Finally, regarding lessons from the past experience for future collaborations between Canadian and Chinese universities, the importance and cost of maintaining networks across the Pacific should be reflected in the budgetary design. We learned from the CCMEP that once the linkages were no longer supported by CIDA, there were no resources for staying in touch with one another. While China's economic success has led to increased scholarship support for study abroad, capacity constraints are present in Canada for hosting visiting scholars. Many requests by government-funded Chinese scholars for office space and other visiting privileges could not be accommodated due to lack of Canadian mentors and physical limitations. The CCMEP experience suggests the inclusion of some networking and seed funds in future project budgets, so that contacts can continue to be nurtured, new initiatives can be started, and abrupt activity stops can be avoided.

Another big challenge for China is to address the shortage of internationally experienced managers. This goes beyond management education as such, because it pertains to the add-on international cultural exposure for Chinese graduates of management programs. With China's ongoing move to market reliance and further opening-up, as reflected, among others, in the China Investment Corporation's global acquisition policy of companies and portions thereof, the need for managers with experience in Chinese and Western settings is huge. This need calls for the provision of internships by receptive and enlightened multinational companies that have not only the means, but also the necessary long-term vision.

NOTES

1 Many individuals have made impressive contributions to the Canada-China Management Education Program projects. On the Canadian side, two in particular must be mentioned as they are no longer alive. The efforts and accomplishments of Myron (Mike) Gordon of the University of Toronto and Cecil Dipchand of Dalhousie University were substantial. For the University of Alberta, former dean Roger Smith was a driving force. On the Chinese side, I am particularly indebted to two individuals: former Dean and Vice-President Wang Yingluo steered the University of Alberta–Xi'an Jiaotong collaboration in the early stages, and remains a strong supporter to this day; and former Vice-Dean Li Huaizu has been a teacher and indefatigable guide on all matters related to China throughout the last thirty years.

Due to the paucity of documented material and constraints on pursuing primary sources, this chapter represents a combination of personal memoir and documented review. The resulting perspective is therefore partial and should not be expected to do justice to all aspects of the Canadian management education transfer to China. The author gratefully acknowledges the helpful suggestions of Brian Evans and Roger S. Smith, while assuming responsibility for any remaining errors.

2 Université Laval's dean of the Faculty of Administrative Sciences, seeing limited room for French-language cooperation, supported the Nankai-York linkage (Singer 1986, 126).

3 Phase I results were summed up by Wallace Crowston as follows: "During the five years of the program, we trained over 20 PhDs and over 100 MBAs. In addition we received visits from 65 Chinese scholars in management, and sent over 80 Canadians to teach or do research in China" (Crowston 1989, 2).

4 Mr Jeff Nankivell brought greetings from the Government of Canada to the conference in a speech made on 10 May 2014.

5 Senior visiting scholars from China could not fully benefit from long stays in Canada due, in most cases, to their lack of language skills. This insight led to a focus on short-term visits by younger staff from the partner universities. Although more travel costs were incurred, with four- to six-month stays rather than stays of one-year duration, junior faculty development, a high priority for the future of China's business schools, became accelerated.

6 The accomplishments of the linkages were added up before all activities had been completed, so the quoted numbers represent underestimates of the achievements.

7 This section draws on Chambers, Cullen, and Hoskins (1989, 91–6).

8 An example of the discipline and patience of Chinese visiting scholars can be gleaned from the following excerpt: "I was lucky to have my application for going to Canada successfully approved by the Division, the Department, the Personnel Department, the Foreign Affairs Department, the Party Secretary, the President of the University, the State Commission for Education, and the Foreign Ministry. The experience was filled with misery and hope, formidableness and fortune" (Letter to the author by visiting scholar prospect T.Y., dated 30 March 1990).

9 "Looks good on paper." *The Economist*, 28 September 2013, 39–40.

5

The Impact of Cross-Cultural Experience on Academic Leadership from Individual and Process Perspectives

XI YOUMIN, ZHANG XIAOJUN,
ZHANG XIAOFENG, NI JIE, AND LI HUAIZU

INTRODUCTION

Since the establishment of the "Opening Up" policy more than thirty years ago, international cooperation has been an important way for China to learn from the West. In the late 1970s, Deng Xiaoping advocated that China's industries adopt the advanced ideas and technologies of the West. A large number of international cooperative programs were created as a result, including international cooperation between higher-education institutions. Deng Xiaoping was particularly concerned about education and technology after the Cultural Revolution, and initiated many critical changes that had a fundamental influence on the development of China's education system. The field of business management in China was significantly changed by this development. According to Deng, Chinese firms should learn about management techniques from Western companies, and Chinese universities should collect knowledge on how to run businesses from Western universities.

The cooperation between the Chinese Ministry of Education (MOE) and the Canadian International Development Agency (CIDA) was the outcome of Deng's advocacy. This collaboration was initiated in 1983 and continued for a second phase in 1990. Several similar international cooperation projects were also established in the last thirty years. Today, many national-level grants and not-for-profit foundations still support Chinese scholars abroad. Although Chinese universities and scholars have been absorbing the Western model for more than thirty years, there is no sign of the suspension of such activities, even though China's education system is now much stronger than before. Rather, the experience of studying abroad has become a critical advantage when seeking a job in China's higher-education system. The "One Thousand Talent Plan" initiated by the Organization Department of the Central Committee of the Communist Party of China is a typical example that indicates how much importance the Chinese government and universities attach to international experience.

However, little specific research exists on whether the overseas experiences of Chinese scholars, as provided by the national-level cooperative programs or not-for-profit foundations, actually do improve their capabilities. Moreover, there is little research on how the impact of such experiences has changed with the development of China. We know little about the value of international cooperation to individuals who were supported in their studies abroad, and how this value evolves over time. Although it is broadly admitted that the "Opening Up" policy has made a great contribution to the success of China's economic development, there is a lack of empirical examinations and theoretical interpretation of this effect over time. In this chapter, by means of a case study of the CIDA program, we aim to determine the influence of overseas experiences on Chinese scholars' academic leadership, and how this influence was derived and has evolved from individual and process perspectives.

THEORETICAL BACKGROUND

Overview of Research on International Cooperative Programs

An international cooperative program is a typical means of internationalization for higher-education institutions in the globalized world. There are several types of cooperation between higher-education institutions in different countries, including degree programs, short-term student and faculty exchange programs, and credit transfer programs. In recent years, a new type of international cooperative higher-education program named the Sino-Foreign Cooperative in Running Universities has been introduced. Considering the irreversible trend of internationalization (Jiang 2006), it seems that international cooperative higher-education programs will be one of the most important phenomena in the future of education.

Many education research studies focus on international cooperative programs. The primary theoretical basis of these studies includes the human capital theory (Blundell et al. 1999), internationalization (Knight 1997), and cross-cultural theories (Barnett 1990). Generally speaking, most of these studies pay attention to national-level and institutional-level motivations behind and effects of international cooperative programs. For example, there are many studies and reports addressing why and how countries and universities launch international cooperative programs and how these programs contribute to the development of these countries and universities (see, for example: Feng and Gong 2006; Knight 1997; Watson 2007; Yang 2006). However, little attention has been paid to the motivations and gains of individuals involved in these programs. The existing small body of research on this topic focuses mainly on the reasons and experiences of individuals participating in international cooperative programs (Dunn 2008; Tam 2007).

It is easy to understand why national-level investigations are important when studying international cooperative programs, since these programs are easily affected by relations between the cooperative countries and by the intentions of the countries involved. For example, due to the strained relations between China and Canada in 1989, and the problem of Chinese scholars remaining abroad after the completion of their visits, the CIDA program was on the brink of being terminated. Many Chinese scholars who were sent to Canada for MBA degrees before 1989 stayed permanently in Canada, leading to a great sense of loss over the disappearance of even more valuable young talent to the West. As a result, the cooperative PhD degree program was cancelled and visits abroad by Chinese scholars were shortened in duration. Similarly, it is vital to understand the intentions of institutions when evaluating their executing roles in the outcome of international cooperative programs.

However, as the individuals (student or faculty) involved are the direct beneficiaries of international cooperative programs, it is essential and indispensible to examine the gains and experiences of these individuals when evaluating the outcome and contributions of international programs. The impact of these programs on individuals is the premise of their impact at the institutional and national levels. Moreover, the fundamental challenges of international cooperative programs lie in how to encourage program participants from one culture to live and study in a different cultural setting. The experience of living in a different culture may cause some conflict and detachment in participants. Therefore, there are many issues and questions deserving deeper investigation when understanding the outcome and contributions of international cooperative programs, such as: Why do people eagerly strive for overseas studies? Why are overseas returnees highly valued? Do scholars with overseas study experiences have clear comparative advantages? What is the potential value of overseas studies in terms of academic development? How do the impacts of overseas studies in the early stages of the Open Door policy differ from impacts today?

Academic Leadership

Existing research related to academic leadership mainly focuses on the holders of formal academic management roles such as vice-chancellor, principal, pro-vice-chancellor, and deans and heads of departments. Academic leadership is traditionally defined as referring to these roles, specifically including leaders who work to direct and align people through personal influence and through organizational mechanisms such as workload allocation, performance review, and research output. Because this type of role is highly relevant to professional management work, Bolden et al. (2012) refer to it as *academic management* rather than academic leadership.

According to Bolden et al. (2012), the term academic leadership can also refer to personal academic excellence or achievement, such as publishing in refereed journals and presenting papers at national and international conferences (Rowley 1997). This form of academic leadership mainly relates to individuals' excellent academic identities or high reputations, which result in a following by other academics. Today, however, the university role and the university environment have changed. As suggested by Margainson and Sawir (2006), the globalization of higher education has transformed a university education into a commodity, and the students into consumers. Traditional modes of academic leadership are becoming outdated. In this chapter, therefore, we define academic leadership differently, as a process through which academic values and identities are constructed, promoted, and maintained (Bolden et al. 2012). Academic leadership can be understood at three levels: the individual level, the program level, and the organizational level. On the other hand, academic leadership covers a broader range than institutional roles and responsibilities, and is most significant in terms of its impact upon academic values and identities. As we define it, academic leadership is mostly concerned with commitment and direction, and is enacted through a process of "self-leadership" (Bolden et al. 2012).

Academic leadership at the individual level operates in a different way than that related to managerial and professional work. According to research conducted by Bolden et al. (2012),

> Academic leadership was shifted from early mentoring relationships with one's research supervisor and early research groups to a form of self-leadership where inspiration and direction came from one's own work, as well as one's teaching team and/or research community (the latter often being located outside one's institution). From this perspective on academic leadership, the role of management was not seen to be one of leadership but instead to provide support, resources and an enabling environment that facilitated, rather than directed, the academic work of others. Academic leadership came from individuals (or groups) that provided inspiration for their academic work. For example, a principal lecturer identified receiving academic leadership from both her students and her colleagues. Meanwhile academic leadership had a significant part to play in shaping the values, direction and sense of commitment to academic work (Bolden et al. 2012, 33).

However, few research studies focus on the improvement of academic leadership in research groups and academic institutions, because academic leadership has not been generally understood as a capability to lead programs and institutions. In this study, we aim to integrate the three-level phenomenon to give a holistic view of improvements in academic leadership.

It is important to consider the context-sensitive characteristics of academic leadership. Academic leadership has significant contextual variations depending on factors such as career stage, job role, gender, academic discipline, and organizational type. As Richard Bolden and his colleagues (2012) identify in their research, there is a stronger tendency for those in senior roles and those with a more extensive teaching focus to regard themselves as having leadership influence within their organizations, a weaker tendency for females to describe themselves as having leadership influence, and a preference for "self-leadership" among established academics. Locke and Bennion (2010a) identify similar differences, including significant variations between countries and staff groups with regards to the experiences and expectations of academics. Considering the rapidly shifting context, and changing perspectives on the nature and purpose of academic work, it is inadvisable to suggest a "best practice" approach to academic leadership and management, and preferable to nurture the development of a culture that respects and acknowledges the importance of academic values and identities in the accomplishment of academic work (Locke and Bennion 2010b). Such an approach draws attention to the importance of context in defining an appropriate leadership and management strategy, and of seeking to nurture and develop mutually beneficial configurations of leadership practice (Gronn 2010). This approach suggests that different people and processes provide important and essential contributions to the accomplishment of academic work.

Although studies have found that academic leadership is context-sensitive, most of the previous research defines academic leadership in relation to academic achievement and the academic management role. Because these definitions differ from the definition used in this study, we are reluctant to adopt the arguments of these studies to understand the phenomenon we examine here. As described above, we define academic leadership in relation to academic identity and values. Since academic identity and values relate strongly to culture at the national level, academics with different cultural backgrounds may have different senses of academic leadership. Culture differences at the national level should be a principal factor influencing understanding of international cooperative programs. Moreover, previous research about academic leadership mainly focuses on the topic within a concrete cultural context, rather than paying attention to academic leadership in different cultures. In particular, previous research ignores the impact of cross-cultural interaction on improving scholars' academic leadership. This is a critical limitation in existing research on international cooperative programs.

Investigating the Impact of Cross-Cultural International Collaborations from Individual and Process Perspectives

In this study, we examine what scholars involved in the CIDA program obtained and learned from studying in Canada, how the participants of international cooperative programs such as this one have been influenced, supported, and given a sense of direction in relation to their academic work, and whether participants' academic leadership has been improved or strengthened by international exposure in the three levels respectively, especially at the early stage. We interviewed many scholars who took part in this program and analyzed the data at the individual level to catch the critical points of each interviewee. In addition, we paid attention to changes in these scholars' academic activities before and after they participated in this program to investigate how their overseas experiences impacted their academic leadership.

METHODOLOGY

Research Design

From individual and process perspectives, we employed an inductive, grounded case-study method in order to capture the impact of cross-cultural experience on the improvement of academic leadership in the rich detail that only international cooperative programs' founders and participants could provide. Drawing on a grounded theory analysis of interview, observation, and archival data about the CIDA program, we explored the improvement of academic leadership through cross-cultural interactions (what) and the process of academic leadership transformation (how). We designed the study along three dimensions: the overseas experiences of pure scholars and of scholars with administrative leadership roles; academic leadership at individual, group, and organizational levels; and time including both the early stage and the later stage of the program (see figure 5.1).

Research Setting

In this study, we focus on analyzing the influence of the CIDA program on the academic leadership of scholars involved in the program. The CIDA program was initiated and supported by CIDA and by the Chinese Ministry of Foreign Trade and Economic Cooperation (MOFTEC) in the context of an increasingly market-oriented economic developing trend in China with 300,000 enterprises operating without trained staff. In the early 1980s, academics in Chinese universities were primarily engineers or Marxist economists. They had limited teaching material on business management and no experience in dealing with the rapidly changing economic environment. Meanwhile, Vice-Premier Deng Xiaoping had indicated that it was essential to learn and acquire foreign advanced managerial knowledge and technologies. Many Chinese companies sent their managers and staff abroad in order to do so. At the university level, the Chinese MOE gave high priority to management education. The MOE had much interest in collaboration with CIDA, and continued this connection even after the Tiananmen event. The Chinese MOE selected

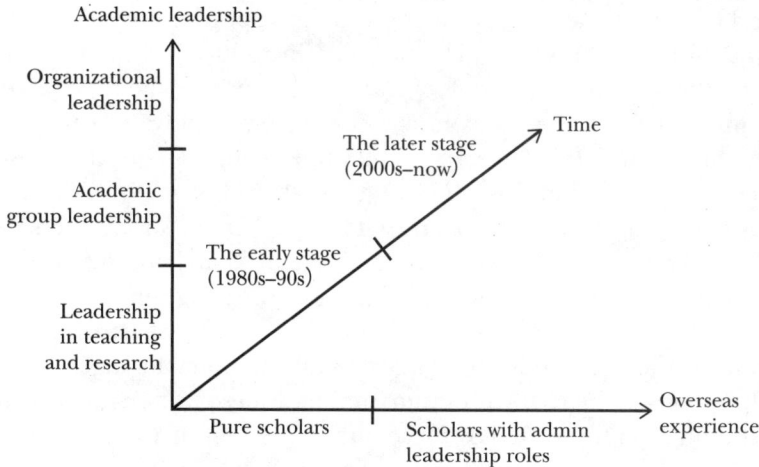

Figure 5.1 The research design for studying the influence of overseas experience on academic leadership

eight leading Chinese universities to create partnerships with eight universities in Canada. For example, Xiamen University (Xiada) was paired with Dalhousie University in Halifax, the University of Alberta (U of A) Business School collaborated with the School of Management (SOM) at Xi'an Jiaotong University (XJTU), the University of British Columbia (UBC)'s Sauder School was paired with the Management School of Shanghai Jiaotong University, and so forth.

The original purpose on the Chinese side in participating in the CIDA program was to develop MBA and management courses to train managers in China, and to give opportunities to Chinese scholars to learn how to conduct management research in a more scientific way. It is said that the main purpose on the Canadian side was to promote the development of China much more rapidly in a globalized environment. There were two main forms of collaboration: sending experienced faculty from the eight selected Chinese universities to engage in research and courses at the paired Canadian universities, and creating a cooperative PhD degree program. This program existed in two main stages: the Canada-China Management Education Program (CCMEP) from 1983 to 1996, and the China-Canada Higher-Education Program (CCHEP) from 1996 to 2003.

The CIDA program, as a national-level collaborating program that surpassed the cooperation between two universities, lasted a relatively long time and involved large numbers of people and large quantities of funding. Through this program, the Chinese universities involved learned a kind of thinking and a knowledge structure appropriate for the establishment of MBA programs. The program introduced Chinese universities to the teaching method of case study in management courses (Beamish, chapter 6 of this volume). Moreover, it cultivated many management personnel and leaders in the Chinese higher-education system (Li et al., chapter 7 of this volume), such as Professor Bing Xiang, the founding dean of Cheung Kong Graduate School of Business, and Professor Youmin Xi, the executive president of Xi'an Jiaotong-Liverpool University in Suzhou. On the Canadian side, the program provided crucial learning to Canadian management schools in how to manage international projects and develop long-term international linkages.

The effects of the CIDA program on the Chinese universities involved are still highly appreciated by these universities, ensuring the value and appropriateness of this study. For example, XJTU, one of the Chinese universities that took part in the program, made full use of this opportunity to collaborate with the Alberta Business School deeply and thoroughly. Professor Li Huaizu, an initiator and coordinator of the CIDA program from the Chinese side, recalled that the SOM of XJTU sent four groups of PhD students to Canadian universities. Each group contained approximately thirty nationally selected students. At the very beginning, the PhD students studied in Canada for one year; soon this time was shortened to half a year due to the low return rate of students. In addition, the SOM sent teachers to study advanced teaching methods and to create international research networks in Canada as visiting scholars. Due to its many years of collaboration with Canadian universities, the SOM of XJTU was recognized as one of the top management schools in China. Moreover, the CIDA program also provided a solid foundation that enabled the SOM of XJTU to pass the Association to Advance Collegiate Schools of Business (AACSB) accreditation. In conclusion, it seems clear that the CIDA program had a significant impact on the development of both Chinese management subjects and Chinese management schools (Mirus, chapter 4 of this volume).

Sample and Data Sources

We selected eight scholars who participated in the CIDA program from the SOM of XJTU as our samples. We used the theoretical sampling method (Glaser 1978; Glaser and Strauss 1967) in selecting our samples. The samples included three program managers and three participants of CIDA's three different stages to ensure that our data was sufficiently comprehensive. Two of our interviewees are now university-level leaders.

In addition, we also generated results based on our decades of observation of those who participated in the CIDA program. To get rich data and understanding of the research subjects, we chose one participant to be our main research subject, and used grounded theory method to observe his daily work. We compared in detail the results obtained from this participant with results from the other seven subjects of our study.

In this study, we collected data from interviews, observations, and archives. Interviews, which were private and conducted face-to-face, were structured to begin with four questions about CIDA's background and how each interviewee was placed in the program. This part lasted approximately ten to fifteen minutes and was used as the basis for eight more questions about CIDA's influence on the interviewee's teaching and researching practices, which took up the remainder of each interview. The interviews ranged in length from fifty to 120 minutes and were audiotaped and transcribed for analysis. In addition, we took some observations that would give clues as to the effect of the CIDA project on scholars' academic leadership; these observations were complementary to our interview data. We also reviewed literature referring to the CIDA project and used it as the basis of follow-up interviews and data analysis.

Data Analysis Process

Given the opportunity to analyze a characteristic instance of a cross-cultural international cooperative program, we wanted both to investigate the improvement of academic leadership and the process of academic leadership transformation. We chose grounded theory methodology (Glaser 1978; Glaser and Strauss 1967) to derive new theoretical insights about the contextualization and process of the improvement of academic leadership.

We first analyzed the data collected from the main subject of our study, who was observed for more than two years; then we analyzed data from the other subjects one by one. Finally, we integrated and compared the results from different subjects in order to generate theoretical concepts and interpretations over the target research questions. Grounded theory advocates analyzing data through three steps: open coding, axial coding, and theoretical coding (Glaser 1978; Strauss and Corbin 1998). In the first step, we simplified our data into categories, which were further abstracted into several themes addressing the research questions of the study. In the final step, we extracted theoretical concepts and processes from our data.

Table 5.1 Results from the study of academic leadership change

		Individual level	Group level	Organizational level
Pure scholars	Early stage	Cognitive enlightenment and limited behavioural impact	Cognitive understanding of teamwork and collaboration	Improved teaching and research standard; discipline construction; human resource development
	Later stage	Behavioural learning, rethinking, and practice	Set up small research teams	
Scholars with administrative roles	Early stage	Cognitive enlightenment and improved leadership capabilities in teaching and research within the organization	Cognitive understanding of teamwork and collaboration; set up small research teams	Improved understanding of Western academic governance structure; set up new institutions with unique governance structure
	Later stage	Behavioural learning, rethinking, and practice	Set up large research teams	

RESULTS

The overall results of the study are illustrated in table 5.1.

Improvement of Academic Leadership through Cross-Cultural Interactions

Our data indicate that the CIDA program had significant impacts on the cognition of participants from the SOM of XJTU. In particular, Chinese scholars who visited Canadian universities recalled that the experience expanded their horizons in a large degree after China had closed its door to the world for nearly three decades. As one interviewee said, "What we [see] in Canada may not be the technical knowledge nor the strategy tool which can be applied into practice right now, but the thing really can change our cognition and enlighten our thinking, this cognition improvement can affect us in daily life unconsciously, what we [see] and what we touch decided our thinking and notion."

We observed cognition improvement in the teachers participating in the CIDA program in three main areas. Firstly, Chinese teachers were introduced to important new teaching methods. In Canada, management teaching mainly relies on the case-study method. Teachers distribute some materials, and students seek out more information and cases relevant to the topic. During class, students present and share their ideas, which are then discussed by the class, while the teacher provides additional comments and advice. The case-study method is prevalent in many overseas management colleges, and was slowly introduced into China at this time. Secondly, we observed cognition development in the understanding of teaching itself. Canadian teachers do not count the quantity of knowledge they convey to students, but rather value what knowledge their students have grasped. Teachers pay attention to the critical and creative thinking students gain through the teaching process, and pay attention to the teaching process itself, creating an environment that inspires students to search for related knowledge, and that encourages them to learn by taking initiative positively. As a result, the burden of learning placed on Canadian students is greater than that placed on Chinese students. By contrast, Chinese students do not want to seek and search for knowledge by themselves. Instead, they wait for their teachers' instruction, and learn passively from their teachers. To some extent, this attitude is a result of Chinese culture, and cannot be changed over a short period of time. Thirdly, we observed increased availability of advanced equipment and better supporting services. One interviewee recalled that in Canadian universities, printers and other teaching equipment are conveniently located and numerous, research conditions are better than in China, and research information is profuse and accessible.

We found that the CIDA program had a positive impact on participants' teaching and research behaviours, in addition to improving their cognition. Our interviewees stated that when they returned to China from Canada, they had a new understanding of their teaching and research work, and they changed their behaviour in their own practices. These behavioural changes occurred in several different areas. Firstly, participants' own teaching methods changed. After participants learned the case-study teaching method in Canadian universities, they applied this best practice in their own classes. They began to encourage students to actively take part in class, have group discussions, and make presentations. According to the case-study method, their new teaching role was to provide related material and references for students, guide student discussions, and provide comments and advice on student presentations. This method is considered to be a good way to develop students' potential, and turns the focus of classroom teaching from what kind of knowledge teachers should address in class to the knowledge that students have really grasped. In recent years, the case-study teaching method has been a primary teaching method in Chinese universities' management classes, and many professors use this method in their classes.

Secondly, participants' behaviours were impacted by what they observed regarding connections between management classes and industry. As management is in essence a practice-oriented subject, the participants found that management classes in Canadian universities had close relationships with management practice in all kinds of industries. One of our interviewees described the cooperation between Canadian universities and various industries as mature and impeccable. It is common in Canada to invite members of the industrial management elite to lecture and give reports to students in management classes. In some courses, the main teachers are managers with abundant managerial experience. In this kind of class, students have the chance to communicate directly and have face-to-face discussions with the industrial elite. They also have the chance to do an internship within an enterprise that interests them. One of our interviewees recalled that this cooperation between universities and industry had inspired her to set up a club for sharing knowledge and practical experience with the managerial elite. In addition to providing the chance for students to learn about this type of cooperation, she also considered the club to be a university-industry cooperation platform to facilitate the collaboration between universities and companies.

Thirdly, participants' behaviours were impacted in terms of research methodology. It is not difficult to imagine this influence, considering the substantial gap between management research in China and that in Canada. Before the CIDA program started, very few Chinese scholars were familiar with scientific research methodology in management, and few researchers adopted empirical methods to develop theories in their research. Rather, conceptual research and system research were the primary research methods, and solving a narrowly focused problem was the research objective. As one of the managers of the CIDA program recalled, many of the students who were recommended to the PhD part of the program rated Canadian research methods, which are normative and empirical oriented, very highly. Based on communication with Canadian scholars, one professor from the SOM of XJTU published an influential book titled *Management Research Methodology*, which systematically introduced the empirical research methodology used in Western management research to Chinese scholars. This book has had a substantial impact on Chinese management scholars' research since its publication. Even now, many researchers learn how to conduct normative management research by referring to this book. Participants also hold that the relatively early contact the SOM of XJTU had with Western research methodology assisted in this school's long-term leading role among other Chinese business schools.

Fourthly, participants' group-level academic leadership was impacted. We found that many overseas returnees set up their own research teams or became team leaders as a result of their learning in Canada. Many of the participants of the CIDA program became team leaders (see Mirus, chapter 4 of this volume, for more detail). Some participants became leaders of degree programs in their department or institution, and some participants became leaders of national key research labs or research projects. Moreover, we found that scholars with administrative roles were more likely to become team leaders or to set up their own research groups.

Fifthly, academic leadership at the organizational level was impacted. One obvious phenomenon is that those management schools that participated in the CIDA program all became top management schools in China. The teaching and research standards of these management schools were greatly improved as a result of the program. Moreover, some participants with administrative roles became leaders at institutional or university levels, resulting in a direct impact on the strategy and operation of these institutions and universities. Several participants even played key roles in setting up new universities or institutions that combined best practices of the West and East. For example, Bing Xiang created the Cheung Kong Graduate School of Business after returning from Canada, and Youmin Xi created the Xi'an Jiaotong-Liverpool University after serving ten years as the vice-president of a top Chinese university.

Although the experience of studying in Canada had obvious positive impacts on the participants in terms of their cognition and academic work behaviour, our data also indicate apparent deviations between participants' cognition of the best practices learned in Canada, and their behaviour in their own academic practice. Almost all of our interviewees expressed their regret about the limitations preventing them from adopting the best practices they learned in Canada in their own work upon their return to China. Although the participants learned many new ideas and greatly improved their understanding of their academic work, they pointed out that many of these best practices could not be adopted in the Chinese context, or that their new thinking on academic work could not be fully realized due to external factors such as social norms and limited educating software and hardware facilities. In this sense, taking part in the CIDA program was more of an experience than a training program to them. It was difficult to apply what they had learned in their own teaching and research practice quickly and directly.

Our data revealed that the difference between Chinese and Canadian contexts in almost all aspects including culture, higher-education systems, and economic development levels was the main cause of this deviation. For example, although all the participants appreciated the case-study teaching method in management courses, it was impossible for them to teach it in the same way as their Canadian colleagues, because this method requires students to be active and self-driven in classroom learning. However, Chinese students prefer to rely on their teachers to provide ready-made knowledge rather than to act positively and take initiative in digging up knowledge from the cases. So it usually happens that Chinese students do little preparation before class and receive very limited knowledge from the case study. By contrast, Canadian students deal with such assignments more seriously than Chinese students, guaranteeing the outcome of the case study.

Besides, although the participants liked the Canadian connections between universities and businesses, it was difficult for them to invite Chinese managerial elite to give lectures in class because there was no close relationship between universities and industries in China, and people in industries had no interest in presenting in universities. By contrast, Canadian universities had a long tradition of close connection with industries, making it easy for Canadian teachers to interact with people in industries. When it came to research methodology, it was difficult for the participants to adopt the Western research methodology paradigm quickly due to the unique history of Chinese management research and the unique evaluation system for scholars' research in China.

However, it is worth pointing out that the deviation between cognition and behaviour has been reduced as the gap between the development of China and that of Canada narrows. Initially, going abroad to learn and communicate impacted Chinese teachers' cognition and broadened their horizons to a great extent, yet the advanced techniques and ideas they learned were hard to implement due to the substantial difference between China and Canada. However, as Chinese education conditions improved and Chinese teachers became more qualified, the gap in cognition between Chinese and Canadian education began to narrow. Today, advanced ideas and teaching concepts can be realized in China. Several interviewees stated that when they visited Western universities again after participating in the CIDA program, it was relatively easier than before for them to implement what they learned in their own teaching and research upon their return to China.

The deviation between cognition and behaviour was also moderated by the work of the participants, that is, whether they were pure scholars or scholars with administrative roles. Pure scholars tended to be constrained to a larger degree than those scholars with administrative roles. For example, with regard to research, it was much more difficult for pure scholars to collaborate with Canadian scholars and set up their own research groups after returning to China. The pure scholars' academic leadership at the organizational level was also improved to a very limited degree as compared to those with administrative roles.

The Process of Academic Leadership Improvement

As indicated by our data, the improvement in academic leadership of participating scholars occurred gradually during their stay in Canada and upon their return to China. In this section, we will present our results on how the academic leadership of the participants was improved from the process perspective. We summarize the five steps we observed in the development process of enhancing academic leadership in Chinese scholars as follows: *understanding* Canadian society at a deep level through field observation in Canada and personal contact; *differentiating* between Chinese and Canadian education and culture; *learning* from the differences; *rethinking* the differences; and finally *practising* what they learned in their own work. As shown in figure 5.2, these five steps form a circulation system that happened in both Chinese and Canadian contexts. (The different shading in the diagram indicates the difference in the development of academic leadership in the two countries at that time.) The distinctions between the academic leadership of Chinese and Canadian scholars and the broad social contexts in which scholars were embedded lay behind these improvement steps.

The first step in the development process, understanding, is based on *what* new things were observed in Canada in the 1980s, at a time when China had just opened its door to the world. Because there was a great gap between the economic and social development of China and that of Canada, scholars going abroad saw many fresh things pertaining to both their lives and their work. In particular, in the early 1980s, at the start-up phase of management research in China, the CIDA program was the first to provide a platform for Chinese scholars to understand management teaching and research in Canada. One executor of the CIDA project on the Chinese side pointed out that the purpose of Chinese scholars' visits was to gain a general understanding of teaching and research practices in Canada. With respect to teaching, the first impressions of one interviewee included the advanced teaching support system and the unique relationship between teachers and students. At that time, the

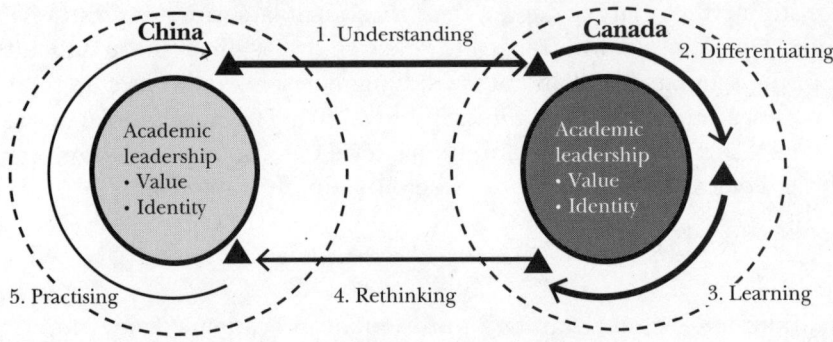

Figure 5.2 The process of academic leadership improvement

teaching support system in Canadian universities, including teaching management systems, software, and facilities, was much more advanced than that in Chinese universities. Canadian teachers were seen to be serious and responsible, and interviewees observed that Canadian students had considerable amounts of homework and pressure to learn both in and out of class. With respect to research, one of our interviewees was deeply impressed by the rigor and scientificity of research in the field of management in Canadian universities, while another interviewee received deep impressions of excellent research conditions, such as special offices, abundant information, and easily collected research resources in Canadian universities.

The second step of the process, differentiating, is based on *what* was different in Canadian universities and *why* these universities had a different system than the Chinese one. Based on their understanding of advanced foreign management methods, participating scholars began to differentiate between Chinese management teaching and research and foreign management teaching and research. Through this differentiating process, scholars gained a deep understanding of the advantages of the Canadian system and the disadvantages of the Chinese system, as well as the reasons for the gap between the two systems. One interviewee noted that management teaching in Canada concentrated more on students. Canadian students prepared material before and after class, and organized panel discussions in class with occasional comments from teachers. The Canadian management schools involved in the program had close relationships with businesses, so many social resources were available in case-study teaching, classes were taken on business tours, and students could study in real companies. In China, on the other hand, management teaching concentrated more on teaching the teachers.

Another interviewee pointed out that Canadian management courses were assigned one year in advance, and that the same course materials were used extensively across Canada, leading to lower administrative costs. By contrast, the institutional cost of teaching was very high in China, and the software and service support systems in Chinese universities were much worse than in Canadian universities.

The third step, learning, is based on participants studying *how* the Canadian system ran, in order to identify the key factors of teaching and research in Canadian universities, and to highlight what could be learned and adopted in their own teaching and research. Through comparing Chinese and Canadian practices, participating scholars actively learned advanced Canadian methods during their visits. For example, one interviewee said she learned in Canada that management science should be applied in practice, and that introducing business tours and business practices into the classroom is conducive to students' understanding and learning. She also learned how to teach the case-study method in management courses. As mentioned earlier, another interviewee published *Management Research Methodology*, a book that has been very influential in Chinese management research, based on his active learning of foreign management methodology in Canada.

The fourth step, rethinking, involves participating Chinese scholars reflecting on *how* their own teaching and research practices could be improved by integrating the best practices they learned in Canada. This step required a critical rethinking process on the advantages and disadvantages of the Chinese teaching and research tradition, and an evaluating process on the feasibility of adapting Canadian teaching and research best practices into the participants' own academic practices. After learning the best practices of Canadian universities, several interviewees pointed out that it was impossible to adopt many of these best practices into their own work directly. For example, one interviewee pointed out that although the gap between Canadian and Chinese research facilities could be narrowed with the fast development of China's economy, the gap in software could not be narrowed in the short term, nor could teaching concepts, which are affected by behavioural differences between Chinese and Canadian students. She insisted that many foreign teaching methods and research strategies have not been well adapted into the practice of Chinese scholars even now. Another interviewee showed very convincing evidence on how he rethought Western and Eastern teaching traditions to create a new teaching model that is superior to both the Western and Eastern models.

Another interviewee indicated that many things could not be learned from foreign management, such as the case-study method of teaching, which was introduced during the CIDA project. Canadian students are willing to ask questions, while Chinese students prefer to be quiet, so the case-study method is more effective in Canada than in China. Foreign MBA programs do not depend as much on written papers as Chinese MBA programs do, and foreign courses have higher homework requirements and more dependence on practical experience. By contrast, Chinese students who enter an MBA program leave their work in business to concentrate solely on learning. Chinese MBA programs are different from international programs in other ways as well. It is common for Chinese MBA students to plagiarize their theses, and *guanxi*, a powerful form of social and business networking in China, can lead to preferential treatment and falsification of results. In Canada, research is dispersive, and there is a set of industry-university-research cooperation mechanisms. In China, although industry-university-research cooperation is a desired ideal, in reality the cooperation among industry, university, and research institutions has been inadequate for a long time.

In consideration of the different macro social environments, it is impossible to directly copy Canadian best practices in a Chinese context. For participants, it was critical to determine how Canadian best practices could be integrated into their practice in China. In the view of one interviewee, foreign concepts and best practices should be adjusted according to Chinese conditions. Through participating in the CIDA project, she learned not only techniques and strategic methods, but also received personal inspiration and learned new ways of thinking. The inspiration and new thinking will impact her own work for the rest of her life, but her ability to use the techniques and strategies she learned are contingent on the context.

The final step in the improvement process, practising, is based on *how* the participants taught and conducted research in a new way after their return to China. Our data suggest that participating scholars have been able to integrate much of the Canadian best practices in teaching and research that they learned into their own work. For example, the CIDA project strongly promoted the construction of MBA and PhD programs in the SOM at XJTU. Many Western management textbooks were introduced into Chinese classrooms through the CIDA project. Additionally, owing to the CIDA project, the SOM paid attention to internationalization earlier than other Chinese universities, and held an international symposium in the 1990s, at a time when most other Chinese universities had not yet realized the importance of internationalization. As described earlier, one interviewee was inspired by the Canadian teaching method that connected classroom learning with industries, and worked to establish a knowledge-sharing club after her return to China. In recent years, several knowledge-sharing clubs have been established in China, and have become the platform for cooperation between universities and industries. Another interviewee told us his story of integrating Western and Eastern teaching and research traditions both in his own academic work and in his university managerial work for many years.

The Dynamic of Academic Leadership Improvement

Based on our data, we found that the contribution of the five steps in the process of improving academic leadership was contingent on the gap between academic leadership in Chinese and Canadian universities at the institutional level. As shown in figure 5.3a, in the early stage of the CIDA program, when the gap between Chinese and Canadian scholars' academic leadership was more significant (as indicated by the different shading in the diagram), Chinese scholars knew little about the Canadian system, so that the main challenge of their studies in Canada was to figure out the whole Canadian system. Therefore, the first three steps of understanding, differentiating, and learning contributed more to the improvement of these Chinese scholars' academic leadership than the last two steps of rethinking and practising (as indicated by the thicker lines in the diagram). By contrast, during the later stage of the CIDA program, illustrated in figure 5.3b, when the gap between Chinese and Canadian scholars' academic leadership was greatly narrowed, Chinese scholars were already familiar with the Canadian system because China had many channels of information from the Western world. For these scholars, the challenge of their studies in Canada was to experience how the Canadian system ran and how they could adopt Canadian best practices into their own work. Therefore, the last three steps of learning, rethinking, and practising contributed more to the improvement of these Chinese scholars' academic leadership than the first two steps of understanding and differentiating.

DISCUSSION

Rethinking the Influence of Cross-Cultural International Cooperative Programs

It is both urgent and crucial to examine the effects of international cooperative programs in higher-education systems in the globalized

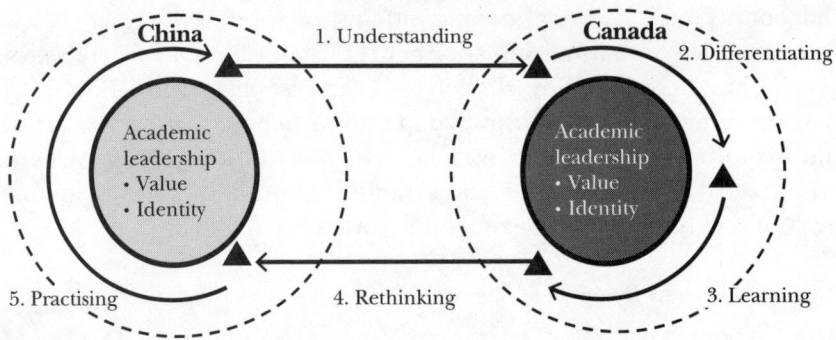

Figure 5.3a Improvement of academic leadership in the early stage of the CIDA program

world. By reviewing the CIDA program between China and Canada, which lasted for nearly two decades, we aim to deepen current understanding of the historical legacy of the program, as well as to provide insights for international cooperative higher-education programs in the future. Our results suggest that the influence of international cooperative programs can be understood from contextual, dynamic, and individual perspectives. Firstly, we consider it necessary to understand the influence of international cooperative programs from a contextual perspective. In other words, it is necessary to consider the effects of contextual factors at national, institutional, and individual levels when evaluating the influence of such programs. Using the CIDA program as an example at the national level, understanding the difference between China and Canada in terms of culture, institutions, and economic development is essential to understanding the gains of both sides through the collaboration. It was the huge gap in higher-education development between the two countries (in particular, the gap between the academic leadership of scholars in the two countries) that caused the most important impact for Chinese scholars to be a *broadening of their horizons in the early phases of the collaboration*. By contrast, a similar program between two Western countries would not require the same focus on context; rather, an analysis of such a program might focus on the behavioural-level collaborations aiming to deal with common challenges.

Secondly, we argue that it is necessary to understand the influence of international cooperative programs from the dynamic perspective. In other words, even when evaluating a single program, it is important to pay attention to the effects of the time dimension. The dynamic of academic leadership improvement during the CIDA program, as discussed

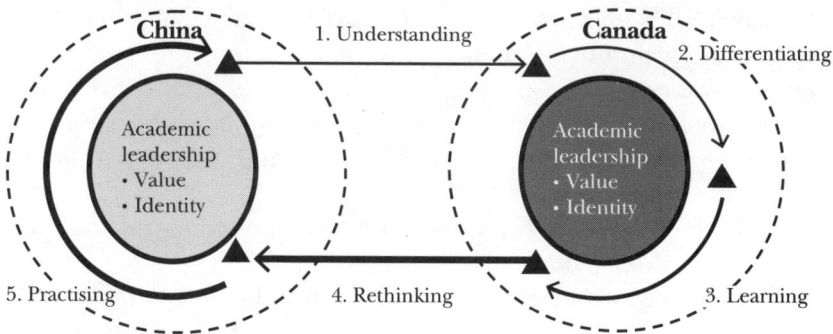

Figure 5.3b Improvement of academic leadership in the later stage of the CIDA program

in the last section, indicates that it is not appropriate to use the same criteria at each time period in evaluating the contribution of the five steps on the improvement of academic leadership.

Finally, we also find it helpful to understand the influence of international cooperative programs from the individual perspective. We chose to highlight the individual level because existing discussion paid much attention to national-level and institutional-level influences of these programs in order to evaluate the performance of the initiators. In fact, we believe the essential influence of cooperative programs should be examined based on assessments of the individual teachers and students who are the real beneficiaries as well as the targets of such collaborations. For example, the objective of the CIDA program was to improve the teaching and research capabilities of scholars involved in the program, both from the Chinese and the Canadian sides. Therefore, the evaluation of this program should address the degree to which the capabilities of participating scholars are improved. Our study, as an investigation on the individual-level influence of the CIDA program, examined cognitive- and behavioural-level impacts in participating Chinese scholars. This type of analysis is hardly ever found in investigations at national and institutional levels.

The Contextualization and Process of Improving Academic Leadership

Our study also yields implications on how to improve academic leadership in university scholars. Our results revealed that the concept of academic leadership is composed of two core elements: *cognition* and *behaviour.* That is, improving scholars' academic leadership includes at least two steps: improving their cognition and improving their behaviour. If only the cognitive dimension is improved, although this is helpful, improvement in academic leadership may not be visible, since the behavioural dimension is critical for scholars to fully utilize their understanding in their academic work.

In addition, our results echo the contextual nature of academic leadership. If we understand academic leadership to be composed of both cognitive and behavioural dimensions, it is not difficult to find that in many circumstances, deviation between cognition and behaviour is the critical reason behind poor academic leadership. Using the CIDA program as an example, the gap between the macro social and economic development of China and that of Canada was a key factor that determined the improvement in academic leadership of participating Chinese scholars. The separation of academic leadership into cognitive and behavioural dimensions gives us an opportunity to better understand the context-sensitive nature of academic leadership, as well as the mechanism of the effects of contextual factors on the improvement of academic leadership.

CONCLUDING REMARKS

It is important to understand the effects of international cooperative programs in the era of internationalization. In this chapter, we described the twenty-year collaborative linkage between XJTU and the U of A, as well as the sister universities of both, supported by the CIDA. We developed the process model of improvement in academic leadership with the influence of international cooperative programs at the individual level, and contextualized the process by considering the impact of the macro social and economic development of the two collaborators. We argue that much more attention should be paid to individual-level investigations on the effects of international cooperative programs in future research.

6

The Case Study Legacy of Ivey's Early Linkages in China

PAUL W. BEAMISH

INTRODUCTION

For the past thirty years, the Ivey Business School at Western University in London, Ontario, has been very active in China, much more so than most university business schools whether from Canada or elsewhere. Many of these activities have been in relation to introducing and popularizing the case method in China. Yet as Exhibit 1 at the end of this chapter suggests, school activities have gone well beyond this emphasis. Of particular note is the fact that Ivey was the very first business school from the US or Canada to establish a full degree program campus in greater China.

This chapter is divided into two sections. The first part examines Ivey's case-study initiatives in China. Several of these started in the Canadian International Development Agency (CIDA) funding era. The second part reflects on the longer-term consequences and contributions from the original university linkages.

PART ONE: IVEY'S CASE STUDY INITIATIVES IN CHINA

1984 marked the beginning of what was known at Ivey as "The China Project." The original phase was a CIDA-funded multi-year linkage with Tsinghua University's School of Economics and Management. At Ivey, there was a clear understanding that the CIDA-funded "China Project" was never intended to be permanent. There was no expectation on our end that funding would be renewed indefinitely. Our premise was that if the original government-funded linkage(s) were to continue after the government funding stopped, this would be a successful initiative.

Not surprisingly, the "China projects" at Ivey and at many of the other Canadian business schools were led by international business professors. All of these professors would be quite familiar with the classic approach to internationalization. Johanson and Vahlne's (1977) well-known model for internationalization describes foreign-market entry as a learning process. Here the organization makes an initial commitment of resources to the foreign market, and through this investment, it gains local market knowledge about customers, competitors, and regulatory conditions. On the basis of their market knowledge, the organization is able to evaluate its current activities, the extent of its commitment to the market, and thus its opportunities for additional investment. It then makes a subsequent resource commitment. Gradually, and through several cycles of investment, the organization develops the necessary levels of local capability and market knowledge to become an effective operator in the foreign country.

One important set of factors is the assimilation of local market knowledge by the subsidiary unit, as suggested by the Johanson and Vahlne model. But other, equally important factors to the foreign organization include its overall level of commitment to the foreign market in question, the required level of control of foreign operations, and the timing of its entry. To help make sense of these different factors, it is useful to think of the different modes of operating overseas in terms of two factors: the level of market commitment made and the level of control needed (see figure 6.1).

Some organizations internationalize by gradually moving up the scale, from exporting through joint venturing to direct foreign investment. Others prefer to move straight to the high-commitment, high-control mode of operating, in part because they are entering mature markets in which it would be very difficult to build a business from nothing. Still others choose to adopt a low-commitment, low-control mode, such as some "born global" companies. "Born globals" establish significant international operations at or near their founding (Calof and Beamish 1995).

Clearly, in the early stages of the China projects, emphasis was on the lower left corner of the figure. Here China was very much the importer of education (see Bild, chapter 3 of this volume). There is initially an exporting of ideas, research ability, and teaching material from Canada to China. This occurred initially via the use of student exchanges and faculty visits. Years later, of course, the internationalization of higher education would include emphasis on the upper right corner of the figure (see

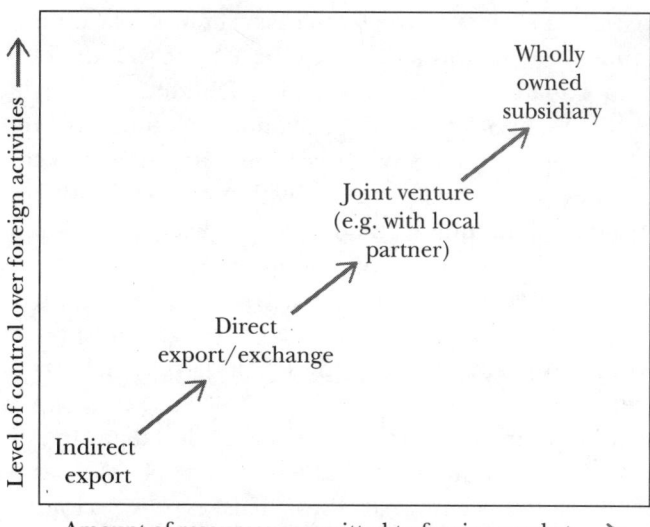

Figure 6.1   Approaches to foreign market entry

for example the Université de Montréal experience in China, Lefebvre, Rigaud, and Steyn, chapter 12 of this volume).

During Phase I of Ivey's "China Project," the school made a commitment to prepare Chinese MBA and PhD students for studies at Ivey, to work with visiting scholars, to provide some short-term instruction in China, and to assist Tsinghua University in the development of its management faculty. Everyone shared in the desire to "train-the-trainers" in order to achieve the desired multiplier effect (Jackson 2003; Mirus, chapter 4 of this volume).

Another goal was to help Ivey become more familiar with China and the conduct of business in that country. While no one questions the importance of understanding the Chinese market now, thirty years ago it was not as obvious to some people. In fact, even during the latter days of our "China Project" in the early 1990s, one associate dean questioned why so much time was being spent "on China."

During Phase I of the project, thirty-five articles, cases, and notes were written; nine Ivey faculty participated in short lecture visits to China; twelve visiting scholars spent one year each at Ivey; there were eight graduates of the MBA program; and all visiting Chinese attended the Case Writing Workshop.

An expanded Phase II of the China Project took place until 1994. A five-year endeavour, the project was a joint venture with the University of Waterloo in Canada, and in China with Tsinghua University, Dalian University of Technology, and the Nanjing Institute of Technology (renamed Southeast University). Ivey's commitment was to continue to assist in the development of Chinese institutional capacity for management education. A unique element was the design, development, and delivery in August 1992 of a program on teaching Joint Ventures (JV), Technology Transfer, and International Trade via the case method. This "train-the-trainers" program was offered through interpreters to academics from across China. All of the teaching material was translated into Chinese.

A large-scale joint publishing effort was undertaken. In April 1992, the first volume of five international business casebooks was published in Chinese by Tsinghua University Press. This series was a joint undertaking of Ivey and Tsinghua University. This series constituted a comprehensive collection of international business cases for Chinese managers and students. In 1992–93, six international texts were published in Chinese by presses arranged through our partner schools in Dalian and Southeast.

These initial efforts laid the groundwork for multiple case-study-related initiatives by Ivey over the next two decades. Each of the following four projects will be discussed in detail:

1 Ivey-Tsinghua Casebook Series (1998–2002)
2 Annual Case Teaching / Writing Workshops at Tsinghua (since 1998)
3 Ivey Publishing's Case Distribution in China
4 Additional Case-Related Linkages in China (since 2010)

1. Ivey-Tsinghua Casebook Series (1998–2002)

In response to the Chinese government's decree that 25 per cent of MBA courses be taught using the case method, together with Tsinghua University's School of Economics and Management, and the China Machine Press (Huazhang Graphic), Ivey embarked on the project "A Total Solution for Management Education Material in China."

Dr Sun Lizhe, president of Multi-Lingua Publishing International Inc., a JV partner with China Machine Press, recognized that the Chinese universities had a great need for high quality teaching materials, and that Ivey was a logical solution. True to the significance of *guanxi*, Dr Sun was a close friend of Chen Xiaoyue, a Tsinghua professor who was among the first group of visiting scholars to Ivey in 1984. Three elements of the model were devised:

(i) Customization of casebooks based on the curriculum needs of the China MBA program
(ii) Recommendation of best text books for the MBA curriculum
(iii) Introduction of case method workshops for MBA instructors across China

In 1998 and 1999, thirty-two volumes of casebooks (sixteen in English and sixteen in Chinese translations) were prepared for the China market. Cases selected for each volume were based on the core curriculum of the MBA program in China. The series was supplemented by subsequent titles based on electives and new topics as the curriculum continued to be revised.

Several elements of this project were considered groundbreaking at Ivey. First, seventeen Ivey faculty members served as editors. They volunteered their time to select cases from Ivey's collection. They consulted with their colleagues in China on the curriculum needs. Each book involved an editor from Ivey and an editor from Tsinghua. The Ivey editor would select perhaps twenty to thirty Ivey cases, which they thought were most appropriate for the topic. From these, the Chinese co-editor would select the fifteen to twenty cases he/she deemed most appropriate for the China market. These would be the cases included in each volume. The Ivey co-editor also provided an introduction for each casebook, speaking specifically to the content and its use in classrooms. Second, as copyright holder to its intellectual capital, Ivey Publishing waived all of its normal permission fees (typically $500/case) to translate and use the cases in the books. More than 300 Ivey cases were translated into simplified Chinese. Third, corporate sponsorships were secured to subsidize the project to ensure affordable price for broad distribution. Each casebook typically had about fifteen cases and was priced in the range of 15–30 RMB (less than US$4). Last, any royalties collected from the sale of casebooks, which were owing to Ivey, were donated to charities in China.

Some of the more popular Chinese casebooks, including Corporate Finance, Human-Resource Development and Management, Management, and Marketing Management, were expanded again in 2001–02 into second editions, along with the introduction of casebooks on three new topics: E-Commerce, International Entrepreneurship, and Organizational Behaviour. The nineteen casebooks are as follows: Business Ethics; Corporate Finance; E-Commerce; Finance and Money Market; Financial Accounting; Human-Resource Development and Management; International Business; International Entrepreneurship; International Trade and International Finance; Management; Management Communications; Management Information Systems; Management Science; Managerial Accounting; Managerial Statistics; Marketing Management; Organizational Behaviour; Production and Operations Management; and Strategic Management.

Ivey also organized eighteen Ivey professors to work with faculty from Tsinghua and consulting professors from other Chinese universities in selecting eighteen of the most highly regarded textbooks in the West for reprinting. Dr Sun had the reprinting rights in China from a number of major US and European publishers. These textbooks represented the state-of-the-art of business education and corresponded to the core courses of the Chinese MBA curriculum. These textbooks were available in major bookstores in China and were priced at 1,500 RMB (US$180) for the set of eighteen.

Coordination of many of the Ivey activities at Tsinghua fell under the oversight of either the Tsinghua dean, Zhao Chunjun, or senior professor Chen Xiaoyue. Chen spent one and a half years at Ivey (during two separate visits) and very much personified the model of enhancing academic leadership of Chinese scholars as developed by Xi, Zhang, Zhang, Ni, and Li (chapter 5 of this volume): "*Understanding* Canadian society at a deep level through field observation in Canada and personal contact; *differentiating* between Chinese and Canadian education and culture; *learning* from the differences; *rethinking* the differences; and finally *practising* what they learned in their own work."

2. Annual Case Teaching/Writing Workshops at Tsinghua (since 1998)

The case-method approach is a relatively new way of thinking for Chinese educators. Rather than lectures, students learn through lively discussion and debate. Traditionally, Chinese students would not confront professors or provide opinions due to the sense of hierarchy and cultural deference to people in positions of authority. Some instructors and even more students were increasingly ready for this non-lecture "Western" approach in the MBA experience. To those unfamiliar with the case method, sharing the "dos" and "don'ts" with experts in workshops, and understanding the opportunities and risks in teaching and learning with cases are critical in building up the confidence to help improve the overall experience for students and instructors.

Ivey has been extremely active in introducing the case method in China. For the past fifteen years, a Hong Kong–based foundation has provided funding to allow us to provide an annual Ivey-Tsinghua Case Teaching and Writing Workshop. Over 1,000 Chinese university professors have attended. In addition to working with Tsinghua, Ivey faculty members continue to offer workshops at other universities throughout China. More than 2,000 additional Chinese professors have attended these workshops to date. Despite such progress, adoption of the case method in China has been highly variable. Certainly those Chinese business schools that are highly ranked are the most regular users of cases in their classrooms. Yet as Hatch and Mu (2014) have noted from their interviews at several dozen business schools in China, impediments exist. These include a lack of reward system for those teaching with cases, a lack of student preparation, and a lack of case culture.

3. Ivey Publishing in China

Ivey Publishing is the world's second largest producer of business school teaching cases, after Harvard. It has over 5,100 items in its current collection. Over 1,000 Ivey cases or Ivey Business Journal (IBJ) articles are already available in simplified Chinese, with 200 additional cases or readings now being translated annually. By practice, all Ivey cases or IBJ articles involving China are translated into simplified Chinese, as are all bestsellers. Ivey Publishing has over 350 cases involving China in its current collection, and Ivey cases are used all over China. Ivey Publishing has dozens of site licences with Chinese business schools, as well as full-time staff members based in China. In June 2013 and July 2014, Ivey hosted at its London, Ontario campus visits by deans and case centre directors from China for a two-day workshop on how to set up and manage a case centre. There are over fifty case centres at Chinese business schools as of early 2014. That Ivey Publishing is so active in China should not come as a surprise. In 2013, there were about thirty million Chinese university students versus half that number at US colleges (see Evans, chapter 2 of this volume).

4. Additional Case-Related Linkages in China

Linkages through the China Management Case-Sharing Centre (CMCC) have been in place since 2010. A Memorandum of Understanding (MOU) on Case Development Collaboration was signed in 2010 to foster the development and dissemination of China-based cases. This collaboration involves over 200 Chinese universities and one non-China based institution: Ivey. An Ivey faculty member often provides a keynote speech at the annual conference, and assistance is provided in helping to raise the quantity and quality of business cases in China. The CMCC is supported by the China National MBA Education Supervisory Committee (CNMESC). With offices at the School of Management at Dalian University of Technology, CMCC operates as a non-profit service organization with a focus on researching, developing, and sharing cases that discuss local business challenges.

Further linkages exist through the China Academic Degrees and Graduate Education Development Centre (CDGDC). In the spring of 2013, a delegation from the CDGDC and the Ministry of Education (MOE) visited Ivey Publishing. The primary responsibilities of the CDGDC are to quality-assure higher education as well as Sino-foreign jointly run schools and programs; to provide recognition services of educational qualifications; to administrate two national examinations in graduate education; and to manage the National Database Centre for China Academic Degrees and Graduate Education. In September 2013, the CDGDC was entrusted with a new task by the Ministry: to build a national-level case centre for professional degrees education in China. There are now nearly forty professional degrees in China, and their proposed case centre is intended to help *all* of them!

In addition, linkages involving case-writing training exist. As of June 2014, Ivey has established six case-writing training initiatives with Chinese business schools. The Joint Case Training Development Project (JCTDP) is designed to leverage Ivey professors' expertise on case writing, something that is highly needed in Chinese business schools. The relevant China school's faculty and Ivey faculty jointly develop a series of cases (up to ten per contract). In May 2014, two workshops were held at the China Europe International Business School (CEIBS), host school for nine Shanghai-area business schools involved with the Shanghai MBA Case Library being developed by the Shanghai MBA Case Development and Sharing Platform. The Platform was established by the Shanghai Government. The two workshops that I led were on "Case Evaluation" and "Advanced Case Writing," both of which went far beyond the introductory workshops in case teaching and case writing which are now common in China.

PART TWO: REFLECTIONS ON LONGER-TERM CONSEQUENCES AND CONTRIBUTIONS

It is hard to know with certainty the long-term consequences of any university's linkages in China. With or without the university linkages, China would have developed economically. Yet I believe that the Ivey linkages did make a positive difference. I have been visiting China every year for over thirty years now, and I have observed extraordinary change, mostly for good. The comments below must be understood as personal reflections. They are considered according to the four questions asked by the editor of this volume.

1. In what ways did universities, acting in partnership, contribute to China's economic revitalization and rapid transformation?

When I first visited China in the early 1980s, the state of management education there was very low. The Open Door policy had only recently been announced, and there was much to be done in regards to moving away from a planned-economy model toward one which included more market economy realities. Research in the 1980s about operating in China reflected the evolving nature of business practices there. My own papers are illustrative (Beamish 1984; Beamish and Carr-Harris 1984; Beamish and Tan 1985; Conley and Beamish 1986; Beamish and Wang 1989).

There is no doubt that Canadian universities were able to make a positive contribution to China's economic revitalization and transformation (see Hayhoe, Pan, and Zha, chapter 1 of this volume). Ivey's university partners in China were able to play an important role in China's economic revitalization because the country supported the very rapid growth in its number of degree-granting business schools. The Canadian business school linkages in China in turn facilitated their role in two primary ways. First, Chinese visiting scholars to Canada learned a great deal during their visits. They were able to observe first-hand how a market economy functioned, and how at least one business school (in this case Ivey) functioned within such a context. Exposure to a viable alternative model allowed them to think about how to bring back to China those elements that might work best. Second, they were introduced to new, current teaching material (both textbooks and case studies) from which they could draw as they deemed appropriate to their new reality. The fact that the Ivey Casebooks for the Chinese market sold hundreds of thousands of copies, and the fact that millions of copies of Ivey cases have been studied in China, suggests that our content was able to contribute to China's transformation.

2. How far did university partnerships foster the spawning of new ideas that would address crucial issues of humane and democratic governance, social justice, and environmental sustainability arising in the train of rapid economic and technological change?

Whether through observation as visiting scholars, or access to more and current teaching materials, university partnerships certainly create knowledge transfer and the introduction of new ideas to one's Chinese counterparts. These new ideas definitely include consideration of governance, justice, and sustainability. Any key-word search of the Ivey Publishing website[1] using the above (and related) terms will return hundreds of relevant examples. All of these cases have long been available for use in China. Whether they are actually used is up to the Chinese professors.

3. What organizational or contextual features of the linkages themselves were important in enabling them to be effective and what serious challenges or hindrances arose?

A major strength of the Ivey-Tsinghua linkage was continuity. Some of the same key people were in place both during and after the ten-year funding period. This continuity allowed personal relationships / friendships / trust to develop, which in turn created an environment in which complex issues could be managed more easily.

A number of hindrances and challenges nonetheless existed or arose. First, if Chinese faculty had limited facility with English, they were unable to derive as much benefit as would have been desirable. Second, the issues around the Tiananmen Square protests of June 1989 resulted in a number of Chinese visiting scholars in Canada not returning to China. This non-returnee problem (see Mirus, chapter 4 of this volume) slowed progress in the linkages. Third, the CIDA contracts required a lot of time to be spent on paperwork and bureaucratic issues.

4. *What lessons for current and future collaboration between Canadian and Chinese universities may be drawn from past experience?*

As described in Beamish, Wong, and Shoveller (2005, 200):

> The experience of working with Chinese colleagues in translating Ivey cases into Chinese was invaluable. It has improved the quality of the original English-language versions by forcing us to recognize and remove colloquialisms, clarify ambiguous works or phrases, and eliminate any ethnocentric biases that may have unconsciously crept in. It reinforced the fact that some cases are "culture bound." In certain instances, we recognized the "inappropriateness" of the Western-style cases and acknowledged the practical needs of the local teachers. Such collaboration has provided opportunities for our faculty to engage in "better" joint case writing with colleagues in China.

From the Ivey side, it was a guiding principle always to treat our counterparts in China with respect. There was a widespread recognition that the state of management education was likely to improve quickly in China, and that eventually our counterparts would have the skills and abilities to be able to teach us as much about the practice of management as we were teaching them. Another important lesson for future collaborations is to retain strong institutional memory. Most players will change over a three-decade period so it is helpful on all sides to understand the past.

EXHIBIT 1: ADDITIONAL CANADA-CHINA
EDUCATIONAL COOPERATION INITIATIVES BY IVEY

Student Teaching Programs in China (since 1994)

Since 1994, Ivey has had a group of its MBA students teach a credit course in Introductory Business to undergraduate students at Tsinghua University. In 2002, MBA students embarked on a pilot teaching program for business students at the Shanghai Institute of Foreign Trade in Shanghai. In 2011, another pilot program was started at Jinan University in Guangzhou. The student-run China Teaching Project (CTP) has engaged as many as thirteen MBA students each year, teaching for the month of May at Beijing, Shanghai, and Guangzhou. In 2005, doctoral students at Ivey launched the Global Teaching Project (GTP). The first country of choice was China.

Ivey's Campus in Greater China (since 1998)

Ivey was the first North American business school to establish a campus anywhere in Asia. Called The Cheng Yu Tung Management Institute, this campus is located in the Hong Kong Convention and Exhibition Centre, and officially opened in 1998. It offers a learning facility specially designed to meet the exacting standards of Ivey's executive MBA program. In addition to the executive MBA (EMBA) program, over 100 non-degree executive programs have been taught in Hong Kong and in mainland China. Literally thousands of Chinese managers have attended the Ivey degree and non-degree programs. In total, Ivey has about twenty full-time staff in its offices in Hong Kong, Shanghai, and Beijing.

The research and development arm of Ivey's Campus in Hong Kong is the Asian Management Institute (AMI). It was established in 1996 to increase the level of intellectual capital in relation to case writing, research, and Asia-knowledgeable faculty. Since the AMI was established, dozens of Ivey faculty members have taught in greater China; hundreds of China-specific teaching cases have been developed, over half having a Chinese co-author; and over fifty China-specific journal articles have been published.

Ivey and the Asia Pacific Foundation of Canada

Ivey has had long-time linkages with the Asia Pacific Foundation of Canada (APFC). We will highlight two areas in particular. First, in 2007, we registered several Research Reports with the APFC, which dealt with toy recalls from China. This work on toy recalls received massive international attention, being quoted in more than 250 newspapers in fifteen countries. Second, for four years, Ivey provided the APFC with a quarterly commentary with case studies, offering executives and researchers insight on business challenges in China and other parts of Asia.

Custom EMBA Program for Chinese Managers

In 2011, in cooperation with the Bank of Montreal, Ivey provided a custom EMBA program in Canada for a group of senior managers from the Agriculture Bank of China (ABC).

Casebooks

In December 2013, four additional casebooks were published in Chinese. These were co-edited by faculty members from Ivey and China University of Political Science and Law (CUPL). These books dealt respectively with Family Businesses, State-Owned Enterprises, Foreign Companies in China, and New Industries. By mid-2014 there were already about ninety books focused on China edited by Ivey faculty members.

Canada China Business Council (CCBC)

Like many business schools in Canada, Ivey has long been a member of CCBC. In late 2012, Ivey was unanimously chosen by an independent judging panel to receive the Gold Award in their inaugural Education Excellence category. The judges noted, "Ivey has demonstrated outstanding achievement in delivering success to research partnerships, recruitment, student and faculty exchanges, alumni relations, institution linkages, executive training, as well as provision of Canadian curricula. As well, Ivey was able to overcome challenges and has successfully built effective and sustainable international partnerships that help students become global citizens."[2]

NOTES

1 www.iveycases.com.
2 Congratulatory letter dated 6 November 2012 from Sarah Kutulakos (executive director of the Canada China Business Council) to Ivey.

PART THREE

Collaboration in Engineering and Environment

7

Canada-China Collaboration in Engineering Education and Its Societal Influences

LI CHONGAN, LÜ SHUNJING, AND YAO LING

INTRODUCTION

The Canada-China University Linkage Program (CCULP) and the ensuing Special University Linkage Consolidation Program (SULCP), running from the 1980s to the early 2000s, were major events in China's international cooperation in higher education after the country's reform and opening-up. Of all the CCULP/SULCP projects and other Canadian International Development Agency (CIDA) programs in higher education, quite a number of them were linkages between engineering universities. These linkages took place during a special historical period in China – a time of technical progress, accelerated industrialization, transformation of the economic system, and reform in engineering education. Some of the industrial ministries in the central government that had founded and run educational institutions were now shut down, so the administrative systems of nearly 100 engineering universities had to change at a fundamental level. The question of what models and paths to follow emerged as a major challenge in engineering education. Relatively speaking, engineering universities often have more direct and extensive contacts than other universities with the economy, society, and even politics. As a result, significant changes in engineering universities are very likely to lead to wider social impacts. The changes and growth at engineering universities that occurred during this critical period in history led to impacts across China.

Eleven of the Chinese cooperative partners of the CCULP, about one third, were engineering universities, largely polytechnical or professional in nature. Located in the eastern, central, and western regions of China, these engineering universities were administered respectively by the State Education Commission (SEdC), by industrial ministries of the State Council, and by local governments. As a group, these eleven universities were a good representation of higher engineering education in China. Table 7.1 lists the participating engineering universities and their CCULP projects.

We have collected data on nine CCULP engineering projects from four project-assessment reports, from publications, from the Internet, and through interviews with fifteen participants from six projects. In this chapter, we focus on the content and scope of these projects, personal information regarding key participants, academic influences on the institutions involved, and the development of these institutions both before and after the projects. We attempt to examine the value of these projects, based on their historical environment, developmental stages, and larger social impacts, paying close attention to participation in and coverage of these projects, and tracking institutional and personal development after the projects concluded. Our key points of concern are: the connection between these projects and the universities' development after the projects; the intersection between progress in industrial technology and the process of national industrialization; and the direct and indirect impacts of these projects on the relationships between universities and industries, governments, and wider society.

In addition, we review case studies from collaborative projects between Canadian and Chinese engineering universities, in order to further analyze the causes of the success of these programs, and their impact on participating universities, China's higher education in engineering, and China's economy and society.

BACKGROUND AND FAVOURABLE CONDITIONS

The CCULP/SULCP projects were considered very successful by the Chinese and Canadian sides, both giving widespread praise of the projects. The success of these projects was by no means accidental; the projects had either luckily coincided with or consciously created all the necessary conditions for ultimate success. As the Chinese put it, the projects enjoyed "favourable climatic, geographical, and human conditions."

Favourable Climatic Conditions: A Receptive Macro-Environment

China's reform and opening-up offered a good opportunity for Chinese-Canadian cooperation. Changes within China had been initiated, the

Table 7.1 Engineering university linkages and CCULP engineering projects

Chinese universities	Current names	Administered by	Canadian universities	Project theme
Chongqing Institute of Civil Engineering and Architecture	Chongqing Univ.	Ministry of Construction	McGill University	Rural planning and environmental health
University of Science and Technology Beijing (USTB)		Ministry of Metallurgy	McMaster University	Mining and metallurgy education and research
Zhejiang Univ.		State Education Commission	Technical Univ. of Nova Scotia (TUNS)	Circulating fluid bed technology
Shanghai Univ. of Engineering Science (SUES)		Shanghai Municipality	University of Waterloo	Building cooperative educational system
Shanghai Institute of Mechanical Engineering	Univ. of Shanghai for Science and Technology (USST)	Shanghai Municipality	Université de Montréal	Land utilization and transport system optimization
Wuhan Iron and Steel Univ.	Wuhan Univ. of Science and Technology (WUST)	Ministry of Metallurgy	Univ. of Toronto	Engineering university reform
Southeast University (SEU)		State Education Commission	Concordia Univ.	Joint doctoral training
Lanzhou Railway Institute (LRI)	Lanzhou Jiaotong Univ. (LJU)	Ministry of Railways	Ryerson Polytechnic University	Computer application
Southwest Institute of Technology (SWIT)	Southwest Univ. of Science and Technology (SWUST)	State Bureau of Building Materials Industry	Laurentian University of Sudbury	Mining industry science and technology
Beihang University of Aeronautics and Astronautics (BUAA)		3rd Ministry of Industrial Machinery	Univ. of Manitoba	Failure analysis and prevention
Beijing Univ./Tsinghua Univ.		State Education Commission	Dalhousie Univ./ Tech. Univ. of Nova Scotia	Environmental impact of water resources development

pace of industrialization was accelerating, and China badly needed valuable information, technology, and experience from overseas for its economic construction and development of science, technology, and education. Industries were hungry for knowledge and external information, and an unprecedentedly relaxed political environment, administrative control, and social atmosphere existed at that time. Other important social characteristics of this development phase included the enthusiasm of the Chinese people for learning and working, and a strong desire for external collaboration on the part of science and education institutions.

China's higher-education development also created favourable conditions for cooperation. Driven by its intrinsic vitality to reform and develop, China's higher-education sector was making rapid and substantial progress in higher-education reforms.[1] The level of respect toward Chinese universities had changed dramatically after the Cultural Revolution, and the universities' influence on the economy and society had been recovered and strengthened. Applied sciences, such as engineering, obtained unprecedented attention, and universities were undergoing radical changes in management systems and a transformation of schooling concepts. CIDA's choice of higher education as the major aid area for China, centred as it was on the development of human resources, was truly in line with China's overall development situation and the core requirements of its higher education (Hayhoe et al. 2012).

The transformation of engineering education in particular provided the opportunity for engineering-related CIDA projects to thrive. The acceleration in industrial development urgently called for the emergence of new engineering talents. Engineering disciplines were transformed, leading to the appearance of new disciplines and cross-disciplinary subjects. As the economy became more market-oriented, the administration of several of the engineering industries changed. No longer administered by industrial ministries, these universities were compelled to look further afield for direction in professional development and to increase their ability to provide social services. The China-Canada cooperative projects came at exactly the right moment during this refreshing transition, satisfying China's urgent needs for reform and development in its engineering education.

Finally, the positive relationship already existing between the two countries provided a good atmosphere and a guarantee of good faith. The Chinese people traditionally have a friendly affection for Canadians, largely due to the work of Dr Norman Bethune, the hero of many Chinese household tales. Good diplomatic relations between the two countries and the commitment and foresight of CIDA and the Chinese cooperative partners helped to cement this relationship.

*Favourable Geographic Conditions:
The Presence of Necessary Infrastructure*

Having gone through the early developmental stage of the reform and opening-up, Chinese universities had already achieved the essential conditions required to cooperate with foreign universities. Firstly, Chinese universities had a strong demand for technology. As major role-players in the fast-moving industrialization process, science and technology universities were powerfully motivated to carry out international exchanges. These universities had a thirst for new science and technology, a desire for advanced international experience, and aspirations for self-development.

Secondly, Chinese universities, through their efforts to recover and to catch up to their international counterparts, had achieved the academic basis and professional conditions that were necessary for international cooperation in some disciplines and educational models.

Thirdly, the necessary human linkages were in place: a number of visiting scholars and overseas students had returned to their universities in China. These scholars and students were often more entitled to speak up than their peers, and more influential in both academic and administrative circles. Their advantages, such as possessing more information and knowledge, proficiency in a foreign language, international contacts, and new ideas, often moved them forward to become pioneers and organizers of international cooperative projects, as well as bridges of communication between cooperative partners.

Fourthly, Chinese universities were equipped with the software, hardware, and other infrastructure required to implement the projects. They had accumulated experience in inviting foreign experts and teachers for intercollegiate exchanges, and could provide organizational support, coordination, and basic service for implementing the projects. For example, most universities had already established a "Waiban" (foreign affairs office), and built an "Experts Building" (a guest house for experts).

Finally, the cultural atmosphere both in and outside the universities was ripe for international cooperation. Chinese universities had worked hard to create and optimize the basic environment and atmosphere required to carry out the projects. The universities were undergoing fundamental changes in all areas, from schooling orientation to logistics service. In general, Chinese people were more ideologically active than ever before, and thus more tolerant and receptive of foreign cultures and of changes in social environment, and more accustomed to adaptive adjustment. All these changes provided a suitable environment both on campuses and in society.

*Favourable Human Conditions:
Harmonious and Efficient Working Relationships*

The CIDA projects in engineering were marked by candid, equal, and unified working relationships, active and enthusiastic participation of faculty and students on both sides, consensus of the joint management teams, and the care and support of the governments and other related organizations in both countries. In such an open and supported environment, participants had the opportunity to display initiative, and the cooperation took place in a pleasant and effective manner.

From project planning and decision-making all the way through to full implementation of the projects, both sides strove to establish mutually beneficial relationships that featured equality, mutual respect and learning, coordinated conformity, and active participation (Leng and Pan 2013). Only a few cooperative partners experienced barriers of communication during the early stage of the projects, but these partners were quick to rectify the situation thanks to their adherence to the principles described above, and henceforth an increasingly friendly and sincere cooperative relationship was established. As compared to the educational and social science projects, the "centre-periphery" relationship of the engineering projects was not generally an issue but was limited to the areas of science and technology, where China had much catching up to do. The equal partnership between China and Canada on the engineering projects,[2] the counterpart funding on the Chinese side, the unconditional technology transfer, and the studies targeting local problems were all conducive to safeguarding the independent status of the parties receiving assistance and avoiding a situation in which they would remain dependent on the assisting parties even after the projects were terminated (as Qiang and Wang question in chapter 11 of this volume).

The projects received constant support and care from the SEdC, the Ministry of Foreign Trade and Economic Cooperation (MOFTEC), and the industrial ministries in charge of the Chinese project universities. A meeting was held each year for project directors on the Chinese side, and officials were dispatched to each participating institution for inspection, guidance, and timely coordination and problem solving. Government departments on both sides offered coordinated support, including on-site guidance, timely coordination, problem solving, and regular exchanges. We did not observe the same high level of support in many other intercollegiate cooperative projects.[3]

In addition, visiting personnel all received considerate and warm-hearted help. Feedback from the many teachers who visited Canada at that time included a universal sense of gratitude for the arrangements and care provided by Canada. This gratitude is still strongly felt today, as we observed during our interviews. The orientation program arranged by the Association of Universities and Colleges of Canada (AUCC) was very helpful to many Chinese teachers on their first arrival in Canada, as were the documents handed out to them to help them adjust to the new life there. They are very grateful, even today, to their many Canadian friends for their care and support during their stay in Canada, which, they believe, not only ensured their success in learning and research, but also gave them life-long benefits.

The increasingly close relationship between Chinese universities and Chinese industries was also essential to the success of the CIDA projects, and strongly benefited the cooperative projects surrounding engineering technology. Universities and businesses were both developing new management systems at that time, based on the transformation from planned to market economy, as well as dealing with waves of new technologies. Their similar focus drew the universities and industries together, making it possible for investigative and training activities and new technologies that were first learned in the universities to be smoothly implemented in associated industries.[4]

CASE STUDIES: A RETROSPECTIVE ON ENGINEERING UNIVERSITY LINKAGES

When assessing the CCULP, the SEdC of China listed six remarkable benefits for the Chinese participating institutions: strengthened discipline and improved academic standards; improved teaching standards and the cultivation of a group of core teachers; increased supply of books and equipment; satisfaction of urgent needs in teaching, research, and medical treatment; amplified influence of participating institutions and substantial supporting funds; and expanding benefits that started with the projects and radiated outward to impact many additional areas.

Looking back at those programs and their benefits nearly twenty years later, we can see their longer-term and wider impacts. The case studies that follow show how the CCULP/SULCP projects were carried out in a few engineering universities, the benefits to the participating universities, and a follow-up of the development started by the projects.

The Lanzhou Railway Institute-Ryerson Polytechnic Institute Linkage

Of the eleven engineering universities that participated in the CCULP, six were established by industrial ministries within the central government. Founded and managed by the Ministry of Railways, Lanzhou Railway Institute (LRI) is a typical example of the specialized engineering colleges run by industrial ministries. The collaborative project between LRI and Ryerson Polytechnic Institute (Ryerson University today) was centred on computer application and information technology. The project covered the introduction of new technologies, staff training, curriculum renewal, technological upgrading of the computer system on campus, and industrial promotion of computer technologies, with the aim to improve the computer application standard of the railway system and of local industries. The five-year project between these universities included eight teachers sent from LRI to Ryerson for training, ten professors sent from Ryerson to LRI for technical assistance, the establishment of five new computer-related courses and the upgrading of nine other courses, a comparative study on the continuing education of technical personnel and a conference on the continuing education of female technicians, and upgrades to the equipment and technical standard of the computer centre.[5]

The successful implementation of this project in the early 1990s, at a time when computer and network technology was still in its early stage, quickly elevated LRI to a high starting point in computer technology and equipment. LRI soon developed the computer interlocking system that was widely applied in railway yards. Since then, LRI has rapidly developed in computer application and information technology, and has built strong disciplines in engineering and computer technology, forming a group of disciplines that have national influence today.[6] The influence of these disciplines started with the railways, but later expanded to many other industries and the local economy. For example, the computer system for logistics monitoring and management developed at LRI is now used extensively in the aviation and railway industries, including Beijing Capital Airport and Guangzhou Baiyun Airport. In addition, Volkswagen has adopted the green film-coating technology and related equipment originally developed at LRI for use in automobile parts film-coating.

Numerous other important benefits resulted for LRI, including elevated quality of teaching and strengthening of students' abilities, the training of academic leaders (one university president, one chairman of a college, three department chairs, and one head librarian), improved administration and concept of schooling, and accelerated internationalization. In 2003, LRI was renamed Lanzhou Jiaotong University (LJU), and today graduating students rarely have difficulty finding jobs, even in the difficult job market. Additionally, LJU has formed dozens of valuable and active connections with international universities.

The Beijing University of Aeronautics-University of Manitoba Linkage

The Beijing University of Aeronautics and Astronautics (now Beihang University) still belongs to the Ministry of Industry and Information today. It was the first aviation institute in China, founded by bringing together the aviation colleges and departments of eight famed universities. It is one of the key comprehensive universities in China (as are the three universities discussed after this one), and the only university co-built by the Chinese Academy of Engineering (CAE), which is a testimony to its important status in China's engineering education, science, and technology.

The collaborative program between Beihang and the University of Manitoba centred on failure analysis and prevention (in mechanical equipment), a multi-disciplinary area in frontier technology. The CCULP project occurred during the critical nascent stage of failure analysis in China and had a strong impact, leading to the founding of the Failure Analysis and Prevention Centre of the Joint Engineering Association in 1994, the International Conference on Failure Analysis and Prevention in 1995, and the establishment of the China-Canada Training Centre in Failure Analysis and Prevention of Mechanical Equipment, also in 1995.[7] One of the two professors in charge of the CCULP project in Beihang was elected as an academician of the CAE, and the other became a member of the Science and Technology Committee of China Aviation Industry Corporation and the deputy director of the Academic Committee of Beihang.

The Chongqing Architectural Engineering Institute-McGill University Linkage

The Chongqing Architectural Engineering Institute (now part of Chongqing University) was the first architectural university in China, founded in 1952 by bringing together nine civil engineering departments from six universities. It was the only national key university affiliated with the Ministry of Construction at that time, and was partnered with McGill University during the CCULP. Initiated in 1988, this CCULP project focused on rural planning and health infrastructure construction. Based on the CCULP project, the Chongqing Architectural Engineering Institute set up the Human Settlement Institute in 1990, headed by a Chinese professor and project director. (This professor later became the first chief of the Planning Bureau of Sanya City, the deputy chief of the planning bureau of Xiamen City, and the chair of the Department of Urban Planning of Xiamen University.) The legacy of this cooperative project was passed on to the four architectural colleges of Chongqing University today, especially the Urban Construction and Environmental Engineering College and the Architecture and Urban Planning College.

The Sichuan Institute of Building Materials-Laurentian University Linkage

The Sichuan Institute of Building Materials, renamed the Southwest Institute of Technology (SWIT) in 1992 and now part of the Southwest University of Science and Technology, was originally founded from a glass property school and a ceramics technology school. At the time of the CCULP, it was affiliated with the Ministry of Building Materials Industry (now the Bureau of Building Materials). This university is competitive in majors such as the use of non-metal resources as building materials, as is Laurentian University (LU), its Canadian partner in the cooperative program.

The objective of the collaborative project between the two universities was to upgrade the capacity and standard of teaching, research, and external service at SWIT, and to boost the economic development of China's western region. During the five-year project, sixteen teachers from SWIT had the opportunity to study at LU, and nineteen professors, technical experts, and senior executives from LU visited SWIT to provide technical support. The visiting scholars from SWIT demonstrated very strong initiative during their short-term studies at LU. Some of them were keen to observe the teaching methods at LU, and learned to organize in-class tutorial discussions. They also opened up micro-design courses after returning to China, in order to encourage interaction between teachers and students. One teacher did a comparative study of geology education between China and Canada, and held a seminar to compare the educational system of the two universities. He also imported Canadian teaching methodology into his own lectures in geochemistry.

Upon completion of the CCULP project, SWIT was able to open up new majors including environmental engineering, computer science, and engineering economic analysis and assessment. Other important benefits from the project included upgraded systems and infrastructure, new courses and seminars, the training of scholars who later became academic and technical leaders, inspiration for SWIT students who went on to outstanding performance in national competitions,[8] and a strengthening of the overall development of the university. For example, based on its Canadian experience, SWIT set up its own board of directors that included community representatives, a pioneering action among Chinese universities at that time. This unique concept and new organizational pattern caused extensive attention nationwide.

Benefits from the CCULP project reached well beyond SWIT itself. For example, a number of joint research programs were done by people from both partner universities that involved investigative study and technological achievements aimed at China's mineral industry. These studies and technologies became widely useful in many industrial and mining enterprises in a number of provinces including Anhui, Jiangsu, and Gansu.

When discussing the reasons behind the success of the linkage between SWIT and LU, both parties stressed the importance of mutual trust, sincerity, understanding, and respect. Other more concrete factors included precise project design, careful selection of a partner university and of exchange scholars, a joint working committee, a good working mechanism, and the serious involvement of top management from both universities. Respondents from the Chinese university mentioned that direct and barrier-free exchange of ideas was important. Those from the Canadian university pointed out the necessity to understand Chinese norms, and admitted that it just would not work to impose Canadian ways to solve Chinese problems. Based on this consensus, the two parties were quick to surmount the difficulties they met in the beginning of the cooperation (further discussed later in this chapter), and developed a very friendly, candid, and efficient partnership (Gerhard 1995).

The Shanghai Institute of Mechanical Engineering-Université de Montréal Linkage

The Shanghai Institute of Mechanical Engineering belongs to a different category than the universities previously discussed here – that of engineering universities founded and administered by provincial or municipal governments. Such universities mainly serve the economic and social development of local regions. The Shanghai Institute of

Mechanical Engineering, belonging to the municipality of Shanghai, is a locally famous engineering university. It was renamed as Huadong Gongye University during the late years of the CCULP project, and renamed again two years later as the Shanghai University of Science and Technology, its current name.

The cooperative partnership between the Shanghai Institute of Mechanical Engineering and the Université de Montréal (UdeM) focused on land use and transportation. With rapid economic development in China, traffic congestion in Chinese cities was an increasingly serious problem. Much of the old planning and infrastructure was insufficient to meet current needs. To tackle this problem, the partner universities began a series of new studies and joint research based on new ideas and the latest methods, and achieved remarkable results both theoretically and practically. The cooperation also included participation from two other universities from South China and Northwest China to form a collaborative network of research. Thus, the research content and the social impact of this cooperative project were extended to a broader area and to different types of cities.

With China's accelerated development in economy and urbanization, problems in land use and urban transport have become increasingly serious constraints on China's sustainable development, social harmony, and the protection of people's livelihood. The contributions made during the CCULP project are therefore a precious legacy today.

*The Shanghai University of Engineering Science-
Waterloo University Linkage*

Like the Shanghai Institute of Mechanical Engineering, the Shanghai University of Engineering Science is an application-oriented local university affiliated with the municipality of Shanghai. Its cooperative project with Waterloo University focused on introducing the cooperative education model to China. Waterloo University is Canada's first university to offer cooperative education courses and is also the biggest base of cooperative education in North America. The Shanghai University of Engineering Science was built on the Electromechanical College of Shanghai Jiaotong University, jointly founded by the university, five industrial bureaus of Shanghai Municipality, and Changning District Government, and on a college jointly founded by the East China Textile Institute, the Shanghai Textile Industry Bureau, and Putuo District Government.[9] Thus, right from the very start, this university has possessed inseparable ties with industries, local governments, and local society, making it an ideal place for the introduction of cooperative education programs to China.

The CCULP project between the Shanghai University of Engineering Science and Waterloo University occurred at a time when cooperative education in China's engineering universities was at its nascent stage, and thus had milestone significance. The project trained research and practice talents for cooperative education in China, and the leaders of the project became proponents of Chinese cooperative education. One of the major participants of the project began to devote time and effort to a systematic study of cooperative education and its daily practice, and became one of the earliest scholars in this area. Not only did the CCULP project help the Shanghai University of Engineering Science become a pioneer of cooperative education in China, both in theoretical study and in practical exploration, the project also helped to gradually improve and expand the university's practice to form a normalized system. Starting from the beginning of the twenty-first century, cooperative education at the Shanghai University of Engineering Science is carried out in all colleges and in 70 per cent of the disciplines, with the participation of more than 8,300 students per year.

Although cooperative education in China is still at a primary development stage of experiment and exploration, persistence in this reform will carry with it certain social influences. The extensive practice of cooperative education can boost close ties between universities and enterprises, and lead to the development and growth of both. By connecting society with the market (with no need for governmental interference), cooperative education leads to direct training and use of talents as well as optimal allocation of resources. This practice will naturally help to raise the status and function of social forces and market mechanisms in social governance, changing the inertia that is characteristic of the thinking and functions of traditional government management, and leading to modernized social governance.

The Southeast University-Concordia University Linkage

Of the eleven Chinese engineering universities involved in the CIDA project, Southeast University (SEU) was the only one that succeeded in entering the second phase of the project (SULCP). Unlike the universities discussed so far in these case studies, Southeast University is directly under the administration of the SEdC. It is one of the earliest established universities in China and is also one of the famous key universities. The president of this university, with a background of overseas education and experience in international exchanges, was particularly far-sighted in international cooperation. She later became an academician of the CAE and the deputy director-general of the State Education Commission, in charge of international exchanges. Even before the CIDA project, the university had begun long-term international exchange programs with Japan's Aichi University of Technology and Switzerland's Zurich Higher Engineering Institute.

The CCULP/SULCP project this university conducted with Concordia University centred on Southeast University's key and specialized disciplines. During the first cooperative project (CCULP 1989–95), ten doctoral students majoring in mechanical engineering and in electronics and information graduated, tutored by professors from both universities. The second project (SULCP 1997–2001) focused on the connecting point between the two disciplines mentioned above: advanced manufacturing technology. This project set up an education and training base at SEU for both university and industrial circles, to promote cooperation and exchanges between the academic world and industries, and to train the talent that was urgently needed for China's rapid development in this area.

It was a pity that the cooperative relationship did not carry on after the completion of the projects. However, the projects still remain fresh in the memory of the person in charge of international cooperation at SEU. He believes that the projects benefited the university by providing funding, experience, teaching assistance, curriculum reform, and by promoting connections between the university and industries. In addition to the exchange visits of dozens of teachers from both partner universities and thirteen doctoral students' study in Canada, five entrepreneurs from Jiangsu Province and Canada also exchanged visits. With the support of the local government, the university ran a series of advanced seminars for Chinese enterprises, and offered technical consultation, training, and cooperation in science and technology. The projects also promoted the rapid expansion of international cooperation at SEU. In 1989, only thirty-five faculty members had the chance to go overseas for academic exchanges (mostly conferences). This number has increased to today's average of 800 to 1,000 annual exchanges.

EFFECTS AND IMPACTS

Thanks to the historic opportunity in China and the success of the projects themselves, the CCULP and the SULCP had an enduring and intensive influence on the participating universities. Some of these influences have spread to other engineering universities and to relevant industries, and even to society and the government. How could these programs be so influential? One major reason is that they focused on human resources development, carrying out a series of intensive interpersonal exchanges through direct talent training. In addition, the CCULP/SULCP projects improved the universities' ability to train future talents with the new models they adopted. The young people trained during and after the projects had extensive influence in academic circles as well as in industry and society. In this section, we discuss the overall effects and impacts of these projects on the participating universities, scholars, students, and their wider environment.

Upgrading Universities' Standards and Overall Ability

The timely upgrades these projects brought to the standards and capacities of the universities made the universities more qualified to face the tremendous challenge of China's rapid move to popularize higher education at the beginning of the twenty-first century. The projects also helped the universities to accumulate experience and resources to expand their international cooperation. The China-Canada cooperation became a new starting point on the road of internationalization for each participating university, and was also a historical event on the road of internationalization of higher education in China, worthy of study and remembrance. When summing up the results of the CCULP, the International Cooperation Department of the SEdC specially mentioned that the achievements of the cooperation focused governments and other institutions' attention on universities, increased funding support in scientific research and international cooperation, and elevated the influence of the universities.

Features of these improvements in standards and ability are as follows:

- The projects improved the quality of education and teaching at participating universities. A large number of faculty exchanged visits during the projects,[10] broadening their knowledge and vision, learning new ways of thinking, and gaining enthusiasm to reform their curriculum content, teaching principles, and methodology. Benefits to the teachers resulted in benefits to the students.
- The projects improved the research and academic standard at participating universities. Strong disciplines at the universities began

to take shape or were reinforced. Returned scholars from Canada set up national academic organizations and served as chairpersons.[11] Some academic centres or research institutes established during the projects are still in existence today.
- The projects improved the infrastructure at participating universities. Many participating universities in China got equipped with advanced computers, CAD/CAM devices, library management systems, and campus LANs that were among the earliest in China to be connected to the Internet. Information technology was introduced into teaching and student management to meet the needs of information and internationalization. These advanced technologies and installations were quite impressive at that time in China.[12]
- The projects improved the universities' ability to serve industries and society by promoting the transfer of new technologies to enterprises and by allowing universities to once again take a leading role in technical innovation and talent training after the Cultural Revolution. The projects not only transmitted new knowledge and technologies, but also provided well-studied technical routes and development strategies, as well as training for senior management business personnel and government officials. Universities thus became more influential in formulating and implementing industrial technology policies. The projects also promoted distance education, continuing education, minority education, and community cooperation, substantially expanding the educational function of the universities as a result.

Boosting Technical Progress and Industrialization

The disciplines covered by the projects all centred on technologies that China needed badly at that time, such as information technology and computer application, resource utilization and environmental protection, biological technology, and reliability and safety of mechanical equipment. These new technologies quickly spread from the participating universities to other institutions and businesses and had a timely and obvious driving effect on technology upgrades in many industries.

Visits to Canada offered new perspectives on technology upgrades as well. Quite a few visiting Chinese scholars observed that in Canadian university labs and in Canadian industries, the latest technologies could coexist in the same system with old equipment. This was a new idea in China, where old systems were usually completely disposed of and replaced entirely by new equipment. Scholars were interested to find that it could sometimes be more economical and efficient to transform and integrate a system rather than simply replace the old with the new.

In addition, several of the projects focused on traps concealed in the industrialization process and their enduring impacts on sustainable development, and tried to find solutions and technologies based on both Canadian experience and Chinese situations.[13] These projects promoted connections with the government and business personnel who were responsible for decision-making and implementation. For example, a big workshop on industrial coal burning held jointly by Zhejiang University and the Technical University of Nova Scotia (TUNS) attracted over 200 participants from across the country.

Technological development has continued after the projects, as the participating Chinese universities have cultivated high-level research and development teams, some of which have joined the ranks of national teams in technological innovation. For example, LRI (now LJU) won the National Award for Science and Technology Progress for its participation in the Qinghai-Tibet Railway Project.

Inspiring the Reform of Engineering Education in China

The projects were carried out during a special period of reform and development of engineering education in China. Each engineering university had no choice but to make multiple choices to tackle a series of rapid, fierce, and profound changes occurring at that time. These changes included new requirements for universities to provide technological support and talent training for the industrial sector, the need to explore a more flexible enrolment system and employment strategies for graduates due to the transition from a planned economy to a market economy,[14] a shift from relying exclusively on government funding to opening up multiple sources of funds, and system changes and readjustments in administration.[15]

In order to respond to all these challenges, each university had to rethink its role and adjust its relationships with the government, industries, and society. The most important mission for engineering universities, though, was to renew their concepts of engineering education, discipline construction, and the teaching process, and to seek solutions to questions on engineering education in China, many of which were historical issues that had been debated and studied for over a hundred years (Hayhoe 1987).

At that time, higher engineering education in China contained heavy traces of the former Soviet Union model and its industrial management system. Higher engineering education was also still characterized by the fact that many universities had been founded for specific industries. The departments and disciplines in these universities were set in accordance with the industrial divisions, and the curriculum system was designed to reflect industry products, equipment, and jobs. Engineering universities that had been founded in this way tended to stress the education and training needed for certain industries but neglect the students' broader academic basis, knowledge and skill repository for further development, and adaptability to a more extensive career environment. Against this background, the question "What is the next step forward for China's higher engineering education?" had already become real and pressing. The experiences, information, and perspectives gained from the China-Canada cooperative projects offered both enlightenment and reference value to Chinese engineering universities. In addition to enacting curricular and teaching reform and exploring new training models, the participating universities also conducted all sorts of structural reform tests during the CCULP projects. Many of these tests became national hallmark events that spawned extensive concern and produced long-term impacts. For example, SWIT was the national pioneer in conducting structural reform to "jointly build and run a school," ultimately making itself the test unit for structural reform of higher education in China.

Profound Influence on People

Most of the Chinese teachers who trained in Canada became the mainstays of their universities in teaching and research. For all the teachers, students, engineering technicians, and organizing managers involved in the projects, their participation became a precious and even critical part of their growth and development. As found by a tracking study of Chinese teachers who trained in Canada, most of these lucky returnees later held important responsibilities in various fields and industries, though concentrated mainly in key academic and administrative positions at universities. According to the tracking statistics, out of fifteen young teachers from two universities, fourteen became full professors, two held top executive positions in multi-disciplinary universities, and twelve worked as deans of colleges or directors of departments.[16] As mentioned in SWIT's assessment report, "We got well trained key players for our school for the next century" (Gerhard 1995). A few scholars took up leadership positions in governments or enterprises. For example, one of the people in charge of the Chongqing project later became the first chief of the Planning Bureau of Sanya City, the deputy chief of the Planning Bureau of Xiamen City, and the chair of the Department of Urban Planning of Xiamen University. One of the doctoral students educated by the Southeast-Concordia project is now the chief technology officer (CTO) of a major international communication technology enterprise. Most of the participants in management training were also soon promoted in governments or enterprises. For example, two of the participants in the management training jointly run by the University of Science and Technology Beijing (USTB) and McMaster University became, respectively, the vice-governor of Anhui Province and the deputy mayor of Benxi, Liaoning Province.

These backbone scholars not only learned new knowledge through the projects, they also broadened their fields of vision, equipped themselves with new ideas, and changed their way of thinking, as they themselves commented. According to the survey conducted at the end of the USTB project, the major influence of the project was on the mindset.[17] Many teachers, equipped with new ideas, actively engaged themselves in teaching and educational reform, resulting in changes in teaching and training methods. As is often the case, the way students are trained at an engineering university will ultimately affect their thinking and ways of handling all sorts of tasks. Beneficial traits include being more practical, ignoring minor factors, and seeking solutions with simple models before verification and amendment for the sake of safety. These traits are remarkably different from those developed by a pure science education, which focuses more on strict logic, complete systems, and ideal states. The traits, encouraged by the CCULP projects, may have helped engineering graduates stand out more easily in the country's industrialization construction. Our statistical study supports this general view: the proportion of engineering graduates within the array of leading cadres is extraordinarily high.[18] Thus, changes in engineering education would later affect the composition of cadres and their behaviours.

Impacts on Concepts, Culture, and Society

The cooperative projects offered a rare and precious opportunity for those involved to observe the outside world more closely. This opportunity naturally helped to "emancipate people's minds," as was advocated then, and influenced the demands and visions for China's reform and opening-up. Reasons for the remarkable influence of these projects on Chinese concepts, culture, and society are discussed below.

Firstly, the project participants on both sides naturally discovered, through frequent exchanges and close cooperation while working in teams, the similarities and differences between the two countries in terms of cultural traditions and value systems. This happened at each important stage of the project. As Chinese intellectuals, many teachers took this chance to actively acquaint themselves with the foreign culture and, through comparison, to understand and appreciate it. The benefits from these cultural encounters and exchanges influenced and permeated systems and habits within the university culture – and this ideological influence was not limited to campuses.

Secondly, the projects involved many different groups of people, including teachers, students, and administrators of universities, technical and administrative personnel of different industries and other social sectors, women and minorities who received favourable care, officials of relevant governments at all levels, and participants of all sorts of training programs. As a result, benefits from the program were directly felt in a variety of different social circles.

Thirdly, the projects encouraged equality and mutual benefit during international exchanges. For many Chinese participants, it was their first time being personally involved in an international assistance project that featured mutual consultation on an equal footing, codetermination, hand-in-hand implementation, and a focus on meeting the needs of the partner accepting support. The principles of "equity, autonomy, solidarity, and participation" were widely agreed on by the Chinese participants and were reflected in their practice of international cooperation in the many years that followed (Leng and Pan 2013).

Fourthly, the Chinese participants developed an understanding of the Canadian people, society, and culture, and increased their friendliness toward the Canadian people. Quite a number of returnees recalled with gratitude the assistance they received in Canada that enabled them to live comfortably in the Canadian culture, and to understand and appreciate it. The friendships they developed are likely to last for the rest of their lives, and have probably affected other people around them.

Finally, most of the engineering projects involved development concepts such as human development, living environments, equal opportunity, resources and sustainability, and regional disparities. These projects were aligned with China's national scientific development strategy, discussed at that time and established a few years later. Several other CCULP projects also touched on these areas, but each project studied and looked for solutions from different angles. For example, the education project focused on the equality of gender and minorities (see Qiang and Wang, chapter 11 of this volume), while the LRI-Ryerson project promoted the continuing education of female technicians, and the SWIT-LU project helped ethnic minorities and people in remote areas to receive better access to engineering education. The CCMEP was designed to train business managers to better face the coming market economy (see Hayhoe et al., chapter 1 of this volume), while the engineering projects were aimed at providing tactics and technical solutions for managers when confronting traps in the process of industrialization. All these projects had a very positive influence on the formulation, understanding, and implementation of development policies in China. As a result, universities were motivated to set up closer ties with governments and the society. The strong development, growth, and increased influence of universities and industries were essential for the ultimate creation of a situation in China where governments, market, and society can work in balanced coordination.

SETBACKS

A story relating to the very successful project between LU and SWIT shows us that a good partnership does not come naturally or easily. When the project was initiated, a serious misunderstanding occurred as a result of poor communication. This "cultural glitch" and the resulting organizational restructuring of the project management team on the Chinese side put the project in hiatus for half a year. As a result, the two parties had to renegotiate later on. Thanks to the acuity, sincerity, and patience of the top executives and project management teams of both universities, the difficulty was overcome and mutual trust was rebuilt. All the people involved also learned through this process to recognize and accommodate the cultural values and preferences of the other side. The Canadian university community showed cultural sensitivity and warmth to visiting Chinese scholars, while the visiting Chinese academics took the initiative to learn about Canadian culture and society, endeavouring to be friendly ambassadors between the two universities and the two countries. Both sides spared no efforts in building a good partnership that ensured the smooth implementation of the project thereafter (Gerhard 1995).

REGRETS

At one or two Chinese universities, it is already difficult to find traces or memories of the CCULP projects. Also, in some cases, the projects were either restricted in scope or relatively isolated events, thus producing limited effect and influence.[19] Possible causes of the reduced success and influence of these projects could include problems with project design, uninspired selection of themes, a narrow range of participation, and a lack of commitment on the part of university authorities.

Quite a few universities, although enthusiastic about continuing cooperation, had to cease the exchanges due to the termination of funding. It would have been a different picture if the projects had been designed from the start to enable at least the professors or cooperative teams to carry on their collaboration even after the project funds ran out.

CONCLUSION

Of course, we cannot say that a China-Canada cooperative project determined the direction or path of development of any particular university all by itself. Neither can we claim that any of the critical changes occurring in China at that time were directly due to an international cooperative project. However, the perfect timing of these projects, occurring as they did during a key period of reform and opening-up in China, resulted in unexpectedly far-reaching influences on China's engineering higher education.

The impacts of the CCULP projects not only affected universities, but also spread beyond them to reach industries, governments, and the wider society. These impacts involved knowledge and technology, ideas and concepts, and systems and cultural levels. Some influences were overt, while others were indirect, hidden, or underlying. All things considered, the projects produced positive impacts that helped promote China's progress in education, science and technology, social politics, and environmental ecology. Some of the more profound influences, especially those on people, had long-lasting effects. Cross-cultural exchanges not only benefited the participants but also enriched universities' resources and capacities. The young people involved were able to realize their human needs and development, and their changes and the active roles they later took on helped to extend social impacts even further.

The China-Canada university cooperation practised and enriched the "Norman Bethune spirit" already revered in China, and furthermore set up what we might call the "Norman Bethune Model" of international cooperation: a model that features sincere help and close collaboration in the pursuit of higher values through international exchanges. Great changes have taken place since then within the higher-education environments in both China and Canada, but the significance of the China-Canada university cooperation still exists. Although Chinese universities are considered today to be less peripheral than in the past, this may only be due to knowledge transmission, or perhaps even fancy buildings. Most universities still lack the clear understanding and sense of obligation required to promote human development and well-being, to boost social progress, and to create a better tomorrow for mankind. Therefore, universities in China cannot do without cross-cultural exchanges and references in addition to their own efforts.

We hope that the important lessons presented in this volume can become the consensus of both sides. As Hayhoe summarized from many years of China-Canada university cooperation, since the global knowledge economy is unsustainable if it fails to address fundamental human needs, modernity is in even more urgent need of redemption or humanization than before, and short-term commercially motivated collaboration will not suffice (chapter 1 of this volume). Evans raised the point that "university partnerships are points of intersection that may be valuable in their own right but ultimately will be judged on whether they produce a larger societal and global good" (chapter 2 of this volume), and this should be the assessment of the ultimate value of the university linkages. On this basis, universities of both countries should select collaborations that focus on the needs of human development and economic/social sustainability, drawing wisdom from the exchanges between two profound cultures to seek better solutions for problems in the development process, and a better life for the people. Universities and intellectuals of both China and Canada can make concerted efforts, through mutual exchanges, understanding, learning, and borrowing between cultures to explore appropriate methods of realizing harmonious coexistence and mutual development of our different civilizations. As proposed by Professor Fei Xiaotong, all cultures should "appreciate their own beauty and that of others; different beauties coexist and work together to create the best world."[20] In this way, we can once again be a convincing role model for the world.

NOTES

1 The National Work Conference on Education was held in 1985 when the CPC Central Committee made the decision to reform the education system. In 1993, the State Council issued and implemented *China Educational Reform and Development Outline* (Central Committee of the Communist Party of China and the State Council, 1993, The National Program for Educational Reform and Development, Beijing).
2 Rather than the pure patron-client relationship, given as a contrasting example by Phirom Leng during the conference on which this volume is based, held at Tsinghua University in May 2014.
3 Mr Fred Bild, then Canadian Ambassador to China, visited the Lanzhou Railway Institute for project inspection, the first foreign ambassador's visit in LRI's history.
4 This experience was quite different from the experience during the CCMEP projects, when Chinese universities invited management practitioners to the classrooms (see Xi et al., chapter 5 of this volume).
5 As described in the Computer Applications Project (1990–95) Final Report, submitted to AUCC/SEdC by the Lanzhou Railway Institute and Ryerson Polytechnic University, Project # 926-282-14218.
6 The technical achievements of several distinguished professors from LRI in such areas as industrial process and auto-control, CAD/CAM, transport information management systems, and mechatronics rival those of first-rate universities in China.
7 As described by Zhong Qunpeng in Baidu Encyclopedia, China's biggest search engine to date. http://baike.baidu.com/link?url=sebLrG1S6LaDf4 Z56EeNVMamyuxjpih9faC_cCsqXtGpMC4g5v1pOeWH2ZfFopKQ.
8 For example, SWIT students won the gold medal and the best technology award in the Third Robot Competition on TV for university students nationwide. They also participated, as the representative of China, in the robot competition for Asia-Pacific university students, where they obtained the silver medal and best technology award.
9 These two colleges were merged in 1985 to form the Shanghai University of Engineering Science.
10 The statistical average of three projects shows that thirteen teachers from each university (and as many as eighteen from SWIT) studied in Canada, and twelve Canadian teachers lectured in China, benefiting even more teachers in China.
11 Examples include the China Metal Deeply Stamping Association and the Failure Analysis and Prevention Centre.

12 We remember clearly that during the early stages of the project, even in Beijing, we had to go to the Telegraph Building on Chang'an Avenue to send a telex to Ryerson.
13 These projects included resource utilization and environmental impact in hydropower development, industrial fire coal and mining metallurgy, land utilization and metropolis transport systems, urban and rural development planning, and human settlement environmental studies.
14 During those few years, freshmen tuition went from totally free to partially free and then a situation where all students pay fees. The employment of graduates changed from jobs assigned by the government to graduates looking for jobs by themselves.
15 Once an industrial ministry or commission no longer existed, should the universities it had founded and administered be handed over to the Ministry of Education or to the local governments? Should these universities run on their own or be merged with other universities? All these were entangling, complex, and varied questions that needed to be addressed.
16 Also, according to incomplete statistics of the Chinese returnees from seven universities, two CAE members, seven university executives, and seventeen department heads emerged after the projects.
17 Of the twenty-three survey sheets collected, fifteen respondents selected "work method" from the six options (specialized knowledge, work method, interpersonal relations, society and economy, English learning, none of the above) as the biggest harvest from their study in Canada. Out of the six options relating to "feelings of administration," eighteen chose "got new ideas for the trend of institutional reform in China" or "increased confidence in and determination for institutional reform."
18 We did statistical analysis of the education background and specialty structures of nearly 500 major leaders in thirty-one provinces of China who were in office from 1978 to 2013 (eight terms of office) and found that those with engineering backgrounds far outnumbered those with other specialty backgrounds. From the late 1980s to 2013, cadres with engineering diplomas made up 40 per cent of all cadres with college diplomas, and up to more than 70 per cent during two terms (1993 and 1998), far higher than the proportion of engineering students among all college graduates thirty years ago and nearly twice as high during three terms (1988–98).
19 Note that these projects were the exception. More representative examples include: the USTB project, which covered sixteen out of all nineteen departments of the university; the LRI project, which drove the progress of many disciplines and elevated the entire university; and the anti-cancer

project between Jilin University and Université Laval, which lasted for over twenty years (see Fred Bild, chapter 3 of this volume).

20 Since it is difficult to find an accurate translation of this proverb by Fei, I provide the original here: "各美其美，美人之美，美美与共，天下大同。" (费孝通 [Fei Xiaotong]. 1997. "反思・对话・文化自觉 [Fansi duihua wenhua zijue – Reflection Dialogue Cultural Awareness]."北京大学报 [Beijing daxue xuebao, Journal of Peking University] 03: 15–22).

8

Impacts of Canada-China Environmental Research

JING M. CHEN, JOSEPH WHITNEY, AND JULIA PAN

INTRODUCTION

Canada-China diplomatic relations were officially established in 1970, and Canada was among the first developed countries to provide China with official development assistance (ODA) immediately after this establishment. The development cooperation program planning mission to China by the Canadian International Development Agency (CIDA) began in 1981, and various development projects started taking place after the signing of a General Agreement on Development Cooperation between the Canadian and Chinese governments in October 1983.

Environmentally sustainable development has been a significant and integral component of CIDA's China Country Development Policy. A milestone of Canada's environmental protection collaboration with China was to support the Chinese government in establishing the China Council for International Cooperation on Environment and Development (CCICED) in 1992 (Hayhoe et al., chapter 1 of this volume), which formed a high-level international consultative and advisory body "to further strengthen cooperation and exchange between China and the international community in the field of environment and development." CIDA has been a key supporter and the single most important international donor of the CCICED to the Chinese State Council, and contributed $20 million in its three phases of operation (1992–2007). The CCICED created the "2020 Vision: China's Environment and Development Task Force," co-chaired by Song Jian of the Chinese State Council and Huguette Labelle, who served several years as CCICED vice-chair while also the president of CIDA.[1]

All Canadian government-sponsored projects engaged in by the University of Toronto (UT) and its partners were to comply with the Country Development Policy Framework issued by CIDA. The policy objectives were as follows:

- To promote China's continuing economic reform in areas critical to the development of a socialist market economy and to promote linkages and partnerships between Canada and China
- To promote environmentally sustainable development in China by enhancing its capacity to manage its environment
- To increase China's capacity to improve governance, respect for human rights, and democratic development processes (CIDA 1994)

UT has been an active participant in international collaboration on environmental research and has led five Canada-China environmental research projects funded by CIDA and the International Development Research Centre (IDRC).[2] In this chapter, we provide a review of these projects, in chronological sequence, to assess their impacts on China's environmental research and socioeconomic development.

SOIL EROSION AND LAND MANAGEMENT IN THE GRANITIC REGIONS OF GUANGDONG PROVINCE (1987–1990)[3]

The co-directors of this project were Professors Shiu-hung Luk of UT and Yao Qingyin of the Guangzhou Institute of Geography. The Chinese University of Hong Kong, South China Normal University, Deqing County Government, and McMaster University also participated in the project (Luk and Yao 1990, 120).

The idea of collaborative projects with China arose from a conference in 1983 at McMaster University in Hamilton, Ontario that involved Canadian and Chinese geographers. Scientists attending the conference generated a list of about thirty potential collaborative research projects. Of all these, the only two that came to fruition were those followed up by Professor Luk and Professor Joseph Whitney of the Department of Geography and the Institute for Environmental Studies at UT. Professor Luk had already made many valuable contacts at the Institute of Geography at the Chinese Academy of Sciences, later renamed the Institute of Geographical Sciences and Natural Resources Research

(IGSNRR), and he was able to use these contacts to invite other participants to the conference. The first collaborative project to emanate from this conference was this IDRC-sponsored study of soil erosion in South China.

Study Region

The Deqing area and the Shenchong Experimental Basin, where the research took place (Luk and Yao 1990), are granitic areas of Guangdong Province characterized by hilly topography, a tropical to sub-tropical monsoon climate, and a deep weathering mantle. These features have contributed to a high erosion potential in the area and over 75 per cent of the county is thus affected. Although sheet erosion is widespread, gully erosion is the most severe form and has done great damage to farming communities. The deposited sediments have raised river beds and exacerbated flooding of productive valley-lands (Luk and Yao 1990, 2-4).

Although there had been much effort during the previous decades to alleviate the problem of soil erosion in the county, four fundamental weaknesses in these efforts were recognized. First, erosion control measures were only evaluated on a trial-and-error basis. Second, erosion control programs in upland and lowland areas were not coordinated and studied as an integrated system. Third, much of the work done was by the conscientious but uncoordinated efforts of local farmers with no overall plan to accomplish the greatest social good. Fourth, the cost-effectiveness of different control measures had never been assessed. It was these weaknesses that the project sought to address.

Basic Aims of the Project

The four basic aims of the project were as follows (Luk and Yao 1990, 1-4, 107-10):

1 To assess the extent and severity of existing soil erosion problems in the Shenchong Experimental Basin in Deqing County and evaluate the major factors that influence soil erosion
2 To investigate the major mechanisms of soil erosion in the study area at the watershed scale
3 To assess the effectiveness of a range of practical erosion control measures

4 To evaluate the biophysical and socioeconomic impacts of erosion and erosion control methods commonly employed in the study region

These aims became the research objectives of four sub-project studies.

Capacity Building

The principal contribution of the project to this goal was the training of both Chinese and Canadian team members in integrated, international research. In 1988, under the aegis of UNESCO and the International Sedimentation Centre in Beijing, the project hosted a training course for Chinese, Canadians, and participants from other countries. In addition, ten Chinese professors and graduate students participated in training in Toronto for varying lengths of time. Members of the Chinese team were also exposed to new soil erosion modeling techniques and the application of Western economic models to the evaluation of complex biophysical and socioeconomic processes. This appears to have been the first time such a type of economic analysis was incorporated into a soil erosion study in China (Cai 2011).

Scientific Achievements

The study produced much data on the unique soil erosion processes found in these granitic areas. Apart from rainfall erosivity, all other erosion factors were adequately assessed (sub-project one), and work on erosivity was continued after the project was completed by members of the Guangzhou Institute of Geography. The aims of sub-project two were also successfully achieved. However, the effectiveness of different control measures (sub-project three) could be only partially achieved for gully control since the Shenchong Basin was already at an advanced stage of gullying. It was therefore impossible to evaluate control measures for other stages of erosion. Among the most important findings of sub-projects one to three was the fact that south-facing slopes were most prone to soil erosion because of heavier rainfall and a higher incidence of solar radiation, leading to soil moisture deficits and reduced plant and crop cover to alleviate the rainfall impact (Luk and Yao 1990, 102).

The economic analysis conducted in sub-project four was successfully completed by means of a multi-objective decision model which evaluated the viability of different combinations of erosion control measures that would meet the objectives of minimizing erosion and maximizing land productivity (Luk and Yao 1990, 77–91). The policy implication from this component of the study was that natural vegetation cover, especially ferns (*Dicranopterus linearis* and *Blechnum orientale*), is effective in controlling erosion, and also has a high economic benefit as a fuel source. Another finding with strong policy and political implications was that upslope control of erosion through maintenance of the natural vegetation may impose significant private costs, since upstream users should maintain natural vegetation cover rather than economically productive crops, whereas the social and private benefits will accrue to those living downslope or downstream. The major policy issue was how to balance the costs and benefits of upstream and downstream inhabitants in an equitable manner. In short, the project was able to examine the weaknesses of previous erosion control efforts and suggest practical and cost-effective methods to remedy them.

Lessons Learned

In general, the project was executed smoothly and as planned, but several unexpected problems along the way resulted in some delays and modification of the original plans. First, the beginning of the project coincided with a period of economic adjustment in China which resulted in drastic changes in the organization of research within the Guangzhou Institute of Geography.[4] This resulted in frequent changes of personnel and lack of continuity in executing research. The Tiananmen tragedy of June 1989 resulted in the evacuation of Canadian personnel and an abrupt change of the research schedule. To compensate for these incidents, IDRC funded field research for an additional six months and the project was successfully completed in May 1990.

Impact and Legacy

This project resulted in many useful and practical recommendations for soil erosion control in granitic landscapes, including reduction in terrace farming on slopes and the use of natural fern vegetation to cover sloping surfaces. Through the use of a multi-objective decision model, this project introduced a systems approach to the analysis of the costs and benefits of erosion control measures at the watershed scale and stressed the importance of upslope land use controls in improving downslope conditions. These recommendations and approaches were well received by the local communities and governments and encouraged the development of more rational soil erosion control policies and practices. Moreover, the links with the participating Chinese and Canadian universities were further strengthened, enhancing collaboration in some of the projects described below.

SOIL EROSION MANAGEMENT GEOGRAPHICAL INFORMATION SYSTEM (SEMGIS I) IN THE WANGJIAGOU EXPERIMENTAL BASIN, LISHI, SHANXI PROVINCE, NORTH CHINA[5]

The co-directors of this project were Professors Joseph Whitney (UT) and Chen Yongzong (Institute of Geography [INSGR], now the IGSNRR, and the Chinese Academy of Sciences [CAS]). The SEMGIS I project was funded by CIDA, under its newly established Canada-China University Linkage Programs (CCULP) from 1988 to 1992. UT, the INSGR, the CAS, Beijing, and the Shanxi Institute of Soil and Water Conservation, Taiyuan, participated in the project.

Study Region

The Loess Plateau region of North China, where the study area was located, is one of the most severely eroded regions in China. Loess is a fine soil (probably wind-blown) that mantles huge areas of North China to a depth of between 10 meters and 100 meters. This fine soil, if properly watered and covered with vegetation, is very fertile and originally provided the agricultural base for early Chinese civilization. Over the centuries, however, increasing population pressure, deforestation, and changes in climate have gradually stripped the land of its original vegetation, allowing excessive erosion to occur upstream and flooding downstream (Whitney and Chen 1992, 1–2; Elvin 2004, 22–30).

The two main concerns about Loess Plateau erosion are: first, the loss of fertility and crops on upper slopes of valleys; and second, and more importantly, the eroded material deposited in the Yellow River system that has raised its bed far above the surrounding plain, and has over the centuries placed many millions of inhabitants in a flood-prone area, giving rise to major loss of lives (Luk 1992, 9–31). Lishi was selected as the site for the project's experimental work because some twenty years of soil erosion and other data had already been collected. However, many of the weaknesses existing in soil erosion control measures in the Guangdong project described above also existed here.

The researchers believed that a Geographic Information System (GIS) and remote sensing (RS), together with a biophysical and socioeconomic modeling approach in association with a Decision Support System (DSS), would be the most effective way to assist land managers in the region to cope with the multiplicity of physical, social, and economic problems of soil erosion which confronted them (Whitney and Chen 1992, 3–7). A team of thirteen Chinese and twelve Canadian researchers was assembled, and project implementation was greatly assisted and encouraged by Mr Sun Jianxuan, vice-minister of soil and water conservation, Shanxi Province.

Basic Aims of the Project

The aims of the project were as follows:

1 To examine and assess the twenty-year soil erosion data that had been collected at the Wangjiagou Experimental Basin for consistency, comparability, and relevance to the new study proposed
2 To create a GIS including a digital terrain model (DTM) for the basin
3 To create a crop production model (YIELD) and soil erosion model (ERODE)
4 To develop an economic model that linked the GIS/DTM YIELD and ERODE models in order to calculate the on-site costs and benefits of each kind of crop production and soil erosion control measure
5 To develop an evaluation model using a multi-criteria approach so that land managers could evaluate the soil erosion and socioeconomic impacts of different developmental and erosion control strategies
6 To train personnel at the Wangjiagou Experimental Station to use and modify, as required, the computer models developed (Band and Fu 1992, 32–43)

Capacity Building

As with the Guangdong project, the main element of capacity building was the experience of working in an integrated, multi-disciplinary, international research team. This was appreciated both by Chinese and Canadian professors and graduate students. In addition, twenty-two Chinese researchers were sent to Canada for further training. Some fifty-four refereed papers based on the research were published in Chinese and international journals (White 2001; Whitney and Chen 1992).

The Chinese team received further specific training in Geographical Resource Analysis Support System (GRASS), which was used as the basis for the GIS employed in the project. The Chinese team was also employed in modifying GRASS to incorporate land cover and agricultural practices.

The Chinese team also received additional training in using and developing the ERODE model that estimated hill slope, valley slope, and channel erosion. Similarly, they were trained in and contributed to the development of YIELD (the crop growth model) and contributed to providing economic parameters for cost-benefit evaluations in China's non-market economy.

Scientific Achievements

The GIS component-based modelling approach to soil erosion problems was the first time such a system had been employed in China. Among other innovative approaches were the sprinkler rain-making experiments designed and conducted by Professor Luk, the associate director of the project, to obtain specific data on soil erosivity, crusting, and tunnelling[6] in the loess soils. These and the other data collected by the experimental station provided the inputs for the ERODE model. The inputs for YIELD were obtained from interviews with local farmers in the experimental basin.

All of the models developed in the study, although completed, could be considered only as prototypes requiring fine-tuning and modification when applied to different areas and types of loess soils. The modelling of tunnel erosion is very complex, and the study concluded that much additional work would be required to model this phenomenon. One surprising finding was that terracing itself may trigger tunnelling along the lower perimeter of the terraced field, thus being a cause rather than a remedy for some types of soil erosion (Whitney and Chen 1992, 22).

Lessons Learned

The Tiananmen tragedy of May 1989 led to the withdrawal of Canadians from China, and the high cost and problems of obtaining meteorological and other data from local authorities resulted in some minor delays. CIDA compensated for these by extending the project for an additional nine months.

In CIDA's final evaluation of the project, the main criticism was that there was an overemphasis on the technical aspects of soil erosion and too little on the socioeconomic aspects, implementability of recommendations, and issues of gender equity (White 2001). A Phase II of the project was, therefore, proposed to remedy these weaknesses.

Impact and Legacy

The introduction of GIS in soil erosion management through this project was an innovative approach for the local governments concerned with soil erosion problems. The new computer technology provided endless possibilities for managing the complex loess landscape to optimize agricultural production and minimize soil erosion, and to maintain the livelihood of the local communities. Some of these possibilities were demonstrated in the project, even though the SEMGIS system was still in its infancy. The idea of using computers for land management was well-received by scientists, local government officials, and farmers. In 1994, SEMGIS I received the Grade II science prize from the CAS. In 1995, a summary report for the ten-year Canada-China cooperation ranked SEMGIS I as the number-one project (Cai 1999). This project laid a solid foundation for the succeeding SEMGIS II project, which made long-lasting impacts on land management in China.

GIS-BASED EROSION MANAGEMENT OUTREACH PROGRAM (SEMGIS II) FOR CHINA (1996–2001)[7]

This project was co-directed by Professors Rodney White (UT) and Cai Qiangguo (INSGR, CAS). Built on SEMGIS I, this Special University Linkage Consolidation Program (SULCP) was aimed at enhancing social and economic impacts of soil erosion control methods. The participating institutions were: the UT Department of Geography and Institute of Environmental Studies; the INSGR; the CAS; the Bureau of Soil and Water Conservation; the Ih Ju League, Inner Mongolia; and the Shanxi Ministry of Water Conservancy.

Study Area

The study area was enlarged to include both the original Wangjiagou Basin in Shanxi Province and the Ih Ju League in Inner Mongolia. In SEMGIS II there was less emphasis on soil erosion research (which had already been completed in SEMGIS I) and more on the management and policy implications of GIS applications and the development of related biophysical indicators (White 2001, 1–5).

Basic Aims of the Project

The aims of the project were as follows:

1 To develop indicators of soil erosion, sustainable land use, and plant productivity rather than the collection of more soil erosion experimental data
2 To develop an agro-forestry component to be added to the new Decision Support System (DSS)
3 To adapt the original SEMGIS I DSS model for PC use, enabling unsophisticated users at the county level to use it
4 To incorporate gender equity and training considerations into all aspects of the DSS
5 To train DSS users to produce land-use scenarios of different cropping and land management strategies
6 To attempt to persuade farmers to adopt some of the recommended practices formulated in the DSS

Capacity Building

In all, 161 Chinese professionals, including ninety-five female local government trainees, some of whom were from the local indigenous minority group, were involved in the project, resulting in nineteen refereed papers. Eight Chinese researchers were sent to Canada for training.

A major thrust of the project was training team members in gender equity considerations in project development and in the development and use of DSS. It was agreed by both parties that gender equity should be applied to both the researchers and the beneficiaries of our research to ensure the equitable treatment of women. Moreover, management strategies that disadvantaged women were to be discarded in favour of those that distributed the costs and benefits equitably (Murck 1997). Programs were designed for outreach training and nearly 100 female soil and water managers were trained in professional networking at the county level.

Scientific Achievements

Instead of using GRASS as in SEMGIS I, SEMGIS II was designed to run on IDRISI or ARCINFO, which are windows-based GIS programs and can be run on ordinary PCs. In addition, an AGROFORESTRY submodel was developed to integrate productivity predictions from YIELD with a new forest growth sub-model. This enabled the impact of various degrees of tree planting in place of annual crops to be assessed.

It was agreed by all the parties that there was little point in developing a DSS to generate recommendations that had little chance of being adopted by farmers. Thus, it was very important to identify the factors that enhance or militate against adoption by farm households (Amott 1999; Maclaren, Amott, Gan, and Feng 2001). As a result, a major component of the project involved surveys to ascertain household perceptions of the impacts of various land-use scenarios on their livelihood. Unfortunately, the final implementation of this latter recommendation could not be completed due to time and budgetary constraints. It was believed that some local authorities would continue this investigation once the project ended.

Lessons Learned

One of the key lessons was the importance of providing sufficient funding to the Chinese partners for the human and material resources they bring to the projects. Our Chinese colleagues have many competing demands on their time, and it is often difficult for them and their research assistants to allocate the needed amount of time to the project. Researchers must also recognize that complex collaborative modelling often takes much longer than anticipated (Hayhoe et al., chapter 1 of this volume), but that unanticipated benefits may sometimes accrue. For example, one of the SEMGIS II partners demonstrated a prototype of the GIS soil erosion model to senior government officials. As a result, the concept of watershed modelling for soil erosion management with GIS was endorsed by the Chinese Ministry of Water Resources.[8]

Cordial personal relationships must be stressed in all projects. The strong working relationship we had with the Institute of Geography in all our projects led to a more efficient work environment. A key player from another Chinese institution, who had taken a degree at UT, felt such a strong commitment to the project that he raised extra funds in China for SEMGIS training activities.[9]

Impact and Legacy

The GIS-based soil erosion model developed in SEMGIS II was first adopted by the Shanxi Ministry of Water Resources and used for soil erosion management for many small watersheds across Shanxi Province, raising local land management to a new level. The use of GIS allowed land-use planning for individual field plots of irregular shapes rather than regular grids, so that it could be closely associated with individual farms. This SEMGIS II method of land-use planning became the most effective and advanced in China at that time and was endorsed by the Chinese Ministry of Water Resources for adoption across the country.[10] In 1995–97, the ministry held a nation-wide competition on GIS for soil and water conservation. The main project participants, Mr Wang Guiping, Professor Cai Qiangguo, and Professor Liu Gaohuan (all members of the research team), were invited as panellists at the competition, in recognition of the advanced expertise shown in the SEMGIS II project. The GIS-based soil erosion modelling system developed in this project was used widely in Shanxi Province for about ten years after this project, and is still being used in some regions. Most importantly, the concepts of land-use management using GIS gained wide acceptance in China, and have created long-lasting impacts.[11]

SUSTAINABLE WATER MANAGEMENT IN THE BEIJING-TIANJIN REGION (1997–2004)[12]

Study Area

In the 1980s and 1990s, the rapid urbanization and industrialization of the North China Plain was beginning to seriously impinge on the water quantity and quality of the supply for many northern Chinese cities, especially Tianjin and Beijing. The Chinese government was anxious to explore innovative approaches to address this problem. In the late 1990s, a consortium of three Chinese and four Canadian universities had been established. The purpose was "to develop close, effective links among these intellectual centres in areas of common interest so researchers and students from both countries could collaborate and benefit from the distinct strengths and perspectives of the partner institutions."[13] In light of China's interest and concern about environmental problems of the North China Plain, this University Consortium, consisting of the University of British Columbia (UBC), McGill University, UT, and Nankai, Peking, and Tsinghua Universities, was encouraged to compete for funding under the new China-Canada Higher-Education Program (CCHEP) project. The Consortium's proposal on Sustainable Water Management in the Beijing-Tianjin Region was one of the eight proposals selected to receive funding. In all, some thirty-three Chinese and twenty-six Canadian faculty members participated in the research, and eighty-four Chinese and twenty-eight Canadian students were trained as research assistants. The project lasted from 1997 to 2004, but was delayed by the SARS outbreak in 2003.

Basic Aims of the Project

The principal aim was to evaluate ways for solving water-resource and pollution problems in the designated region.

Capacity Building

Canadian and Chinese participants undertook extensive reviews of the data and literature available on water resources and pollution of the region, and these were summarized in a number of position papers that were presented in seminars to the whole team. Criticisms from both Canadian and Chinese participants were valuable and led to modification of the papers before submission for publication and/or presentation to relevant local authorities[14] (Centre for Human Settlements, University of British Columbia [CHSUBC] CD Report, n.d.).

Scientific Achievements

The team carried out a multi-objective modelling exercise to approximately quantify the water deficit that would occur if current water use trends continued and no action was taken, and then to judge the impact of various water-management options on reducing this deficit (CHSUBC Report 2003).

Lessons Learned

Since the project was created in a decidedly top-down manner by the presidents of the universities involved, few of the collaborators from the various institutions knew one another at the outset. The participants joined the project in the interest of fulfilling their respective president's desire for collaboration rather than as a high-priority item on their own personal research agendas.[15] Few of the Canadian faculty members had previous experience in China, and the specific research interests and skills of the individual participants did not always align well with the project's objectives. Moreover, at the outset, the Canadian participants were somewhat chagrined to discover that the project appeared to have been made redundant because a major World Bank study on a similar topic had just been completed.[16] Nonetheless, even though the project did not result in any major breakthroughs or any long-term, post-project research collaboration, the participants agreed that they had benefitted from contacts with some superb researchers from both the Chinese and Canadian universities, and gained insights into regional resource issues in China. Above all, our students benefited from the opportunity to carry out their work in China in collaboration with outstanding researchers. As one Canadian participant stated, "The interactions between the participants, who had in a sense been thrown together by circumstance (rather than on a self-selection based on interests and perhaps past interactions), led to an elevated level of enthusiasm to work together. Everyone seemed to want to contribute, even if it was hard to imagine how to pull the whole project together."[17]

Progress on the project was also halted by, among other things, the SARS outbreak in 2003, and by reluctance on the part of some local authorities to provide water resource data that might reflect badly on China's bid for the 2010 Olympic Games in Beijing.[18]

Impact and Legacy

Although the funding for the project was moderate, the project produced a set of position papers by leading Canadian and Chinese experts on the water-deficit issues in the Beijing-Tianjin region and evaluations on water-management options to address these. It is believed that these high-level position papers have influenced water-management strategies by local governments in the area. However, the extent of this influence is mostly anecdotal and lacks formal documentation.[19]

CONFRONTING GLOBAL WARMING: ENHANCING CHINA'S CAPACITY FOR CARBON SEQUESTRATION (2002–2006)[20]

This project was co-directed by Jing M. Chen of UT and Liu Jiyuan of the IGSNRR of the CAS. It was established on the bases of very strong links of the institutional and personal relationships that had been formed during the previous environmental projects in China. The appointment of Professor Jing M. Chen, Fellow of the Royal Society of Canada (FRSC) and Senior Canada Research Chair in 2000, at UT was timely for the initiation of this project. Other participating institutions included the

Nanjing Institute of Soil Science, the Lanzhou Cold and Arid Regions Environmental and Engineering Research Institute of CAS, Nanjing University, Nanjing Forestry University (NFU), Nanjing Agriculture University, Beijing Normal University (BNU), Environment Canada, and Natural Resources Canada.

Study Area

All China's forests were covered in this study using remote sensing images. Ground study sites were selected in five pilot ecological regions which represented different biomes and environmental conditions and where previous research had been carried out and data collected (see figure 8.1).

As shown in figure 8.1, three of the five sites (Changbaishan, Liping, and Heihe) are considered to be the core sites, at which all field data collection and investigation were conducted. The other two (Xingguo and Baoying) are considered to be supplementary sites to augment some components of the project. Xingguo is representative of large areas of southeastern China and therefore the ground data are useful for developing a remote sensing algorithm for that area. Baoying is in an area where plantations of poplar trees are frequently found and are intensively studied by NFU.

Basic Aims of the Project

The overarching goal of the project was to "build China's ability and capacity to increase ecosystem carbon stocks through the development of technical and human resources that will result in more informed and effective land-use, forest management, and a more solid scientific base for environmental and land-use policy making" (Chen et al. 2007, 516–23).

The project had the following objectives:

1 To facilitate the transfer of knowledge and technology in GIS and remote sensing as applied to ecosystem carbon cycle monitoring and modeling in order to estimate China's potential for carbon sequestration (CS) in forest ecosystems. An important component of this objective was to test the degree to which field instruments, remote sensing algorithms, and ecosystem models developed in Canada could be applied to terrestrial carbon estimation for Chinese forest ecosystems.

Figure 8.1 Distribution of three core sites (■) and two auxiliary sites (●) for the project titled "Confronting Global Warming: Enhancing China's Capacity for Carbon Sequestration." (The assistance of Byron Moldofsky of the University of Toronto with the preparation of this map is gratefully acknowledged.)

2 To undertake forest and soil assessments in pilot ecological regions to validate and calibrate existing carbon models in China, and to evaluate the potential to use these models for developing balanced afforestation policies.
3 To conduct integrated assessments (IA) on various forest CS options by considering their social, economic, and environmental impacts in order to develop carbon-favourable and sustainable land-use options. Of particular concern were the impacts of the Grain for Green (GFG) program on the livelihood of farmers, particularly women and minority groups.

Capacity Building

In terms of forest carbon budget estimation, the primary objective of this component was to transfer Canadian expertise in the application of GIS and remote sensing techniques to estimate the potential for carbon sequestration in China's forests. This task required the testing and validation of remote sensing algorithms and ecosystem models developed in Canada for various ecological conditions in China using *in situ* measurements and high-resolution satellite data (objective 2). The transfer of Canadian algorithms and models was achieved through training Chinese scientists in technical workshops and their active participation in all phases of the project. Nearly 100 Chinese scientists participated in three training workshops at the beginning of the project. In addition, some thirty-five of the latter spent extended periods of time in Canada to learn the operation of field instruments, remote sensing algorithms, and carbon cycle models. In all, a solid base of expertise was established in China through these means.

A scientific basis for more effective carbon sequestration in land-use policy and planning was essential for the success of the project. In particular, this required the transfer of other land-uses to forest and the evaluation of the implications of these changes in terms of sustainability, economic well-being, and gender equality – all priority considerations for CIDA and CCICED. Such a transfer to forest was part of the GFG program that was introduced to mitigate soil erosion and provide alternative employment in rural areas. This project took a holistic approach to evaluating the GFG program not only in terms of soil erosion control and economic costs and benefits, but also in terms of the value of carbon sequestration. It demonstrated net benefits to farmers during the seven-year GFG program with government subsidy and net losses after GFG, when the subsidy was withdrawn. Particular attention was paid to these costs and benefits as they applied to the 70 to 80 per cent minority peoples who lived in the Liping study area.

The scientific basis for this assessment was conducted in the pilot study areas with the use of state-of-the-art tools such as Goal Programming and the Analytical Hierarchy Process. These efforts allowed planners to assess the carbon sequestration and socioeconomic impacts of required land use changes.

Successful technology transfer requires mechanisms for ensuring continuity after the project is completed. Among these were the establishment of an institutional home in the Chinese National Forestry Administration and a computerized decision support tool (DST) package that could be applied in a user-friendly manner by planners and community organizations at the local level. The DST produced could be used in combination with relevant documentation to assess the impact of a range of land-use decisions.

Scientific Achievements

As a result of research undertaken in the project, the remote sensing algorithms and carbon cycle models originally developed in Canada were validated for a variety of ecological zones in China ranging from cold-temperate to sub-tropical. Geospatial national data sets at 1 km resolution were made available for leaf area index phenology, improved estimates of net primary and net ecosystems productivity in recent years, and annual carbon source-sink distributions in China's forests over a 200 year period (1901–2100) with consideration of the impacts of forest stand age dynamics and climate change, atmospheric CO_2 enrichment, and nitrogen deposition on forest growth.

The project demonstrated that the RS/GIS modeling approach could provide information rapidly and effectively over wide areas and that the information was valuable for effective land-use planning and environmental reporting.

At the end of the project, a special issue entitled "Carbon Sequestration in China's Forest Ecosystems" was published in the *Journal of Environmental Management* (Chen et al. 2007) containing twenty-six original research papers and two summary and commentary papers. Some twenty papers were published elsewhere in international journals. Some of the papers were the basis for the research theses of ten doctoral and master's students in China and four in Canada.

Lessons Learned

A results-based management approach was implemented in this project whereby the allocation of funds could be adjusted according to the requirements and performance of the participating Canadian and Chinese institutions and individuals, and this mechanism allowed for some timely solutions when problems occurred that could have delayed the progress of the project.

In the four years of the project duration, China experienced a period of rapid economic growth and rapid expansion of research investment and activities. As a result, some key Chinese participants shifted their attention to other larger projects. The special issue in the *Journal of Environmental Management* helped galvanize the attention of all participants and encouraged the completion of project tasks with sufficient thoroughness and depth. Graduate students and their supervisors provided much of the incentive for completing the papers in this special issue.

The project lasted for four years, an extension from the original three-year plan, because of the SARS outbreak in China in 2003, during which project activities in China were temporarily halted. This one-year extension was very helpful for fine-tuning the project and for better preparation of the field data collection in the following years. The original three-year plan would have been too short to complete all tasks, especially the social and economic synthesis analysis. The SARS outbreak therefore inadvertently helped the completion of the project in a timely manner!

Impact and Legacy

The project occurred at an opportune time when both developed and developing countries were preoccupied by the concerns of carbon emission reduction requirements under the Kyoto Agreement. China, as an Annex 2 country, supported the Kyoto Agreement, albeit without immediate obligations for emission control, but was facing mounting international pressure because of its rapid increase in carbon emissions. This project produced, for the first time, annual carbon source and sink distributions in all China's forests for the period from 1901 to 2100 using remote sensing, climate, and soil data based on a well-calibrated process model. The annual sink values for the past and future were highly relevant for central government climate policy formulation with consideration of forest sinks as part of the emission control strategy. These values were quoted in a climate policy report of the Chinese Commission of Development and Reform. The Climate Change Office (formerly the Carbon Sinks Office) at the project's "home institution," the Chinese National Forestry Administration, was interested in the DSTs produced in this project, and sent key office staff member Dr Zhang Dongsheng to Toronto for six months of training in using the DST. These tools were later used to provide sink estimates for forest carbon sequestration projects in China invested by the Chinese National Forestry Administration.

The expertise gained in forest structural measurements on the ground, remote sensing of forest types and structural parameters, short-term carbon-cycle modeling using remote sensing inputs, long-term carbon-cycle modeling using both short-term remote sensing and long-term climate data, and integrated assessment methods have been useful for subsequent carbon-cycle research in China. Many project participants have become leading scientists in this field of research in China. In 2010, many of them formed a team and successfully applied for a large grant (around Can$5 million) from the newly established Global Change Key Program of the Chinese Ministry of Science and Technology to carry out a five-year research project entitled "Mechanisms controlling the carbon cycle in different regions of the globe, and its optimized calculations." This is an extension of the research scope of the CIDA project from China to the whole globe. Professor Jing M. Chen was selected to be the PI of this project and remains active in China's carbon-cycle research to the present day. The special issue in the *Journal of Environmental Management* is a milestone for China's forest carbon cycle research, and the instruments, algorithms, and models are continuously used in most of the participating institutions, and have become more widely used by more than twenty-three major universities and institutes in recent years.

CONCLUSIONS

Thirteen centuries ago, the philosopher and essayist Liu Zongyuan rebuked the way society was destroying its forests and causing soil and fertility loss and sedimentation of streams and irrigation systems: "Great-girthed trees of towering height lie blocking the forest tracks / A tumbled confusion of lumber, as flames on the hillside crackle / Not even the last remaining shrubs are safeguarded from destruction; / Where once the mountain torrents leapt – nothing but rotted gullies" (quoted in Elvin 2004, 19).

The five projects discussed in this chapter are directly or indirectly related to Liu's observations of over a millennium ago. The first three are projects that seek ways to remedy, in two contrasting regions, the damage done by deforestation over the centuries. The fourth project, while only indirectly related to deforestation, is concerned with the depletion and pollution of groundwater resources due to reduced infiltration rates, rapid population growth, and urban and industrial development. The fifth project examines the ways in which revitalized reforestation practices across China can sequester more carbon and offset the global warming effects of the country's rapid growth, while incidentally reducing soil erosion and enhancing water quality.

We will now examine the ways in which these five projects are related to the four key questions posed by Professor Hayhoe and her colleagues in chapter 1 of this volume.

> *1. In what ways did our projects contribute to China's economic revitalization and rapid transformation?*

While not contributing directly to China's rapid development, the projects initiated policies and practices that will mitigate some of the harmful environmental effects of that development and those of previous centuries. The implementation of the carbon sequestration policies and practices from the carbon project will go a long way to convince the world that China is serious about its support of the Kyoto Agreement, and thus will counteract some of the international criticisms levelled at its environmental record.

> *2. How did the projects foster the spawning of new ideas that would address crucial issues of humane and democratic governance?*

All five projects introduced new ideas and methodologies that were or could be applied at either the local or national level. They all stressed that the introduction of such innovations must be evaluated by their impacts on gender and minority-group equity, and where the negatives outweighed the positives, the innovations should be scrapped or modified. Great emphasis was placed in all the projects on providing training at the local and university level for women, so that the power derived from knowledge should be shared across genders and ethnicities (Walls, chapter 9 of this volume). The research work from the carbon project was published in a special issue of the *Journal of Environmental Management*, providing a wide global and Chinese audience. The other projects produced numerous peer-reviewed journal articles in Chinese and international journals that have had a similar impact.

> *3. What organizational or contextual features of the linkages were important in enabling them to be effective and what serious challenges arose?*

The fact that all five projects were based on the participation of Chinese and Canadian colleagues who had prior academic and friendly relationships was a key factor in their success. Where this had not occurred to the same extent (as in the water management project), the partnership suffered to some degree. The Five Constant Virtues and the Middle Way as keys to a successful project (Walls, chapter 9 of this volume) were exemplified in all five projects and were essential components of their success.

The predominant view held among the Chinese participants interviewed was that the Canadian aid to China's environmental development through the five projects was highly effective and preferred to that of other countries. Annual advisory board and project meetings were generally well-organized and helpful for project execution. The annual Chinese New Year parties held at the Canadian Embassy in Beijing for the main project participants allowed them to maintain and expand their scientific and social networking ties. These parties are fondly remembered![21] Canadian students working on the China projects benefitted greatly from the experience and several have gone on to take up responsible government and university positions – one becoming Canada Research Chair in Watershed Sciences at the University of Western Ontario (UWO). The Canadian faculty involved in the various research projects in China enriched their teaching and research from the experience gained. The subsequent careers of the Canadian and Chinese faculty and students will be the ultimate legacy of these five projects.

4. What lessons for current and future collaboration between Canadian and Chinese universities may be drawn from past experience?

The most important lesson learned from the five projects is that the skills, comradeship, and trust developed among participants has, since CIDA funding ended, provided the basis for further collaborative work in China funded from indigenous or international sources.

For example, one of UT's Chinese graduate students who participated in both SEMGIS projects has since become Deputy Mayor of Shuocheng, a city of 1.7 million people situated in the Loess region of Shanxi Province, North China. With the expertise gained in the two projects and advice from former fellow participants, he was able to initiate, using prefectural funds, some new GIS-based soil and water control measures in the rural areas of the nearly 6,000 square kilometres under his jurisdiction.[22]

Another example is from the Carbon Sequestration Project described earlier. A number of Chinese faculty and graduate students collaborating in the project have created their own research team and obtained a large grant from the Chinese government to apply models developed in the project to the carbon dynamics in different parts of the world. This new project continues to be directed by the Canadian Professor Jing M. Chen.

These two examples illustrate that some projects take on a life of their own and continue self-sufficiently, breaking away from the "dependency model" that characterized so many earlier development projects (Hayhoe et al., chapter 1 of this volume). We believe that this development is the blueprint for future Canadian international collaborative projects.

NOTES

1 Kent Smith, Canadian Embassy, Beijing, Meeting Notes (18 November 2005).
2 A government-funded agency based in Ottawa, Canada.
3 IDRC funding: $495,000.
4 Personal communication with M.K. Woo, 24 April 2013.
5 CIDA Funding: $580,000.
6 Tunnelling is the creation of (usually) vertical cavities formed by poor drainage at the back edge of terraces.
7 CIDA funding: $600,000.
8 Interview with Professors Cai Qiangguo and Liu Gaohuan, IGSNRR, CAS, Beijing, 20 August 2013.
9 Interview with Wang Guiping, Beijing, 11 May 2014.
10 Ibid.
11 Interview with Liu Gaohuan and Cai Qiangguo, Beijing, IGSNRR, CAS, 20 August 2013.
12 CIDA/AUCC funding: $750,000.
13 Kent Smith, Canadian Embassy, Beijing, email on 6 November 2013.
14 Director, CHSUBC, email message to author, 27 August 2013.
15 A.P. Lino Grima, email message to author, 11 April 2013.
16 Director, CHSUBC, email message to author, 27 April 2013.
17 A.P. Lino Grima, email, 11 April 2013.
18 Ibid.
19 Michael Leaf, email message to author, 27 April 2013.
20 CIDA funding: $2.3 million.
21 Notes from interview with colleagues at IGSNRR, CAS, 20 August 2013.
22 Interview with Wang Guiping, Beijing, 11 May 2014.

9

Society, Economy, and Environment: Minorities in the Collaboration between China and Canada

JAN W. WALLS[1]

INTRODUCTION

In China, 8.4 per cent of the population is of non-Han ethnicity (CIA World Factbook 2014), traditionally called *shǎoshù mínzú* (minority nationalities). Minority nationalities in China, like indigenous minorities around the world, face a fundamental cultural challenge: how to gain access to the benefits of the mainstream without abandoning or sacrificing what is positive, comfortable, meaningful, and self-affirming in their own cultures and their identities. Moreover, women in minority nationality communities, like women in most societies around the world, traditionally have enjoyed a smaller share of rights and benefits than the men in their communities. From 1990 to 2001, the David Lam Centre at Simon Fraser University (SFU) and the senior administration of Minzu University[2] collaborated to address and improve the situation among minority nationality communities, especially through the Canada-China University Linkage Program (CCULP) and the Special University Linkage Consolidation Program (SULCP) in the following specific regions: Ningxia, Yunnan, Inner Mongolia, Guangxi, and Hainan. Collaborative partnerships such as these have played major roles in internationalizing both Chinese and Canadian universities. In the words of Professor Hayhoe, "The partnership modality created a large platform for Chinese universities to adapt Canadian models and approaches to the Chinese context, and draw upon leading areas of expertise in Canada that were valuable for China's development needs" (Frolic 2011, 28). Our partnership began with the CCULP.

CCULP: THE FIRST STAGE (1990–1993)

Our relationship began through the Canadian International Development Agency (CIDA)-sponsored, Association of Universities and Colleges of Canada (AUCC)-administered CCULP project called the "Minority Area Development Research Project."[3] The goals that the then Central Institute for Nationalities had in joining this project were: to meet the research and teaching needs of the new economic and social conditions in China; to contribute to the success of the economic reforms, especially in minority areas; to help local minority nationality leaders create a sound development strategy for their regions; and in general to play a more important role in the transfer of needed human resources to minority areas. The David Lam Centre for International Communication at SFU agreed with these goals and offered assistance in the areas of resource and environmental management as well as by providing technological and social science expertise in project development and evaluation.

A detailed discussion of needs revealed that we would have to compile and create new curricula and provide a range of teaching materials, including audio-visual and computer equipment. A central component of the plan was the provision of trained teachers to effectively utilize the new opportunities created for modernization. A training course for local level administrators was chosen as a significant part of these efforts, as it would have the advantage of creating direct links with the base level, where external relations with minority nationalities were and are considered more sensitive than those with the majority Han Chinese.

In the area of research, our efforts involved: attempts at the adaptation and application of social sciences research, especially anthropology and cross-cultural communication, to local development needs; the introduction of environmental impact research methods; environmental and resource management research; and project planning and evaluation research. These were part of a broader effort to bring about a basic change in direction for the Central Institute of Nationalities (now Minzu University): from an administrative and arts training institute to a more comprehensive university, capable of helping to develop skilled administrators, teachers, and technicians for minority nationality areas.

Our CCULP project involved four types of exchange: (1) mutual visits by Chinese and Canadian scholars, which included three young scholars from Minzu University who spent a whole semester at SFU to prepare them for teaching in the training program to be conducted jointly with scholars from SFU and Minzu in Beijing; (2) a study tour for senior administrators and scholars conducted by SFU to familiarize them with their Canadian counterparts;[4] (3) participation by SFU faculty and graduate students in joint research programs in Inner Mongolia, Ningxia, and Yunnan; and (4) the joint development and joint delivery of the training course for local level cadres and teachers from local nationality institutes, which was conducted at Minzu in Beijing.

Project publications were produced in China for use by Minzu as well as by other nationality institutes and post-secondary institutions. In preparation for the first training course, Minzu published a textbook that was developed from lecture notes taken by the Chinese instructors during their SFU courses. Following completion of the training course and the joint field research, Minzu published English-Chinese bilingual versions of SFU faculty lecture notes and the joint field research reports. These publications were used as textbooks for courses conducted at Minzu and other nationalities institutes at local levels.

At the conclusion of their joint research visits, SFU faculty presented seminars on their preliminary research results, usually in the field but also upon their return to Minzu. SFU faculty also presented seminars to the visiting senior administrators and faculty from Minzu outlining the areas they planned to cover in their lectures to the joint training class. In addition, they conducted seminars for Minzu faculty and graduate students while teaching in the training courses.

As agreed to by representatives of Minzu and SFU, faculty from both institutions jointly planned and taught a training course on local and regional economic and social development. Students in the course included local level cadres from the three research areas, and teachers from local nationality institutes and schools. Minzu prepared a text for this course, which was based on lecture notes written by the Minzu faculty members who were teaching classes in the program. In addition, Minzu published further texts for the course including lecture notes taken during SFU faculty lectures as well as from project reports arising from our joint research efforts. These texts were made available to other nationality institutes and schools that planned to run similar courses.

According to the original plan, this training course was to be repeated each year with SFU faculty to participate in the second year, and then subsequent courses to be taught entirely by Minzu faculty. However, the Minzu leadership decided (wisely, in retrospect) to no longer offer the training course every year, but rather to have the new course contents integrated into regular Minzu course curricula. Consequently, SFU faculty members who went to teach in the second round were able to lecture directly to Minzu students (primarily graduate students). This had the advantage of insuring a permanent place for the new courses in the regular university curriculum, and also insured that students would all receive full university credit for the courses. At the same time, it meant that the original goal of establishing an ongoing training centre for base level cadres had to be put aside.

Three representatives from local authorities visited Canada: the magistrate of Yinnan Prefecture in Ningxia, the chief hydrological engineer of Yunnan Province, and the director of the Foreign Affairs Office of the Hailar District in Inner Mongolia. They held discussions with SFU faculty and visited development projects both on and off of First Nations reserves in British Columbia. This visit helped familiarize them with our project and its goals, which was crucial because they were the individuals who would be in charge of the implementation of the joint research projects in their respective localities. In general we had very good relations with and received the strong support of local leadership.

One of the main lessons we and our colleagues at Minzu learned from our CCULP experience, which contributed greatly to the success of our subsequent SULCP partnership, was that involving Chinese university administrative leaders and local government leaders in the very earliest planning stages and in initial site visits cleared the way for smoother implementation of projects when unanticipated obstacles or opportunities arose and speedy permission was required to adapt the project to new conditions. We made certain that all SFU administrators and faculty, Minzu administrators and faculty, and minority nationality local officials were involved in every stage of planning and implementation for this project. As Professor Zha points out in his study, Chinese universities draw on extensive networks, members of which include governments, private enterprises, and community groups, which in turn can disseminate the ideas and initiatives as well as the influence far more broadly and help to forge lasting impacts (Zha 2011a).

SULCP: THE SECOND STAGE (1996–2001)

Thanks to the CCULP "Minority Area Development Research and Training Project," Minzu University was able to increase its capacity to conduct teaching and research relevant to the social and economic development of minority areas through training in Canada and China, workshops, curriculum development, and the development of teaching materials. The main geographic areas affected by the project were Inner Mongolia, Ningxia, and Yunnan.

SFU and Minzu University continued their collaborative efforts to foster development in minority regions under the SULCP with an increased focus on the environment. A major challenge facing most minority regions in China is the rapid deterioration of the environment. The underlying premise for the "Three Sustainables" project[5] was that environmental deterioration problems in minority regions cannot be solved solely by technological innovation or legal stricture. This premise resonates with the assertion by Hayhoe, Pan, and Zha (chapter 1 of this volume) that strategies focusing only on instrumental-technical rationality, while failing to address fundamental human needs, are clearly unsustainable. The remedies required can best be achieved through culturally appropriate education leading to public awareness and by providing economic development strategies that are consistent with minority people's values, while at the same time meeting regional and national development priorities.

The goal of the "Three Sustainables" project was to provide coordinated programs in environmental protection and culturally appropriate economic development for three minority regions in China: Ningxia, Guangxi, and Hainan. The project was to achieve its goal through public information, training and research, scholarly exchanges, and a pilot project aimed at specific development problems. The delivery of training programs both for Chinese faculty members and for local personnel from the three minority regions would prepare them to address environmental, economic, and social sustainability as part of their own development planning. A leading university in each region played a facilitating role.

By the end of the SULCP project, we saw an increased capacity at Minzu University and at Ningxia University to conduct training in environment, culture, and economy. Eight new courses attended by 630 students at Minzu and at Ningxia Universities were developed and taught as a result of training sixteen Chinese faculty and three local administrators at SFU.

More than 3,000 faculty, students, and local stakeholders from Minzu and the three minority regions increased their awareness of issues relating to economic development and environmental and cultural sustainability through participation in twenty-one presentations involving eight Canadian scholars. New textbooks, developed by Canadian and Chinese partners, were used in new courses delivered in Beijing, Ningxia, Guangxi, and Hainan.

All SULCP workshops and training initiatives addressed gender equality. About forty representatives from government and academia achieved an increased understanding of the role of women in social, economic, and environmental development and protection as a result of participating in the "Consultative Workshop on Women's Roles and Contributions to Social, Economic, and Environmental Development" held at Minzu University.[6] This workshop resulted in the bilingual publication of *Women and Development: The Role of Women and their Contributions to Social, Economic and Environmental Development* (Walls and Liu 1999).

Eight senior Minzu faculty members and three local administrators received training in environmental protection in social and economic development at SFU and coastal areas of British Columbia in the spring of 1997, resulting in the preparation of a textbook developed for courses at Minzu University and the three minority regions in China.

The participants were oriented to the need for sustainability, capacity building, and institutional development through their participation in the SULCP project. The delegates then used their newly acquired knowledge and skills to write research papers on their subject of study, to draft curricula for new courses, and to teach their students upon return to their home institutions in China.

Eight scholars (five of them female) from Beijing, Guangxi, Hainan, and Ningxia received four months of advanced study in English language and culture programs, interpretation training, international communication, resource and environmental management, and tourism policy and research. One member of this group studied at SFU for a full eight months before returning to Beijing. The scholars subsequently taught eight new courses for seventeen classes in environment, financial strategies, anthropology, and so on, to more than 632 students at Minzu and at Ningxia Universities. More than 90 per cent of students at Minzu are from minority nationalities and the majority returned to their home regions to teach at all three levels of education or to work in local government.

Two textbooks written by Chinese and Canadian SULCP scholars were published in 1998 and 2001. The collaborative texts, entitled *Economy, Culture and the Environment*, were used in courses at Minzu and in the minority regions (Walls and Liu 1998 and 2001). Copies were also sent to the Chinese Ministry of Education (MOE), the Ministry of Foreign Trade and Economic Cooperation, and the Canadian Embassy in Beijing, as well as to CIDA and AUCC.

INDIVIDUAL TRAINEE EXPERIENCES AND RESULTS

To more fully illustrate the longer-term results of our teaching, training, and publication efforts, it may be useful to follow the subsequent career paths of seven individual academic trainees and administrators involved in our SULCP project.

1. Professor LIU Yuming

A Ningxia University faculty member from China's Ningxia Hui Autonomous Region, Professor Liu participated in the SULCP project in 1997 at SFU. In his own words:

> From January through May 1997, I studied and did research in the School of Environment and Resource Management at Simon Fraser University. In addition to taking related graduate courses, I followed Professor Chad Day down the west coast of Canada and the US to investigate issues like coastal erosion, environmental resource management and environmental protection countermeasures in major coastal cities. Through several months of study and investigation, I gained an understanding of US and Canadian issues related to environment and development, and this greatly expanded my field of vision, laying a good foundation for my work after returning to China.
>
> After returning to China, I created and taught such new courses as "Environment and Sustainable Development," "Environmental Impact Assessment," and "Basic Principles of Environmental Studies." In 1998 I was promoted to become chairman of the Department of Biochemistry, concurrently head of the Research Institute for Natural Resources and Environmental Preservation in China's Ethnic Regions. I added new specialized fields of study, such as Environmental Science and Ecology, which since the year 2000 have been recruiting undergraduate majors. At the same time, based on the foundation of Ecology, I received authorization to create a Master's Degree Program, which began recruiting students in 2001, and in 2009 I began to take in PhD students in Ethnoecology. I have made path-breaking progress in departmental and research field development. To date, I have trained over 1,000 undergraduates in Ethnic Region Environmental and Sustainable Development work, and over 100 master's degree students.
>
> Since returning to China, my main progress is seen through my promotions in academic and administrative duties. Starting in 2000, I became Secretary of the General Party Branch in the Biochemistry Department. In 2002 the Biochemistry Department was upgraded to the present College of Life and Environmental Sciences, of which I

am the General Party Branch Secretary. Since 2006 I have been the Chair of the school's Employee Representative Congress. Since 2001 I have been a Master's Degree Student Supervisor, promoted to Full Professor in 2004, and have served as a PhD Student Supervisor since 2010. I have supervised nine Environmental Science Master's degree students, of whom eight have already graduated and are now working in environmental science related research projects, environmental management and teaching. Presently I am supervising two PhD candidates in Chinese ethnic minority traditional medical science.[7]

2. *Professor DAI Chengping*

A lecturer at Minzu University's Department of Ethnology, Professor Dai entered our project with both a bachelor's degree and a master's degree in ethnology. She studied international communication at SFU in the fall of 1997.

After returning to China, she developed and taught new courses in anthropology, archeology, and cultural history. She was appointed associate dean of ethnology, responsible for undergraduate programs in 2003, and promoted to the rank of associate professor in 2004. While working full time, she began part-time study for a PhD degree in ethnology, which she received in 2011. She has published numerous academic studies of cultural symbolism among China's minority nationalities.[8]

3. *Ms PAN Hui*

As deputy commissioner for the Baise District in the Guangxi Zhuang Autonomous Region, Pan Hui was the most senior administrator of all the SULCP scholars who studied at SFU and was probably the most capable of influencing and affecting change after her return to China. Though she was a relatively young woman, she had already held several key positions within the government and appeared to be moving upwards quite quickly. She was extremely self-confident and presented herself well. Pan Hui held a bachelor's degree in international finance and a master's degree in minority economics. She upgraded her English language proficiency in Vancouver in September 1997.

After returning to China, and having broadened her vision while studying at SFU, Ms Pan took measures to promote economic development with the alleviation of poverty as a core task. In Baise, she implemented projects to improve the living conditions of the poor, including the provision of food and clothes, supplying work opportunities, creating courtyard economies, and generally improving the quality of life and provision of infrastructural support. As a result, electricity, clean water, and housing were provided for every household, a new highway was opened to traffic, and a trading market for agricultural products, two new schools, and a clinic were established. Consequently, the net income per capita for villagers in Baise increased from tens of RMB to over 1,500 RMB. The food and clothing problems for villagers were solved two years earlier than originally anticipated. She also put forward ideas of how to increase tourist visits to Baise. She now holds a doctor of laws degree, a post-doctorate in economics, and another post-doctorate in psychology. She is currently vice-president of the Guangxi College of Education, and member of the Experts Evaluation Committee of the China Entrepreneurial Citizens Commission. She is a research associate on the National Construction and Harmonious Society Task Force, and a research associate in the Fudan University Industrial Development Research Centre. She is also head of the Guangxi College of Education Psychological Research Institute.

4. Professor ZHU Haibing

Professor Zhu Haibing was vice-dean of the Tourism Department at Qiongzhou University in Sanya, Hainan Province. She held a bachelor's degree in political education and had done graduate level studies in economics. She lectured on tourism in a program that had some 200 students. She was well placed to use the results of whatever training and studies she acquired in Canada to benefit her students – many of whom were of the Li minority nationality. She was a bright, ambitious woman who was keenly interested in advancing her knowledge of tourism. Professor Zhu studied in the Advanced Interpreter Training Program at SFU to enhance her proficiency in English. As well, she studied under the guidance of Dr June Francis in the Faculty of Business Administration and worked with Professor Peter Williams in the tourism program at SFU in September 1997.

Since her return to Qiongzhou University, she has become associate professor in the newly created Tourism Management Institute, Party Branch Secretary, and vice-president of the Sanya Campus.[9] In her own words:

> I came to SFU as a visiting scholar from August 1997 to January 1998, under the supervision of the Dean of the School of Environmental

and Resource Management Professor Peter Williams, studying "Tourism Policy and Planning" courses for professional development. I also took part in tourism research with another mentor, Professor June Francis in the Faculty of Business Administration. As a visiting scholar the main benefits to me were:

1 I greatly broadened my horizons and acquired new theoretical knowledge;
2 I became familiar with Canadian economic, cultural, environmental, and other advanced scientific concepts in environmental protection; sustainable development concepts; planning in advance for tourism development; concepts of taking into account the advantages to local residents when developing plans; the need to focus on the protection of minorities and cultural diversity, et cetera;
3 I learned about clarifying the status and function of governmental, business, and local resident beneficiaries in tourism development;
4 While in Canada, through theory and practice as a visiting scholar, I accumulated valuable experiences in Canadian tourism development, and after returning home was able to participate in the development of the local tourism economy; and
5 I accumulated a large amount of truly valuable material that allowed me to continue to engage in tourism management professional teaching and research.[10]

5. *Professor JI Yongqiang*

Professor Ji Yongqiang received his bachelor's degree in chemistry in 1982 and a master's degree in physical chemistry in 1987 at Beijing Normal University (BNU). He was the vice-chairman of the department at Ningxia University prior to his departure for Canada. He arrived in Vancouver on 12 January 1998. He took a course entitled "Environmental and Social Impact Assessment" taught by Professor Chad Day, and another entitled "Energy Management and Policy" taught by Professor Mark Jaccard in the School of Resource and Environmental Management at SFU in January 1998.

Upon returning to China, Professor Ji established the first Environmental Assessment Laboratory in the Chemistry Department at Ningxia University. He wrote a research paper on sustainable development of Ningxia migration projects and developed teaching materials for a new course entitled "Environment and Development." The course was offered in September 1998. Altogether, 138 students enrolled in his two classes. He ran a seminar at Ningxia University for young teachers, and invited Canadian professors to give presentations on the practice of environmental protection in practical situations in Ningxia. Ten young teachers attended the seminar. Professor Ji also established an Environmental Assessment Centre for the Department of Chemistry. The Centre has completed assessment reports on seven projects for the Ningxia Hui Autonomous Region. Experts spoke very highly of his reports. In January 2000, he was awarded a Grade B Certificate for Environmental Assessment issued by the State Environmental Protection Bureau. The bureau appointed Professor Ji as a Bureau Expert.[11]

6. Mr YANG Guangfu

Mr Yang Guangfu, Head of Longlin County in Guangxi, did not come to SFU to study, but through the seminars given by Canadian scholars in China, he learned new ideas for economic development and poverty alleviation. For example, he encouraged women to engage in economic activities such as weaving bamboo-wares and raising sheep and pigs. As a result, the annual income of villagers increased dramatically and poverty was essentially eliminated in his county. He developed and encouraged the wider use of marsh gas and, after one year, 1,700 marsh gas reservoirs had been constructed. The development and use of marsh gas also led to the following improvements in Longlin County:

1 Protection of vegetation and forest cover increased from 27 to 65 per cent.
2 As a result of better soil and water quality, the total output of grain harvest in recent years has increased to around 210 million catties. Thus, Longlin County no longer needs to import grain from other regions.
3 There was an increase in livestock breeding. In 1998, there were 341,556 heads of livestock; by the end of 1999, the number had reached 412,534. With the increase of livestock, the average annual income of villagers also increased from over 300 RMB in the late 1980s to nearly 2,000 RMB by the end of 1999. The financial revenue of the county increased from 8 million RMB in the late 1980s to 160 million RMB in 2000.
4 The standard of health in the village has also improved. Since 1998, there have been fewer outbreaks of infectious diseases.
5 The status of women in Longlin County has been improved. Women can now receive training and are able to contribute to the financial well-being of their families.

6 Financial stability has also contributed to the well-being of family and village life. As many families and villagers become richer, there have been fewer conflicts between family members and villagers due to financial hardship.
7 In 1990, 260,000 of the county's total population of 330,000 had inadequate food and clothing. By 2001, 340,000 had adequate food and clothing and 150,000 were leading a comfortable life.

Longlin County has become one of the hundred counties with the highest earnings per capita in Guangxi.[12]

7. Dr Bamo Ayi

Bamo Ayi, a member of the Yi nationality, became involved with our SULCP project in its later stages through her role as director of the Minzu University Office of Foreign Affairs. Born and raised in the Liangshan Yi Nationality Autonomous Prefecture in Sichuan Province, her association with Minzu University has been a long-lasting one. In 1984, after taking the National Higher-Education Entrance Examinations, she was admitted to Minzu University, and later became the first member of the Yi nationality to receive a bachelor's degree. She went on to complete her master's degree at Minzu, and in 1991 became the first Yi nationality ever to receive a PhD degree. Apart from her administrative work in cooperation with SFU, she has been involved in research projects at the University of Washington, the World Bank, and the Harvard-Yenching Institute. As a scholar, she has published an impressive number of research papers on Yi nationality culture and religion, as well as ethnic relations and national identity.

Currently, in addition to being a professor in the Philosophy Department of Minzu University, she is vice-director of the International Office at the State Ethnic Affairs Commission, and an elected delegate to the Haidian District People's Congress in Beijing.[13]

CONCLUSIONS

The return on our investment of time and resources on this academic training, research, and publication partnership can and should be measured by countable statistics such as the number of new courses created, the number of students who benefited from the teacher training and textbooks published, and the subsequent career paths of the faculty, administrators, and government officials who were involved in the project. But this does not mean that successful partnerships such as "The Three

Sustainables" CCULP/SULCP linkages can or need to be taken as models for emulation in future Canada-China university cooperative projects. The political, economic, social, and academic contexts in China have changed so much since the 1990s. The close communicative relationships we developed and the direct involvement we maintained with senior academic administrators and local government officials, most of whom were involved only to insure their understanding and support of the relationship, no longer need to play quite as big a role in the project as it did back then. We would like to say that the very success of our project has influenced this favourable development, but in fact it is also just one of the positive results of the economic and political reforms that have changed the entire system in China.

Working together with Chinese minority nationalities in future, we must explore all options to ensure that, having proven the feasibility of modernizing their material culture through environmentally and economically sustainable development, they can make enlightened decisions regarding the "modernization" of their cultural heritage. The dangers of technological innovation to cultural value systems in general has been made abundantly clear by scholars like Neil Postman in books like *Technopoly*: "The accusation can be made that the uncontrolled growth of technology destroys the vital sources of our humanity. It creates a culture without a moral foundation. It undermines certain mental processes and social relations that make human life worth living. Technology, in sum, is both friend and enemy" (Postman 1998, xii). Studies have revealed, for example, that ethno-tourism often creates unreal spaces in which identity is contrived or even staged in such a way that it conforms more to a visitor's expectations than to the way an ethnic community sees itself. It has even been argued that the reconstruction of identity for tourism purposes begins with the gaze of the outsider acting as a reference point for identity creation (Hitchcock 1999). Helping minority cultures set up scenarios like this runs the risk of turning their communities into anthropological museums and themselves into museum pieces.

In working with minority nationalities, we need to be respectful both of their right to "modernize" and of their commitment to retaining aspects of their cultural life that are meaningful to them and which they want to preserve. One way of integrating the two is to develop home-stay placement cooperative enterprises in which participating families become members of the coop enterprise. For example, the Lijiang Xintuo Ecotourism Company is a community-owned company, composed of twenty-two Naxi minority nationality village families, that strives to empower local people in northwestern Yunnan Province. The participants follow ecotourism international criteria, bring awareness about local minority cultures, and develop community-based employment opportunities that will improve the local standard of living, allowing for the construction of schools, of hospitals, and of proper sanitation. This is done by employing local Naxi and Yi ethnic minority locals, with 10 per cent of their profit given to a conservation and community development fund that provides services to the local community and schools.[14] Locally owned and operated tourism development projects such as this one allow local families to benefit directly from the tourism industry, but without having to become waitresses and janitors in foreign-owned five-star hotels. Again, I am not suggesting that upscale hotel employment opportunities be discouraged, only that more "culturally autonomous" local community-based development opportunities be made available as viable alternatives to participation in the "international mainstream" tourism industry.

Future Canada-China university linkages will not be able to benefit from CIDA financial support because China is no longer regarded as a poor country reliant upon international development aid, so other sources of financial support will need to be found. Indeed, today many of my Canadian university colleagues are envious of the resources now available to their Chinese counterparts. But whatever form future university linkages may take, some of the relationship practices we applied with success in "The Three Sustainables" project may be expressed in terms that Chinese have been familiar with for over two millennia, and are just as relevant in the twenty-first century as they were back then. They are the "Five Constant Virtues" and "The Middle Way."

The Five Constant Virtues are Empathy (*rén*), Duty (*yì*), Protocol (*lǐ*), Knowledge (*zhì*), and Trust (*xìn*). Mutually beneficial relationships must begin with empathy, the ability to understand and share the feelings of another, to form what Professor Qiang Zha describes as "a shared intersubjective meaning and a partnership of a unity with diversity" (Zha 2013). Confucius himself is quoted in the *Analects* as having said, "People with empathy (*rén*) are those who, desiring to sustain themselves, sustain others, and desiring to develop themselves, develop others" (*Lún Yǔ* VI, 28). Without an empathetic understanding between collaborators, there will be a lack of motivation to address the misunderstandings that inevitably will occur.

Empathy must be paired and balanced with a sense of duty (*yì*) to do the right thing and to abide by the rules no matter how much empathetic feeling one partner has for the other. Both sides must understand and agree with this. A certain amount of prescribed behaviour (*lǐ*) is required if the relationship is to be stable and predictable. Canadians tend to look upon protocol as an unfortunate necessity and a constraint on creativity, but without protocol there is no foundation from which to recognize and appreciate innovation. Ritualized ceremonies also give an official excuse to celebrate and reaffirm the good will and commitment of both sides to the success of the project. The knowledge required for an effective relationship includes practical, technological, institutional, and cultural knowledge. The Chinese word (*zhì*), which I translate as knowledge, also means wisdom, which is the ability to understand the likely long-term consequences of applying acquired knowledge. The critically sympathetic, and sometimes sympathetically critical, knowledge on each side about how the partner thinks, feels, and acts, contributes much to the success of collaboration.

The fifth Constant Virtue is trust (*xìn*). If the two sides cannot trust each other to faithfully practise the other four virtues, the project will not end well. In the rock garden beside the Institute of Asian Research at UBC, there are five large stones of diverse sizes and shapes, each engraved with one of the Five Constant Virtues. The stone placed in the centre, surrounded by the other four, is trust. The central placement is highly symbolic.

The Five Constant Virtues must be observed and applied while keeping a dynamic balance between the letter and the spirit of each in mind. This means keeping all of the relationships balanced as cooperation progresses and circumstances change; the tried and true Chinese ideal and practice for maintaining such balance is to follow "The Middle Way" (*zhōng yōng*). The Middle Way is so fundamental, so important in Chinese culture that a classic treatise by that name is one of "The Four Books" attributed to Confucius himself. It simply counsels against all forms of excessive or extreme behaviour, because all other angles can be viewed and assessed holistically only from the perspective of the middle point. Implicit in the belief and practice of the Middle Way is that even the Middle Way should not be adhered to dogmatically or mechanistically. And if you can understand and accept this notion, congratulations! You are a sinologist!

APPENDIX: TEACHERS, ADMINISTRATORS, AND OFFICIALS INVOLVED IN THE SULCP

Chinese Project Staff

Professor Ha Jingxiong, project director, SULCP project; president, Minzu University

Professor Guo Zhaolin, project coordinator, SULCP project; director,
    Office of External Affairs, Minzu University
Professor Shen Youling, assistant project coordinator, SULCP project;
    deputy director, Office of External Affairs, Minzu University
Professor Bamo Ayi, Office of External Affairs, Minzu University

Canadian Project Staff

Dr Jan W. Walls, project director; chair, SFU Management Committee;
    director, David Lam Centre for International Communication
Ms Alison Winters, project coordinator, David Lam Centre for
    International Communication (SFU)
Dr Chad Day, member of SFU Management Committee; professor,
    School of Resource and Environment Management, SFU
Dr June Francis, member of SFU Management Committee; assistant
    professor, Faculty of Business Administration, SFU
Dr Mark Jaccard, member of SFU Management Committee; professor,
    School of Resource and Environment Management, SFU
Dr Peter Williams, professor, School of Resource and Environment
    Management; director, Centre for Tourism Policy and Research, SFU
Dr Tom Perry, professor, Department of Linguistics; associate dean
    of arts, SFU
Dr John Nyboer, School of Resource and Environment Management, SFU
Dr Diana Lary, professor, Department of History, UBC

Chinese in Canada

Minzu University President Ha Jingxiong (10–26 July 1996 and April
    to May 1998)
Professor Guo Zhaolin – Minzu University (10–26 July 1996 and April
    to May 1998)
Professor Shen Youling – Minzu University (10–26 July 1996,
    26 February to 13 March 1997, April to May 1998, and February
    to March 1999)
University of Qiongzhou President Li Zhenru (February to March
    1999)
Vice-President Liu Shusong – Minzu University (26 February to
    13 March 1997 and February to March 1999)
Professor Shi Zhengyi – Minzu University (26 February to 13 March
    1997)

Professor Li Wenchao – Minzu University (26 February to 13 March 1997)
Professor Ma Qicheng – Minzu University (26 February to 13 March 1997)
Professor Qi Qingfu – Minzu University (26 February to 13 March 1997)
Professor Yu Chen – Minzu University (26 February to 13 March 1997)
Mr Ma Fenghu – deputy director of Minority Affairs Commission of Ningxia Hui Autonomous Region (26 February to 13 March 1997)
Mr Nong Futian – deputy director, Baise Prefecture, Guangxi (26 February to 13 March 1997)
Governor Zhang Tingdeng – governor, Tianyang County, Guangxi (26 February to 13 March 1997)
Professor Liu Yuming – Minzu University (January to April 1997)
Ms Dai Chengping – Minzu University (August to December 1997)
Mr Feng Xiao – Minzu University (August to December 1997)
Ms Pan Hui – deputy commissioner for the Baise District (August to December 1997)
Ms Song Jie – Minzu University (August to December 1997)
Mr Su Yucheng – Minzu University (August to December 1997)
Professor Tai Lin – Minzu University (August to December 1997)
Professor Zhu Haibing – Qiongzhou University (August to December 1997)
Mr Ji Yongqiang – Ningxia University (January to April 1998)

Canadians in China

Dr Jan W. Walls (11–30 June 1997 and May to June 1999)
Dr Chad Day (October 1996 [20 days] and 20 May to 3 June 1999)
Dr Judie Bopp (October 1996 [20 days])
Dr Tom Perry (11–30 June 1997)
Dr June Francis (11–30 June 1997 and late September to early October 1998)
Dr Diana Lary (late September to early October 1998)
Dr Peter Williams (20 May to 3 June 1999)
Dr John Nyboer (20 May to 3 June 1999)

NOTES

1 I would like to thank Professor Shen Youling, now retired from the Minzu University Office of Foreign Affairs, for her eleven years of enlightened

management of the Chinese side of our CCULP and SULCP projects, and for her valuable assistance in accessing and pulling together much of the archival information used in this chapter.
2 Formerly known as the Central Institute for Nationalities (CIN), later the Central University for Nationalities (CUN), most recently renamed Minzu University.
3 CCULP Project number 928-282/14218.
4 Familiarization visits like these should not be confused with "junkets," since senior academic administrators and local government officials were held personally responsible for cooperative relationships they signed off on.
5 SULCP Project number 005-282/19156.
6 12–14 May 1999.
7 Personal correspondence with the author.
8 Information contained in personal correspondence with the author.
9 As party branch secretary and vice-president of Qiongzhou University's Sanya Campus, she has enormous power and influence in developing the new Tourism Management Institute.
10 Personal correspondence with the author.
11 Information from a joint quarterly report submitted to AUCC by Minzu and SFU project directors.
12 Information from a joint quarterly report submitted to AUCC by Minzu and SFU project directors.
13 Information from a joint quarterly report to AUCC by Minzu and SFU project directors.
14 Compare with http://www.ecotourism.com.cn for detailed descriptions.

PART FOUR

Education and Equity

10

The Educational Dimension of China's Transformation: From the Perspective of the Canada-China University Linkage Projects

QIANG ZHA AND RUTH HAYHOE

INTRODUCTION

Education has been a key element in China's dramatic transformation since 1983 when Deng Xiaoping called for China to open itself to modernization, the world, and the future. In this chapter, we will look at major educational reforms that have unfolded, including teacher education and curricular change at the basic education level, as well as intense efforts to improve higher education after the Cultural Revolution fiasco. The most recent decade has seen a huge expansion of higher education and an explicit commitment to greater equity in educational access and provision at all levels. In this chapter, we first examine the role played by education in the reform and transformation of Chinese society. Next, we try to fit three major education projects within the Canada China University Linkage Program (CCULP) into the big picture, explore how they contributed to China's educational reform, and reflect on their possible long-term outcomes. The first project supported the training of doctoral students in education at seven Chinese normal universities, and then supported the returned students in research around issues of moral education, gender and education, and bilingualism and minority cultures. The second project offered nationwide support to higher-education administration and leadership through a partnership between the University of Alberta (U of A) and the National Academy of Educational Administration (NAEA). The third project involved a partnership between the University of Regina and the Jilin Institute of Education, which supported leadership training for schools throughout

China's northeastern region. Two of the three projects were sustained for a second phase under the Special University Linkages Consolidation Program (SULCP).

Educational institutions, and universities in particular, have often been regarded as key agents in processes of social change and development. The most explicit role they have been allocated is the production of human capital and knowledge output to meet perceived social and economic needs. However, to this role may be added – especially during periods of more radical change – roles in building new institutions of civil society, in encouraging and facilitating new cultural values, and in training and socializing members of new social elites. Much of the recent literature on the roles of education in processes of social transformation and modernization has tended to be circumscribed within a specific national context: focusing on what universities ought to do and what is planned for them to do in the landscape of national policy strategies. This chapter attempts to gather some empirical evidence to bring to debates about the social roles of universities as derived from their international functioning. The data were gathered through interviews with fifteen participants in both Canada and China in the aforementioned CCULP/SULCP projects. All interviewees were selected through the knowledge and network of one of the authors who proposed and founded the first project that partnered the Ontario Institute for Studies in Education (OISE) with seven normal universities in China. The time span for data collection ranged from July 2011 to May 2012, and each interview lasted one to one and a half hours.[1] All interview sessions were recorded (but not transcribed), and the researchers took detailed notes on site.

All the data collected were then analyzed through a lens focusing on the cultural role played by universities, under the assumption that universities have been important in providing both a route for the entry of external ideas and experiences into otherwise closed societies and a repository for national sentiments that can come out of "storage" when time and circumstance permit. There can be tensions between these "national" and "international" elements that may result in contradictions of identity and purpose within individual universities as well as in the broader society. Therefore, the exploration and dissemination of successful experiences become necessary and pivotal. In this sense, we feel that the study reported in this chapter should make a contribution to the literature and be of significance for the field of education in an era of globalization.

THE EVOLUTIONARY ROLE OF EDUCATION IN CHINA

Educational policies and strategies in China over the past six decades have been characterized by bold moves, major shifts, and reversals. Educational change is inextricably linked to changes in society at large, which in turn provides us with an opportunity to scrutinize the role of education in China's transformation. In the first thirty years after the founding of the People's Republic of China in 1949, the approach to national development was characterized by continuing class struggle and revolution to transform the social relations of production, and by placing communist politics and ideology at the core of social life. Being a part of the super-structure of society, education was viewed as an important means of political indoctrination and maintaining political loyalty, and the Chinese state exerted tight control over education. In doing so, a highly centralized educational system, which was characterized by unified planning, administration, syllabi, curricula, textbooks, enrolment, and allocation of school and university seats, was developed in Maoist China (Hao 1998), in contrast to the reform era that came after this. Under this centralized system of education, the state assumed the responsibility for formulating educational policies, allocating educational resources, exerting administrative control, recruiting teaching staff, and deciding on curricula and textbooks (Ngok and Kwong 2003).

In this period, despite policy oscillations from time to time, between "redness" and "expertise" (that is, between education for political/ideological development versus education for economic development; between education for the masses versus education for preparing a well-trained elite; and between treating intellectuals and high-skilled personnel as antagonists and suppressing versus enlisting them to serve socialist development), the successive political campaigns marked a general antagonism against intellectuals until the close of the Cultural Revolution. Examples are the Anti-Rightist Movement in 1957–59, the Great Leap Forward in 1958–61, and the Cultural Revolution in 1966–76. The political and ideological function of education held dominance over the acquisition of expertise for economic production. Promotion of social equality was a key national-development goal and was to be achieved through a substantial expansion of access to education for peasant and working-class children. Mao's educational perspective set into motion a rapid quantitative expansion of education at all levels, the proliferation of new schools (especially work-study schools) for children from peasant households, and the incorporation of political education and manual activities into the educational curriculum at all levels.

When the Cultural Revolution came to an end in the late 1970s, Deng Xiaoping led China into a new era, one featuring the economic transition to a "market-oriented socialist economy." With a focus on economic development and modernization, Deng's fundamental policy of reform and opening up to the outside world succeeded in achieving rapid and sustained economic growth and a clear improvement in the living standards of the Chinese people. Under this new policy principle, the Chinese state has been increasingly concerned with the role that education plays in improving China's economic competitiveness and its place in regional and global markets. The concern that education should serve the new economic vision prompted a kind of depoliticization of Chinese education, that is, the emphasis on education as a political and ideological instrument was now downgraded. This does not mean that education lost its political function, nor does it mean that the government abandoned its commitment to socialism and embraced the free market ideology integral to the global economy. Depoliticization only means that politics no longer figure prominently in the school curricula. The political function of education has now given way to an educational strategy that would accelerate China's march toward modernization (Rosen 1997). This would, inevitably, result in dramatic curricular changes, as well as new pedagogical needs. One example of such changes and needs can be seen in the fact that the Chinese state organized, within narrow time intervals, three rounds of revising the country's classifications of instructional programs in universities and colleges, respectively in 1982–87, 1989–93, and 1997–99, from a basis in the 1963 classification which closely followed the Soviet patterns. The successive revisions showed enormous efforts to adapt higher-education program offerings to the new social realities and a market-oriented economy. During these processes, many existing programs were merged in order to enlarge their knowledge base and increase their flexibility, and many new programs were added, especially in humanities and social sciences. Needless to say, such efforts required the backup of new theoretical concepts and professional expertise, as they represented serious attempts at breaking the boundaries of the old patterns.

On the other hand, the over-centralization and stringent regulation in the Maoist period were viewed in the reform era as stifling the initiative and enthusiasm of local governments and educational institutions, and resulting in the inadequate provision of education. The Chinese state alone had been unable to assume the responsibility for satisfying people's increased demand for education. These different perceptions of the role of education had encouraged the central government to relax control and roll back on its role in education, and thus justified retrenchment in government funding and shifting the load to other sectors. In this way, along with depoliticization, a process of decentralization occurred in Chinese education, which refers to the relinquishing of central government control and the assigning of responsibility for the provision and management of education to the local levels. Two milestone reform documents specifically pushed for the decentralization process. The *Decision on the Reform of the Education System* (Central Committee of the CCP 1985), or the 1985 Decision, called for the institution of nine-year compulsory education and stipulated a multiple sponsorship of primary education in rural China. Under the new model of educational finance, primary schools are sponsored by villages (*cun* 村), junior high schools by towns and townships (*xiangzhen* 乡镇), and senior high schools by counties (*xian* 县). Such a financial arrangement indicates that the central government has completely rolled back from sponsoring primary education, and financing primary education has now become the responsibility of grassroots governments and rural communities. The decentralization policy was extended to the higher-education sector in the early 1990s with the promulgation of the *Outline for Educational Reform and Development in China* (Central Committee of the CCP and State Council 1993), or the 1993 Outline. In order to make the higher-education sector suitable for the emerging market-oriented economy, the 1993 Outline included the decision to further the education reform, especially reforming the governance structure of higher education. The core of the decentralization policy was to empower provincial governments in the role of financing and administering higher education. Provincial governments were encouraged to cooperate with the central government via the Ministry of Education (MOE) to coordinate and sponsor all central-ministry-led universities located in the provinces. With the increasing role of local governments in higher education, a new trend of localization of higher education emerged in China. As a result, more and more universities are now administered by provincial governments and even city governments.

This policy has not only allowed local and grassroots governments (at provincial, city, and county levels) to have a greater say in educational matters, it has also opened the way for private organizations and even individuals to operate schools. The measures of decentralization and the involvement of private forces in educational provision have in turn led to the marketization of education: the creation of an educational market where private individuals and organizations can compete with the public schools for clientele and can even run schools for profit. The adoption of this policy of marketization against a background of a market-oriented economy has resulted in deep and far-reaching changes in the organization of education. Through these policies of decentralization and marketization, the Chinese state opened the doors for fundamental changes in the orientation, financing, curriculum, and management of education (Agelasto and Adamson 1998). This in turn raised new and pressing human-resource demands for managing and supporting Chinese education. While those who worked at local grassroots levels used to practise their jobs in close compliance with the detailed policies and instructions from the top in a centralized regime, they now have to take care of new initiatives and strategic planning for their own jurisdictions and institutions.

Perhaps the inscription that Deng Xiaoping wrote for a high school in Beijing[2] in 1983 best expressed the fundamental changes required for Chinese education in the reform era: orienting itself toward modernization, the world, and the future. Deng's vision for Chinese education had crucial significance. Shortly before this slogan was widely heralded, there was a debate over whether or not the reform of Chinese education should primarily conform to the ideas and practices in the period that immediately followed the founding of socialist China before the distortions of the Cultural Revolution, that is, the seventeen years from 1949 to 1966. The policies, strategies, and practices of that period had been perceived as being correct. Yet it was apparent that Deng's idea was not to put the educational reform programs back on the old track, but to orient them toward a new space. Essentially, his vision put two major demands on Chinese education. One was to serve economic growth and national development via nurturing a labour force with modern knowledge and skills. The other was to modernize itself through adopting new educational concepts, values, content, and delivery methods including information technology. All these notions were later included and elaborated in the 1985 Decision. Now the major challenge facing Chinese education was how to implement these ideas, as they embodied a path that had not existed before on Chinese soil. It would need to involve a wide range of inputs and resources in order to push forward the educational reform programs, from curriculum development to leadership transformation. Naturally, China turned to the outside world, primarily the West this time, for norms and patterns, and against this backdrop, the CCULP and SULCP nicely fit into the landscape of China's educational reform.

THE THREE CCULP/SULCP PROJECTS AND THEIR TIMELINESS FOR CHINA'S EDUCATIONAL TRANSFORMATION

The CCULP (1988–95) was supported by the Canadian International Development Agency (CIDA) with a total of $19 million in funding, and with the goal to assist China in developing its human resources in key areas and building up human and institutional contacts between Canada and China. As the largest higher-education project under CIDA's Country Program, the CCULP supported thirty-one university linkage projects in a wide range of fields including public health, education, agriculture, transportation, engineering, environment, biotechnology, mining and minerals, administration, diplomacy, and human settlements, with each linkage project receiving approximately $500,000 over three to six years. It was expected at the end of the program that the institutional capacity of the Chinese partners would be strengthened and serve as change agents in China's rapid economic and social development. Based on the huge success of the CCULP in general, eleven CCULP projects with the best sustainable development potential were chosen to be funded in Phase II, the SULCP (1996–2001), with a total of $10 million in funding. The SULCP was to build on the successful CCULP projects, consolidate their impact, make them sustainable in long-term institution building, and maximize the mutual benefits. Throughout the CCULP and SULCP, the priorities were placed on institutional development, women in development, environmental development, and the sustainability of linkage projects. The combined span of the CCULP and SULCP (1988–2001) coincided with a period of pivotal changes in Chinese society, and they both aimed at maximizing human contacts and multiplying contacts at the thinking level. In the following space, we focus, in a chronological order, on three CCULP projects in educational fields, and elaborate their timeliness and fit with respect to China's needs for transforming its education system.

The OISE CCULP/SULCP Projects: Supporting Curriculum and Pedagogy Development at Both University and School Levels

The CCULP project that linked OISE with seven normal universities[3] across China supported the development of doctoral study in the field of education in China, and lasted from 1989 to 1995. It took an approach of not simply "upgrading" academic programs in China on the basis of

Western expertise, but rather seeking a process of mutual enrichment, whereby Chinese students and scholars would have an extended exposure to the Canadian academic environment and Canadian students and scholars would learn from the wealth of educational knowledge and experience in China's rich tradition. In total, the project enabled eleven affiliated faculty members at OISE to go to China for short-term teaching and joint graduate student supervision, twelve OISE doctoral students to spend periods of study in China, and twenty-two Chinese doctoral students and young scholars to come to Canada to do research related to their doctoral programs and to broaden their academic experience (Hayhoe and Pan 1995; Hayhoe, Pan, and Zha 2013). In addition, six senior Chinese professors who supervised doctoral students in education visited faculties of education in Montreal, Toronto, Edmonton, and Vancouver as well as taking part in a conference.

The CCULP project was then sustained under the SULCP from 1996 to 2001[4] in a project entitled Women and Minorities as Educational Change Agents. This project aimed to build research capacities of normal universities in China in order to advance educational reform programs regarding gender education, moral education, and minority culture and bilingual education. Specifically, the SULCP project sought to support women faculty members and students in higher-education institutions to participate in gender-sensitive forms of teaching, research, and curriculum development that would enhance their leadership capacity, support both female and male teachers in secondary schools in their role as moral educators and reflective practitioners in the current period of rapid social change, and help both female and male minority teachers in primary schools integrate indigenous knowledge into the curriculum to facilitate the interpenetration of minority cultures into mainstream schools and to develop more effective approaches to bilingual education (Boyd and Pan 2003). In this second phase, in addition to those who participated in the first project and then returned to China, many others joined in and spent shorter times doing collaborative research in Canada.

The OISE CCULP/SULCP projects occurred at a time when educational scholarship in China was greatly in need of new ideas and perspectives, and the projects indeed served such a purpose. In this regard, perhaps the story of one participant in the CCULP phase can illustrate this timeliness. With a political education background, her career was at a crossroads when China started the transformation of its economy and society, whereby the Soviet-style political education started to be seriously challenged. In 1994, she was selected for the OISE CCULP project and spent eight months in Canada, an experience that opened a new career world for her. She had wanted to develop her doctoral research in a feminist framework, but experienced difficulties, as the field of gender studies did not exist in China at that point. Her period of study in Canada truly opened up this world of scholarship. She was thus at the forefront of the development of gender studies in China. Indeed the OISE CCULP project resulted in the first textbooks on gender and education at the post-secondary level in China, *Gender and Women's Development* (《社会性别与妇女发展》) and *Development and Education of Female University Students in China* (《中国女大学生发展与教育》), published respectively in 1999 and 2000 by Shaanxi Education Press. These textbooks had an impact on the development of curriculum on women's issues at universities across China (Boyd and Pan 2003). Therefore, on her return, this participant started a whole series of textbooks and courses, taking part in very active ways in the field. Later, she received projects from the Ford Foundation and chose to send her students to Canada to study gender in education, a move prompted by her own positive experience in Canada. Also with the Ford Foundation funds, she helped to organize a large-scale feminist pedagogical workshop in Canada in 2001, which provided training on gender-education teaching methods to women scholars sent by ten Chinese universities (see Hsiung, chapter 13 of this volume). These women scholars are now the leaders in this field in China.[5] Also drawing on her experience in Canada, this scholar spearheaded the research on multicultural education in China, and now heads the Multicultural Education Research Centre at a top university in China. The Centre recently gained the status of a national centre of excellence.

Similarly, moral education, another focus area of the OISE CCULP/SULCP projects, shows how timely this project was. In this area, the project was designed to work with researchers, teacher educators, and schoolteachers (at the junior high school and high school levels) to develop research projects, curriculum materials, and pedagogical strategies that address more directly the moral educational needs of adolescents in a transitional society like China's. Such work involved introducing current research theory, methodology, and teaching instruments that were useful in exploring the moral education problems perceived by the teachers. It further included facilitating teachers' familiarity with pedagogical strategies that work with such theories and materials. In this regard, the project outcomes that have best mirrored such efforts as well as the collaboration between the Canadian and Chinese participants included

Moral Education: Action Research in Secondary Schools, a book published in 2000 by Jilin Education Press. If these efforts are projected onto the large context of moral education development in Chinese schools, the project's significance stands out even more.

The timing of the CCULP project (1989-95) overlapped with a period in which moral education in elementary and secondary schools went through a major transition in China, 1985-96 (Tan and Ban 2008). Moral education was restored in schools after the Cultural Revolution, but suffered from too much emphasis placed on nurturing the political quality of the students and meeting political needs of the state. In addition to politicization of the moral education curriculum, the curricular materials were dominated by adult logic and rhetoric. In the meantime, little attention had been paid to the physical and cognitive development of adolescents and their real-life scenarios. All these factors resulted in a kind of fragmentation between moral education curriculum/pedagogy and the realities of adolescents. The concern had thus been that these approaches were too politicized, teacher-centred, didactic, prescriptive, and dogmatic, which essentially worked against the need to support the development of character and critical judgment on the part of students. This project responded in a timely way to such tensions and concerns that called for depoliticization and transformation of moral education in China, in particular through developing the teachers' capacity to help students focus on moral dilemmas that they themselves saw as relevant to their lives, in a way that was characterized more by student-student critical discussion than by didactic orientations, and had multidimensional angles. Furthermore, the project enabled the participating teachers and principals to see the conflict between economic values and moral values, in a time when morality and environment were to a large extent neglected in the pursuit of economic benefit.[6] Such approaches are still much needed today, and not limited to the sphere of moral education in China.

On looking back now, we discovered that the OISE CCULP/SULCP projects nurtured a generation of young scholars who became leaders in education fields, and who were spread across China. Among the twenty-two Chinese scholars who came to study in Canada, twenty returned to China, and fifteen are still active in educational leadership, teaching, and research, including one university president, two vice-presidents, four deans, and a number of department chairs. Two of these scholars, when interviewed by us, offered insights into the farseeing nature and pioneering significance of the projects. One scholar had just stepped down from the position of dean of the School of Education at a top normal university in China. He stressed the point that the OISE projects exposed China's education research community to the outside world, and he used his own story to illustrate this point. With a background in Chinese literature and philosophy, he used to believe he had a deep understanding of educational issues in the Chinese context. Therefore he did not feel any need to study abroad, and did not really appreciate scholars abroad who were researching Chinese education. After spending nearly one year in Canada, he came to understand that educational problems were looked at very differently in Canada and the United States, and thus realized the need to have a cultural understanding of how educational scholars in different countries would view and analyze similar problems.[7] Considering China was not really open until after 1993, he viewed the OISE projects as truly pioneering ones that had opened up Chinese educational research circles, in terms of methods, ideas, and patterns. This reflection has inspired him to find ways of communicating core educational values and perspectives from the Chinese tradition on a global stage through promoting publications about Chinese education in English. Today, Chinese universities lead the wave of internationalization, and educational studies have become one of the frontiers of international collaborations. This scenario should be tracked back to early efforts including the OISE CCULP/SULCP projects.

Another participant scholar recalled what he saw in Canada set against what he had learned in China. He remembered vividly the first time he went into a primary school in Canada. That was the first time that he saw an open classroom, with small groups and many pupil activities. (The pupils he observed were sitting on the floor, using toys for learning mathematics that day.) This scene contrasted sharply with the rows of chairs and desks typical of a Chinese classroom environment, in which children had very little opportunity for activity, and only listened passively. He felt that it was an entirely different learning environment, and that relations between pupils and teachers were also entirely different. After visiting many similar classrooms, he realized that the whole way of organizing classrooms in Canada was different from the organization of formal classrooms in China. He felt that there was a need to introduce this type of classroom organization to China. Later, he moved to the National Institute of Education Science (NIES) in Beijing, and became a leader there. In that capacity, he started a research institute on educational experimentation in 1995, the first one in China of this kind, and then a national educational experimentation association. The institute set up a number of experimental schools across the country, and promoted interactive and activity-based teaching and learning in schools.[8] His work was pioneering in nature, and many ideas nurtured in his experimentation projects can be perceived as seminal to national curricular reforms initiated in 2001, and reflected in the more recent *National Outline for Medium- and Long-Term Educational Reform and Development* (2010–20) (State Council of China 2010). The ideas he brought back now sit firmly at the core of those policy initiatives that aim to push the reform of Chinese education further, which will in turn serve the sustainable and organic development of Chinese society and economy.

The Alberta-NAEA CCULP Project: Strengthening Institutional Leadership and Preparing Strategic Planning in China's Universities and Colleges

Between 1990 and 1994, the U of A and the NAEA worked together on a CCULP project pursuing human-resource development and strategic planning capacity goals. The mandate of NAEA included the preparation and training of administrators for China's then over 1,000 universities and colleges. It was thus charged with providing educational leadership in China's reform programs geared toward modernization and decentralization of the education system. In the duration of this project, the U of A faculty and staff paid twenty-three person-visits to NAEA to hold project activities there, and seven NAEA scholars (including two women) spent a period of nine months in Canada, all assigned with tasks of developing courses to be taught in NAEA. In specific terms, this amounted to the preparation of course outlines and the assembly of related literature. The course topics included administration of higher education, foundations of higher education, comparative adult education, moral education, management psychology in higher education, and policies, laws, and regulations of higher education. In addition to such personnel exchanges, other project activities included six short courses (each two and a half weeks in duration) offered in Beijing to Chinese higher-education administrators and NAEA faculty, three leadership seminars (of two weeks each) offered in Beijing to senior Chinese education officials, collaborative research focusing on reform in higher education, and expansion of NAEA library holdings in educational administration and provision of computers for research, instruction, and administration.

Notably, the Canadian side was very sensitive to the issue of whether or not the academic content rooted in Canadian context might successfully and sensitively transfer across cultures (Haughey 1992). Therefore, the

Canadian participants adopted a "cultural neutrality" position toward the content; that is, making it clear to their Chinese counterparts that they were dealing with issues in higher-education management as dictated largely by experience in Canada. Accordingly, the Canadian participants agreed that their Chinese colleagues should have the discretion to adopt what they believed useful for China and reject what was unsuitable. Furthermore, the Canadian participants tried hard to find case examples that had particular relevance for the Chinese milieu. Such an approach "greatly strengthened the conceptualization and delivery of the project" (F.J. Morgan Enterprises 1994, 9). When taking our interview, a former project leader on the Canadian side repeatedly emphasized that reciprocal learning was intended at the beginning, though he experienced enormous difficulties to make this a reality in the project. Reflecting on his experience of this project, he became aware that some of the Chinese colleagues involved in the project might now understand education far better than the Canadian colleagues.[9]

Another notable achievement of this project is that of introducing the concept and tools of strategic planning to the context of Chinese higher education. A joint research theme followed by the two sides was strategic planning as a tool of reform and forecasting future reforms (Haughey 1994). Strategic planning in higher education requires, first and foremost, active and quick actions taken by higher-education institutions in response to changes in the environment. Literally, strategic planning conflicted with the norms and structures of decision-making at that time in Chinese higher education, which featured a central planning approach, often driven by a political agenda. Notwithstanding this conflict, China was indeed at the dawn of distinguishing administrative from political roles in the early 1990s, since the tenets of educational reform programs starting from the mid-1980s had preceded strategic planning at the institutional level. The Alberta-NAEA project successfully transferred to China's higher education sector the concept that administration is a "science" that should be entrusted to competent experts, which was very new but timely and necessary at that point in the reform era (Paltiel 1992; Haughey 1994). In this process, the Canadian participants exhibited an insightful understanding of the reality that politics would remain in command in China, and political savvy would be the indispensable "leadership science." As one of them observed, the Chinese administrative elite would have to be prepared to cope with some of the critical political and economic dynamics that would test the Chinese system. Therefore, "the extent to which strategic planning can aid in the refinement of the Chinese system of higher education" is very much left in the hands of Chinese colleagues (Haughey 1994). When reading this remark twenty years later, we are still amazed by its foresight.

The Regina-Jilin CCULP/SULCP *Projects:*
Contributing to Gender Equity in Jilin Xchools

With CIDA's sponsorship, the University of Regina and the Jilin Institute of Education formed a partnership which lasted five years, from 1991 to 1995. This project supported the establishment of the Education Management Training Centre in Changchun, which had the capacity to provide in-service professional development training to educational leaders in Jilin Province. During the tenure of this project, forty-eight Canadian scholars and project staff travelled to China for project work, and fifty-six Chinese went to the University of Regina.[10] As a result, the project provided comprehensive professional development training in educational administration to ninety-two in-service school administrators, and held seminars that introduced theories of educational administration for another 591 school administrators (Zhao 2000). The Education Management Training Centre continued to run follow-up seminars and workshops, which have benefitted an additional 2,300 school staff and teachers throughout Jilin Province. Based on the success of the CCULP, the University of Regina went on to obtain funding to continue the project through the SULCP. The Consolidation of the Management Training Project: Educational Policy Implementation and Gender Equity in Human-Resource Development (abbreviated as the Educational Policy and Gender Equity Program, or EPGEP) thus resulted in 1996, which supported in-service training of ten faculty members of the Jilin Institute of Education and approximately 100 school administrators in Jilin, with half of them being female.

While Canadian values always put an overriding priority on gender issues,[11] it was not initially an easy task to secure a gender balance in the CCULP project, against the backdrop of persisting gender inequity in China (Bartels and Eppley 1995; Hershkovitz 1995; Wang and Staver 1995). Males continued to dominate significant administrative positions in the schooling system, and played a key role in program planning and decision-making concerning all aspects of school management (human, material, and financial), a situation which in turn served to perpetuate gender inequity in Chinese schools. Some argued that the gender inequity was rooted in the Confucian tradition that survived the revolutionary era, and continued to prescribe a subordinate role for women (Hopper 1991; Rosen 1992). Others maintained that the socialist regime was merely rhetorical in its stance on the gender imbalance in education, rather than taking effective actions at the practical level to remedy gender discrepancies in schooling (Rosen 1992; Hershkovitz 1995). Consequently, females comprised a declining percentage of the student body as they moved further up the hierarchy of educational grade levels (Tan 1994). The Regina-Jilin CCULP project, though originally planned as comprising 50 per cent female in-service school administrators, saw initially only ten female participants on the Jilin side. Meanwhile, there was no mechanism to ensure selecting female candidates to participate in the project, and the Canadian side had little control over the process of selection.

Therefore the SULCP project placed a high priority on gender parity among its participants selected from all the nine regions in Jilin Province; that is, making sure to include equal numbers of male and female participants in all of its seminars and workshops. Over the CCULP/SULCP projects' duration, six women were selected to participate as writer/translator seminar team members, seven women were selected as delegation members for place-based learning experiences in Canada, and seventy-one female participants attended the seminars offered through the CCULP/SULCP projects. Together the Education Management Training Program and its extension, the Educational Policy and Gender Equity Program, developed in-service leadership and curriculum-development training for female educational administrators through the Education Management Training Centre, provided opportunities for women to train as trainer/consultants and participate directly in school administration and curriculum planning, assisted senior provincial educational officials in implementing policy that better included women in school administration and curriculum planning, helped provincial educational officials identify systemic problems causing the high dropout rate of school-aged girls, and worked with provincial education authorities to ensure opportunities for school-aged girls to complete a middle school education.

The CCULP/SULCP projects between the University of Regina and the Jilin Institute of Education helped to not only train a cohort of school administrators who were urgently needed for China's decentralization and the transformation of the schooling system, but also to reinforce the awareness and understanding of gender issues among educational officials and school administrators in Jilin. It is perceived that only when school administrators take an active part with teachers in the gender-equity-in-education programs can such programs be implemented successfully and benefit the students substantially (Sadker and Sadker 1982, 1994). This is particularly true in the Chinese context where educational officials and school administrators had significant positional power, and could function as decisive agents for change. Through the CCULP/SULCP projects, those Jilin educational officials and school administrators who were involved, together with other participants, came to understand that gender equity in education should be more than putting female students on an equal footing with their male peers, but acting to eliminate the barriers and stereotypes that existed and limited opportunities and choices for women (Zhao 2000). This point is perhaps best summarized in the words of a scholar who participated in the CCULP project from the Jilin Education Institute: "change is not a choice," a new concept he learned from his Canadian experience.[12] Today, female students outnumber their male peers in many Chinese universities. Certainly we can't see this change as the direct outcome of the CCULP and SULCP projects, but it might be fair to say the Regina-Jilin projects were part of the catalyst that led to such a positive change in Chinese education and society today.

CONCLUSION

Universities can be effective partners for global development. As agents of change, they are highly effective at channelling ideas and stimulating initiatives in specific target communities and in the society at large. Also, universities are long-term, permanent institutions, which provide a socially liberal environment that promotes, among other things, such values as gender equality, and independent and critical inquiry. Furthermore, universities draw on extensive networks, members of which include governments, private enterprises, and community groups, which in turn can disseminate the ideas and initiatives as well as the influence far more broadly and help to forge lasting impacts (Zha 2011a; see also Evans, chapter 2 of this volume). Research on knowledge networks shows that the diverse memberships of these structures are most effective in generating innovation and learning, and facilitating productive "encounters" between global and local knowledge. As a result, universities possess the comparative advantages that other development actors do not necessarily have, evident in (but not limited to) such features as people-to-people exchanges, cross-border knowledge mobility and joint research, which are in turn instrumental in easing the possible tensions between the "national" and the "international" elements. Such comparative advantages are clearly illustrated by the three CIDA-supported education projects involving OISE, U of A, and the University of Regina, as well as by the similar narratives in other chapters included in this volume (for examples, see chapters 2, 3, 4, and 7). Their capacity-development strategies served to multiply these comparative advantages. As a result, they established enormous networks of education scholars, in particular women scholars, many of whom went on to play key leadership roles in their institutions and fields of study. More detail on this can be found in this volume in chapter 11 by Qiang Haiyan and in chapter 13 by Ping-chun Hsiung.

Between 1981 and 2001, CIDA provided some $250 million in grants to support more than 100 linkage projects between Canadian universities (and colleges) and Chinese universities (Jackson 2003). When involved in those projects, Canadian universities served as effective organizational vehicles to enable the opening up of the Chinese education system (and in turn the society at large), and to optimize institutional capacities of the Chinese partners, as the experience of the above-mentioned projects illustrates. This experience, unfortunately, stands in contrast to Canada-China higher-education exchanges in the current context, in which Canadian universities lag behind their competitors and fail to take up the challenge of seeking long-term, stable funding for advancement of knowledge and mutual understanding with Chinese partners. Thus, Canadian universities need to retool themselves for future cooperation with their Chinese counterparts, and mobilize a new generation of faculty members and graduate students for the sake of creating knowledge networks with their Chinese partners. These are steps that should be taken by Canadian universities in preparing for the future. To strengthen this point, we would like to quote the words of a visionary colleague, Paul Evans, who said at the Tsinghua conference: "University partnerships are points of intersection that may be valuable in their own right but ultimately will be judged on whether they produce a larger societal and global good." He makes his point even more specifically in his chapter in this volume: "Getting China right will depend in large part on the expertise, understanding and relentless interactions that have no better home than universities" (chapter 2, 51). For its part, the Canadian government should understand the important and unique role played by the universities to ensure and enhance Canada's influence on the future of China's development, and provide Canadian universities with the necessary funding for the purpose of producing, together with Chinese universities, meaningful development results for a future world with complex and changing development needs. As an endorsement to this view, the German government recently announced a policy alteration, which would continue its development aid to China – not in a conventional manner, but through collaborative research between the universities, in particular in areas of health, environmental, and agricultural sciences.

NOTES

1 In accordance with the terms of the ethical protocol that was adopted for this SSHRCC supported research project, we are not at liberty to identify the names of interviewees.
2 The school is named Jingshan School (景山学校), and has been designated a pilot school for experimenting in educational and pedagogical reform programs since the early 1960s.
3 These included Beijing Normal University (in Beijing), Shaanxi Normal University (Xi'an), Northwest Normal University (Lanzhou), Northeast Normal University (Changchun), Nanjing Normal University (Nanjing), East China Normal University (Shanghai), and Southwest Normal University (Chongqing).
4 Most of the same Chinese universities continued their involvement and some new ones joined in the SULCP project, while a second Canadian university, the University of British Columbia (UBC) came on board. Now the Chinese partner institutions were Shaanxi Normal University, Northwest Normal University, Northeast Normal University, Nanjing Normal University, East China Normal University, and the Higher Education Research Institute of Huazhong University of Science and Technology (Wuhan).
5 Interview with Chinese CCULP participant on 5 July 2011 in Beijing.
6 Interview with Chinese CCULP/SULCP participant on 4 July 2011 in Beijing.
7 Interview with Chinese CCULP participant on 1 July 2011 in Beijing.
8 Interview with Chinese CCULP participant on 4 July 2011 in Beijing.
9 Interview with a Canadian CCULP project leader on 18 May 2012 in Edmonton.
10 Interview with two Canadian CCULP/SULCP project leaders on 6 October 2011 in Regina.

11 CIDA's *Policy on Women in Development and Gender Equity* set explicit objectives to "promote and support policies and activities among CIDA's partners ... which enable them to integrate gender considerations effectively into their development work" and to "support partners in voicing their concerns on gender issues" (Canadian International Development Agency 1995b, 2).
12 Interview with Chinese CCULP/SULCP participant on 13 May 2012 in Changchun.

11

Nurturing a Leadership Cohort for Chinese Faculties of Education

QIANG HAIYAN AND WANG JIAYI

INTRODUCTION

In this chapter, we reflect on two Canadian International Development Agency (CIDA) projects in education, using some concepts from dependency theory as our framework of analysis. First, we provide a general introduction to the two CIDA education projects. Second, we discuss the main concepts and how we will use them as a framework of analysis. Third, we explore the content of the CIDA projects to see if they are related to neocolonialism. Fourth, we examine the process of the project to see if any dependency existed during the cooperation. Fifth, we search the long-term progress of Chinese normal universities after the completion of the projects, to study their changes as they moved away from their periphery status. In the final part of the chapter, we relate the key concepts of dependency theory to the real experience of the two projects, and discuss perspectives for future partnerships.

INTRODUCTION TO THE TWO CIDA PROJECTS

Canada/China Joint Doctoral Programs in Education

The Canada/China Joint Doctoral Programs in Education was the first of the two CIDA projects in which we participated. Part of the Canada China University Linkage Program (CCULP, 1989–95), this project involved seven Chinese normal universities in six provinces: Beijing Normal University (BNU), Northeast Normal University (NENU), East China Normal University (ECNU), Southwest Normal University (SWNU), Shaanxi Normal University (SNU), Northwest Normal University (NWNU), and

Nanjing Normal University (NNU). The project objectives were: (1) to enhance doctoral programs in education in both countries in ways that would lay a sound basis for cooperative research in the future; (2) to support the development of innovative curricula in China; and (3) to assist the field development in educational administration in China (Hayhoe and Pan 1995).

The purpose of the project was to create cross-cultural knowledge transfer and cooperation. The hope for the project itself was to encourage reflection on various cultural and knowledge bases, leading to more mutually beneficial forms of cultural exchange. It was also a part of the internationalization of higher education in China and in Canada. The project improved teaching, research, and institution-building on both sides. It was the beginning of shared knowledge and understanding between these countries, paving the way for the formation and dissemination of new knowledge.

This project provided learning opportunities in Canada for Chinese doctoral students, and for some more experienced visiting scholars from different regions and provinces in China. They were able to work on their doctoral research or increase their academic capacities more generally at the main Canadian partner institution, the Ontario Institute for Studies in Education of the University of Toronto (OISE), and at a few other Canadian universities. The effects of the project went far beyond the participating institutions. More than 200 secondary school principals, university administrators, and teacher educators from northwest and northeast regions of China and from the Chinese Tibetan area directly benefited from this project (AUCC 2001a).

Women and Minorities as Educational Change Agents

The eleven CCULP partnerships that were considered to be the most effective were selected through a competitive process to be continued as part of the Special University Linkage Consolidation Program (SULCP, 1996–2001). The Canada/China Joint Doctoral Program in Education was one of the CCULP projects chosen, and a second project, Women and Minorities as Educational Change Agents, was built on its success. The first project had involved seven Chinese normal universities. For the second project, two well-known Canadian higher-education institutions – OISE and the University of British Columbia (UBC) – were linked as partners with five of the original Chinese normal universities and a science and engineering university, the Huazhong University of Science and Technology (HUST). Many of the key participants on the Chinese side of the project were returned scholars/doctoral graduates from the seven original Chinese institutions involved in the CCULP project. Thus, the CCULP project was the base and precondition for the SULCP project. Together with their Canadian partners, these key participants developed the SULCP project proposal: to enable women and minorities to become driving forces for educational reforms in China. The objectives of the SULCP project focused on supporting women and minority teachers at all three levels of education in forms of professional development that enabled them to become dynamic agents of social change (Qiang 2001, 1).

The SULCP project had three themes – women's participation in higher education and social progress, moral education, and cultural and language issues in minorities' schooling – and worked on these themes mainly through a series of activities involving educational innovation in China. The project helped women and minority teachers from the six provinces of Shaanxi, Hubei, Jiangsu, Gansu, Qinghai, Jilin, and Shanghai City at three educational levels: higher education, secondary education, and elementary education. Through professional training, the project enabled them to become facilitators of and contributors to educational reform, social progress, and economic development in China (AUCC 2001a).

Features of the Two Projects

These two projects were among the largest in scale of the CIDA projects, including as they did many universities and schools, and hundreds of administrators, teachers, and scholars. The projects were also some of the earliest pilot joint programs in education in China after its opening up; they also lasted the longest, for a period of twelve years, from 1989 to 2001. They were well planned and systematically implemented, and emphasized institutional and personnel development, as well as research and scholarship. They were enjoyable projects due to the cultural climate they formed, and the way they were developed by the people on both sides.

FRAMEWORK OF ANALYSIS

As mentioned by Hayhoe et al. in chapter 1 of this volume, dependency theory has been an influential theory in comparative higher-education research, being "formally presented as a methodological tool, which is most promising for educational analysis" (Velloso 1985, 207). Use of this theory has contributed to the avoidance of an uncritical acceptance of international cooperation in education, and its alleged benefits to the recipient countries. It has long been recognized that cooperative activities and projects have often been conducted mainly in the interest of developed countries, as in the case of Latin America (Velloso 1985). This chapter will use the key concepts of dependency theory – centre/periphery, dependency, and neocolonialism – as a framework to analyze these two CIDA-supported projects in education, in order to discover the indispensable conditions and factors for successful international cooperation.

Centre and Periphery

According to dependency theory, the world's higher-education system can be divided into two categories: centre and periphery. Universities in developed countries are in the centre, while universities in developing countries are in the periphery. The concept of centre and periphery has been a way of thinking about inequalities, hierarchies, and differing roles of higher education in the world (Altbach 1981).

The institutional and intellectual "centres" give direction, provide models, produce research, and function as the pinnacles of the academic system (Altbach 1981). The centres benefit from a full array of resources, and are part of an international knowledge system. They are research-oriented, with large libraries and well-equipped laboratories. They have access to the bulk of research funds, and produce a high proportion of the world's doctoral-level research degrees (Altbach 2006).

The "peripheries" copy developments from abroad, and are not at the frontiers of knowledge. Peripheral universities are distributors of knowledge through the training of students and the replication of research developed at the centres (Altbach 1981). Factors that keep universities in a peripheral position include: "brain-drain" problems, inadequate libraries, scarcity of research funding, language, and limited access to publication networks (Hayhoe et al., chapter 1 of this volume).

In this chapter, we will analyze how the Canadian partner universities as the centre worked with the Chinese partner universities as the periphery, and whether the Chinese position as periphery changed after the CIDA projects ended.

Dependency

The emphasis of dependency theory is to question the appropriateness of metropolitan country practices to peripheral countries (McLean 1983). Dependency theory shows a relationship in which peripheries are dependent in many ways on the centres for research, the communication of knowledge, and advanced training (Altbach 2007). In many ways, the actual needs of the universities in developing countries are not met through this kind of assistance (Altbach 1981).

In this chapter, we will examine whether the projects involved any dependencies in which the Chinese partner universities relied on their Canadian partners. We ask the question: Did these projects cause equity problems?

Neocolonialism

Neocolonialism describes the foreign policies used by developed countries to maintain their influence and domination over developing countries. Education is one dimension of such policies. The major practices of such policies are: foreign aid programs, which result in the continuity of dependency relations; the transplant of reinforced Western models; and the impeding of indigenous models (Qiang 1993).

Foreign aid programs that offer considerable benefit to the recipients – scholarships to study abroad, high-quality textbooks, scientific equipment, and other resources – often have the result of continuing relationships of dependency. Help from Western "experts" often reinforces Western models of academic research, Western curricula, and other aspects of Western higher education (Altbach 1981). Developing countries accept foreign educational assistance for a variety of reasons. To some degree, it is felt that any help is a useful increment toward development (Altbach 1981).

Foreign assistance in education is regarded as a double-edged sword, maintaining patterns of dependence while at the same time often providing needed technical help. However, third world nations in many instances have been too willing to accept aid without considering the manifold results (Altbach 1981). Therefore, foreign aid projects must be examined carefully for their consequences. Acceptance often means increased ties to the donor countries and institutions, and long-term dependence (Altbach 2007).

Financial support for the two CIDA education projects was provided by CIDA, and technical support was provided by Canadian universities. This chapter will carefully examine the two projects to find out whether they created or played into a continued dependency on the part of Chinese partner universities, and what significant factors contributed to the nature of dependency in the projects.

NEOCOLONIALISM OR GENUINE BENEFIT TO THE RECIPIENT?

CIDA's Human Research Development (HRD) program in China was shaped largely in response to China's initiation of an Open Door policy in 1978 and its rapid modernization process, as well as by Canada's broad-based interest in China. Canada responded to China's development plans (Boyd and Pan 2003). When the CCULP reached its end in 1995, it was due to the momentum of cross-cultural exchange and understanding between the two countries that CIDA carried out a follow-up program, the SULCP, lasting until 2001.

The duration of the CCULP and SULCP coincided with a period of significant social and economic reforms in China, which was opening up to the outside world and becoming involved in global economic life. The CCULP and SULCP projects laid particular emphasis on helping capacity-building in Chinese universities, in order to enable these higher institutions to better solve the problems caused during the development process of the country. The SULCP projects included the areas of health, education, environment, minorities' development, engineering, and agriculture, all of which were priorities of social and economic development in China (AUCC 2001a; see also chapters 3, 7, 8, 9, and 10 of this volume).

COMPARING THE NEEDS OF THE PERIPHERY WITH THE OBJECTIVES OF THE CCULP PROJECT: CANADA/CHINA JOINT DOCTORAL PROGRAM IN EDUCATION

The Need to Develop Doctoral Programs in Education

The CIDA projects had a great influence in the early years of China's Open Door policy. In the early 1980s, China began to establish doctoral programs in universities with high academic reputations. The policy in China at that time was to encourage joint training of doctoral students in all fields. In fact, there were only a few normal universities that provided doctoral programs in education, and these only enrolled two or three doctoral students every year for each doctoral program. Leading Chinese professors supervised these doctoral students, but it was a challenge for the professors because it was a new commitment. There was an urgent need for joint projects to support and develop doctoral programs in education in China. Therefore, the joint training of doctoral students in education was a main concern in the early development of our project, which exactly met the need of China's higher education at that time, especially the need of Chinese normal universities in different regions of the country.

Needs in Developing Curricula and Educational Management

During the initial decade of China's Open Door policy, we saw large gaps between China's universities and the world standard. These gaps were due to poor resources generally, a lack of resources for curriculum development, and poor English-language proficiency. Members of the faculties of education at Chinese normal universities were very interested in participating in international projects because they were aware of their periphery status and had a strong desire to move forward.

For many years, the field of education in China, including curriculum and programs, had been very narrow, as it exclusively followed the ideas of Kairov, a Soviet educator. At the beginning of these projects, sending young Chinese scholars abroad was a valuable endeavour, having the effect of updating scholars' professional knowledge and transferring new knowledge to them from more academically advanced countries. These opportunities were much-needed at the time, especially for teachers in normal universities.

The people in the periphery wished to raise their curricular and research standards, but very little funding was available to them, especially in the northwest region of China. With this large international project and its funding, it became possible to facilitate the development of faculties of education in normal universities. In this case, China's educational reform and Open Door policy made the international opportunity significant. The lack of financial support within China was a crucial causal factor to its dependency. Thus, being dependent on an international project was the choice and preference of the periphery people and their institutions, partly because it helped significantly to solve their financial shortage.

Another need during the 1980s and the early 1990s was that of educational management reform and the development of related programs in normal universities. Along with the economic reform that occurred as China shifted to a socialist market economy, both macro- and micro-management in higher-education systems needed reform. Unfortunately, between the 1950s and the early 1980s, no field or program of educational management existed in Chinese universities. Thus the reform of educational management required both theoretical and professional training, support, and guidance.

In order to meet these urgent needs in Chinese normal universities, the three objectives of the CCULP project noted earlier were constructed. The first objective involved enhancing doctoral programs in education in China and Canada for the mutual benefit of both countries, and developing a sound basis for future cooperative research. The other two objectives involved supporting the development of innovative curricula in China, and assisting programs in educational administration (Hayhoe and Pan 1995).

COMPARING THE NEEDS OF THE PERIPHERY WITH THE OBJECTIVES OF THE SULCP PROJECT: WOMEN AND MINORITIES AS EDUCATIONAL CHANGE AGENTS

The SULCP project aimed at building the capacities of universities in China, especially normal universities, to advance education reform in regard to gender, minority, and moral education. The project objectives focused on supporting women and minority teachers at higher education, secondary, and elementary education levels, in professional development that would enable them to become dynamic agents of social change (Boyd and Pan 2001).

The first project objective focused on schooling in minority cultures. For many years there had been a general lack of culturally relevant and bilingual curriculum for minority groups in China. This lack resulted in considerable resistance from minority families to compulsory-level schooling, based on both cultural and economic concerns (Boyd and Pan 2001).[1] Since the curriculum material did not include respectful attention to important aspects of their culture, minority parents were concerned that schooling was not relevant to their cultural heritage. Furthermore, the issue was exacerbated by the lack of material in minority languages, particularly since such material can be a successful vehicle for cultural maintenance (Qiang 2001). Being aware of these cultural and language concerns, the first project objective focused on helping women and minority teachers to integrate indigenous knowledge into the curriculum in order to ensure that minority cultures were included in mainstream teaching and to develop more effective approaches to bilingual teaching and learning (Boyd and Pan 2001).

The second project objective focused on moral education. There had been a growing awareness among moral educators in the 1990s that traditional Chinese pedagogical approaches were not appropriate for addressing democratic processes of social change. In short, the concern was that these approaches were too teacher-centred, didactic, prescriptive, and dogmatic. They were seen as working against the need to support the development of students' critical judgment for dealing with moral issues in their lives and in society (Qiang 2001). Thus this objective sought to support both female and male teachers in their roles as moral educators and reflective practitioners during the period of rapid social change in China (Boyd and Pan 2001).

The third objective focused on women faculty members at higher-education institutions. During the 1980s and 1990s, along with the economic development in China, there were a number of interrelated challenges and barriers to the development of gender equity in Chinese institutions of higher education. Career and job opportunities for female college graduates became more difficult, and women's participation in academic work was constantly discouraged by significant barriers to promotion (Qiang 2001). In fact, women had much less opportunity than their male colleagues to study overseas, participate in academic conferences, and obtain research funds. The economic reforms did not automatically create better opportunities and development for women in higher education. Therefore, this objective offered teaching and research opportunities to women faculty members in institutes of higher learning to enhance their leadership capacity (Boyd and Pan 2001).

The three objectives of the SULCP project were facilitative and identical in their provision of both financial aid and technical support to meet the urgent needs of the periphery.

THE CENTRE'S INFLUENCE ON CHINESE RETURNEES

According to dependency theory, "brain drain," or the issue of non-returnees, is a common problem for periphery universities in developing countries. It is believed that brain drain has negative impacts on academic development for the periphery universities (Altbach 2007). Therefore, the effects of advanced training abroad should be examined more carefully from the viewpoint of the Third World (Altbach 1981). Two indicators should be used to analyze the effects of overseas studies: one is, of course, the return rate; the other is the relevance of what has been learned abroad.

During the two project periods, and especially during the first project, the relationship between Chinese educational institutions and their Canadian partners was a dependent centre-periphery one in which brain drain was a very serious concern. These two projects successfully solved this problem and achieved a very high return rate by carefully selecting candidates to study abroad, by choosing appropriate programs and courses, and by bearing responsibility for the projects' commitment to the Chinese partner universities. However, it is still crucial to find out what Chinese participants learned in Canada, how they benefited from their experience in Canada, and the relevance of what they learned to their own professional work and to educational development and reform in China.

Fruitful Learning Experiences and Outcomes

Their studies in Canadian partner universities had a great and life-long influence on Chinese scholars and doctoral students. This opportunity increased both their research abilities and their theoretical level. Specifically, the English proficiency of Chinese scholars and doctoral students was greatly increased by their studies abroad. Due to English, as an international language, being essential for worldwide communication, increasing English proficiency is a very meaningful step for people moving from the periphery toward world standards, allowing them to expose themselves to current research in their areas.

Chinese universities during the 1980s and 1990s had very little academic information and very few Western books. At that time, Chinese scholars and students were highly dependent on "centre" libraries and their abundant research outcomes and findings. Thus, the academic information present in Canadian libraries was very beneficial to visiting Chinese scholars and doctoral students.

Understanding of Canadian Education Systems

In this multicultural world, it makes sense to obtain cross-cultural understanding in education. Most of us, as Chinese educators, knew nothing about Canada and its education system before the two projects started. It was almost a cultural shock to see Canadian schools and their classroom teaching and learning environments. Visiting Chinese scholars and doctoral students also took the opportunities provided by "after-class curricula" to experience Canadian culture and education in many ways, such as watching films on women's issues, joining voluntary social activities, visiting aboriginal people and their universities, and visiting special schools and learning-resource centres. They were curious about how Canadian scholars worked and how their institutions were managed, and found many things to appreciate or to compare with their own practices. Therefore, many of these returnees integrated their knowledge about Canadian education with their own experiences in Canada in order to produce courses upon their return such as "Comparative Education," "Western Educational History," and "Modern Education in Western Countries."

Enriched Curriculum and Improved Pedagogy

These two projects had the important effect of enriching Chinese curricula by integrating new knowledge into curriculum contents. Educators' experiences in Canada supported the development of new ideas and curricula in education. For example, Wu Kangning's *Educational Sociology*, a textbook for graduate-course teaching based in part on his experiences while visiting Canada, introduced many new ideas and approaches.

The projects helped Chinese returnees to improve their teaching at their home universities. They learned to provide course outlines for their classes and to encourage students to express their opinions.

The Development of New Curricula and Textbooks

The new textbooks and course activities introduced by the projects emphasized indigenous cultures and the value of women's participation in education, rather than transferring the Western or centre's values and models into the periphery. For example, the *Tibetan Culture Reading Book* is a "first of its kind" in China. This textbook was the outcome of innovative collaborative work between Chinese returned scholars, minority scholars, and teachers. It filled a glaring gap in the development of indigenous knowledge-based curricula to aid minority students in maintaining their cultural inheritance, and it received favourable attention from the Department of Minority Education of the Ministry of Education (MOE), provincial governments, Tibetan communities, and minority schools. The textbook was used in many Tibetan schools (Qiang 2001).

The Development of New Fields of Studies

Chinese returnees from the two projects developed new fields of study in education, gender-equity education, multicultural education, and special education for their home universities. Here we take gender-equity education as one example.

Before the CIDA projects, Chinese scholars and teachers were unaware of the term "gender-equity education," which was not a field in China at that time. Chinese experiences in Canada played an important role in initiating and developing this field in China. In particular, the projects had a strong emphasis on women's participation, and helped Chinese women scholars lay a foundation for the future development of studies on women and gender-equity education (Hsiung, chapter 13 of this volume).

The project's onset, which involved women scholars studying in Canada, was perfectly timed on the wave of the women's movement in China. After studying gender-equity issues in Canada, this field became Zheng Xinrong's mainstream work in China. Her textbook *Women and Social Development*, along with other books on the topic of gender and education produced by returned woman scholars, have had a major impact on the development of curricula on women's issues at universities across China (Qiang 2001). Meanwhile, the field of women's studies benefited not only in terms of women's equal participation in higher education, but also in terms of academic development. Both male and female scholars benefited from the new content and the new feminist methods of research that were introduced.

The Exploration of New Ways of Thinking

Chinese participants in the projects learned many new theories and approaches, advanced research methods, and different perspectives toward education, as well as cross-cultural understanding in Canada. All of these had a part in helping people to think differently. The CIDA project activities also opened people's minds and stimulated their ways of thinking. We take an example from the sub-project focusing on moral education.

The moral education project activities had a significant influence on the Chinese scholars, teachers, and principals involved. Participants learned how to analyze their decisions from moral, environmental, political, and economic perspectives; that is, how to analyze an issue from various angles. Having learned it themselves, teachers were then able to instruct children to look at issues in multi-dimensional perspectives and to compare different points of view and values. This new way of thinking helped both adults and school children to make better decisions on moral issues. It was also a way to help teachers to shift their teaching approaches away from the teacher-centred, didactic, and dogmatic, and toward a more reflective moral education. In fact, this shift has been encouraged by the National Curriculum Reform for Basic Education in China.

INEQUALITY OR EQUITY-ORIENTED PARTNERSHIP?

Equity Awareness through Cross-Cultural Learning and Communication

Equity awareness was present from the very beginning of the first project, and all the way through the whole process of the two projects. The CCULP provided plenty of opportunities in cross-cultural learning and communication, both by the doctoral students exchange program, and by specially planned conferences. As noted in chapter 10, both the Canadian and Chinese sides of the project were determined that their partnership would not simply be a conventional effort to "upgrade" academic programs in China on the basis of Western expertise, but rather be a process of mutual enrichment. Canadian students and scholars would learn from the wealth of educational knowledge and experience in China's rich civilization, while Chinese students and scholars received extended exposure to a Western academic environment.

In addition, senior scholars in education from Chinese normal universities were invited to come to Canada to make presentations at conferences and to visit doctoral programs in education across Canada. This process opened up a "dialogue between civilizations" involving mutual respect and cross-cultural learning (Hayhoe and Pan 2001). The theme of the second conference during this project, "Indigenous Knowledge and Cultural Interchange: Challenges to the Idea of the University," directly addressed some of the ways in which Eastern approaches to knowledge, and the institutional patterns of higher education in Eastern traditions, might contribute to a rethinking of the university in the twenty-first century. The conference activities and its proceedings, entitled "East-West Dialogue in Knowledge and Higher Education," were great opportunities for mutual learning for many Chinese and Canadian faculty members and students (Hayhoe and Pan 1996).

After experiencing a Western environment, Chinese participants realized the importance of cross-cultural communication and understanding. They found that Canadian cultural approaches and ways of looking at educational problems were very different from those in China. Therefore, going abroad and the ensuing cross-cultural communications were important to enable Chinese scholars and doctoral students to open up their minds. On the other hand, research done by "insiders" within China, along with the insiders' viewpoints, were seldom introduced into Western countries. In order to facilitate cross-cultural learning and communication, Qiang Haiyan gave a talk on women's education in China at OISE as a visiting scholar in 1991. This talk attracted many of OISE's professors and graduate students. It was very rare in the early 1990s to have a scholar from the periphery give an academic talk in a "centre" institution.

Partnership Principles and Strategies for Cooperation

Despite the well-recognized and significant dangers of cultural imperialism – which, based on dependency theory, are inherent in international aid projects, as well as anchored in and inherently tied to Western culture, interests, and economic power – Professor Ruth Hayhoe's belief is that it is possible to orient projects in potentially positive ways (Boyd and Pan 2003, 53). The partnership between the two sides of the Special University Linkages Consolidation Program (SULCP) project justified her belief. This was a truly collaborative relationship: jointly designed, and jointly implemented, managed, and evaluated. The partners on both sides felt respected and treated equally (see chapter 1 of this volume).

Hayhoe interprets Galtung's four guiding principles that can function as constraints on tendencies to imperialism or dependency as follows: "'Equity' suggests project aims and forms of organization that are reached through full mutual agreement between centre and periphery. 'Autonomy' requires that centre participants respect the theoretical perspectives rooted in peripheral culture and gain a thorough knowledge of this culture. 'Solidarity' means that forms of organization should encourage maximum interaction among peripheral participants and growing links between them and their fellow researchers. 'Participation' indicates an approach to knowledge that does not stratify in a hierarchical way but assumes the possibility of a creative peripheral contribution from the very beginning" (Hayhoe 1989, 134). The project's strategies for cooperation clearly reflected the principles of "equity," "solidarity," and "participation." "Autonomy," however, is a very challenging principle for people in the "centre," and there were difficulties to be overcome in realizing this principle.

The cooperative strategies of the SULCP project mainly involved joint workshops and subsequent research activities at the six sites in China: SNU, Xi'an; HUST, Wuhan; NWNU, Lanzhou; NENU, Changchun; NNU,

Nanjing; and ECNU, Shanghai. Two sites concentrated on each of the three project objectives (described earlier in this chapter). Each workshop lasted seven to ten days. A team of two Canadian scholars from OISE/UT and/or UBC collaborated with Chinese colleagues led by Chinese participants of the CCULP project to provide theoretical, methodological, and pedagogical perspectives that might be used by Chinese scholars and teachers in the six universities to address perceived educational problems. The research topics pertaining to these problems were collaboratively designed in the first workshop, which was conducted by the Chinese participants, and were then discussed with the Canadian team in a subsequent workshop before being carried out. Results from the research were then analyzed, refined, and published in the form of books, journal articles, and curricular innovations, facilitated by extended visits of Chinese scholars to the two Canadian institutions. As a final activity, an international conference took place in Lanzhou, China, at which scholars shared and disseminated their research findings and the practical implications of their research (Qiang 2001).

Cooperation as a Learning Process

The CCULP project invested a great deal of money in activities to stimulate cross-cultural understanding and communication, laying a significant foundation for the deep cooperative research and developmental work of the SULCP project. However, challenges, misunderstandings, and frustrated feelings did occur to "centre" partners during the cooperative process. It was quite difficult for them to gain understanding of the deep perspectives rooted in peripheral culture, and a *thorough* knowledge of them. This effort was mandated and shaped in large part by the principle of "equity," but its realization involved challenges (Boyd and Pan 2003). We relate here an interesting story about these challenges.

At the very beginning, Canadian partners recognized the need to involve potential Chinese partners in a substantive way. The actual work for the project proposal had to address the needs articulated by the Chinese participants. In a spirit of partnership, the Canadians attempted to elicit concrete indications from their Chinese counterparts, such as specific ideas about research interests, materials needed, and the kinds of input that were required from the Canadians. However, for the most part, this process was not successful. Initial responses were in the general form of "We would like to hear from the Western experts – please give us some lectures." In response to requests for substantive reaction to a number and variety of topic suggestions, the reply was always in the form of "Yes, that's fine," causing frustration to Canadian team members (Boyd and Pan 2003).

However, the picture was different when looked at through Chinese eyes. There were three reasons for these types of responses, one of which was the language insufficiency. The place of English at the pinnacle of scientific communication gives a significant advantage to those who speak English as a native language. Others must communicate in a foreign language and conform to unfamiliar academic norms (Altbach 2007). The English language was a big challenge for the Chinese participants, especially when they were in the joint planning process. Many of them did not clearly understand what their Canadian partners were talking about, so it was hard to respond in specific and concrete ways, and they were reluctant to ask "I beg your pardon?" too many times.

The second reason was the mental status of periphery scholars. The Chinese partners realized their periphery situation, which might be described as "poor," "lower level," "lower quality," "disadvantaged," or "less developed." They understood that Canadian partners were in a "centre" position, very advanced, very developed, with high research standards and a high quality of education. As the periphery, their sense of inferiority was an obstacle that affected their free expression of ideas. Therefore, their frequent responses were "Yes, that is fine," indicating agreement with the centre. This was the attitude of dependency upon the centre.

The third reason stemmed from culturally rooted behaviour patterns. According to Chinese culture, modesty is the most appreciated behaviour and attitude toward others. In addition to their inferiority mentality and their motivation to push forward China's modernization, the Chinese participants behaved like very good learners, as shown in the many responses of "We would like to hear from the Western experts – please give us some lectures."

Canadian partners also encountered difficulties in China due to not understanding the Chinese language. As one Canadian put it, "We are treated like instant experts in a Confucian society where teachers are revered, but we experience ourselves as a caricature of the expert, marginal to the central undertaking. We are asked to speak and quoted to provide authority like a Confucian text, but our words are reinterpreted in ways we have no control over, and often are not particularly happy with" (Boyd and Pan 2003, 64).

It is crucial to anticipate and plan for difficulties in communication. The implementation of a project like this one is a process of learning for partners on both sides, especially in developing cross-cultural sensitivity and deep understanding.

Friendship-Building through Cooperation

One of the most significant factors contributing to the success of the two projects was Professor Ruth Hayhoe. She is a symbol of the friendship in education between Canada and China. She has a deep understanding of China's culture, history, and education, and speaks fluent Chinese. Throughout the cooperative projects, she was an excellent role model on building friendships between cultures. She hosted many Chinese scholars and doctoral students in her home. Even during a very personal family event, Hayhoe considered the education of rural children in China: at her request, instead of gifts, guests at her wedding donated Can$2,000 to rural schools in Guansu Province to buy books for small libraries in rural schools and to provide scholarships for girl students from poor families.

The cooperative project was also a process of friendship-building between participants. For example, through the language immersion cooperative work, Professor Linda Siegel and her Chinese partners developed deep friendships. They called each other "Canadian mother" and "Chinese mother," meaning that they took care of each other and those they were mentoring in all ways. Dr Julia Pan, a Chinese-Canadian and co-director on the Canadian side, had an important role in building bridges between Canadians and Chinese participants. Not only did she help Canadian scholars understand Chinese culture, she also made close connections with Chinese project directors, and offered a great deal of help in meeting any and all needs of visiting Chinese scholars and doctoral students in Canada.

STAYING AT THE PERIPHERY OR MOVING TOWARD THE CENTRE?

The CCULP and SULCP projects finished successfully nineteen and thirteen years ago, respectively. Reviewing the projects' history and reflecting on the changes after them will help us to identify the current status of Chinese normal universities in relation to their former Canadian partner institutions, in terms of centre-periphery.

Context and Resources

With China's rapid economic development over the last twenty years, universities' infrastructure in China has improved significantly, and the Chinese government's investment in research is increasing every year.

Chinese universities are no longer in the periphery in terms of resources. However, the context of globalization demands the internationalization of higher education, thus international exchange activities and cooperative research are highly valued in Chinese universities.

Therefore, Chinese universities still have a strong motive for international partnerships in education and research, but are no longer dependent on foreign aid programs. The national and provincial governments, as well as the universities, finance a great many teachers, scholars, and students every year to go abroad for academic and educational experience. The return rate is now very high, so brain drain is almost no longer a problem. All universities in China are expected to be international. In many normal universities, one year of overseas study experience is even a necessary requirement for academic promotion. The School of Education in NENU has a training plan for young teachers abroad, and many Chinese education professors have gone to Canada on educational visits, supported by their own research funds, while exploring the possibilities for cooperation.

The Academic Gap between Periphery and Centre

There are two stories we cannot forget about the conditions in Chinese universities during the 1990s. Wang Jiayi was a doctoral student in the CCULP project. When he returned to China, the project gave him a computer to take back for his research work at his home university. This became great news that spread throughout the project's circles in China, because at that time having a computer was a luxury. When Qiang Haiyan became one of the Chinese directors of the SULCP project, she was the first and only person to use email in SNU. Even a vice-president and a science professor asked her to help them in sending email messages!

With the rapid development of Chinese higher education and its massification, and with improved teaching and research conditions, much better conditions exist now at China's universities in terms of equipment, libraries, and hardware of various kinds. Since the beginning of the twenty-first century, information technology in China has allowed the convenience of obtaining academic resources from the Internet and from databases. Scholars in Chinese universities are no longer dependent on visiting "centre" universities to search their on-site libraries of research literature.

In terms of scholarship, China has made great progress, and significantly upgraded its standards. The two CIDA projects in education were especially helpful in facilitating the academic upgrading of Chinese scholars and teachers. For example, gender studies in China now produce high-quality research and have a high academic reputation. Women leaders in Chinese universities now have a scholarly basis to support them in exerting leadership and in making their voices heard in male leadership circles. Many reforms and improvements in research methods and scholarship have been carried out in the field of education. Graduate programs in education have also been opened and enhanced. For example, one third of graduate students in comparative education at South China Normal University (SCNU) now have the chance to go abroad as exchange students, 60 per cent of doctoral students in comparative education at SCNU have degrees from foreign countries, and almost all Chinese doctoral students go abroad for course learning or field study for their dissertations.

A Leadership Cohort Nurtured for International Cooperation in Education

These two CIDA-supported projects have nurtured a leadership cohort in education in China for international cooperation and exchange programs. After the projects' completion, the participating Chinese universities and scholars continued to work with their former Canadian partners, and also began cooperative initiatives with new partners from other countries, resulting in many cooperative projects and programs for research and professional development.

Chinese Professor Zheng Xinrong and Canadian Professor Ping-chun Hsiung have continued their cooperation long after the projects finished. Together, they organized a summer institute on feminist pedagogy (see chapter 14 of this volume). Chinese scholars and the Institute of Moral Education in NNU continued their research on moral education in partnership with Canadian professors Mary Lou Arnold, Dwight Boyd, and Charles Helwig as adjunct professors and foreign advisers and as expert members of the Academic Advisory Board for the *Chinese Journal of Moral Education*.

The capacity Chinese scholars built through their cooperation with Canadian partners helped them a great deal in expanding the concept of partnership to include other countries, and also in enabling them to successfully lead and manage other international projects. Since then, these scholars have been invited as visiting scholars to other Western countries, including as part of the US Fulbright program. Many have taken on other new and exciting roles, such as becoming a consultant for the UK's Department for International Development (DFID), being placed in charge of a United Board For Christian Higher Education in Asia project, becoming education consultants for the World Bank, being placed in charge of a UNICEF project, becoming an official staff member in UNESCO's Beijing office, and being in charge of joint projects with American, Japanese, and British partners. The link between Qiang Haiyan's team in China and Linda Siegel's team in Canada in English immersion education has already lasted seventeen years, and will continue into the future. Their joint efforts for an English immersion program in China have also attracted American scholars and their universities to participate.

Many Chinese scholars in education have attended international conferences to present their papers, resulting in papers jointly or independently published in leading English journals of education in Western countries. For example, the journal of *International Education* in the US has a special issue dedicated to the research findings on English immersion in China. These Chinese scholars with experience in international projects have a mission to step out on China's behalf to do international development work or to provide models for other countries. From this leadership cohort in international relations in education, we can see a significant movement away from the periphery.

A Cohort of Academic and Educational Leaders Nurtured for Domestic Development

The CIDA projects have also nurtured a cohort of leadership in education in China. These leading academics have been making great contributions to their faculties of education and normal universities, to both local and national education reforms, and also to the educational development of disadvantaged groups in China. They have become leaders of educational and academic institutions, playing important roles in decision-making related to educational reforms, and in making efforts to move China from its periphery status in education.

The former Chinese doctoral students in the joint doctoral programs and the young teachers returned from Canada are now leaders in different areas of education as leading professors, doctoral program supervisors and directors, directors of research centres or research institutes, deans and vice-deans of faculties of education in normal universities, chairs or associate chairs of academic/professional associations at provincial and national levels, one president and several vice-presidents of normal universities, and a director of a provincial education bureau.

CCULP visiting scholar Fang Junming developed the first doctoral program in special education in China, and has become one of the top three academic scholars in that field nationwide. CCULP doctoral student Tian Huisheng served as vice-president of the National Institute of Education Sciences in Beijing (NIES, 2002–11), which established the first research institute on educational experimentation in China and the National Educational Experimentation Association.

CCULP doctoral student Zheng Xinrong is now a member of the Beijing People's Political Consultative Committee. She was involved in drafting China's most recent Five Year Plan in Education, and was influential in shaping the national research priorities established in it, as well as in promoting the development of educational research in gender issues across the whole country (Qiang, 2001).

The government has established centres of regional curriculum reform at six universities, and the one at NWNU is responsible for some of this curriculum-related research and for developing relevant regional curriculum in the northwest region of China. Two leading specialists of the CIDA projects, Wang Jiayi and Wan Minggang, are actively involved in these efforts (Qiang 2001). The leading scholars nurtured by the CIDA projects have contributed significantly to the national base for moral education at NNU, for minority education at NWNU, and for rural basic education at NENU (Qiang 2001).

CONCLUSION

The Relationship between Centre and Periphery

The issues of educational borrowing and dependency are of continuing concern and importance. The centre-periphery concept is still given a crucial place in educational dependency analyses. Studies emphasize the impact of educational transfers from developed states to the less-developed. In many cases, these studies document the influence of one metropolitan nation or its agencies on a third world county. As described by McLean, "When the centre-periphery concept is linked to ideas of underdevelopment and dependency it is assumed that transfers from the metropolis to the periphery are harmful ... Broader inquiries would probably throw doubt on this argument. More analysis is required of instances of appropriate transplants as well as dysfunctional and unwelcome transfers" (1983, 33).

Through the case analysis of these two CIDA projects, we find that the relationship of centre-periphery does not inevitably result in dependency, and that the dependency of periphery upon centre is neither inevitably unequal nor a matter of domination. "The approach should be not to show simply that dependency is harmful but to analyze the degree to which it is accepted by local governments and the circumstances in which this acceptance takes place" (McLean 1983, 39). In fact, the participants in the periphery in the two CIDA projects played an active and positive role during the whole process. Periphery participants also have an active role in reacting toward the influence of the centre (Qiang 1993). Noah and Eckstein (1990) pointed out that dependency theory neglects the fact that people in the periphery are not simple subjects to be controlled and dominated.

In addition, dependency theory neglects the value and meaning of educational borrowing, which is a worldwide phenomenon and a mutual learning process with multiple dimensions. Centre and periphery can learn from each other and can share knowledge across civilizations. The relationship between centre and periphery in the two CIDA projects was equal in nature, with mutual respect, mutual understanding, and mutual benefits.

The Relationship between International Projects and Neocolonialism

International projects and foreign aid programs do not necessarily result in neocolonialism. However, equity, mutual respect, and mutual benefit are not automatic outcomes of such projects and programs either. Obtaining such mutuality requires a great deal of endeavour by both sides, especially on the part of the centre. Professor Ruth Hayhoe, the leading scholar and core designer of the two CIDA projects, played the key role for this endeavour on the Canadian side, and acted as a bridge for the Chinese side.

The four principles for partnership insisted on by Hayhoe – equity, autonomy, solidarity, and participation – can be seen through the whole process of the two CIDA projects in designing, reaching agreement on objectives, implementation, cooperative work, outcomes sharing, communication, and evaluation.

By reviewing the two CIDA projects, we discover that a successful international project or foreign aid program is based on the following essential factors: project objectives must meet the urgent needs of the periphery; project planning and implementation must be participated in and decided on by both centre and periphery; participants from both sides should develop their awareness, knowledge, and capacity in cross-cultural understanding; and overseas studies in centre institutions must be relevant to the domestic development needs of the periphery.

As a great achievement of the two CIDA projects, Chinese academic standards in education, faculties of education, and normal universities are moving away from the periphery and toward centre positions. Even though Altbach (1981) believed that movement from the periphery to the centre was not impossible, he saw it as very difficult. The two CIDA projects have helped make this movement not only possible, but also successful.

Expectations on Future Partnerships in Education

"Globalization in higher education and science is inevitable ... Modern technology, the Internet, the increasing ease of communication, and the flow of students and highly educated personnel across borders enhances globalization. No academic system exists by itself in the world of the 21st century" (Altbach 2007, 38). As globalization underscores the importance of cross-cultural experience, the number of students in overseas exchange programs in Chinese universities has increased enormously. Studying abroad has become a very popular phenomenon in Chinese higher education.

Higher education in China is experiencing rapid development, building up flagship universities such as 98/5 and 21/1 universities, and expanding the numbers of institutions and their enrolments. China has increased access to the human, physical, and informational resources needed to produce higher education at the highest level of excellence, to build universities' research capacity in a post-industrial knowledge economy, and to push forward scientific and technological frontiers. From 1995 to 2005, the number of articles published by Chinese scholars in leading scientific and engineering journals more than quadrupled. Only the US, the UK, Germany, and Japan account for more publications (Levin 2010, 15). The development of Chinese normal universities has a similar trend and direction, driving for excellence in education and research in a strong movement toward the "centre."

However, although the gap between higher education in China and Canada has narrowed considerably, it still exists. Canadian universities' reputations are among the highest in the world. When comparing Canadian teacher education and academic research in education, Canadian universities rank higher than their Chinese counterparts.

Therefore, we would like to work with top-class Canadian universities to further improve our teaching quality and research capacity in various areas of education science in which Canada is still a "centre." In these areas, China is no longer peripheral, but might be seen as having a "semi-periphery" status.

In the future, we would like to cooperate with Canadian partners in joint research at deeper and higher levels, in joint doctoral programs, and in university-level collaborations. The context of globalization demands internationalization of higher education. We expect to explore further collaboration in education with potential Canadian partners. We have moved from the periphery to the semi-periphery largely due to the two CIDA projects described in this chapter. Even though financial aid is now neither urgent nor necessary to Chinese universities, technical support will continually be helpful to the Chinese side. We hope to continue learning and borrowing from Canadian education systems. In the future, Canada-China university linkages and collaborations will continue to play a very important role.

NOTE

1 Qiang Haiyan's 2001 project report, which is listed in the bibliography, was incorporated into Boyd and Pan's (2001) paper entitled *Final Assessment: Women and Minorities as Educational Change Agents*. This chapter draws many points from these two documents.

12

Sino-Canadian Legal Partnerships in Law and Education: Genesis, Groundwork, and Growth

GUY LEFEBVRE, MARIE-CLAUDE RIGAUD, AND ELIZABETH STEYN

INTRODUCTION

In his seminal work *The Way*, Taoist philosopher Lao Tzu famously remarked, "A journey of a thousand miles must begin with a single step." Our first step took the form of the Canada-China Senior Judges Training Project. This project provided the spark for close and continued collaboration with the China University of Political Science and Law (CUPL) and with other Chinese universities on a bilateral basis. In turn, it established our credibility in China and helped us to develop valuable relationships and a reputation that ultimately enabled us to explore other collaboration opportunities, first within China and now looking beyond its vast frontiers, with China as our partner.

This chapter will trace the evolution of our Sino-Canadian legal partnerships from that initial spark. First, we will consider the Judges Training Project in its socio-historical context, explain its conceptual functioning, and analyze the lessons learned and perspectives gained. Second, we will look at some contemporary initiatives, including our collaboration with CUPL and other Chinese institutions, our master of laws (LLM) Business Law in a Global Context, and the Université de Montréal (UdeM) China Scholarship Council Doctoral Program for Chinese students. Third, we will draw some conclusions on the benefits and challenges inherent in international partnerships and reflect on the future of our expanding model of cooperation, both within China and with China as our partner.

As a preliminary observation, we wish to point out that the international education business has grown by leaps and bounds over the last four decades, a phenomenon that is particularly striking with regard to Asia. The number of foreign students internationally increased threefold during the period 1975–2007 to three million (Vincent-Lancrin 2011, 94).[1] In mobility terms, Asia accounted for 49 per cent of all international tertiary-level students in the OECD area in 2007 (Vincent-Lancrin 2011, 96). It is clear, therefore, that the time was ripe for the launching of our Sino-Canadian partnerships – and, as can be seen below, the need was pressing.

GENESIS ("THE JUDGES")

Socio-Historical Context: Legal Reform in China

In a widely publicized 1996 speech, President Jiang Zemin pointed to the rule of law as being indicative of the level of social progress attained by a society, as well as its civilization. He concluded that it was accordingly required for the successful construction of a modern socialist state in China (Chen 2000, 127). This idea gained concrete form in 1997 when the Central Committee of the Chinese Communist Party (CCP) formally adopted the program of "governance according to law," a decision that had the effect of equating the importance of the policy status of governance according to law with the policy of economic reform and modernization (Biddulph 2010, 272).

In March 1999, the National People's Congress (NPC) adopted a constitutional amendment that formally changed Article 5 of the Constitution of the People's Republic of China to provide that: "The People's Republic of China shall practice ruling the country according to the law, and shall construct a socialist rule-of-law state" (Chen 2000, 128).[2] The Supreme People's Court (SPC) immediately announced a five-year plan to build a "fair, open, highly effective, honest, and well-functioning" judicial system, with "judicial fairness" (*sifa gongzheng*) at its crux (Gechlik 2006, 98).[3] This would provide the necessary institutional framework for the Judges Training Project, which took place from 1997–2001. Complementary to this, developments in Chinese legal training would create the necessary demand for the project, as can be seen from the section below.

Socio-Historical Context: Legal Training in China

Since the re-establishment of the Ministry of Justice after the Cultural Revolution in 1979, China's contemporary legal education environment has been distinguished by a significant augmentation in law school and student numbers,[4] as well as an improvement in institutional and educational resources for these schools.[5] In addition to legal practice, legal education has been considered to be a good preparation for a career in business or in the government service (He 2006, 147). This has meant that both political and legal institutions in China have often required candidates for top-level positions to pass a law exam[6] (Gechlik 2006, 110), giving rise to a generation of "lawyer-statesmen [who] are brokers between market and state" (Liu 2013, 687).

Zou (2003, 161) estimates that legal education has played a critical role in the Chinese reform era, dating back to 1978,[7] and Biddulph (2010, 260) emphasizes that it has underpinned programs of economic modernization, as well as legal governance.[8] Due to the market-oriented economic development, a high degree of demand has furthermore developed for sophisticated legal services.[9]

It is against this background that the Senior Judges Training Project came into being and that the later bilateral cooperation agreements with CUPL and certain other Chinese universities were concluded.

Senior Judges Training Project: Project Description

The Senior Judges Training Project drew its origins from a letter of intent signed in 1994 between Premier Li Peng of the People's Republic of China and Canadian Prime Minister Jean Chrétien. It was a $4.2 million project, promoted by the United Nations Development Program (UNDP) and funded by the Canadian International Development Agency (CIDA).[10]

The project spanned the years 1997–2001, and comprised two generations of trainees. It was aimed at assisting China with the new demands that globalization placed on the judiciary (UdeM Consortium 1999b, 1).

There were three main objectives to the project: an introduction to Western legal theory and practice; the training of judges "to become agents for change"; and a process of empowerment to allow the judges to become educators of other judges (UdeM Consortium 1999a, 6). In this way, it was hoped to contribute to the development of judicial independence, the sensitization of the profession to gender issues and ethnic differences, as well as the enhancement of the rule of law.[11]

The project consisted of three blocks and had legs in both China and Canada. The first phase, dubbed the In-China Training Program, lasted for three months and served as preparation for the second, the In-Canada Training Program. During the first phase, the judges were introduced to

Canadian legal systems, legal English, and the teaching of law. At the end of the block, candidates were selected among the participants to continue with phase two in Canada.

Phase two, the In-Canada Training Program, was divided into two parts: eight months' formal training followed by two months' internship with law firms and judges. Formal training consisted of two units on substantive law[12] and one unit each on legal theory, judicial practice, and adult education.[13]

Judicial practice seminars were held once a week for twelve weeks over two semesters. They consisted of sessions hosted by judges of the Appeal Court, the Superior Court, the Provincial Court of Quebec, the Federal Court, and by officers from other jurisdictions such as the Securities Commission.[14] The internships were intended as practical exposure to the Canadian legal system[15] and involved the participation of both litigation lawyers and judges as mentors and peers (UdeM Consortium 1999b, 7–8).[16]

The third phase, known as the Graduate upon Return Program, contained two units: the development of a fifteen-hour course portfolio on various aspects of law covered during phase two, for delivery to senior judges in China, and activities aimed at developing skills in using different teaching media.[17] The project furthermore included the organization of six joint seminars in China.[18] The program culminated with the judges obtaining a graduate degree from the UdeM.

Senior Judges Training Project: Conceptual Explanation

The UdeM viewed the Judges Training Project as a pilot. Early on, it was recognized as "the first and most elaborate project of its kind to be conducted by CIDA in China" (UdeM 2002, 2.2).[19] The project methodologies applied were both innovative and conceived specifically for purposes of the project.

Open exploration of commonalities and differences between the Canadian and Chinese systems was integral to the approach, which took place in an educational setting of mutual learning. The instructional approach was learner-focused, in that learning experiences were conceived bearing in mind the context in which the judges had operated in the past and would again operate in the future. Thus the design systematically used Chinese law as a departure point, enabling trainees to reflect on the values underlying their own system as the window through which alternative legal models and values were introduced. Accordingly, the Canadian professors were required to familiarize themselves with the basic features of Chinese law from sources in English or French. They were thus empowered to explain Western law in a way more easily accessible to the judges (Canada/China Senior Judges Training Project 1998, 2). Finally, the learning model linked legal practice and theory back to their social, political, and economic contexts (UdeM Consortium 1999b, 1).[20]

Senior Judges Training Project: Analysis

Throughout the project, we expressly recognized that we were dealing with vastly different cultures and legal systems, being careful to work from a basis of mutual respect.[21] We strived to give effect to our understanding that simply because our Chinese students had a different way of viewing things did not render those views ill-founded or misplaced.[22]

One of the most important lessons we learned was the importance of preparing agents for change in developing countries, so as to enable them to intervene effectively when opportunities arose.[23] This turned out to be crucial given the rapid pace of reform in China, law being known to both respond to and influence societal change (UdeM 2002, 3.1).[24]

We gained some important perspectives from our interactions with various aspects of Chinese culture,[25] which in turn led us to reflect on and re-evaluate aspects of our own legal tradition.[26] We refer here to Confucian ideas such as: mediation as preferred dispute resolution mechanism; moral governance; flexibility in the enforcement, education, and reform of offenders; and the importance accorded to achieving a balance in the interests of society's members (Baraban 1998, 1254).[27]

GROUNDWORK AND GROWTH ("THE PRESENT")

The Context of Internationalization

The trend toward internationalization of higher education has multiple contributing causes.[28] Canadian universities have undergone important change relating to efforts to internationalize their curricula, the encouragement offered to students to study abroad, as well as efforts undertaken to attract international students to Canadian campuses (Farr 2007, 32).[29] The UdeM is no exception, formulating its first comprehensive internationalization strategy in 2000 and intrinsically revising it in 2006 (UdeM 2006).

In its recently published policy document, *Canada's International Education Strategy*, the Canadian government unveiled ambitious internationalization goals: it aims to double the number of long-term (six months or longer) international students in Canada by 2022 from a total of 239,131 in 2011 to more than 450,000 in 2022 (Government of Canada 2014, 11). In doing so, it will target six specifically identified markets, one of which is China[30] (Government of Canada 2014, 10). In 2012, Chinese long-term students in Canada numbered 80,638 and made up 30.4 per cent of the total student population (Government of Canada 2014, 20). In 2012, there were 38,114 international long-term students in Quebec, accounting for 14.4 per cent of Canada's international student population and showing an annual growth rate of 5.9 per cent for the period 2007–12 (Government of Canada 2014, 27). Given that the government's objectives include "leverag[ing] Canada's bilingual, multicultural identity in marketing efforts and in building strategic partnerships" and "highlight[ing] Canada's French-language strengths to increase Canada's share of the international francophone student market," we can expect these numbers to rise significantly (Government of Canada 2014, 17).[31]

With reference to Asian students, Chen (2006, 77) makes the crucial point that international graduate students fulfill an important function in Canadian graduate education in that both the learning environment and society derive academic, cultural, and economic benefits from their presence. Upon completion of their studies they thus become "ambassadors of Canadian education to the world."[32]

In this vein, Waincymer (2010, 70–4) identifies a dual purpose for internationalized legal training: preparation for international legal practice at home or practice abroad, in addition to the preparation of students for their future roles as leaders of the community and ethical global citizens.[33]

It is clear, therefore, that the time was ripe to pursue collaborative efforts in the field of legal education. We were eager to both expose Canadian students to China and Chinese law, and to introduce Chinese students to Canada and Canadian law.[34] We also wanted to develop research relationships[35] and to facilitate faculty exchange. This, then, became our next objective.

Groundwork: China University of Politics and Law (CUPL)

The Senior Judges Training Project provided the spark for us to solidify the goodwill that was established and the relationships that were nurtured carefully over the course of the project into concrete initiatives in China.[36] During the course of the project, we had the good fortune of collaborating with a CUPL professor, a relationship which proved to be very valuable when establishing formal links with CUPL.

In 2002, shortly after completion of the Judges Training Project, we held our first summer school for future law graduates from the UdeM and other Canadian universities at the CUPL in Beijing, which has allowed more than 500 Canadian students to receive basic training in Chinese law over the past twelve years. The CUPL reciprocated in 2006 by co-hosting with our faculty its first summer program for Chinese students in Montreal. This summer program is now open to students from East China University of Political Science and Law (ECUPL), the University of Macau, and Zhongnan University of Economics and Law. Since 2006, more than 200 outstanding Chinese students have been trained in Canadian law. The collaboration between the parties has gone from strength to strength over the years, including research collaborations and the hosting of visiting scholars (Faculty of Law UdeM, 10).

In order to celebrate ten years of partnership between CUPL and the UdeM, a ceremony was held in Beijing on 24 October 2011.[37] At this occasion, the President of CUPL, Professor Huang Jin, outlined the principal elements of the partnership (including summer schools, student and scholar exchanges, conferences, and joint publications). He bestowed the Medal of Merit of CUPL on the then UdeM Law Faculty vice-dean, Guy Lefebvre, in recognition of his "exceptional involvement in establishing the linkage between CUPL and the UdeM, as well as his remarkable contribution in the domain of international business law between Canada and China." For his part, our then dean, Gilles Trudeau, highlighted the importance of this partnership and its considerable exposure for our faculty. He also mentioned the importance accorded to China by the Canadian legal sphere and referred to the UdeM's long-standing involvement with the training of Chinese lawyers, even preceding the ten-year period in question. He subsequently presented the Faculty Medal to two of the principal architects of the partnership: Dean John Mo and Professor Jiao Jie, both from the Faculty of International Law. During the afternoon, a joint conference was held on comparisons between public Chinese and Canadian law, with the papers subsequently being translated into Mandarin and published in the CUPL *International Law Review*.[38]

Another interesting example of collaboration between CUPL and our faculty was a joint conference on international law, hosted at the UdeM in November 2012. The conference papers, which were delivered by scholars from both CUPL and the UdeM, have been published in our law journal, *La Revue juridique Thémis de l'Université de Montréal*.[39]

There have been multiple articles co-authored by faculty from our two universities over the years,[40] as well as reciprocal research and lecturing visits. For example, one of us acts as visiting professor at CUPL and is also the Canadian director of the Sino-Canadian Law Research Centre at CUPL.

The Sino-Canadian Law Research Centre is a partnership between CUPL and our faculty, established to mark ten years of collaboration between us.[41] In May 2014, the Centre hosted an international conference on "Canadian Law and Natural Resources: Contemporary Challenges," aimed at exploring challenges and opportunities in Canadian natural resources development. Key Canadian scholars and experts in the field of energy and natural resource law delivered papers, followed by Chinese perspectives on the subject.

We will also open up a Sino-Canadian Centre at the UdeM in 2014 in collaboration with CUPL and other Chinese and Canadian partners, including a leading Canadian law firm, in a marriage of enterprise and education. In this way, we seek to establish relationships that cross-over both national and situational boundaries. The main activities and projects of the Centre will include: the holding of conferences and colloquia for Canadian and Chinese professionals and business enterprises in Canada and in China; the training of Chinese law students in Canada and their subsequent integration into the Canadian or Chinese legal market; the training of Canadian law students on Chinese law; academic research projects on a broad spectrum of subjects, in relation to Chinese and Canadian law;[42] Sino-Canadian professional training programs and exchanges, involving professionals;[43] the publication of scholarly articles or of a journal on subjects relating to Sino-Canadian law; and the attribution of scholarships encouraging students to pursue training or research on Sino-Canadian law or on Sino-Canadian social realities impacting law.

Growth: Broadening Our Involvement

Building on the success of our venture with CUPL, we have been fortunate to establish relationships that have led to collaborations with several other Chinese universities. Thus began our bilateral phase in China. To date, our projects have included summer school participation, a summer program in China for Quebec lawyers, faculty and student exchanges, and double degrees. In addition to CUPL, we have entered into cooperation agreements with some of the best law schools in China, including Wuhan University, East China University of Political Science and Law, Shanghai Jiao Tong University, and Macau University.

In 2010, double LLM degrees were implemented between the UdeM and CUPL and the UdeM and ECUPL. A similar agreement followed in 2013 with the University of Macau.

In 2011, we held a summer school for Quebec lawyers in China in conjunction with CUPL and ECUPL. Twelve Quebec lawyers participated in a two-week visit to China with the objective of learning more about Chinese law and Chinese culture. They spent the first week at CUPL in Beijing and the second week at ECUPL. During this time, they received an introduction to Chinese law and they also had the opportunity to visit Chinese law firms. We are currently studying ways of reintroducing this program.

In 2012, we entered into a cooperation agreement with the Chinese Academy of Social Sciences (CASS). Under the terms of this agreement, we are currently hosting a Chinese professor who has received a six-month research grant from the Canadian government. We also entered into an agreement with Zhongnan University of Economics and Law, and students from this reputable institution attended our summer program last year.

Not only have we received a steady stream of visiting scholars from multiple Chinese universities, including CUPL, ECUPL, and CASS, but one of us acts as visiting professor at CUPL, ECUPL, as adjunct professor at the University of Macau, and as a fellow at the Centre for Public Law of the Institute of Law, CASS.

Two additional initiatives between the UdeM and China deserve detailed discussion: the master of laws (LLM) Business Law in a Global Context and the Doctoral Scholarship for Chinese Students Program.

Master's of Laws (LLM) Business Law in a Global Context

Created in 2007, the master of laws Business Law in a Global Context is a degree that was tailor-made to the requirements of international law students (Faculty of Law UdeM, 3). It is, in fact, the first LLM program in Canada designed exclusively for foreign graduate students (Faculty of Law UdeM, 4). Although entry is not restricted to Chinese students, the degree is extremely popular amongst them and we have specific agreements with Chinese universities in this regard, such as the Memorandum of Understanding (MOU) signed in 2010 with CUPL.

The program is intended to provide students with analytical and research skills in the spheres of comparative, international, and North-American business law that will be of great value to their careers. It will enable them to work more effectively within the global context and it will assist them in developing critical appraisals of the main legal traditions as well as international business law. Other objectives of the program are to increase students' awareness of difficulties allied to questions of governance and to develop their problem-solving capacity relating to different legal categories from diverse legal systems or from international business law, thus enabling them to respond creatively to complex legal problems (Faculty of Law UdeM).

Like the Judges Training Program, the emphasis is not solely on theory. The program also provides opportunities for informal discussions with Canadian law professors, lawyers, and officials. Students are furthermore exposed to local law firms, Courts of Justice, and business enterprises (Faculty of Law UdeM). The program itself comprises sixteen compulsory courses with both theoretical and practical content.[44]

The MOU signed with CUPL in 2010 provides a good illustration of how the degree functions in the Chinese context. The MOU has a term of five years and speaks specifically to this program. CUPL full-time postgraduate students in their first-year master's program may apply to be admitted to our LLM Business Law in a Global Context program during their second year of studies.[45] Upon successful completion of the one-year study at the UdeM, they are granted the LLM degree. They then return to China for a further year's study in order to be granted a master's degree by CUPL; however, the credits earned from the UdeM are recognized by CUPL (MOU CUPL 2010, 1).

In terms of reciprocity, students holding a master's degree of laws from or enrolled in a master's program at the UdeM may apply to be admitted to the master's program in Chinese law for international students of CUPL. If accepted, they will be awarded a master's degree from CUPL upon successful completion of one year of study.[46] The credits earned from the UdeM are recognized by CUPL (MOU CUPL 2010, 1).

The above MOU serves as an example; as mentioned, we now have similar agreements in place with ECUPL and the University of Macau.

We take great care to maintain contact with our Chinese graduates and have an interest in following their progress in the world. Many of them go on to make their mark in Chinese public, business, and legal office, but there are also those who stay on to pursue their studies at the doctoral level, under the auspices of the program we will consider next. Others choose to pursue an LLB, enabling them to become members of the Quebec bar – which offers them the possibility of bi-jurisdictional practice. It is a popular program that has to date yielded more than 125 graduates, many of them fulfilling an important function in Chinese life.

The Doctoral Scholarship for Chinese Students Program

The Doctoral Scholarship for Chinese Students Program takes place within the context of an agreement signed between the UdeM and the China Scholarship Council (CSC)[47] in terms of which the UdeM will award a maximum of twenty fellowships to Chinese students annually in the first three years of the Program. Thereafter, there will be a maximum of sixty ongoing doctoral Chinese students per year (UdeM 2012a, 1).

The agreement was signed against the background of the CSC Doctoral Scholarship Program that was launched in 2007 and that envisaged sending 6,000 Chinese students abroad from 2007–11. To this end, the CSC has entered into contracts with forty-nine top Chinese universities, allotting a scholarship quota to each of them (UdeM 2012a, 1).

In order to enable excellent Chinese candidates to undertake doctoral studies at the UdeM, the University has signed an agreement with the CSC and fourteen institutions, including the CUPL, the Beijing Normal University (BNU), Peking University, Wuhan University, Tsinghua University, and Central China University. Students from these fourteen universities, as well as students from other universities who have an agreement with the CSC, may apply for scholarships under this Doctoral Scholarship Program (UdeM 2012b, 1).

In terms of the Doctoral Scholarship Program, the UdeM waives the tuition fees of the successful candidates, while they can apply to the CSC for a living allowance (including student health cover), return airfare to Canada, and visa application fees (UdeM 2012b, 1).[48] Students may apply to be admitted to any PhD program offered at the UdeM, but programs within *inter alia* the field of law are prioritized.[49] Although we only make up 3.9 per cent of the UdeM as law school, we attract between 30 and 60 per cent of these candidates annually.

A good example of an agreement signed within the ambit of the Chinese Doctoral Scholarship Program is the *Cooperation Agreement Concerning Candidates at the Doctoral Level* that was signed between Renmin University (RU) of China and the UdeM in August 2012.[50]

Since doctoral students form lasting relationships with their host universities that augur well for future collaborative research once the students have returned to their home countries (Sakamoto and Chapman 2011, 6), we work hard at maintaining ties with these students, thus adding them to our ever-expanding network of relationships.

CONCLUSIONS

Benefits and Challenges of International Partnerships

A major advantage of teaching law across borders is the exposure to different legal cultures and different ways of legal thought, which leads to an enhanced understanding of the strengths and weaknesses of one's own legal system (Tan, Bell, et al. 2006, 16). We have also discovered that the learning is mutual, in that over the period of our collaboration the students on either side have learned much from one another, as have they and the professors, both in respect of matters pertaining to culture and law.[51]

Typical challenges defined by literature – namely equity of access for students in terms of financial means and linguistic ability,[52] quality assurance in the absence of international standards,[53] the legitimacy and recognition of qualifications thus obtained,[54] and the "brain drain"/"brain gain"/"brain train" phenomenon[55] – are not considered to have hindered us in pursuing a fruitful relationship.

Past and Future Reflections

Our cooperation with China over the past sixteen years has been a very enriching experience.[56] We feel validated in knowing that we have managed to guard against cultural imperialism[57] in the understanding that we need to demonstrate sensitivity to China's history and traditions [58] and to approach our partnership in the context of differing cultures and value systems.[59]

A partnership principle of importance is that interactions between partners should, to the greatest extent possible, be horizontal and balanced (Shivnan and Hill 2011, 156), meaning that all partners should participate fully from the beginning in a relationship built on equality and reciprocity.[60] The latter concepts should not be understood on a literal one-to-one basis, but rather in the more global context of give-and-take.[61] We have learned a great lesson in the sphere of give-and-take from our Chinese students who, fuelled by a sense of collective responsibility, actively seek ways to give back to China, for example in the form of contributions to a forthcoming book published by CUPL in Chinese about Quebec business law under auspices of the two Sino-Canadian Legal Research Centres, or by creating orientation guides for new students, aimed at easing their transition into Canadian student life.

We are currently in the process of discussing a new project of continued legal education with China. We also aim to increase the number of Canadian graduate students that are sent to China, and to do so for a longer time, so as to improve their understanding of Chinese culture, language, legal system, and society. As future Canadian lawyers, this will present them with an incredible opportunity to learn about a different culture and way of thinking, to gain a better understanding of values beyond their immediate frame of reference.[62]

We also look forward to welcoming new generations of Chinese students to our programs including, but not limited to, the LLM Business Law in a Global Context. We are proud to offer a learning experience in a bilingual context in both civil and common law, at a world-class university situated in a culturally diverse city that welcomes variety and difference.

Ultimately, this has been about a journey. It began with the establishment of key contacts, credibility and relationships during the Senior Judges Training Project. We then solidified our relationships into a formal collaboration with CUPL, and built on the success of that program to create bilateral programs with other Chinese institutions such as ECUPL, the University of Macau, the CASS, and the CSC.[63] Strengthened by the lessons learned over the years, we believe that we are now ready to take the next logical step: the pursuit of multilateral relations with our Chinese partners.

The Consortium for Global Governance and International Legal Order, founded in 2012 with the CUPL, Nankai University, Wuhan University, Xiamen University, the University of International Business and Economics of China, the University of New South Wales, and the University of Helsinki, has as a goal the implementation of an international PhD in Science, Technology, and Innovation. As a complementary measure, we intend to launch a multilingual law journal to publish research and contribute to the formation of future leaders in this area. In our view this translates into a more inclusive, multilateral, multicultural approach. We have learned a lot from our Chinese partners on a reciprocal basis over the years.

And thus we continue onto the next journey of a thousand miles.

NOTES

1 For additional information, see Guo, Schugurensky, et al. (2010, 76).
2 The extent to which China adhered to the "rule of law" prior to 1996 is subject to a much broader debate on "rule of law," "rule by law," and "rule of man" that falls beyond the scope of this chapter. See in this regard: Chen (2000, 125–65); Zeng (2002, 707–09); Mo and Li (2002, 176, 202); Gechlik (2006, 97–8); He (2006, 150–1); Hou (2006, 293–4); Gillespie (2008, 659); Head (2010, 38–52); Taylor (2010, 221); and Zhao and Hu (2012, 221). On the role and importance of the rule of law generally, see: Haggard, MacIntyre, et al. (2008, 11); Magen (2009, 45); Skaaning (2010, 63); and Haggard and Tiede (2011, 39).
3 SPC President Xiao Yang announced in 2003 that the reforms as envisaged in the plan had been mostly completed (Gechlik 2006, 99).
4 When formal university education was restored in 1977, there were only two law schools, namely those of Jilin and Beijing Universities (Tan, Bell, et al. 2006, 2), and there were just 600 law students in 1978 (He 2006, 145). This figure had augmented to 300,000 law students enrolled in some 600 law schools by 2008 (Irish 2008, 250). He (2006, 148) is critical of this explosion in numbers, arguing that it has been detrimental to China's judicial reputation since it has led to a dilution in the *pro rata* equation between legal education and students. In the same vein, Zhao and Hu (2012, 358) point out that quantity does not equate to quality and emphasize that China has greater need of the latter than the former. See Evans (chapter 2 of this volume) on the "staggering expansion" that has characterized Chinese universities as a whole.
5 Biddulph (2010, 266) cites the example of East China University of Politics and Law: prior to the Cultural Revolution, its collection comprised 350,000 books. In 1980, it had 80,000 books and 520 journals. By 2005, the collection had grown to 670,000 books and 1,200 Chinese and foreign-language journals. Students furthermore had access to specialist international legal databases such as HeinOnline and Lexis.
6 A unified judicial exam was introduced in 2002, meaning that there is a single entry requirement for lawyers, judges, and procurators. This is applauded by Zou (2003, 174–5), who links the legal profession's entry standard to conformity with the rule of law.
7 For a detailed historical overview, see: Mo and Li (2002, 177–90); Wang (2002, 103–06); Zou (2003, 161–4); He (2006, 139–45); Hou (2006, 294); Irish (2008, 246–8); Zhao and Hu (2012, 331–5); and Chen and Huang (2013, 92–101).

8 Also see: Taylor (2010, 221) and Zhao and Hu (2012, 344).
9 Zou (2003, 161) notes: "To meet this new demand, the Chinese government underscored the importance of having legal workers, particularly practicing lawyers, to provide a pool of legal experts who 'know law, know economics, and know foreign languages' (*dongfalu, dongjingji, dong waiyu*)."
10 A consortium was formed for its execution, consisting of the UdeM (leading partner), McGill University, the Canadian Institute for the Administration of Justice (Canadian executing agency), and the National Judges College (Chinese executing agency) (UdeM 2002, 1.1).
11 A significant portion of the trainees was from a criminal law background and a substantial portion of the training was devoted to rule of law and human rights topics (UdeM 2002, 2.2). This enabled the trainees to address issues of democratic governance and social justice arising from the rapidly transforming environment in which they found themselves. See Hayhoe et al. (chapter 1 of this volume) on the second of four key questions that we were asked to consider for the purposes of this book. Also see the comments of Bild (chapter 3 of this volume) on the effect of the "newly awakened Canadian emphasis on human rights."
12 For purposes of the first generation of trainees, the substantive law emphasis was placed on private and economic law; for the second generation it was on public law, including international, constitutional, and administrative law (UdeM 2002, 1.2).
13 Topics covered ranged from contracts and torts, property law, and economic crime in the substantive law units, to constitutional law and rule of law, judicial independence and equality, and social diversity in the legal theory unit (UdeM Consortium 1999b, 4).
14 Issues addressed included the independence of the judiciary, the organization of the courts, judicial ethics, and judgment writing.
15 Given that legal education pertains not only to "training in the substance of law, but also training in professional skills, values, and culture," Woo (2001, 450) postulates that in creating an international exchange program it is necessary to consider the inclusion of both substantive areas of law and pertinent aspects of skills, values, and culture from the legal system in question.
16 Objectives included familiarizing the judges with court proceedings, the management of trials and "judicial ends available to Canadian judges," and the exchange of views with their mentors and peers (Canada/China Senior Judges Training Project 1998, 6–7).
17 These activities included two in-house seminars, with presentations being rendered by the trainees themselves – the first topic being "How to behave

as a judge in critical situations" and the second being "How to hear, analyse, decide, and handle caseload efficiently" (UdeM 2002, 1.2).

18 The first, on "Crimes against Market Economy," was held in Beijing in October 1998. In January 1999 a second seminar was held in Kunming on "Drug Crimes and Prevention." The seminar included a moot trial with jury with more than 100 judges and judiciary personnel in attendance. The third seminar took place in Beijing in June 1999 and related to "The Reform of Contract Law in China." A fourth seminar followed in Beijing in November 1999, this time on "Gender Considerations, the Law, and the Judiciary." In June 2000, the fifth seminar was held in Beijing on "Canadian and Chinese Perspectives on WTO: Legislative and Judicial Impacts." The final seminar took place in November 2000 and was themed "Judicial Review: Comparative Analysis, Practices and Perspectives" (UdeM 2002, 1.2, 2.2).

19 By November 1996, CIDA and other Canadian organizations had reportedly spent an additional $159,000 on Chinese criminal code modernization and prosecutor training; $284,000 in support of research on good governance and human rights; $500,000 on training for Chinese lawyers; and $2.5 million as assistance with the establishment of the Chinese Institute of Judges (Baraban 1998, 1270).

20 These, then, are the contextual features of the Judges Training that we consider to have rendered the program most effective. See Hayhoe et al. (chapter 1 of this volume) on the third key question that we were asked to consider. We did not encounter any serious challenges or hindrances.

21 This is probably the most important lesson that may be drawn from our project for purposes of current and future collaboration between Canadian and Chinese universities. See Hayhoe et al. (chapter 1 of this volume) on the fourth key question. Beamish (chapter 6 of this volume) reaches a similar conclusion.

22 See McCubbin, Seymore et al. (2007, 295–6).

23 In response to the first of the four key questions that we were asked to consider for the purposes of this book, we would thus consider this to be our most important contribution to China's revitalization and transformation. See Hayhoe et al. (chapter 1 of this volume).

24 There has been much speculation as to the reasons for legal reform in China, a matter that falls beyond the scope of this chapter. Reasons advanced during the course of the project included China's accession to the WTO, as well as interest in reforming the criminal process due to factors such as "an upsurge of crime and the appearance of new crimes, the development of legal institutions in other areas, a desire for greater

regularity and rationality, an increased professionalization, and institutional differentiation within the three agencies that administer the criminal process, growing rights-consciousness among Chinese, and the influence of international practice and the sting of international criticism" (UdeM 2002, 3.2). See generally: Chen (2000, 17); Wang (2002, 1211); He (2006, 138); Irish (2008, 250); Gillespie (2008, 668); Waincymer (2010, 76); and Taylor (2010, 221).

25 In its *Stratégie d'internationalisation de 2e génération*, the Université de Montréal emphasizes how important it is to retain respect for cultural diversity and to remain sensitive to national characteristics when dealing with international students (2006, 8).

26 As Atwood, Silveira et al. (2005, 549) comment, "[O]ne's understanding of a legal regime or legal structure is sharpened when it is contrasted with possible alternatives situated in different legal cultures." Woo (2001, 449) notes that such an increased understanding will result in a decreased perception of superiority pertaining to the Anglo-American legal system and more respect for the legal systems of others. Also see Sexton (1996, 330).

27 Also see Woo (2001, 451), who highlights the differences between Chinese and American legal culture.

28 These include factors such as: the increased global integration; the increased mobility of skilled employees in a globalized economy; the diminishing costs of transport and communication and the development of novel communication technologies; the desire of universities to raise their profile both nationally and internationally; the desire of universities to generate additional income in a lucrative segment of the market and their need to source a greater portion of their own funding; local constraints in terms of educational capacity and sometimes quality in developing countries linked to an increasing demand in post-secondary education; the desire of countries to encourage university and cultural exchanges; and the desire of universities to attract top talent in terms of students and staff and to strengthen their research capacities (Knight 2011, 17; Vincent-Lancrin 2011, 93–4, 107).

29 Ryan and Carroll (2005, 8–9) identify important advantages to increased numbers of international students, including the incentive for teachers to review their teaching methodologies and the opportunity for the university to reassess its institutional role as being either "transformative" or "reproductive."

30 An ongoing annual funding of $5 million, primarily directed at primary market efforts, has been earmarked by the government to support the objectives of the International Education Strategy (Ryan and Carroll 2005, 13).

31 Also see Evans (chapter 2 of this volume) on the scope of current Sino-Canadian university relationships.
32 His research findings on the motivational factors that attract East Asian students to Canadian universities are also interesting. He found that the largest group reported Canada to have been their first choice and motivated it with reference to "the positive Canadian environment – safe, diverse, and multicultural." Issues of specific importance in their decision included "safety, discrimination and tolerance (being accepted), diversity and multiculturalism within a city and within an institution." These are certainly values on which the City of Montreal and the UdeM pride themselves.
33 He emphasizes that it is not sufficient to add on *ad hoc* elements of internationalization to the legal curriculum; rather, internationalization needs to be entrenched in the legal educational framework as such.
34 This offers the additional advantage that the student is enriched by travel and exposure to a foreign culture. See Knight (2011, 18 and 31). Louie (2005, 24) points out that it also endows students with the opportunity and skills to critically appraise their own culture.
35 Casey (2010, 30–1) points to the "synergistic possibilities that arise from cultural differences" when performing international research collaboration.
36 In commenting on the positive side of Sino-Canadian collaboration, Hayhoe et al. (chapter 1 of this volume) report a "strong sense of family relations" arising between the project members on either side. This has certainly been our experience. Also see in this regard the contribution of Bild (chapter 3 of this volume). In his contribution, Beamish (chapter 6 of this volume) points out that continuity gave rise to strong personal relationships, which assisted with the management of complex issues.
37 Hayhoe et al. (chapter 1 of this volume) highlight the importance that the partnership literature accords to lengthy time frames when it comes to continued and expanded collaboration.
38 UdeM faculty contributions include: Rigaud (2013, 309); Gaudreault-DesBiens (2013, 327); Leclair (2013, 350); Karazivan (2013, 364); and Valois (2013, 377).
39 It is also an indication of the degree of our commitment to our Chinese partnerships that the article summaries in our faculty law journal have been translated into five languages since January 2013, one of which is Mandarin.
40 See for examples: Jiao and Lefebvre (2013, 10); Lefebvre, Rigaud et al. (2012, 8); Lefebvre, Rigaud, et al. (2012, 7); Jiao and Lefebvre (2011, 116); Lefebvre and Jiao (2011d); Lefebvre and Jiao (2011c); Lefebvre

and Jiao (2011b); Lefebvre and Jiao (2011a); and Lefebvre and Jiao (2002, 36).

41 A second important point gleaned by Hayhoe et al. (chapter 1 of this volume) from the partnership literature centres on the "importance of collaborative research ... around issues of common concern on both sides."

42 Including alternative conflict resolution, governance, access to justice through technology, international business transactions, and natural resources.

43 For example, training seminars for business people or lawyers and three-week judicial training programs.

44 The courses include topics such as: "Western Legal Systems," "Electronic Commerce Law," "International Economic Relations," "International Contract Law," "International Commercial Disputes," "Legal Aspects of International Finance," "Globalization and Emerging Economies," and "International Economic Crimes" (Faculty of Law UdeM, 4).

45 The bachelor obtained need not be with a law major, but it must have been completed with at least five law-related courses in order to qualify for admission into the program.

46 However, it is a prerequisite that they should hold their master of laws from the UdeM before the beginning of the first term of their master's program at CUPL.

47 The CSC is a non-profit institution affiliated with the Ministry of Education. Its objective is to provide financial assistance to Chinese citizens wishing to study abroad and to foreign citizens wishing to study in China with the goal of developing educational, scientific, technological, and scientific exchanges and to strengthen economic and trade cooperation between China and other countries (UdeM 2012b, 1).

48 One of the entry criteria and conditions of eligibility is that the candidate signs with the CSC an "Agreement for Study Abroad for CSC Sponsored Chinese Citizens," promising to return to China upon completion of his/her research and within the agreed time frame (UdeM 2012a, 2). This is a good example of what Guo, Schugurensky, et al. (2010, 76) term "'brain return' strategies." These are not idle fears, as are illustrated by Hayhoe et al.'s interview with Tsinghua professors as recorded in chapter 1 of this volume). Also see Bild (chapter 3 of this volume) on his experience of the situation from a diplomatic angle, and Xi et al. (chapter 5 of this volume) for a Chinese perspective. Mirus (chapter 4 of this volume) identifies two factors that may have contributed to the issue: inaction on the part of the Canadian government and the loss of jurisdiction by the universities once the students had graduated.

49 The other priority fields are: Arts and Sciences, Environmental Planning and Design, Health Sciences, Animal Health Sciences, and Pharmacy. Within the field of Law, priority is given to Biotechnology Law, Information Technology Law, Computer Law, Business Law, and Electronic Security (UdeM 2012b, 2).

50 It is clear that the agreement envisages long-term collaboration: clause 7 stipulates that while the UdeM will provide the principal academic advisers for the Project, co-supervision between the UdeM and RU will be encouraged where possible, in light of the fact that the two institutions have as a goal the development of long-term research collaboration between them. In the same vein, clause 9 provides for a term of three years from date of signature, automatically renewable for further periods of three years (UdeM 2012a, 3–4).

51 Zha and Hayhoe (chapter 10 of this volume) highlight a similar insight on the part of a Chinese professor who through personal experience came to realize "the need to have a cultural understanding of how educational scholars in different countries would view and analyse similar problems." Also see the contribution of Qiang and Wang (chapter 11 of this volume) on the importance of cross-cultural communications.

52 Also see Chesterman (2008, 65), who critiques the new global legal education as "simply a discourse of the rich" and "an elite phenomenon," but notes that at the same time that it is cardinal that lawyers be able to deal with diversity.

53 See: Davis (2007, 40); Hénard, Diamond, et al. (2012, 20); and Vincent-Lancrin and Pfotenhauer (2012).

54 The OECD guidelines recommend specifically in this regard that, where appropriate, members develop or encourage bilateral or multilateral recognition agreements for the recognition or equivalence of the individual countries' qualifications (Vincent-Lancrin and Pfotenhauer 2012, 60).

55 "While 'brain drain and brain gain' are well-known concepts, research is showing that international students and researchers are increasingly interested in taking a degree in Country A, followed by a second degree or perhaps internship in Country B, leading to employment in Country C and probably D, finally returning to their home country after eight to twelve years of international study and work experience. Hence the emergence of the term 'brain train'" (Knight 2011, 31).

56 See Ryan and Carroll (2005, 9) on the importance of welcoming international students as "bearers of alternative knowledge, perspectives and life experiences."

57 See Moliterno (2008, 280).

58 See Baraban (1998, 1275) who cautions in the American context that failure to take these enduring traditions into consideration in the pursuit of individual rights and free-market values will have China "recoiling into nationalism."

59 See Hayhoe et al. (chapter 1 of this volume) for an interview with a Chinese dean of education. Xi et al. (chapter 5 of this volume) warn of the risks of "conflict and detachment" inherent in international cooperative programs due to cultural differences. This is also borne out by the literature. Shivnan and Hill (2011, 155) caution that many nations and cultures perceive the dominance of western values and culture as threatening. In the same vein, they distinguish between the individualistic cultures predominant in North America and Europe, and the collectivist cultures found throughout Asia, Africa, and South America, noting that, "In collectivist cultures, constituting 70 per cent of all cultures, loyalties of the individual to the group can outweigh individual rights. In individualistic cultures the rights of the individual are central, and must be balanced against the common good" (155–6).

60 Also see Qiang and Wang (chapter 11 of this volume). This provides a contrast with the "somewhat dictatorial stance of some project leaders at Canadian universities" as reported on by Hayhoe et al. (chapter 1 of this volume).

61 For instance, there is the issue of demographics when comparing Canada to China – Canada neither could nor should aspire to send the same number of students to China as it is receiving in return. The important thing is that there be a flow of students, scholars, and research collaborations in both directions.

62 See in this regard the excellent summary by Walls of the "Five Constant Virtues" and "The Middle Way" (chapter 9 of this volume).

63 See Bild's comment in this regard (chapter 3 of this volume).

13

Gender and Development in CIDA's Programs: A Reflection on the *Doing* of Feminist Collaboration

PING-CHUN HSIUNG

INTRODUCTION

In March 2014, the Canadian International Development Agency (CIDA) completed all its projects and contract work in China. A prominent piece of CIDA's legacy in China is its Gender and Development (GAD) program. With well-articulated objectives and clearly defined measurements of gender equality results and assessing framework, much of CIDA's legacy of GAD is documented through multiple reports that demonstrate success through charts, statistical figures, and/or indicators of progress (CIDA 1997a; 1997b; 1998; 2005; 2007). These results are confirmed by chapters in this book. For example, Mirus and Li (chapters 4 and 7) point out how CIDA's GAD objectives are incorporated in management projects and in engineering projects. Zha and Hayhoe (chapter 10) and Walls (chapter 9) cite publications that prominently feature women in education and in social, economic, and environmental developments. Qiang and Wang (chapter 11) discuss extensively how CIDA projects provide opportunities to Chinese women scholars.

Missing from CIDA's archival documents are testimonials of the concerted effort and unwavering human commitment that not only made CIDA's vision on GAD imaginable but a reality. To commemorate CIDA's legacy of GAD in China, I reflect upon the *doing* of feminist collaboration that I have had the good fortune to be a part of since the 1990s. Empirically, I call upon narratives and exchanges to accentuate the process and efforts associated with feminist collaboration as initiatives sponsored by CIDA and other funding agencies are planned and executed at the micro level. I also privilege evidence of women as change agents. Theoretically, my writing focuses on the *doing* of feminist collaboration. I problematize the criteria used to produce a particular type of knowledge about GAD where women inadvertently become the targeted objects rather than empowered subjects in feminist collaboration.

CIDA'S LEGACY OF GENDER AND DEVELOPMENT IN CHINA

The objectives of CIDA's GAD are to (1) "advance women's equal participation with men as decision-makers in shaping the sustainable development of their societies," and (2) "support women and girls in the realization of their full human rights" and "reduce gender inequalities in access to and control over the resources and benefits of development" (CIDA 2007, v). To make its work accountable, CIDA has used its "Gender Equality Results Categorization" to demonstrate how CIDA's "Framework for Assessing Gender Equality Results" is operationalized (CIDA 2005). Functioning as a knowledge production system to account for the GAD program, for example, women's equal participation in decision-making with men is measured by indicators such as "capacity for public participation," "representation among decision makers," and "household and individual decision." Examples provided of "the ways in which a project or other investment could contribute to particular gender equality results" include "increase in independent decision-making by women on matters such as voting and mobility" and "increase in shared decision-making at the household level on matters such as expenditure, activities, et cetera" (CIDA 2007, 17). The corporate measurements are then used to compile statistics to credit CIDA's achievement. For example, the 2010–11 report on CIDA's achievement in human rights states, "More than 250,000 young men and women have received information about trafficking for labour exploitation and their rights as migrant workers, and more than 35,000 women and children have received support services from women's homes and community service centres in order to prevent or address trafficking/labour exploitation" (CIDA 2013, 3). Its report on prevention of labour trafficking states, "The project's awareness-raising campaigns have reached over 750,000 young migrant workers. In addition, education departments in the four migrant-sending provinces of Anhui, Hunan, Guizhou, and Yunnan are integrating information on the prevention of trafficking in middle- and high-school curricula; this information has already reached 1.5 million students and over 500 teachers have been trained through the project" (CIDA 2013, 3).

Although these statistics provide an overview on results of various GAD projects, they say nothing about the process and efforts that have brought them about. In fact, in its "Framework for Assessing Gender Equality Results," CIDA states specifically that its focus is on "development results rather than processes, inputs, or efforts" (CIDA 2005, 3). Therefore, individual skills and collective labour imperative to the planning and executing of GAD programs become invisible in CIDA's reports, which will stand as the primary sources about its legacy from now on. To counterbalance this official knowledge, this chapter examines meaningful encounters and tangible outcomes that go beyond statistical figures and corporate measurements. My writing on the *doing* of feminist collaboration underscores the process and efforts that have produced CIDA's stellar records of GAD in China.

DOING FEMINIST COLLABORATION – CONNECTING THE TRACK AND BEYOND

A diverse range of women's organizing initiatives have emerged since China's market reforms. The idea of "connecting the track" (*jiegui*, 接轨) captured Chinese activists' enthusiasm to align to and be enlightened by the international women's movement when the United Nations decided to hold its Fourth World Conference on Women in Beijing in 1995. As a Chinese diaspora, feminist researcher, and trained qualitative sociologist in Canada, I have been involved in several collaborative engagements since the early 1990s. I formally assumed the role of a facilitator in the process of "connecting the track." It soon became clear that there were not readily, pre-defined "tracks" to be connected with. As my Chinese collaborators and I "crossed the river by feeling the stones" (*mozhe shitou guohe* 摸着石头过河), we needed to actively identify fruitful points of engagement, assertively articulate our vision, and deliberately lay down new pathways. In retrospect, if it was not immediately apparent at the time, many of the meaningful encounters and tangible outcomes I will discuss later in this chapter have come about because the Chinese participants have been the active partakers, rather than passive recipients. Empirically speaking, therefore, the idea of "connecting the track and beyond" highlights the interactive process and unfailing determination allotted to the collaborative endeavour.

Theoretically, my reflection is anchored by Mencius's statement that encapsulates the Confucian wisdom in governance: "Virtue alone is not sufficient for the exercise of government; laws alone cannot carry themselves into practice" (徒善不足以为政，徒法不足以自行) (Mencius; 《孟子.离娄上》).

This statement problematizes a simplistic understanding of the power of moral leadership imposed from above, and identifies the space between policy/law and local governance. It recognizes the process through which policy/law is implemented in local governance. Since "virtue alone is not sufficient for the exercise of government," I am compelled to examine the planning and execution that constituted the implementation of CIDA's GAD program. The notion that "laws alone cannot carry themselves into practice" encourages me to document and to analyze concerted efforts and deliberate actions made by individuals in the in-between space, which are imperative in the implementation of CIDA's GAD programs. Together, I discuss opportunities and challenges I have encountered as seeds were sown. My analysis fills the gap between the objectives of CIDA's GAD program and its "development results" appraised by a specific set of corporate measurements. Hence, theoretically speaking, "connecting the track and beyond" echoes Mencius's position. It questions the existing practices and discourse that focus exclusively on *results*. By making visible the processes and efforts of feminist collaboration, I privilege nuances and expand the lexicon to commemorate CIDA's legacy of GAD programming.

I focus on three key undertakings in which I have participated, both as a facilitator and as a "comrade" in the eyes of my Chinese colleagues: the Xi'an Workshop (funded by CIDA); the Summer Institute on Feminist Pedagogy and Curriculum Development (funded by the Ford Foundation); and the Workshop on Chinese Women Organizing (funded by the Ford Foundation, the Davis Fund, the Great Britain-China Centre, The Reuter Foundation, the Sino-British Fellowship Trust, and the Universities' China Committee). Calling upon narratives, exchanges, and personal reflections, I document meaningful encounters and tangible outcomes of these three undertakings.

THE XI'AN WORKSHOP

The Xi'an group was one of the two groups focused on women as educational change agents in the CIDA-sponsored project, entitled Women and Minorities as Educational Change Agents.[1] In 1997, I was approached to work with Professor Qiang Haiyan, the vice-dean of Education at Shaanxi

Normal University (SNU), to provide social science research training to enhance the research capacity of junior female faculty members in higher education, in order to help them become educational change agents. We organized two training workshops (December 1997 and June 1998). In addition to presentations on substantive issues pertinent to women and higher education in China and Canada, the primary objective was to provide training on social science research methods so that each participating junior female faculty member would complete an independent research project under the supervision of the team leaders from China and Canada. The plan saw the participating faculty members develop their research proposals during the first workshop, gather and analyze data between the first and second workshops, and finalize and present their work at the closing conference.

As a trained sociologist in qualitative research (QR), I was responsible for working with workshop participants interested in using QR for their research projects. To facilitate the objectives of cultivating the participants into educational change agents, I adhered to the premise of QR where methodological principle, epistemological position, and method(s) are interconnected. Perceiving QR as a means of knowledge production, I worked with the participants so that they not only acquired research techniques in QR, but also learned to examine the implicit methodologies and epistemologies being employed. My pedagogical practice consisted of three key aspects: introducing QR as a legitimate means of social science inquiry; practicing an inductive, bottom-up pedagogy; and incorporating feminist epistemology into an inquiry.

Qualitative Research as a Legitimate Means of Social Science Inquiry

In my lectures at the first workshop, I compared and contrasted QR and a quantitative approach as two distinctive research paradigms. I discussed qualitative interviewing and ethnography, calling upon my research on class stratification, gender inequalities, and Taiwan's economic development. I demonstrated how my research was informed by feminist epistemology, which eventually allowed me to challenge the state's developmental policies, tease out the interconnectedness between class stratification and gender inequalities, and examine the ways in which women's productive and reproductive labour was activated for economic development that catered to the global market.

While a few participants found my presentation refreshing, many were doubtful about QR. For some, doing fieldwork and conducting interviews were seen as not dissimilar from Mao Zedong's legendary Investigative

Research (*diaocha yanjiu*调查研究, IR). QR was not welcome because Mao's IR was considered responsible for the policy failure during the Great Leap Forward (1958–62) that had resulted in an estimated thirty-five to forty-five million Chinese deaths. For others, QR was less appealing than the quantitative paradigm because its findings were perceived as not objective, scientific, or generalizable. At the workshop, I was particularly intrigued by comments made about QR and its perceived similarities to Mao's IR. I was also alarmed by examples of misfits mentioned by workshop participants when they applied statistical models and survey questionnaires transplanted from the West to study Chinese society. As I will discuss later in this chapter, the discussion enticed me to explore the methodological and epistemological principles of QR in the Chinese context.

Eventually, I worked closely with seven workshop participants who wanted to employ QR for their individual research projects; four of them were junior faculty members from four different normal universities, one was a junior faculty member from a Tibetan college, one was a local journalist, and one was a staff member from the local Women's Federation. During our group sections, I covered how to develop an interview guide, how to frame specific interview questions, and ethics-related matters in qualitative interviewing. During the first workshop, each participant carried out an interview and transcribed it. I provided written comments on their transcripts. I also led discussions on silencing, attentive listening, and power relationships in the interview context. Using their transcripts as examples, I covered coding, memoing, and writing up in QR.

During the six months between the first and second workshops, each participant carried out and transcribed ten interviews. They were instructed to bring their transcripts and drafts of their final papers to the second workshop.

Sowing Seeds through an Inductive, Bottom-Up Pedagogy

Throughout the project, I adopted an inductive, bottom-up pedagogy to work with the participants. From the beginning, I asked the participants to develop a research project that would address an issue or problem they had observed or experienced at work. This pedagogical instruction not only adhered to QRs methodological principles but also facilitated the project's vision of junior female faculty members as change agents.

This turned out to be quite an empowering impetus. For one thing, it had never occurred to them that social science inquiry could be personally meaningful. Through active engagement, doing research was no longer an abstract, useless academic exercise with no tangible relevance to their lives and realities. Furthermore, it was particularly exciting for the participants to realize that research findings could lay the foundation for local activism. Employing QR as a means of inquiry provided them with a new entry point not only as intellectuals but as change agents. This is evident in the following three comments made by the participants:

- "In the past, I was never interested in doing research because it only plays around with all those abstract concepts. To me, such research is useless and meaningless. Everything is different now. I'm now very eager to get involved in research because we can actually 'discover' problems through research. With the applied aspect, our findings are going to make a real difference."
- "Knowing this approach is more important than anything else. Producing articles is only secondary. The main thing is to have learned this method and to use it to study and analyse what is happening. I feel I have finally found my destiny."
- "After learning this approach, I have a completely new perspective. This perspective allows me to see new meaning in my life ... it is like making a turn in my life. Now I know what I'll do the rest of my life. I told my husband, 'I have come to understand why there are people who sacrifice their own lives to protect certain principles.' I feel I have become such a noble person now."

Instead of seeing and positioning themselves as the authority, I encouraged them to perceive their informants as "experts" who were in the position to articulate their own experiences from their unique perspectives. The interviews were therefore an opportunity for the researcher to "learn" from the informants. This conceptualization was in startling contrast to existing practices where the researcher has habitually assumed the authority position.

When it came to data analysis, I worked closely with each participant. Through reading their transcripts repeatedly, conducting line-by-line coding, and teasing out layers of meanings, the participant came to appreciate the meaning of "giving voice" to the informant. They were particularly shocked by the extent to which their own preconceived notions and unchecked assumptions had prevented them from hearing what their informants had said. Workshop participants eventually came to reflect upon the inductive logic in QR and its implications. One of the most salient sentiments expressed by the participants about QR was, "When more people come to accept it, China will undergo some fundamental changes." This was captured by an elaboration made by a participant in a matter-of-fact manner:

> If the real essence of this approach is to shed light on positions and existing problems from the feelings and experiences of the subject, I think we can apply the same principle to broader areas. [In doing this] it will bring the democratic spirit to the so-called authority in our country ... [We should always ask] from whose perspectives. It's not only certain people's words that count, not only the leader who has the final say. For example, if I were a worker or a female textile worker, I would be the authority on my feelings and beliefs. That's it. In this way, everyone can have a chance to speak up. People's voices will be respected and answered. This will raise the degree of our [nation's] democracy.

The notion of having "multiple authorities" is particularly essential in the effort of incorporating feminist epistemology into QR.

Incorporating Feminist Epistemologies

As a whole, I was mindful about the Chinese Communist Party (CCP)'s legacy on women's liberation, the role of the All China Women's Federation, and positions articulated by newly emergent women's NGOs. I had applied a feminist critique of the state in my own research on Taiwan's economic development. I discussed how the state's policies perpetuated, rather than challenged, gender inequalities. I used examples from my research to illustrate what a feminist epistemology entails and how to apply the legendary notion that the "personal is political" into one's inquiry. In our small group discussions, individual participants called upon incidents in their own lives that resonated with this notion. For example, a participant shared a story about a house renovation in which she did not have a say about which side the doors of her kitchen cabinet should open to even though she's the person who did most of the cooking in her family. According to her, she had been bothered for years by the inconvenient design single-handedly made by her husband. However, she could not figure out why until our discussion. She said, the "light bulb just went on" during our discussion. Others talked about specific incidents at work in which they, as women, were ridiculed in, or excluded from, decision-making processes.

I was pleasantly surprised and utterly impressed when individual participants began to turn the critical lens toward their own roles and positions. Reflecting upon how they exercised their power as a mother, teacher, journalist, or administrator, they no longer saw themselves as powerless objects. They came to interrogate the way power and authority is exercised in daily practices.

The breakthrough made by a staff member of the local China's Women's Federation was particularly remarkable. Jiang Yen was responsible for a financial aid program for girls, and for raising its profile. To that end, she frequently sought to involve the financial aid recipients in public or broadcast events. All along, she had attributed the recipients' reluctance to participate in public events to their introverted personalities. One of her primary goals for her research project was to find ways to make them less camera shy. When she first reported the results of her research findings, she recounted her interview with a recipient who had walked out from a TV interview:

> [We] once arranged a TV interview to publicize our program. A student recipient asked the journalist if it was all right to have the interview recorded off camera. Without thinking, the journalist responded, "Does your TV at home have only voice, with no images?" The student retorted, "We don't have a TV at home." The journalist didn't apologize. He had no responses at all, but kept saying "you should stand over here," "you should face the camera that way," etc. The student eventually refused to be interviewed and walked out. One of her teachers said to her "you should go see a psychotherapist."

When Jiang Yen learned the details of the incident from the student, she thought the encounter had caused grave harm to the student and promised to pursue an apology from the teacher and journalist. However, it was only through line-by-line coding that Jiang Yen came to realize how the program's operation had inadvertently stigmatized the students as "financial aid recipients." In her words, "I realized that the very process of accepting financial aid and the people, events, and activities [involved in the program] have all intensified the student's recipient status." She eventually changed the name of the program from "financial aid" to "scholarship."

Although some participants were wary about the term "feminism" for its widely subscribed negative, politicized connotation, they were empowered by their newfound voices and a sense of collective identity. Most importantly, their critical lenses were not only directed toward others but inwardly toward themselves. Their narratives and reflective notes captured the essential attributes of a transformative process that a successfully executed feminist collaboration entails. During the final days of the second workshop, a male colleague jokily commented that there was no need to worry about having too many feminists around because "you will all quickly work yourselves to death." The joke attests to the intellectual efforts and emotional labour that were dedicated to the undertaking but never appeared in the official reports that relied on statistics and corporate measurements to showcase results.

Discussion: Meaningful Encounters and Tangible Outcomes

The workshops offered a platform for meaningful encounters. First, the participants' newfound meaning and personal commitment to doing research emerged as a critique to the dominant mode of research practice associated with the mill-treading mentality of "writing papers" (*xie wenzhang*, 写文章). By grounding their research projects locally, the participants were able to detach themselves from "[playing] around with all those abstract, meaningless concepts" in the mindless effort of *producing* publications. They came to uphold their research as "pursuing knowledge" (*zuo xuewen* 做学问). The notion of "pursuing knowledge" invoked a truth-searching endeavour that resonated with the Chinese intellectual tradition of knowing and doing (*zhixing heyi* 知行合一) that sanctions an interconnected and mutually reinforced relationship between knowing and doing or implementing.

To be a change agent, the local scholar must take ownership to define "the problem." This is an important but easily neglected aspect of international encounters and dialogue. Such exercises are only meaningful when they are grounded in the local, cultural context. Thus, by carrying out locally grounded research projects guided by the principles of QR, workshop participants went through a transformative journey in becoming change agents facilitated by an inductive pedagogy and epistemological shift that sanction *pursuing knowledge* as a dissenting position to challenge the dominant norms and practices of *writing papers*.

Furthermore, a feminist epistemology enabled the participants to turn a critical eye to their own biases and/or blindness. After making sense of their data through line-by-line coding, it became clear that the participants' initial reading of their data was filtered through their own unchecked perceptions influenced by dominant norms and/or official discourse. For example, instead of recognizing the mechanism that has perpetuated higher dropout rates among elementary-school girls than among boys, several participants used transcripts of teachers to reach the conclusion that parents' traditional ideology and girls' low self-esteem were the primary causes. When I first used the notion "subverting the dominant discourse" (*dianfu zhuliu huayu* 颠覆主流话语) to emphasize QR's critical perspective, the participants were rather startled by the term "subvert" because of its political connotation in the Chinese context. I was therefore particularly delighted when several participants jokingly claimed that they have eventually "subverted" their own unchecked perceptions and assumptions after realizing how their own conceptual baggage had compromised their endeavours.

Central to the meaningful encounters is an inductive methodology that underlines the investigative inquiry. Critical perspectives and technical know-how enable the participants to recognize the mechanisms that have perpetuated patterned relationships and social structures. Rather than remaining aligned to official rhetoric that blames the disempowered, they came to identify processes that produced and reproduced the victims. Much of the epistemological breakthrough is catalyzed by individual trust, commitment, and determination that bonded the participants and instructors and infused the teaching/learning of the workshops. As change agents, the workshop participants came to tackle issues not only relevant to their local, daily challenges but also matters essential to the advancement of democracy and civil society at large.

Many of participants shared their earthshaking experiences through their reflective narratives. For example, a senior scholar at the workshop noted the meaning and political implications of the inductive approach and QR: "The research methodology [we have studied] is indeed a new way of looking at things. It's a new perspective and theoretical approach. It also requires a transformation of the researcher ... I believe it can transform our society as well. That is, change it for the better. So, 'subversion' may not be a bad thing."

These reflections demonstrate that the workshops have definitely gone beyond the original parameters of GAD. As the facilitator, I feel professionally entrusted by the workshop participants to relay the encounters to a broader audience. The conference report, entitled "Transformation, Subversion, and Feminist Activism: Report on the

Workshops of a Developmental Project, Xi'an, China," bears witness to the encounters (Hsiung 1999).

Since the Xi'an Workshop, I have conducted workshops on critical QR in Nanning (Guangxi Province), Guiyang (Guizhou Province), Kunming (Yunnan Province), Nanjing and Hangzhou (Zhejiang Province), and Beijing and Tianjin (Hebei Province). Although these workshops were not funded by CIDA, the intellectual curiosity about QR and feminist epistemology was contagious. Collegial bonds and the trust initiated by the Xi'an workshop were imperative especially because there was no readily available institutionalized support to sustain such collaborative endeavours. As professional networks continued to expand, those subsequent workshops drew participants from faculty members in the humanities and social sciences at universities, researchers from the All China Women's Federation and the Chinese Academy of Social Sciences (CASS) at the provincial levels, and activists from newly emerging women's NGOs. Many of the conversations I had with the workshop participants during the off-hours centred on how to create institutional foundations to indigenize the collective endeavour on QR and on feminist endeavour.

My paper, entitled "*Zhixing Yanjiu Fangfa Chuyi: Laizi Shehui Xingbie Shijiao de Tansuo*" (质性研方法刍议：来自社会性别视角的探索, "On Qualitative Research: Engendering Sociology from Feminist Perspectives"), is published in *Shehuixue Yanjiu* (社会学研究 *Sociological Research*), brought out by the Institute of Sociology, CASS (Hsiung 2001). This is the first publication in China that critically reviews perspectives and practices of social science inquiry in China from the perspectives of feminist epistemology. It challenges the deductive logic that permeates social science inquiry. In addition to insights from my study about class stratification, gender relations, and social change in Taiwan, I draw several excerpts from participants of the workshops to substantiate my critique. Much of my discussion on feminist perspectives in this paper captures the notion of women as change agents.

My curiosity about Mao's legacy of Investigative Research led to my current project on investigative research during China's Great Leap Forward (1958–62) that aims to map out the genealogy of social science inquiry in China, a genealogy that is distinctively different from the trajectory that has been constructed by Denzin and Lincoln based upon the development of QR in the United States.[2] In recent years, as I engaged in dialogue with scholars outside of China about the importance of writing country-specific genealogies of social science research, I recall various comments made by my Chinese colleagues at the Xi'an workshop. In this sense, the female junior faculty members who participated in the Xi'an workshop are not the only beneficiaries. The rippling effects of the CIDA-sponsored initiative have made their way to the global stage with the potential to redraw the intellectual map about practices and development of social science research at the global scale. It is important to note that the intellectual seed was sowed accidentally in China more than a decade earlier.

THE SUMMER INSTITUTE: FEMINIST PEDAGOGY AND PROGRAM DEVELOPMENT IN WOMEN'S STUDIES

After the United Nation's Fourth World Conference on Women, held in China, 1995, the Ford Foundation provided a major grant to help establish and support women's studies programs at key Chinese universities in four disciplines: history, education, sociology, and literature. Much of the work involved translating and publishing feminist scholarship, primarily from the United States, into Chinese, providing training for local scholars, and expanding professional networks throughout China.

In 2002, I worked with Professor Du Fangqin to organize the Summer Institute on Feminist Pedagogy, hosted by the University of Toronto Scarborough (UTSC). This undertaking started from a conversation when Professor Du and I casually talked about what was next for the Curriculum Development Project. We eventually agreed on the need to explore feminist pedagogy – the pedagogical practices that facilitate the teaching and learning of feminism. The main objective was to provide the most "ready" candidates additional training and opportunities to advance women's studies programs through course development and pedagogical practices. I invited Professor Ruth Hayhoe, the CIDA program director, and Professors Margrit Eichler, Renita Wong, and Julia Pan, the CIDA program facilitators, to participate in the Summer Institute.[3] I designed the program to allow the participants to witness feminist principles in practices during their visit. The participants considered three program activities to be the most meaningful. These activities are discussed below.

Insights of Chinese Graduate Students

I recruited four graduate students originally from China, Taiwan, and Hong Kong to be research assistants for the Summer Institute to translate English publications on feminist pedagogy in Canada and United

States and to provide simultaneous English/Chinese translation throughout the Summer Institute. They also presented at a roundtable session to reflect upon their own learning experiences as female minority students in Canada. As students from China, Taiwan, and Hong Kong, they discussed their struggles to make their voices heard in Canadian classrooms. Their stories covered a wide range of issues: what it was like to be surrounded by an audience that was neither knowledgeable nor culturally ready to appreciate their intellectual contribution; the sense of alienation when most of the assigned readings on women's and gender studies did not speak to their personal experiences as members of a minority in Canada; the effects of silencing in the classroom; the mechanism and pedagogical practices that had perpetuated such in-class dynamics; and their strategies to confront the silencing effects in a classroom in which each was the only non-white student. Together, these four Chinese graduate students identified attributes of an effective, inspirational feminist teacher.

These students' insights were particularly appreciated because the workshop participants all belonged to the Han ethnic majority group in the Chinese context and have never had personal knowledge of being a minority. They could easily relate to stories of the students because of their shared ethnic and cultural background. The conversation was particularly effective because no English-to-Chinese translation was involved. The students digested and synthesized their experiences, and articulated what it was like to be discriminated against. Many workshop participants commented on the rare opportunity for them to reflect upon their own privileged position as the Han majority in China and what it would take to incorporate such new insights into their teaching. For the students, it was exuberating to be part of the workshop as the catalysts. Being the workshop presenters brought a particular sense of satisfaction for them because their insights were appreciated and their status elevated.

*Visits to the Women and Gender Studies Institute
and Transitional Year Program*

The Chinese participants were interested in learning about the efforts it had taken to set up the recently established Women and Gender Studies Institute at the University of Toronto (UT). They were surprised as well as somewhat relieved to realize that building an institutional foundation for women's and gender studies was no less trying in Canada than in China. The Chinese participants also observed classroom teaching. It was eye-opening for them to see how specific strategies were used by the instructors to facilitate student-centred, experiential-based learning. For example, in order to ensure that students would not shy away from asking "stupid questions," Professor Kathryn Morgan, a philosopher and seasoned teacher, asked students in her graduate seminar to write down questions on pieces of paper provided by her. She then collected the paper and questions. When she addressed the questions one by one, the focus was on the question without any inferences made to individual students who had raised the questions in the first place. When the Chinese participants later developed their own syllabi and lesson plans, many of them included publications and resources they had acquired through the Summer Institute. Such text-based outputs, however, do not adequately capture moments of meaningful engagement that allow for a nuanced understanding of principles of feminist pedagogy.

The Chinese participants also paid a visit to the Transitional Year Program (TYP). The TYP is a well-established program that provides support to adults from underprivileged communities who did not have an opportunity to finish high school because of financial problems, family difficulties, or other circumstances beyond their control. I arranged the visit and conversation in order to show the institutional structure and pedagogical support needed to address systematic inequalities in higher education. Two faculty members from the TYP provided information about its history, a program overview, and accomplishments. Two TYP students presented their experiences and explained what higher education meant to them and their families.

The Chinese participants were surprised to learn that UT, an internationally acclaimed, prestigious institution, established the TYP in the 1970s and has sustained the program for decades. It was eye-opening for many participants that the program was set up for members of the Indigenous, African-Canadian, and LGBTQ communities, sole-support parents, persons with disabilities, and individuals from working-class backgrounds of all ethnicities. They found this virtually inconceivable, because the participants perceived the Chinese educational system as a merit-based, fair system; students must prove their academic excellence through strict competitions to enter universities. It did not occur to them that the material foundation of such a merit-based system was systemic and hierarchical. They were particularly moved by the TYP students who shared their personal trials and triumphs – how the TYP program has given them a second chance. The instructors' commitment and devotion also deeply touched the participants. At the Q & A session, the participants raised questions such as: "How has the program managed to secure support from the administration?" "What have been the most challenging aspects of running the program?" "How does the program get connected to local communities?" and "How do students handle stigma?" Much of the conversation touched upon issues beyond the conventional scope of women's and gender studies. While some participants emphasized the unfortunate, necessary evil of the Chinese educational system, others commented and reflected upon the blindness and shortcoming of a merit-based, elite-centred educational structure that systematically and simultaneously values the privileged and talented groups and denies access to the marginalized, disadvantaged others.

Conversation with the Officer of the Sexual Harassment Office

In order to capture the institutionalized aspects of gender and equity, I invited the officer of the Sexual Harassment Office (SHO) to talk to the participants. The officer discussed the historical context of the SHO's establishment and mandate. She provided a detailed description of the SHO's services to undergraduate, graduate, faculty, and staff, the procedures of making a complaint, and the resolution process. The officer used individual cases to elaborate on the SHO's responsibilities and practices. For the Chinese participants, this was the first time they had come across an office established at a university that was responsible for addressing sexual harassment related issues. They were particularly impressed by the insights presented by the seasoned officer. As one of the participants stated, "This is certainly the most profound, down-to-earth feminist activism I've ever seen."

The SHO is an exemplar of a feminist-inspired institutional setup intended to disrupt the systematic patriarchal norms and practices that are embedded in academic daily encounters, and that often disable and dis-empower women as equal partners. Although the Summer Institute was centred on feminist pedagogy and the development of curriculum in women's studies in China, conversation with the SHO officer provided opportunities for the Chinese participants to appreciate the need to institutionalize feminist principles in diverse areas. Curriculum and program development in women's studies should be perceived as a critical but only initial step of feminist praxis in universities.

Discussion: Meaningful Encounters and Tangible Outcomes

The Summer Institute was organized to facilitate the development of women's studies programs in Chinese universities. It called upon institutional resources at UT as a means of engagement. Most importantly, personal narratives and local, accumulated knowledge were activated for the Chinese participants to mull over as they embarked on their respective journeys. As the Summer Institute drew to an end, Professor Du and I decided to bring out a CD-ROM entitled Feminist Pedagogy (*Xin Nushu* 新女书), to solidify the endeavour and disseminate teaching resources and pedagogical practices for the advancement of women's studies programs in China.

The CD-ROM includes samples of syllabi developed by Chinese scholars who had already designed and taught gender-related courses at the time. Based upon discussions held at the Summer Institute, I compiled and addressed questions and issues instructors encounter in the classroom, referring to the literature and pedagogical resources. Although this did expand my own understanding and knowledge on the subject matter, it is not my area of research, nor have I had opportunities to develop it substantively. When the unit committed to produce the CD-ROM at UTSC was closed down as result of administrative restructuring, a colleague picked up and worked on the project as a "work of love." In China, the CD-ROM is distributed through professional networks rather than being marketed formally through commercial venues. This informal, do-as-we-go approach attests to the pioneering nature of our work. To a large extent, established professional resources were either non-existent or virtually beyond our reach. The non-institutionalized attribute of our effort makes sustainability challenging, if not impossible.

In his preface, Dr Kwong Loi Shun, the vice-president of UT and principal at UTSC at the time, commented on the international scope and interdisciplinary nature of the Summer Institute. He also praised the innovative merit of the CD-ROM. To highlight its transformative potential, Dr Shun referred to the Chinese saying, "It takes ten years for trees to grow. It takes a hundred years for educational endeavours to flourish" (*shinian shumu, bainian shuren,* 十年樹木, 百年樹人).

CHINESE WOMEN ORGANIZING

Over the last decades, women's groups in China have been continuously and concertedly seeking to carve out a space to articulate their position and speak with their own voices somewhere between the CCP state, feminist theories, and the international women's movement. Maria Jaschok, Cecilia Milwertz, and I co-organized the workshop entitled "Chinese Women Organizing" at Oxford University, United Kingdom, in July 1999. A book of the same title was later published (Hsiung, Jaschok, et al. 2001). The project provides a platform for Chinese scholars and activists to document and analyze women's activism in contemporary China. To the English-speaking audience, it challenges the image of Chinese women as passive, docile, and victimized, which continues to linger in much of Western literature. It also offers contextually grounded nuance to address the NGO debates which have often fixated on Western-framed questions such as "whether or not there are *real* NGOs in China" or "whether or not the All China Women's Federation is an NGO." In contrast, the work of the Chinese Queer (*Tongzhi*) Group, the East Meets West Feminist Translation Group, and the Chinese Society for Women's Studies testifies that engaging in women's organizing has compelled Chinese academics and activists to contextualize and transcend the East-West boundaries.

At the workshop, simultaneous English-Chinese translations were arranged to ensure that neither the English nor the Chinese-speaking participants were inhibited by language barriers. This was particularly liberating for the Chinese participants whose self-expression and communication capacity are often constrained in the international arena by the hegemony of English, being held as the "international language." Not just on a linguistic level but on other discursive levels, the workshop and book were intended to benefit from differences across feminist praxes. Although only selected presentations at the workshop were included as chapters in the final volume, debates and diverse positions presented at the workshop were transcribed and excerpted. Rather than presenting a definitive position, which tends to close off conversations, the sections entitled "Other Voices – Other Conversations" were presented to preserve and continue dialogue on multiple levels of interaction. Instead of assuming ourselves to be professional experts in the subject fields, the co-editors and I rendered ourselves to be facilitators of the Chinese women's organizing. Thus, what set this project apart from the conventional academic exercise was the organizers' deliberate effort to resist intellectual elitism that would privilege scholarly theorizing over empirical-based exploration. This enabled Chinese academics and activists to speak for themselves as the subjective agents, rather than being represented by the experts as the objectified "others."

The workshop served as a catalyst in various ways. This is captured by the post-workshop reflections from the participants. For some, the workshop enabled academics and activists in China and from the West to engage in hot debates. For the Chinese participants from China, it bridged the hierarchical divide between the academics and activists, the Han majority and religious/ethnic minorities, and the urban and rural-based organizations. For the activists in particular, sharing exuberating and frustrating moments of activism at the workshop was like taking a vow to continue the work and to pass on the torch. It sustained them by keeping the internal flame of the campfire that had brought them into the movement in the first place. For the organizational path-breakers, telling their own histories was a "process of building identity and cementing it solid" (Stearns 2001, 268).

The book provides in-depth descriptions and analyses of grass-roots activities surrounding the Chinese women's movement in the 1980s and 1990s. Conceptualizing women's organizing as a process, the narratives and reflection presented in the book capture the emerging spaces and constraining forces, the feisty push and strategic halt, and the progressive developments and regressive impediments. To portray a gradually emerging but constantly reconfigured mosaic, the volume includes the work of academics who concentrate on research and curriculum development at universities; that of activists focusing on community mobilizing; the articulations of Muslim women transgressing the religious and ethnic boundaries; the work of representatives of international donors keenly aware of their power in shaping the directions of local movements; the positions of the state-sponsored Women's Federation; and dissenting voices of newly established women's NGOs.

Discussions: Meaningful Encounters and Tangible Outcomes

The most significant tangible outcome of the project is accounted by Gao Xiaoxian, the founder of the Shaanxi Association for Women and Family (SAWF). Gao founded the SAWF in 1986 to advocate for research and to carry out local initiatives to address gender inequalities. According to Gao, the SAWF has always been conceived as simply a means to "do things." Discussions at the workshop led her to reflect upon the SAWF as an *organizing* site which embodied processes and practices. Although the SAWF has been in operation for fourteen years, "there is no thorough, healthy system of decision-making or management." Gao raised questions such as "What is similar, or different, in the principles and objectives of feminist women's organizations when compared to those of patriarchal organizations?" and "How do we conceptualize 'organizing/organization' so that it is participatory, empowering, and carried by sisterhood?" (Gao 2001, 259). Seeking answers to those questions in practice, Gao invited experts to assess the SAWF's organizing practices. As a result, the SAWF's strategic planning for the following five years was set to "improve the institution and work of the Association; to enhance the ability of its members; to build participatory, democratic, and sustainable modes of women's popular organizing activities" (Gao 2001, 260). Gao considered the workshop to have been the most fruitful conference she attended in recent years. As one of the most prominent activists on gender issues, her analysis on the *politics of organizing* and her subsequent action to democratize the SAWF materialized the potential of the workshop through transcending the boundaries of East-West and academia-activism.

CONCLUSION

By writing about the *doing* of feminist collaboration, this chapter focuses on *process* and *efforts*, two aspects of the GAD program that disappeared when CIDA's legacy was written up into official reports. The notion of meaningful encounters allows me to demonstrate, for example, that at the Xi'an workshop, the transformative process was brought about by the workshop participants' proactive engagement and risk-taking. By conducting locally situated research projects, the workshop participants not only found value in "conducting research" but saw themselves as change agents in local activism. The inference some of them made about the implications of QR for China's democratic future echoes the ultimate goal of CIDA's involvement in China. In the case of the Summer Institute, a broadened scope of engagement covered topics such as race/ethnicity, pedagogical strategies of student-centred curriculum, an inclusive higher-education system, and feminism-informed workplace environments. The process of engagement was facilitated not only by researchers/scholars but by undergraduate and graduate students, instructors, and staff.

By switching sole attention from results to process, it becomes possible to capture tangible outcomes that do not fall into the framework and categorization that CIDA has developed to accredit its GAD program in China. The most illustrative example is the undertaking assumed by Gao Xiaoxian that eventually turned SAWF from an NGO working for women's causes to a platform of democratizing practices. The seed was sowed at the Oxford workshop on Chinese women organizing. It has taken more than a decade before I could attend to comments made at the Xi'an workshop about QR, qualitative approach, and Mao's Investigative Research. The ripple effects attest to the diverse potentials and uncharted territory embedded in the *doing* of feminist collaboration. As local knowledge, none of these can be adequately covered by statistics and corporate measurements. Thus, description and analysis of the process provide insights and raw materials for future academic theorizing and government's policy planning.

My focus on *efforts* is a call to make visible the invisible emotional and intellectual labour that infuses the GAD program. Neglecting the emotional labour is particularly problematic. As it has been well argued in the literature on parenting and housework, a disproportionate amount of the emotional labour in GAD, and arguably in other developmental projects, is carried out by women. Not acknowledging these efforts is equivalent to turning a blind eye on gender inequalities implicated in women's unpaid reproductive labour.

Furthermore, as my analysis in this chapter has demonstrated, much intellectual labour is called upon to plan and implement CIDA's pathmaking program. Clearly marked, already-paved tracks do not exist in feminist collaboration. For example, as a person of diaspora, to initiate discussion on the relationship between the state and women's issues in China, I apply my research about gender relationship, family structures, and the roles of the state in Taiwan's economic development. It is intellectually fulfilling to step out of the academic ivy tower to realize the vision of public sociology advocated by M. Burawoy when he calls his colleagues in sociology to find collective calling in his capacity as the president of the American Sociology Association. Nevertheless, values in the *doing* of feminist collaboration are not necessarily recognized. In fact, my work in feminist collaboration as a Chinese diaspora was questioned when my department's chair at the time asked, "You're paid by Canadian taxpayers, why are you doing work in China?" The merit and integrity of such work are undermined by statements such as "if you continue to do this type of work, you will never get promoted."

By focusing on *process* and *efforts*, this chapter explores opportunities presented by CIDA's GAD program. It has not explicitly addressed challenges to sustain the GAD program. This is particularly important as CIDA completes its involvement in China. To a large extent, the projects discussed in this chapter are consummated through pre-existing institutional setups and local practices. To sustain and to institutionalize the meaningful encounters and tangible outcomes I have laid out in this chapter require additional resources, on-going commitment, and path-breaking leadership beyond the scope of any particular projects. For example, it only became apparent to me after the Xi'an workshop had been completed that it was impossible for me to provide on-going support to the workshop participants who had then returned to their own universities or other work units. As the sole qualitative researcher locally, it was extremely trying for each one of them to sustain their newly acquired intellectual interest. Although faculty members who took part in the Summer Institute have all offered gender-related courses in their own disciplines, women's studies programs at all involved universities continue to struggle. Women's NGOs in China must simultaneously assert their positions and collaborate with other players in the field. Whether or not seeds sown at specific GAD initiatives come to germinate and flourish is worth exploring after CIDA leaves China.

NOTES

1 For a description of the project, see Boyd and Pan (2001). The project is also discussed in some detail in Qiang and Wang (chapter 11 of this volume).
2 Over the years, Denzin and Lincoln have revised their writing about the development of QR in the United States. Their latest version is in Norman K. Denzin and Yvonna S. Lincoln, *The Sage Handbook of Qualitative Research* (Thousand Oaks: Sage Publications, 2011). Alasuutari has presented an alternative framework to understand the development of QR. For Alasuutari's counterargument, see Pertti Alasuutari, "The Globalization of Qualitative Research," in *Qualitative Research in Practice*, ed. Clive Seale, Giampietro Gobo, Jaber F. Gubrium, and David Silverman, 595–608 (Thousand Oaks: Sage Publications, 2004).
3 The Canadian facilitators include: Leslie Chan (Information Technology, UTSC); Afua Copper (History, UT); Teresa Dawson (Teaching and Learning Centre, UTSC); Margrit Eichler (Sociology, Institute of Women's and Gender Studies); Ruth Hayhoe (Education, Ontario Institute for Studies in Education, OISE); Ping-chun Hsiung (Sociology, UT); June Larkin (Education, Institute of Women's and Gender Studies); Julia Pan (Education, OISE); Paddy Stamp (the Sexual Harassment Office, UT); Renita Wong (Social Work, York University); the Transitional Year Program (TYP); and Anne Wu, Zhu Ni, Rachel Zhou, and Fei Wu (graduate students).

14

Closing the Circle: Reflections on Past and Future Partnerships across the Disciplines

RUTH HAYHOE AND CHRISTY HAYHOE

CLOSING THE CIRCLE

This volume began with a description of the conference held at Tsinghua University, where we gathered leading scholars from across nine disciplines who had been involved in collaborative projects between Chinese and Canadian universities, supported by the Canadian International Development Agency (CIDA), in the first two decades after the end of China's Cultural Revolution. It was a remarkable group of intellectual leaders, and a rare opportunity for specialists in areas such as marine-earth sciences, agriculture, medicine, and environment to sit down with scholars of political science, management, anthropology, education, and law to share what they had learned in this cross-cultural journey. We were delighted that twelve of the keynote speakers were able to craft chapters for this volume. The main purpose of this concluding chapter is to draw together the themes that emerged, and reflect on their implications for current and future collaboration.

First, however, we need to complete the circle of the conference by providing a brief overview of keynote papers in three scientific areas that were presented in the conference program but not subsequently developed into chapters. It was a great honour that each of these leading scientists found time in their busy schedules to come to Beijing – from Nanjing, Wuhan, Winnipeg, and Changchun – and make dynamic presentations.[1] We thus regard them as important contributors to this volume, and are including their biographies in the list of contributors. Meanwhile, it is our honour to provide a summary of the collaboration that took place in coastal and ocean sciences, agriculture, and medicine in this chapter. For each case, we will start with the genesis of each project, then go through its chronology and summarize the major impacts and ongoing outcomes.

Collaboration in Marine-Earth Sciences

Professor Wang Ying of Nanjing University's School of Geographic and Ocean Sciences is an academician of the Chinese Academy of Sciences (CAS) who has been personally engaged in collaboration with a number of Canadian universities over a period of thirty-five years. Her history of collaboration began in February 1979, when she was sponsored by the Chinese government as one of three pioneer visiting scholars to work as a research fellow at Dalhousie University's Department of Geology and at the Atlantic Geoscience Centre of Bedford Institute of Oceanography. She returned to Nanjing University in 1982, and immediately organized discussions and workshops with Canadian partners, leading to a successful project supported by Canada's International Development Research Centre (IDRC) on the "Sedimentation Process of Tidal Embayments and their Relationship to Deep Water Harbour Development along Hainan Island, China." This project lasted from 1988 to 1992 and resulted in the establishment of a laboratory in coastal ocean research at Nanjing University, as well as the successful development of harbours in three coastal areas of Hainan Island. A total of twenty-two young scientists were trained through this project and continue to serve at Nanjing University, and a conference held in 1990 resulted in an edited book containing fifty-eight related papers (Wang and Schafer 1992).

The second phase of collaboration continued the focus on coastal zones of Hainan Province with environmental training for integrated monitoring and management, this time supported by CIDA's Canada-China Higher-Education Program (CCHEP), which had followed the Canada-China University Linkage Program (CCULP) and Special University Linkages Consolidation Program (SULCP).[2] The Canadian partners in this collaboration were the University of Waterloo, the University of Guelph, and Wilfrid Laurier University, and the project ran from 1997 to 2002. This project had a significant impact on the local community and government in Hainan. Many of the fifty students and trainees who participated are now employed in local government, research institutions, and the private sector. In addition, a training base was established during the project for ongoing environmental monitoring.

The third phase of collaboration was also supported by CIDA, and ran from 2002 to 2007 as a Tier One project parallel to that of the University of Toronto (UT) over the same period.[3] The project was titled "Eco-planning and Environmental Management in Coastal Communities." The Dalian University of Technology and Hainan Province were formal partners in this project, alongside Nanjing University and the University of Waterloo. Although the focus remained on Hainan Province and the Hainan Research Academy of Environmental Sciences, Jiangsu Province was also involved, with some support for Yangkou Harbour construction and coastal tourism development.

These years of scientific collaboration, which involved four schools within Nanjing University's Faculty of Earth Sciences – Earth Sciences and Engineering; Geographic and Oceanic Sciences; Atmospheric Sciences; and Environmental Sciences – have now blossomed into the establishment of a Sino-Canadian College on the Nanjing University campus as a platform for promoting international academic cooperation and exchange with the University of Waterloo. Established in 2005, the college already has four cohorts of graduates, and a strong emphasis on the geo-sciences and environmental sciences in its programs. It also fosters research collaboration, workshops, and exchange visits of all kinds. A visit in 2013 by the Honourable David Johnson, Canada's Governor General and a former president of the University of Waterloo, provided the opportunity for a high-level lecture on the "Diplomacy of Knowledge" that emphasized the importance of scientific and educational exchange in this era of the knowledge economy (Wang 2014). This institutionalization of the many collaborative linkages of the past takes us back to the comment by a senior scholar of education in chapter 1, who noted the need for an organization at the university level which could give long-term continuity to changing forms and themes of partnership.[4]

Collaboration in Agricultural Sciences

The collaboration in agricultural research between the University of Manitoba (UM) and the Huazhong Agricultural University (HAU) that led to the development of canola as a health-enhancing edible oil has been one of the most celebrated of the CIDA-supported projects, due to the combination of scientific achievement and commercial success it embodied, as was noted earlier.[5] We were fortunate to have senior scientists from both the HAU and the UM's Department of Plant Science presenting keynote papers at the conference, and so we were able to hear reflections on the experience from both the Chinese and Canadian sides. Since Professor Zhou Yongming and academician Fu Tingdong of HAU were involved in the collaboration from its inception, while Professor Dilantha Fernando of UM joined during Phase II, we will begin with insights from the HAU account.

The genesis of the project lay in a visit from UM's vice-president, leading a delegation of five, to HAU in June 1986. This trip included visits to the Departments of Agronomy, Agricultural Economics, and Soil Chemistry, as well as to related labs, and a bilateral agreement for cooperation and exchange was signed. The two universities then jointly applied to CIDA for inclusion in the CCULP, which was granted in September 1988. The initial phase of the project involved the training of four PhD students and twelve postdoctoral fellows from HAU at UM, shorter visits by eight senior visiting scholars to undertake cooperative research at UM, and visits by twelve UM faculty to give lectures at HAU. These exchanges gradually blossomed into ongoing interaction and long-term collaborative research relating to the development of disease-resistant wheat and rapeseed, and the application of research results in farming communities in both countries. This project was one of eleven selected for a second phase as part of the SULCP, which ran from 1996 to 2001. On the Canadian side, the University of Saskatchewan, the University of Guelph, and several research institutes under Agric-Food Canada were drawn into Phase II of the project. HAU was both a participant and a leader in a series of Sino-Canadian Agricultural University Presidents Forums. In addition, a number of collaborative programs for students at undergraduate and master's levels evolved during this second phase, as well as collaborative research programs among faculty on both sides (Zhou and Fu 2014).

Professor Dilantha Fernando, a high-level expert in plant diseases, particularly diseases affecting rapeseed, provided his perspective on the project based on his involvement from the beginning of Phase II in 1996 up to the present (Fernando 2014). In his conference lecture, he explained how Professor Baldur Steffansson of UM's Department of Plant Science had pioneered the development of a variety of rapeseed that could be used as edible oil in the 1970s, and was regarded as the "Father of Canola." Given that Canada and China are the two leading rapeseed-producing countries in the world, they have a common interest in expanding the growth of this valuable commodity. The economic outcomes of this collaboration have been nothing less than spectacular, with canola becoming Canada's most important cash crop in 2012, surpassing wheat. On the Chinese side, both economic and social contributions have also been striking. Chinese farmers have benefitted hugely from a crop that is less labour-intensive than others; in fact, this crop is particularly suited to the increasing number of women taking up agricultural roles as young men move to the cities, with as many as one million rural women positively affected by its use. On the environmental side, the collaboration has also had a significant impact, since many cultivars have been developed that are resistant to pests and pathogens, reducing the use of environmentally harmful chemical fungicides. Canola seed meal, a byproduct from the extraction of canola oil, has also become a nutritious food supplement as animal feed.

Professor Fernando explained that initially the collaboration arose in UM's Department of Plant Science, but over time the Departments of Animal Science, Food Science, and Human Ecology also joined in, as all three departments had scientists working on the oil and meal of rapeseed/canola. The main participants on the HAU side were breeders, cytogeneticists, molecular biologists, and pathologists from the Institute of Crop Genetics and Breeding. Project research included breeding for high oil content and for low saturates, a study of land races for genetic diversity, and new genes with resistance to blackleg and Sclerotina.

While the formal collaboration supported by CIDA's SULCP came to a close in 2001 with a high-level conference that brought together more than 150 researchers, this was only a beginning. Professor Fernando noted that participation in this conference opened up many opportunities for research collaboration in agricultural institutions across China, as well as visits to farming communities. The training of students and researchers from both sides has continued, and 43 per cent of the international students at UM are now from China, while numerous UM students went on exchange to China between 2007 and 2012.

UM faculty members have won external research grants of $6.4 million in collaboration with Chinese partners over the past ten years. There has also been a related program funded by CIDA to support collaboration in HIV/AIDS research between UM's Faculty of Medicine and the West China School of Public Health at Sichuan University (2007–12). In addition, UM's Faculty of Social Work and the China Women's University were supported by CIDA in developing rural social work services in Sichuan, Inner Mongolia, and Shandong, where there was a focus on reducing gender inequality for rural women. Tuula Heinonen, a senior UM professor of Social Work, presented a paper at the conference about this project (Heinonen and Liu 2014).

Two CIDA-supported projects have thus blossomed into a wide network of collaborative-research activities that have created fruitful training opportunities for students and young scientists on both sides. Of equal significance have been the economic, social, and environmental benefits.

Collaboration in Medical Science and Cancer Care

Collaboration in cancer research began with Professor Liu Guojin, who went to Université Laval's Faculty of Medicine in 1986 for a two-year postdoctoral fellowship in the thoracic surgery division. The fact that Professor Liu came from China's Norman Bethune University of Medical Science (NBUMS), located in the northeastern city of Changchun, may have given a certain impetus to early considerations of collaboration – given the history of Dr Norman Bethune, a colourful Canadian doctor who supported Mao's revolution. We were privileged to have Professor Liu's former student and mentee, Professor Fan Zhimin, as a keynote speaker at the conference. Professor Fan is the current director of the Breast Surgery Department at the No. 1 Hospital of Jilin University, a part of the NBUMS that has been integrated through merger into the larger Jilin University.

The Bethune-Laval collaboration began through a visit of a small group of surgeons from Laval to Changchun in 1989, facilitated by Professor Liu Guojin, and discussions that led to a decision to focus on collaboration in the area of oncology. This collaboration was to include the establishment of an oncology unit in the first hospital of NBUMS, and appropriate training for health professionals working as a multidisciplinary team. The collaboration also included a plan for developing a tumor registry for the purpose of identification, follow-up, and treatment. Professor Jean Couture, retiring director of Laval's Department of Surgery, took the initiative to apply to CIDA for inclusion in the CCULP, and was successful in gaining a grant from 1990 to 1995. Over this period, a first group of eighteen Chinese doctors, nurses, epidemiologists, and technologists came to Laval. On their return, they took up positions in a newly established Bethune-Laval Oncology Unit (BLOU) in the First Teaching Hospital of NBUMS (Deschenes 2014). In 1993, a major conference was held in Changchun, where it was recognized that the BLOU could be a good model for other hospitals in China.[6]

Under Professor Couture's dynamic leadership, the two universities were successful in competing for the SULCP. The additional five years of this second phase of the project, from 1996 to 2001, made possible the development of a set of "mini-BLOUs" in Inner Mongolia, Shenyang, Zhuhai, Qingdao, and Shenzhen, as well as the development of palliative care units. The culminating conference in 2001 attracted more than 300 participants from all over China as well as from Quebec. Although this conference marked the end of the CIDA funding, the collaboration continued, moving into new areas and regions (Liu 2014).

There was great concern in China at that time about the prevention of lung cancer in a country of smokers, and Professor Couture was able to get support from the government of Quebec to launch a major campaign of public education against smoking in the North and West of China from 2003 to 2006. All kinds of media were used, and crucial help came from the involvement of Mark Rowswell, a Canadian known throughout China for his skill in comic dialogue. A well-loved public figure in China, Rowswell is sometimes seen as the Norman Bethune of the contemporary period!

As China became more and more prosperous, it took responsibility for the funding of ongoing collaboration that involved mutual exchanges between 2007 and 2013. Five Laval students and one senior medical professor went for study and research in Changchun each year, while more than twenty scholars and several doctoral students came from Changchun for study and research collaboration at Laval.

This collaboration between Laval and NBUMS has had a major impact on cancer research and cancer treatment at a national level in China. One of the features that led to its success was the continuity of leadership on the Laval side, with project leadership passing from Professor Couture to his successor as director of surgery, Professor Luc Deschenes, and subsequently to Professor Yvan Douville, who was present at the conference with a delegation of eleven from Laval's Faculty of Medicine. The greatest challenge now on the Chinese side relates to issues of health provision for China's huge population, and to reforms in the health system that make treatment widely available.[7]

COMMONALITIES AND LEGACIES OF THE CIDA PROJECTS

The projects discussed in this volume, as well as those summarized in the first half of this chapter, covered many disciplines, including: environmental, agricultural, and medical science; engineering; management and cooperative education; education, law and gender-equity issues. Dozens of universities and hundreds of scholars, teachers, and students, both Chinese and Canadian, participated in the projects. However, despite such a wide range of knowledge fields and institutions, strong commonalities exist among the projects. Their timing during a period of rapid growth and development led to greater influence than might have been expected. Their focus on human resources development, or "training the trainers," led to wide-ranging and long-lasting influence in some cases. Their focus on gender-equality and concern for minorities enabled and empowered these often disenfranchised members of Chinese society. Many of the Chinese universities that participated in the projects were strengthened internally and some rose to exert considerable influence on a national and even international scale. Finally, the impacts of the projects were felt not only on-campus, but in industry, political circles, and general society.

In addition, participants on both sides of the projects reported similar experiences and learning. The authors of this volume, as well as many of those interviewed for this volume, reported on learning the importance of mutual respect for each others' culture and norms, the value of in-kind contributions from both sides, and the benefits of strong working and personal relationships, many of which have lasted to this day. A strong sense of gratitude pervades most responses.

Common Starting Points and Results from the CIDA Projects

As mentioned throughout this volume, the CIDA projects took place during a remarkable and opportune time in Chinese history.[8] China was open to the world for the first time in decades, and Vice-Premier Deng Xiaoping had specifically advocated the need for China to learn from advanced foreign countries. As economic, industrial, and education reforms took hold, China was experiencing an increasing need for knowledge, experience, and technology in a wide range of fields. In addition, friendly relations were already in place between China and Canada for a number of historical reasons, including the contribution of noted Canadian Dr Norman Bethune to China's revolution.

The importance of the projects' timing has been remarked on again and again in this volume. For example, in chapter 4, Mirus discusses how China's requirement of elite administrators to implement new economic policies provided the ideal setting for management cooperation projects. In chapter 7, Li et al. note that due to the reorganization of the industrial ministries that had formerly controlled them, many engineering universities were in the process of changing their entire administrative systems, and looking for models and paths to follow. Linkages between engineering universities in China and Canada provided the support that was needed in a time of growth and change. In chapters 10, 11, and 13, the authors mention that the SULCP project focusing on training women faculty members in higher education occurred during the emergence of the women's movement in China. Thanks in part to these and many other examples of serendipitous timing, the CIDA projects exerted greater influence in China than might have been expected. In addition, by responding directly to China's clear and expressed needs, the CIDA projects ensured their relevance and usefulness.

Another reason for the projects' great influence was their focus on human resources development, or "training the trainers." As Li et al. point out in chapter 7, the CIDA projects improved existing programs within universities and helped with the development of new ones. These programs, along with the training received by scholars and teachers, provided universities with the ability they needed to train future leaders. It is worth noting that many Chinese participants of the projects are now highly placed in Chinese academic and political circles. For example, Mirus lists many respected Chinese leaders who were once part of the University of Alberta (U of A) university linkage in chapter 4. Similar lists can be found in chapters 7 to 11.

Not only did these projects exert great influence at the time, in many cases the influence has proved to be long lasting. In chapter 3, Bild maintains that the training and development that occurred during the linkage programs have left "serious indelible marks in the minds of all participants" and have left participants with a general receptivity to products of other cultures. Long-standing relationships and partnerships derived from the projects are mentioned specifically in chapters 4, 6, and 11, and are implicit throughout this volume.

Yet another commonality of the CIDA projects was the emphasis on gender equality, and a special focus on minorities where appropriate. Although only a few of the projects specifically focused on women or minorities,[9] CIDA's Gender and Development Program's objectives were incorporated into many other projects, including management, engineering, environmental science, and education.[10]

The Chinese universities involved in the Canada-China university linkages were strengthened by their participation in the projects, and some experienced elevations in status in the years following them. For example, the School of Management of Xi'an Jiaotong University became one of the top management schools in China after its projects in management education with the U of A.[11] The Lanzhou Railway Institute (LRI) benefited from its linkage with Ryerson Polytechnic Institute (now Ryerson University) with improved teaching methods, administration, and research, and eventually won the National Award for Science and Technology Progress[12] (chapter 7 of this volume). Similar results are mentioned in this volume for almost every Chinese institute of higher learning involved in the Canada-China Management Education Program (CCMEP), CCULP, and SULCP projects. As Li et al. remarked in chapter 7, "The timely upgrades these projects brought to the standards and capacities of the universities made the universities more qualified to face the tremendous challenge of China's quick popularization of higher education at the beginning of this century" (155).

Finally, the CIDA projects, while having a large impact on campuses across China, also had an impact on non-academic circles including industry, politics, and general society. In chapter 2, Evans states that international cooperative projects such as these have played an important part in aiding economic and social change in China. Examples abound to back up his point. In chapter 3, Bild describes a Canadian specialist in transportation from the Université de Montréal (UdeM), who worked among Chinese universities during the CIDA projects in the field of light rail transit (LRT). The impacts from this scholar's work affect China's transportation systems even today. In chapters 4, 5, and 6, the authors describe how Chinese management students and teachers were fascinated to see the close connections between Canadian management schools and various industries, and how they worked to develop such connections for themselves. In chapter 7, Li et al. describe how the growing relationships between Chinese universities and industry allowed new technologies that were developed in universities to be "smoothly implemented" in relevant industries. They provide the example of how the computer system for logistics monitoring and management developed at LRI is now used in Beijing Capital Airport. In chapter 8, Chen et al. describe how erosion management projects assisted farmers in rural China, and in chapter 9, Walls describes how the deputy commissioner of a province returned home after studying at Simon Frasier University (SFU) and took emphatic and effective steps to reduce poverty in her region.

Impacts in political circles are harder to judge, but several authors have remarked on project participants who have gone on to enter politics, and on politicians and government officials attending training sessions.[13] Furthermore, simply by their focus on human-resource development, the new ways of thinking introduced during these projects are likely to have spread far via the interconnectivity of human relationships and dialogue.

Common Experiences of the CIDA Projects

Many project participants were interviewed on their experiences during the CIDA projects, and the authors, most of whom led these projects, have numerous recollections of their own. Each participant has his or her own story, but common threads are woven throughout the individual experiences described in this volume. Almost every author mentions the lessons learned by both sides on the importance of respecting and understanding each others' culture and norms. Terms such as "mutual trust," "understanding," and "mutual respect" are used again and again to describe how project participants from the two sides came to regard each other.[14]

In fact, mutual trust and respect were indeed essential, since collaborations included joint decision making, planning, implementation, and analysis.[15] The other in-kind contributions provided by both sides – funding and training from the Canadian side balanced by the human and material resources provided by the Chinese side[16] – also helped to maintain equity between partners, which is essential in reducing dependency, as discussed in chapter 11. Equally important was the fact that both sides benefited from the projects. For example, Lefebvre et al. state in chapter 12 that "the learning was mutual," and in chapter 5, Xi et al. describe how the management education projects provided "crucial learning" to Canadian schools on managing international projects and linkages.

The importance of good working relationships is also mentioned repeatedly in this volume,[17] and these relationships have in some cases developed into life-long friendships, such as the "Chinese mother" and "Canadian mother" relationship described in chapter 11. And finally, one of the most pervasive of these common threads is a sense of appreciation and enrichment. Chinese visiting scholars and students recall their welcome and care in Canada with strong gratitude and both Chinese and Canadian participants express their sense of achievement and personal enrichment from their involvement.

CONCLUSION

In summary, we take a last look at the four questions posed by the editors to each of the chapter authors:

1. In what ways did universities, acting in partnership, contribute to China's economic revitalization and rapid transformation?

By responding directly to China's development needs, and by providing universities with the training, technology, and programs they required to successfully operate and to train new talent, the CIDA projects helped enable the universities to respond to China's economic and social reforms.

2. How far did university partnerships foster the spawning of new ideas that would address crucial issues of humane and democratic governance, social justice, and environmental sustainability arising in the train of rapid economic and technological change?

During their studies in Canada, Chinese scholars and students were exposed to new ideas, ways of thinking, and methodologies, many of which were specifically aimed at aiding the Chinese in dealing with the traps and issues that come with rapid development.[18] Canadian scholars also came and lectured in China, bringing these new ideas to many more. In addition, the projects' focus on gender and minority-group equity, as well as environmental concerns, ensured that participants encountered and learned to deal with social justice issues.

3. What organizational or contextual features of the linkages themselves were important in enabling them to be effective and what serious challenges or hindrances arose?

Strengths of the projects included the continuity of the same participants throughout the duration of a project or succeeding projects,[19] mutual trust and respect (throughout), and joint decision-making (throughout). However, setbacks did arise. For example, during the management education project, participants encountered difficulties in introducing the case-study method to Chinese learners due to the typical (at that time) Chinese learning behaviour of passive listening.[20] Similar limitations in importing Western methods into Chinese settings were noted by many interviewees.[21] During the linkage between Laurentian University and the Southwest Institute of Technology described in chapter 7, poor communication led to a serious misunderstanding, placing the project in hiatus for some time.

The Tiananmen tragedy of June 1989 caused a severe disruption in Canadian-Chinese relations, and resulted in changes to some of the projects. However, the Canadian government chose not to withdraw support from these endeavours, and in at least one case even sped up their efforts: the Université Laval-Norman Bethune University linkage, described in chapter 3.

Other significant issues included the Chinese government's concern with the problem of "brain-drain," particularly after the Tiananmen event,[22] and the fact that many successful linkages could not continue once funding was withdrawn at the end of the projects – although this was not always the case, as evident in chapters 3, 4, 7, and 8.

4. What lessons for current and future collaboration between Canadian and Chinese universities may be drawn from past experience?

On the Canadian side, the project experiences were deemed "invaluable" (Beamish, chapter 6) in learning to work with China and other cultures. Additional lessons included the importance of respect and equality between partners (throughout), the value of the relationships developed during a project, which can lead to further collaborations as seen in chapter 8, and the importance of a focus on humanization and sustainable development as emphasized in chapters 7 and 9.

In chapter 11, Qiang and Wang describe a successful international project as meeting both the urgent and the development needs of the recipient, being planned and participated in by both sides, and including efforts on both sides to develop cross-cultural understanding. In chapter 9, Walls describes an ideal partnership as being based on the Five Constant Virtues of empathy, duty, protocol, knowledge, and trust, and makes the point that these "must be observed and applied while keeping a dynamic balance between the letter and the spirit of each in mind" (204).

The strongest statements given in this volume in regards to future partnerships insist that China-Canada partnerships are still necessary for, desired by, and beneficial to both countries, even though China is no longer in a peripheral position, and that universities have a key role to play in these partnerships. We conclude with some of these statements:

- "Learning to live with global China may eventually prove more daunting than living with China of the Maoist period. Getting China right will depend in large part on the expertise, understanding and relentless interactions that have no better home than universities" (Evans, chapter 2, 51).

- "Thus, as China enters this far more critical phase of its development, it is through true and long-lasting partnerships that Canadians can further their own interests and those of the world's future, in general" (Bild, chapter 3, 74).
- "Universities and intellectuals of both China and Canada can make concerted efforts, through mutual exchanges, understanding, learning, and borrowing between different cultures, to explore appropriate methods of realizing harmonious coexistence and mutual development between different civilizations" (Li et al., chapter 7, 163).
- "In future, Canada-China university linkages and collaborations will continue to play a very important role" (Qiang and Wang, Chapter 11, 253).

NOTES

1 Powerpoints for all four presentations can be found on the conference website, under the names of each of the keynote speakers. http://www.oise.utoronto.ca/cidec/Research/conference_2014.html.
2 See Hayhoe et al., chapter 1 of this volume, 15, and Mirus, chapter 4 of this volume, 88.
3 See Chen et al., chapter 8 of this volume, 178–80.
4 See Hayhoe et al., chapter 1 of this volume, 17–18.
5 Ibid., 22–3.
6 See Bild, chapter 3 of this volume.
7 See Hayhoe et al., chapter 1 of this volume, 28.
8 See chapters 3, 4, 5, 7, and 10 of this volume for further discussion.
9 See chapters 9, 11, and 13 of this volume.
10 See chapters 4, 7, 8, and 10 of this volume.
11 See chapters 4 and 5 of this volume.
12 See chapter 7 of this volume.
13 See chapters 7, 8, 9, and 11 of this volume.
14 See chapters 3, 5, 7, and 12 of this volume for examples.
15 See chapters 6, 7, 10, and 11 of this volume for examples.
16 See chapters 4 and 8 of this volume.
17 See chapters 3, 7, and 8 of this volume for examples.
18 See chapters 7 and 8 of this volume.
19 See chapters 6 and 11 of this volume – the same was not true for a project in chapter 8, and was noted as an issue.
20 See chapters 4, 5, and 6 of this volume.
21 See chapter 5 of this volume.
22 See chapters 2, 3, 4, and 5 of this volume.

References

Abrami, Regina M., William C. Kirby, and Warren McFarlan. 2014. *Can China Lead? Reaching the Limits of Power and Growth.* Boston: Harvard Business School Press.

Agelasto, M., and B. Adamson. 1998. *Higher Education in Post-Mao China.* Hong Kong: The University of Hong Kong Press.

Altbach, Philip, and Viswanathan Selvaratnam. 1989. *From Dependence to Autonomy: The Development of Asian Universities.* The Netherlands: Kluwer Academic Publishers.

Altbach, Philip. 1981. "The University as Centre and Periphery." *Teachers College Record* 28(4): 601–21.

– 2006. "Globalization and the University: Realities in an Unequal World." In *International Handbook of Higher Education,* edited by James Forest and Philip Altbach, 121–39. Dordrecht, Netherlands: Springer.

Amott, N. 1999. "Decision-Making Structures for Soil Erosion Management in Rural North China." MA Research Paper, University of Toronto. Distributed as SEMGIS II Working Paper No.1.

Association of Universities and Colleges of Canada (AUCC). 2000. *Canada-China University Partnerships: Answering Community Needs,* March. Ottawa: Association of Universities and Colleges of Canada.

– 2001a. *Executive Summary: Final Report of the Special University Linkage Consolidation Program (1996–2001).* Ottawa: Association of Universities and Colleges of Canada.

– 2001b. "Final Report of SULCP Projects (1996–2001)," Chinese version, unpublished. [Translated from Association of Universities and Colleges of Canada (AUCC). 2000. *Canada-China University Partnerships: Answering Community Needs,* March. Ottawa: Association of Universities and Colleges of Canada.]

Atwood, Barbara, Graciela Jasa Silveira, Nicole Laviolette, and Tom Oldham. 2005. "Crossing Borders in the Classroom: A Comparative Law Experiment in Family Law." *Journal of Legal Education* 55: 542–59.

Band, Larry, and L.Y. Fu. 1992. "Structure and Operation of SEMGIS." In *Soil Erosion Geographical Information System in North China*, edited by Joseph Whitney and Chen Yongzong, 32–43. Toronto: University of Toronto, Institute of Environmental Studies.

Baraban, Cynthia Losure. 1998. "Inspiring Global Professionalism: Challenges and Opportunities for American Lawyers in China." *Indiana Law Journal* 73: 1247–75.

Barnett, R. 1990. *The Idea of Higher Education*. Buckingham: The Society for Research into Higher Education and Open University Press.

Beamish, Paul W. 1984. "The Long March to China Trade." *Policy Options*, November, 5(6): 30–3. Edited version reprinted as "Doing Business with the Chinese." *Exchange*, February, 2(5).

– 2010. "Engaging the Chinese Market." In *Cross-Enterprise Leadership: Business Leadership for the Twenty-First Century*, edited by M. Crossan, J. Gandz and G. Seijts, 121–55. Hoboken, NJ: Wiley.

Beamish, Paul W., and Hugh Carr-Harris. 1984. "High Tech Road to China: Case History." *Canadian Export World*, December, 1(5): 35–6.

Beamish, Paul W., and Hui Wang. 1989. "Investing in China via Joint Ventures." *Management International Review* 29(1): 57–64.

Beamish, Paul W., and Lorraine Spiess. 1991. "Post-Tiananmen China: Should You Invest?" *Business Quarterly*, Spring, 55(4): 67–72.

Beamish, Paul W., and Wei Wei Tan. 1985. "Improving Canadian-Chinese Economic Ties." *Proceedings of the Southeast Asia Region of the Academy of International Business*, April, Hong Kong.

Beamish, Paul W., Gigi Wong, and Joanne Shoveller. 2005. "Meeting China's Need for Case Based Teaching Material: The Ivey Business School Experience." In *Business and Management Education in China: Transition, Pedagogy and Training*, edited by J. McIntyre and I. Alon, 195–203. New York: World Scientific Publishing Co. Inc.

Biddulph, Sarah. 2010. "Legal Education in the People's Republic of China: The Ongoing Story of Politics and the Law." In *Legal Education in Asia: Globalization, Change and Contexts*, edited by Stacey Steele and Kathryn Taylor, 260–77. Oxon: Routledge.

Bild, Fred. 2007. "China." In *Ambassador Assignments: Canadian Diplomats Reflect on Our Place in the World*, by David Reece, 235–8. Markham, Ontario: Fitzhenry & Whiteside.

Blundell, R., L. Dearden, C. Meighir, and B. Sianesi. 1999. "Human Capital Investment: The Returns from Education and Training to the Individual, the Firm, and the Economy." *Fiscal Studies* 20(1): 1–23.

Bolden, R., A. O'Brien, K. Peters, M. Ryan, and A. Haslam. 2012. "Academic Leadership: Changing Conceptions, Identities and Experiences." UK *Higher Education, Research and Development Series*.

Boyd, Dwight, and Julia Pan. 2001. *Women and Minorities as Educational Change Agents: Final Report*. Toronto: The Ontario Institute for Studies in Education of the University of Toronto. http://home.oise.utoronto.ca/~women-minority_project/final_assesment.html.

– 2003. "Working and Worrying Partnership: A Case Study of a Long-Term Academic Development Project in China." *Canadian Journal of Development Studies* 24(1): 51–72.

Cai, Q.G. 1999. "A Summary Report on Fifteen Years' Joint Research with Department of Geography & Planning and the Institute for Environmental Studies of University of Toronto (1984–1998)." Institute of Geographical Science and Natural Resources Research, Chinese Academy of Sciences.

– 2011. "SEMGIS II Project Annual Report (1999–2000)." Institute of Geography, Chinese Academy of Sciences.

Calof, Jonathan, and Paul W. Beamish. 1995. "Adapting to Foreign Markets: Explaining Internationalization." *International Business Review* 4: 115–31.

Canada-China Senior Judges Training Project. 1998. *In-Canada Training Programme: Draft PIP*, 14 July: Université de Montréal.

Canadian International Development Agency (CIDA). 1992. CIDA *Programs in Asia: China*. Hull: Asia Branch, CIDA.

– 1994. *China Country Development Policy Framework*, November.

– 1995a. CIDA *Current China Bilateral Projects*. Beijing: Canada China Cooperation Support Unit, CIDA.

– 1995b. CIDA*'s Policy on Women in Development and Gender Equity*. Gatineau, Quebec: CIDA.

– 1997a. *Guide to Gender Sensitive Indicators*.

– 1997b. *A Project Level Handbook: The Why and How of Gender-Sensitive Indicators*.

– 1998. CIDA*'s Policy on Women in Development and Gender Equity*.

– 2005. CIDA*'s Framework for Assessing Gender Equality Results*. Gatineau, Quebec: Canadian International Development Agency.

– 2007. *Gender Equality Toolkit:* CIDA *China Program*. Gatineau, Quebec: Canadian International Development Agency.

– 2013. "Project Profile for Labour Rights: Prevention of Labour Trafficking (China)." Accessed 3 September 2014. http://www.acdi-cida.gc.ca/cidaweb/cpo.nsf/vWebCSAZEn/3AB97F62471E4EF88525765F00371C3B.

Cao, Huhua, and Vivienne Poy, eds. 2011. *The China Challenge: Sino-Canadian Relations in the 21st Century*. Ottawa: University of Ottawa Press.

Casey, James J. Jr. 2010. "The Guirr International Research Collaborations Project: Towards a Greater Understanding of International Collaboration." *University of Daytona Law Review* 36: 29–64.

Central Committee of the Chinese Communist Party (CCP). 1985. *Guanyu jiaoyu tizhi gaike de jueding [Decision on the Reform of the Education System]*. Accessed 16 September 2001. http://www.edu.cn/special/showarticle.php?id=301.

Central Committee of the Chinese Communist Party and State Council. 1993. *Zhongguo jiaoyu gaige he fazhan gangyao [Outline for Educational Reform and Development in China]*. Accessed 16 September 2001. http://www.edu.cn/special/showarticle.php?id=298.

Centre for Human Settlements University of British Columbia (CHSUBC). 2003. "Sustainable Water Resources Management in the Beijing-Tianjin Region." University of British Columbia, Centre for Human Settlements, CD. Report.

Canadian Federation of Deans of Management and Administrative Studies (CFDMAS). 1993. "1992–1993 Annual Activities Report," 18 October. Canada-China Management Education Program Phase II.

Chambers, E.J., D. Cullen, and C. Hoskins. 1989. "A Chinese MBA? The Problem of Technology Transfer." *International Journal of Educational Development* 9(2): 91–6.

Chen, Jiefang. 2006. *Theories of Cooperative Education and the Practice in China – Research on Work-Integrated Learning*. Shanghai: Shanghai Jiaotong University Press.

Chen, Albert H.Y. 2000. "Toward a Legal Enlightenment: Discussions in Contemporary China on the Rule of Law." *Pacific Bin Law Journal* 17: 125–65.

Chen, Jing M., Sean Thomas, and Yangquan Yin, eds. 2007. "Carbon Sequestration in China's Forest Ecosystems." *Journal of Environmental Management* 85(3), November Special Issue.

Chen, Liang-Hsuan. 2006. "Attracting East Asian Students to Canadian Graduate Schools." *The Canadian Journal of Higher Education* 36(2): 77–105.

Chen, Linhan, and Danyan Huang. 2013. "Internationalization of Chinese Higher Education." *Higher Education Studies* 3(1): 92–105.

Chesterman, Simon. 2008. "The Globalisation of Legal Education." *Singapore Journal of Legal Studies*, July: 58–67.

CIA World Factbook. 2014. "China: People and Society." https://www.cia.gov/library/publications/the-world-factbook/geos/ch.html.

Conley, Terrance W., and Paul W. Beamish. 1986. "Joint Ventures in China: Legal Implications." *Business Quarterly*, November 51(3): 39–43.

Crowston, Wallace B. 1989. "Editorial." *Phase II Newsletter* 1(1).
Cummings, William. 2010. "Is the Academic Centre Shifting to Asia?" In *Border Crossing in East Asian Higher Education*, edited by David Chapman, William Cummings, and Gerard Postiglione, 47–76. Hong Kong: Comparative Education Centre, University of Hong Kong and Springer Press.
Davis, Kenneth B. Jr. 2007. "Six Uneasy Pieces." *Wisconsin International Law Journal* 24: 31–40.
Deschenes, Luc. 2013. "Canada-China University Linkages: Building a Cancer Control Network." Unpublished paper, Université Laval. http://www.oise. utoronto.ca/cidec/UserFiles/File/Research/CIDEC_Projects/ Conference2014/Luc_Deschenes_paper.pdf.
Dorsen, Norman. 2001. "Achieving International Cooperation: NYU's Global Law School Program." *Journal of Legal Education* 51: 332–7.
Dunn, L., and M. Wallace, eds. 2008. *Teaching in Transnational Higher Education: Enhancing Learning for Offshore International Students*. New York and London: Routledge.
Elvin, Mark. 2004. *The Retreat of the Elephants: An Environmental History of China*. New Haven and London: Yale University Press.
Evans, Brian. 2012. *Pursuing China: Memoir of a Beaver Liaison Officer*. Edmonton: University of Alberta Press.
Evans, Paul. 2014. *Engaging China: Myth, Aspiration and Strategy in Canadian Policy from Trudeau to Harper*. Toronto: University of Toronto Press.
Evans, Paul, and Michael B. Frolic. 1991. *Reluctant Adversaries*. Toronto: University of Toronto Press.
F.J. Morgan Enterprises. 1994. *Summative Evaluation Report. Canada/China University Linkage Program*. University of Alberta (Edmonton, Canada) and National Academy of Educational Administration (Beijing, China). Edmonton, Alberta.
Faculty of Law Université de Montréal (UdeM). 2013. *Master of Laws: Business Law in a Global Context*. Accessed 18 October 2013. http://www.droit. uMontreal.ca/deuxieme_cycle/fichiers/BLGC_2009-2010/Master_of_ Law_3_Ed_Web.pdf.
Farr, Moira. 2007. "Universities Embrace Internationalization." *University Affairs* 48(9): 31–2.
Feng, G., and S. Gong. 2006. "Sino-Foreign Joint Ventures: A National, Regional and Institutional Analysis." *The Observatory on Borderless Higher Education*.
Fernando, Dilantha. 2014. "An Extreme Makeover of Canola/Rapeseed Genetics for Poverty Alleviation in Rural China: A Successful CIDA Funded Partnership." Paper presented to the conference on "Transforming Canada-China Educational Cooperation: Significant Legacies and Future Challenges," Tsinghua Univer-sity, 9–10 May. http://www.oise.utoronto.ca/cidec/UserFiles/File/ Research/CIDEC_Projects/Conference2014/Dilantha_Fernando_paper.pdf.

Frolic, B. Michael. 1996. "Everybody Benefits: Canada's Decision to Establish a CIDA China Aid Programme in 1981." Paper presented at the Canadian Political Science Association, Brock University, 4 June.

– 2011. "Canada and China at 40 – With a Response by Professor Ruth Hayhoe." *Asia Colloquia Papers* 1(1). Toronto: York Centre for Asian Research. www.yorku.ca/ycar.

Gao, X. 2001. "Post-Workshop Reflections." In *Chinese Women Organizing: Cadres, Feminists, Muslims, Queers*, edited by P.-C.Hsiung, M. Jaschok and C. Milwertz, 257–71. Oxford: Berg.

Gaudreault-DesBiens, Jean-François. 2013. "Diversity and the Law in Canada" (in Chinese). *China University of Politics and Law International Law Review*: 327–49.

Gechlik, Mei Ying. 2006. "Judicial Reform in China: Lessons from Shanghai." *Columbia Journal of Asian Law* 19: 97–137.

Gerhard, W. 1995. "End of Project Evaluation: Sichuan/Laurentian Mineral Sciences Cooperative Exchange, A CCULP Project between Laurentian University and the Southwest Institute of Technology." Project No. 924–282/14218.

Gillespie, John. 2008. "Towards a Discursive Analysis of Legal Transfers into Developing East Asia." *New York University Journal of International Law & Politics* 40: 657–721.

Gladney, Dru C. 1994. "Representing Nationality in China: Refiguring Majority/Minority Identities." *The Journal of Asian Studies*, February, 53(1): 92–123.

Glaser, B.G. 1978. *Theoretical Sensitivity: Advances in the Methodology of Grounded Theory*. Mill Valley, CA: Sociology Press.

Glaser, B.G., and Strauss, A.L. 1967. *The Discovery of Grounded Theory*. Chicago: Aldine.

Government of Canada. 2014. *Canada's International Education Strategy. Harnessing Our Knowledge Advantage to Drive Innovation and Prosperity*. Canada. Accessed 19 January 2015. http://international.gc.ca/global-markets-marches-mondiaux/assets/pdfs/overview-apercu-eng.pdf.

Grenon, Aline, and Louis Perret. 2002. "Globalization and Canadian Legal Education." *South Texas Law Review* 43: 543–57.

Gronn, P. 2010. "Hybrid Configurations of Leadership." In *Sage Handbook of Leadership*, edited by A. Bryman, D. Collinson, K. Grint, B. Jackson, and M. Uhl-Bien. London: Sage.

Guo, Shibao, Daniel Schugurensky, Budd Hall, Tonette Rocco, and Tara Fenwick. 2010. "Connected Understanding: Internationalization of Adult Education in Canada and Beyond." *The Canadian Journal for the Study of Adult Education* 23(1): 73–89.

Habermas, Juergen. 1984. "Modernisation as Societal Rationalisation." In *The Theory of Communicative Action* 1, 157–241. Boston: Beacon Press.

Haggard, Stephan, and Lydia Tiede. 2011. "The Rule of Law and Economic Growth: Where Are We?" *World Development* 39(5): 673–85.

Haggard, Stephan, Andrew Macintyre, and Lydia Tiede. 2008. "The Rule of Law and Economic Development." *Annual Review of Political Science* 11: 205–34.

Hao, Keming, ed. 1998. *Zhongguo jiaoyu tizhi gaige ershinian [Twenty Years of Educational Reform in China]*. Zhengzhou: Zhongzhou guji chubanshe.

Hatch, James, and Fengli Mu. 2014. *The Case Method in China*. Unpublished monograph.

Haughey, Denis J. 1992. "A Survey of the Perceptions of Selected Canadian Academics Regarding the Design and Delivery of Educational Short Courses in China." Paper presented at the conference "Knowledge across Cultures: Universities East and West," Toronto, 7–10 October.

– 1994. "Strategic Planning and the Reform of Higher Education." Paper presented at the culminating research conference of the Canada-China University Linkage Program between the National Academy of Educational Administration, China, and the Faculties of Education and Extension, University of Alberta. Canada, Beijing, China, May.

Hayhoe, Ruth E.S. 1984. "Chinese-Western Scholarly Exchange: Implications for the Future of Chinese Education." In *Contemporary Chinese Education*, edited by R. Hayhoe. London: Croom Helm.

– 1986. "Chinese Higher Education and the International Community." Background paper commissioned by the OISE Evaluation Team for CIDA's Canada-China Management Education Program Evaluation. Mimeo.

– 1987. "China's Higher Curricular Reform in Historical Perspective." *The China Quarterly* 110: 196–230. doi: 10.1017/S0305741000019883.

– 1989. *China's Universities and the Open Door*. Toronto: OISE Press.

– 2000. "Redeeming Modernity." *Comparative Education Review* 44(4): 423–39.

Hayhoe, Ruth, Jun Li, Jing Lin, and Qiang Zha. 2011. *Portraits of 21st Century Chinese Universities: In the Move to Mass Higher Education*. Hong Kong: Comparative Education Research Centre, University of Hong Kong and Springer.

Hayhoe, Ruth, and Jian Liu. 2010. "China's Universities, Cross-Border Education and the Dialogue among Civilizations." In *Border Crossing in East Asian Higher Education*, edited by David Chapman, William Cummings, and Gerard Postiglione, 76–100. Hong Kong: Comparative Education Centre, University of Hong Kong and Springer Press.

Hayhoe, Ruth, and Julia Pan, eds. 1996. *East-West Dialogue in Knowledge and Higher Education*. New York: M.E. Sharpe.

Hayhoe, Ruth, and Julia Pan. 1995. *Canada/China Joint Doctoral Programs in Education – A Final Evaluation Report.* Toronto: published informally by the Higher Education Group, OISE.
– 2001. "Introduction: A Contribution to the Dialogue of Civilization." In *Knowledge across Cultures: A Contribution to Dialogues among Civilizations (2nd edition),* edited by Ruth Hayhoe and Julia Pan. Hong Kong: Comparative Education Research Centre, the University of Hong Kong.
Hayhoe, Ruth, Julia Pan, and Qiang Zha. 2013. "Lessons from the Legacy of Canada-China University Linkages." *Frontiers of Education in China* 8(1): 78–102.
Hayhoe, Ruth, Pan Nairong, and Zha Qiang. 2012. "Guanyu Zhongjia Daxue Hezuo De Lishixing Fansi." In *Waiguoren Kan Zhongguo Jiaoyu,* edited by Yuan Guiren. Gaodengjiaoyu Chubanshe. [许美德, 潘乃容, 查强. 关于中加大学合作的历史性反思, 袁贵仁主编 外国人看中国教育, 高等教育出版社 2012年.]
He, Weifang. 2006. "China's Legal Profession: The Nascence and Growing Pains of a Professionalized Legal Class." *Columbia Journal of Asian Law* 19: 138–51.
Head, John W. 2010. "Feeling the Stones When Crossing the River: The Rule of Law in China." *Santa Clara Journal of International Law* 7(2): 25–83.
Heinonen, Tuula, and Meng Liu. 2014. "Collaboration between China Women's University and the University of Manitoba in Social Work Education." Paper presented to the conference on "Transforming Canada-China Educational Cooperation: Significant Legacies and Future Challenges," Tsinghua University, 9–10 May.
Hénard, Fabrice, Leslie Diamond, and Deborah Roseveare. 2012. *Approaches to Internationalisation and Their Implications for Strategic Management and Institutional Practice: A Guide for Higher Education Institutions.* OECD. http://www.oecd.org/edu/imhe/Approaches to internationalisation-final-web.pdf.
Henders, Susan J., and Mary M. Young. 2012. "'Other Diplomacies' and the Making of Canada-Asian Relations: An Interdisciplinary Conversation." In *Asia Colloquia Papers* 2(1). Toronto: York Centre for Asian Research, York University.
Hershkovitz, L. 1995. "China Gender Equity Strategy." Unpublished paper prepared for the Canadian International Development Agency China Program.
Hirai, Naofusa. 1983. "Traditional Cultures and Modernization: Several Problems in the Case of Japan." In *Modernization in Asian Countries: Proceedings of Kokugakuin University Centennial Symposium.* Accessed 9 April 2014. http://www2.kokugakuin.ac.jp/ijcc/wp/cimac/hirai.html.
Hitchcock, Michael. 1999. "Tourism and Ethnicity: Situational Perspectives." *International Journal of Tourism Research* 1: 17–32.

Hooper, B. 1991. "Gender and Education." In *Chinese Education*, edited by I. Epstein, 352–74. New York and London: Garland Publishing, Inc.

Hou, Xinyi. 2006. "Modern Legal Education in China." *Oklahoma City University Law Review* 31(2): 293–9.

Hsiung, P.-C. 1999. "Transformation, Subversion, and Feminist Activism: Report on the Workshops of a Development Project, Xian, China." *Bulletin of Concerned Asian Scholars* 31(3): 47–51.

Hsiung, P.-C. 2001. "Zhixing yanjiu fangfa chuyi: laizi shehui xingbie shejiao de tansuo" (A Preliminary Discussion on Qualitative Research Methods: An Exploration from the Perspective of Gender and Society) in *Sociological Review* 5: 17–33. [熊秉纯 (2001). "质性研究方法刍议：来自社会性别视角的探索." 社会学研究 5: 17–33.]

Hsiung, P.-C., M. Jaschok, and C. Milwertz, eds, with R. Chan. 2001. *Chinese Women Organizing: Cadres, Feminists, Muslims, Queers*. New York: Berg.

Institute for Environmental Studies. 2007. "Confronting Global Warming: Enhancing China's Capacity for Carbon Sequestration: July 2002 – September 2006." General Report, University of Toronto. http://www.utoronto.ca/cccs2002/.

Irish, Charles R. 2008. "Reflections on the Evolution of Law and Legal Education in China and Vietnam." *Wisconsin International Law Journal* 25: 243–54.

Jackson, Edward T., Marielle Gallant, Wang Xiaoqun, and Guo Yingtong. 2001. "Relationships, Respect, Results: Report of the China Higher Education Program Assessment." Report prepared for the China Program, Asia Branch, Canadian International Development Agency.

Jackson, Edward T. 2003. "Lessons from 20 Years of Canada-China Cooperation in Higher Education." *Canadian Journal of Developmental Studies* XXlV(1), 41–9.

Jiang, Xiaoping. 2006. *Impacts of Globalisation and the Knowledge Economy upon Higher Education in China and New Zealand: Interculturalisation in the Making*. Guangzhou, China: Guangdong People's Publishing House.

Jiao, Jie, and Guy Lefebvre. 2011. "The Carrier's Responsibility and the Rotterdam Rules: A Critical Voice (in Chinese)." *Journal of Comparative Law, China* 116(4): 112–25.

– 2013. "International Trades Usages (in Chinese)." *Chinese Legal Review* 10: 21–34.

Johanson, Jan, and Jan-Erik Vahlne. 1977. "The Internationalization Process of the Firm – A Model of Knowledge Development and Increasing Foreign Market Commitments." *Journal of International Business Studies* 88: 23–32.

Karazivan, Noura. 2013. "Key Features and Philosophical Foundations of Canadian Constitutional Law, A Global Overview" (in Chinese). *China University of Politics and Law International Law Review.* 364–76.

King, K. 1990. "The New Politics of International Collaboration in Educational Development in Northern and Southern Research in Education." *International Journal of Educational Development* 10(1): 47–57.

– 2009. "Higher Education and International Cooperation: The role of academic collaboration in the developing world." In *Higher Education and International Capacity Building: Twenty-Five Years of Higher Education Links*, edited by D. Stephens, 33–49. Oxford: Symposium Books.

Knight, Jane. 1997. "Internationalisation of Higher Education: A Conceptual Framework." In *Internationalisation of Higher Education in Asia Pacific Countries*, edited by J. Knight and H. de Wit, 5–19. Amsterdam: European Association for International Education.

– 2011. "Higher Education Crossing Borders – A Framework and Overview of New Developments and Issues." In *Cross-Border Partnerships in Higher Education, Strategies and Issues*, edited by Robin Sakamoto and David W. Chapman, 16–41. New York: Routledge.

Krucken, G. 2003. "Learning the 'New, New Thing:' On the Role of Path Dependency in University Structures." *Higher Education* 46(3): 315–39.

Kwan, Covina Y.W. 2013. "Cultural Diplomacy and Internationalization of Higher Education: The Experience of Three Confucius Institutes in Canada." *Frontiers of Education in China* 9/1:110–26.

Leclair, Jean. 2013. "The Substance and Scope of Aboriginal Rights in Canadian Constitutional Law" (in Chinese). *China University of Politics and Law International Law Review.* 350–63.

Lefebvre, Guy, and Jie Jiao. 2002. "Les Principes d'Unidroit et le Droit Chinois: Convergence et dissonance." *Revue Juridique Thémis* 36: 519–37.

– 2011a. "The New Rotterdam Rules on Maritime Transport: Part 1" (in Chinese). *International Business Daily*, 23 March.

– 2011b. "The New Rotterdam Rules on Maritime Transport: Part 2" (in Chinese). *International Business Daily*, 2 April.

– 2011c. "The New Rotterdam Rules on Maritime Transport: Part 3" (in Chinese). *International Business Daily*, 9 April.

– 2011d. "The New Rotterdam Rules on Maritime Transport: Part 4" (in Chinese). *International Business Daily*, 23 April.

Lefebvre, Guy, Marie-Claude Rigaud, and Jie Jiao. 2012. "International Trade Usages: Uncertainties for Commercial Operators, Chinese Lawyer: Part 1" (in Chinese). *Chinese Lawyer* 7: 63–4.

- "International Trade Usages: Uncertainties for Commercial Operators: Part 2" (in Chinese). *Chinese Lawyer* 8: 68–9.
Levin, Richard. 2010. "The Rise of Asia's Universities." President of Yale University, Seventh Annual Lecture of the Higher Education Policy Institute, delivered at the Royal Society, London, England, 1 February.
Liu, Guojin. 2013. "Canada-China University Linkages: The Results and Achievements on Cancer Control Network." Unpublished paper. http://www.oise.utoronto.ca/cidec/UserFiles/File/Research/CIDEC_Projects/Conference2014/LIU_Guojing_paper.pdf.
Liu, Sida. 2013. "The Legal Profession as a Social Process: A Theory on Lawyers and Globalization." *Law and Social Inquiry* 38: 670–93.
Locke, William, and Alice Bennion. 2010a. *Supplementary Report to the HEFCE Higher Education Workforce Framework*. London: Centre for Higher Education Research and Information (CHERI).
- 2010b. *The Changing Academic Profession: The UK and Beyond*. London: Universities UK.
Louie, Kam. 2005. "Gathering Cultural Knowledge: Useful or Use with Care?" In *Teaching International Students: Improving Learning for All*, edited by Jude Carroll and Janette Ryan, 17–25. Oxon: Routledge.
Luk, Shiu-hung. 1992. "Soil Erosion and Land Management in North China." In *Soil Erosion Geographical Information System in North China*, edited by Joseph Whitney and Chenyong Zong, 9–31. Toronto: University of Toronto, Institute of Environmental Studies.
Luk, Shiu-hung, and Qingyin Yao, eds. 1990. "Soil Erosion and Land Management in the Granitic Regions of Guangdong Province, South China: Final Report." Toronto: University of Toronto and Guangzhou: Guangzhou Institute of Geography.
Macdonald, Deirdre. 2010. "Beijing Diary." In *UofT Magazine*, summer. http://www.magazine.utoronto.ca/feature/beijing-diary-claude-bissell-canadian-in-china/.
Maclaren, Virginia, N. Amott, G.H. Gan, J.L. Feng, and H.Y. Zhao. 2001. "Household Economic Benefits from the Adoption of Soil Erosion Management Measures on the Loess Plateau." *Proceedings of the SEMGIS II Conference*. Taiyuan, China.
Magen, Amichai. 2009. "The Rule of Law and Its Promotion Abroad: Three Problems of Scope." *Stanford Journal of International Law* 45: 51–115.
Manning, Kimberley. 2012. "Pacific Imaginaries: Rebuilding Chinese Studies in Canada." *Research Reports*, 15 March. Asia Pacific Foundation of Canada. http://www.asiapacific.ca/sites/default/files/filefield/researchreportv9.pdf.

Marginson, S., and E. Sawir. 2006. "University Leaders' Strategies in the Global Environment: A Comparative Study of Universitas Indonesia and the Australian National University." *Higher Education* 52: 1–39.

Marginson, Simon, and Marijk van der Wende. 2007. "The Impact of Global Rankings in Higher Education." *Journal of Studies in International Education* 11(3/4): 306–29.

Maybee, Jack. 1985. "The China Policy of the Canadian International Development Agency." Paper presented at the Conference on Canada-China Relations, presented in Montebello, Quebec, 9 May.

McCubbin, Patricia Ross, Malinda L. Seymore, Andrea Curcio, and Llewellyn Joseph Gibbons. 2007. "China's Future Lawyers: Some Differences in Education and Outlook." *Asper Review of International Business and Trade Law* 7: 293–303.

Mclean, Martin. 1983. "Educational Dependency: A Critique." *Compare* 13(1): 25–42.

Mirus, Rolf, and Monica Wegner. 2010. "The University of Alberta's School of Business in China 1983–2003." Unpublished report.

Mo, John, and Weidong Li. 2002. "Legal Education in the PRC." *Journal of the History of International Law* 4: 176–203.

Moliterno, James E. 2008. "Exporting American Legal Education." *Journal of Legal Education* 58: 274–89.

MoU CUPL. 2010. *Memorandum of Understanding between the Faculty of Law of the Université de Montréal and the China University of Political Science and Law on Postgraduates Master Program*. Université de Montréal. Accessed 19 October 2013. http://www.international.uMontreal.ca/China_University_of_Political_Science_and_Law_PMP.pdf.

Murck, Barbara. 1997. "SEMGIS II: Gender Equity Strategy." Toronto: University of Toronto, Institute for Environmental Studies, Working Paper.

Murray, Victor V., and Geoffrey Bonnycastle. 1993. "CCMEP II: Accomplishments to Date and Their Value for Canada." Toronto: York University.

Ngok, King-lun, and Julia Kwong. 2003. "Globalization and Educational Restructuring in China." In *Globalization and Educational Restructuring in the Asia Pacific Region*, edited by Ka-Ho Mok and Anthony Welch. London: Palgrave.

Noah, Harold, and Max Eckestein. 1990. "Dependency Theory in Comparative Education: Twelve Lessons from the Literature." In *Theories and Methods in Comparative Education*, edited by Jürgen Schriewer and Brian Holmes, 165–92. Frankfurt: Peterlang.

O'Brien, Maire. 2000. "The Implementation of CIDA's China Program: Resolving the Disjuncture between Structure and Process." PhD thesis, York University.

Paltiel, J. 1992. "Educating the Modernizers." In *Education and Modernization: The Chinese Experience*, edited by Ruth Hayhoe, 337–57. Oxford: Pergamon.

Phirom Leng, and Julia Pan. 2013. "The Issue of Mutuality in Canada-China Educational Collaboration." *Canadian and International Education / Education canadienne et internationale* 42(2): Article 6.

Postman, Neil. 1998. *Technopoly: The Surrender of Culture to Technology*. New York: Vintage Books.

Purvis, B. 1991. *Barefoot in the Boardroom*. Australia: Allen & Unwin Ltd.

Qiang, Haiyan. 1993. "On Centre-Periphery." *Journal of Shaanxi Normal University* (Chinese version), May: 24–8.

– 2001. "Women and Minorities as Educational Change Agents, a Brief Final Report." Unpublished.

Qiang, Haiyan, and Kang Yeqin. 2011. "English Immersion in China as a Case of Educational Transfer." *Frontiers of Education in China* 6(1): 8–36.

Rigaud, Marie-Claude. 2013. "The Transnationalisation of International Commercial Arbitration" (in Chinese). *China University of Politics and Law International Law Review.* 309–26.

Ronning, Chester. 1974. *A Memoir of China in Revolution: From the Boxer Rebellion to the People's Republic*, 235–9. New York: Random House.

Rosen, Stanley 1992. "Women, Education and Modernization." In *Education and Modernization*, edited by R. Hayhoe. New York, NY: Pergamon Press.

– 1997. "Education and Economic Reform." In *The China Handbook*, edited by C. Hudson, 250–61. Chicago and London: Fitzroy Dearborn Publishers.

Rowley, Jennifer, 1997. "Academic Leaders: Made or Born?" *Industrial and Commercial Training* 29(3): 78–84.

Ryan, Doris W. 1987. "Evaluation of the Canada-China Management Education Program," January. Toronto: OISE.

Ryan, Janette, and Jude Carroll. 2005. "'Canaries in the Coalmine': International Students in Western Universities." In *Teaching International Students: Improving Learning for All*, edited by Jude Carroll and Janette Ryan, 3–10. Oxon: Routledge.

Sadker, Myra Pollack, and David Miller Sadker. 1982. *Sex Equity Handbook for Schools*. New York, NY: Longman, Inc.

– 1994. "Gender Equity in the Classroom: The Unfinished Agenda." *College Board Review* 170, 14–21.

Sakamoto, Robin, and David W. Chapman. 2011. "Expanding across Borders – The Growth of Cross-Border Partnerships in Higher Education." In *Cross-Border Partnerships in Higher Education, Strategies and Issues*, edited by Robin Sakamoto and David W. Chapman, 3–15. New York: Routledge.

Sexton, John Edward. 1996. "The Global Law School Program at New York University." *Journal of Legal Education* 46: 329–35.
Shambaugh, David. 2013. *China Goes Global*. Oxford and New York: Oxford University Press.
Shivnan, Jane C., and Martha N. Hill. 2011. "Global Nursing – Sustaining Multinational Collaboration over Time." In *Cross-Border Partnerships in Higher Education, Strategies and Issues*, edited by Robin Sakamoto and David W. Chapman, 153–68. New York: Routledge.
Singer, Martin. 1986. *Canadian Academic Relations with the People's Republic of China Since 1970*. Ottawa: Ottawa International Development Research Centre.
– 1996. *Academic Relations between Canada and China 1970–95*. Report published by the Association of Universities and Colleges of Canada.
Skaaning, Svend-Erik. 2010. "Measuring the Rule of Law." *Political Research Quarterly* 63(2): 449–60.
State Council of China. 2010. *Guojia zhong chang qi jiaoyu gaige he fazhan guihua gangyao (2010–2020) [National Outline for Medium- and Long-Term Educational Reform and Development (2010–2020)]*. Accessed 7 August 2011. http://www.gov.cn/jrzg/2010-07/29/content_1667143.htm.
Stearns, Lisa. 2001. "Post-Workshop Reflections." In *Chinese Women Organizing: Cadres, Feminists, Muslims, Queers*, edited by Ping-Chun Hsiung, Maria Jaschok and Cecilia Milwertz, 257–71. Oxford: Berg.
Steele, Stacey, and Kathryn Taylor. 2010. "Introduction: Globalization, Change and Contexts." In *Legal Education in Asia: Globalization, Change and Contexts*, edited by Stacey Steele and Kathryn Taylor, 3–19. Oxon: Routledge.
Strauss, Anselm, and Juliet Corbin. 1998. *Basics of Qualitative Research: Grounded Theory Procedures and Techniques*, 2nd ed. Newbury Park: Sage Publications, Inc.
Tam, R. 2007. "Transnational Education: International Branch Campus Operation: A Case Study of a Joint Venture between a British University and Its Partnership in China." Unpublished master's dissertation. University of London Institute of Education.
Tan, Cheng Han, Gary Bell, Xuan Hop Dang, Joongi Kim, Keang Sood Teo, Arun Thiruvengadam, V. Vijayakumar, and Jiangyu Wang. 2006. "Legal Education in Asia." *Asian Journal of Comparative Law* 1(1): 1–22.
Tan, Chuanbao, and Ban Jianwu. 2008. "Zhong xiao xue deyu kecheng de bianqian yu fazhan [Moral Education Changes and Developments in Elementary and Secondary Schools]." In *Gaige kaifang 30 nian zhongguo jiaoyu jishi [A Record of Chinese Education in 30 Years since Adopting the Policy of Reform and Opening Up]*, edited by Gu Mingyuan and Liu Fuxin. Beijing: Renmin chubanshe.

References

Tan, Shen. 1994. "Dangdai zhongguo funv qingkuang de fenxi yu yuce [Analysis and Forecast of Circumstance of Contemporary Chinese Women]." *Funv yanjiu jikan [Women's Studies Quarterly]* 4: 18–26.

Taylor, Veronica L. 2010. "Legal Education as Development." In *Legal Education in Asia: Globalization, Change and Contexts*, edited by Stacey Steele and Kathryn Taylor, 214–40. Oxon: Routledge.

Trubek, David M., Yves Dezalay, Ruth Buchanan, and John R. Davis. 1993–95. "Global Restructuring and the Law: Studies of the Internationalization of Legal Fields and the Creation of Transnational Arenas." *Case Western Reserve Law Review* 44: 407–98.

Tunney, Tom. 2000. "Canada-China University Linkages to Strengthen Basic Education." In *UniWorld*, October: 11–12. http://www.aucc.ca/wp-content/uploads/2011/11/uniworld-unimonde-oct-20001.pdf.

– 2001. "Reflecting on Canada-China Partnerships." In *UniWorld*, October: 4–5. AUCC. http://www.aucc.ca/wp-content/uploads/2011/11/uniworld-unimonde-oct-2001.pdf.

Université de Montréal Consortium. 1999a. *Canada-China Senior Judges Training Project (1998–2001)*.

– 1999b. *In-Canada Training Programme – Presentation of the Programme*. Université de Montréal.

Université de Montréal. 2002. *Canada-China Procuratorate Reform Cooperation Project*. Université de Montreal, Faculté de Droit, SEL: 01-A-021723-01.

– 2006. *Stratégie d'internationalisation de 2e génération*. Université de Montréal. Accessed 18 October 2013. http://www.international.uMontreal.ca/documents/pdf/StrategieInternUdeMnov2006.pdf.

– 2012a. *Cooperation Agreement between Renmin University and Université de Montréal Concerning Candidates at the Doctoral Level*. Université de Montréal. Accessed 18 October 2013. http://www.international.uMontreal.ca/entente/documents/CSC_renmin_2012_000.pdf.

– 2012b. *Doctoral Scholarships for Chinese Students – Université de Montréal and China Scholarship Council – 2013–14*. Université de Montréal. Accessed 5 November 2013. http://www.fesp.uMontreal.ca/fileadmin/Documents/International/CSC_VA.pdf.

University of Alberta. 1988. "Articles of Arrangement and Proposal." Canada-China Management Education Program Phase II, U of A-XJTU Linkage, 19 December. Mimeo.

Valcke, Catherine. 2004. "On Global Law Teaching." *Journal of Legal Education* 54: 160–82.

Valois, Martine. 2013. "Canada Administrative Law: Challenges Faced by the History, Principles and Contemporary." *China University of Politics and Law International Law Review.* 377ff.

Van Zandt, David E. 2004. "Globalization Strategies for Legal Education." *University of Toledo Law Review* 36: 213–20.

Velloso, Jacques. 1985. "Dependency and Education: Reproduction or Conspiracy?" *Prospects* 15(2): 205–12.

Vincent-Lancrin, Stéphan. 2011. "Cross-Border Higher Education and the Internationalization of Academic Research." In *Cross-Border Partnerships in Higher Education, Strategies and Issues*, edited by Robin Sakamoto and David W. Chapman, 93–114. New York: Routledge.

Vincent-Lancrin, Stéphan, and Sebastian Pfotenhauer. 2012. *Guidelines for Quality Provision in Cross-Border Higher Education: Where Do We Stand?* OECD. Paris, France. Accessed 20 October 2013. http://www.oecd.org/edu/49956210.pdf.

Waincymer, Jeff. 2010. "Internationalization of Legal Education: Putting the 'Why' before the 'How.'" In *Legal Education in Asia: Globalization, Change and Contexts*, edited by Stacey Steele and Kathryn Taylor, 68–88. Oxon: Routledge.

Walls, Jan, and Liu Shusong, eds. 1998. *Economy, Culture and Environment* I. Beijing: Minzu University Press.

– 1999. *Women and Development: The Role of Women and Their Contributions to Social, Economic and Environmental Development*. Beijing: Minzu University Press.

– 2001. *Economy, Culture and Environment* II. Beijing: Minzu University Press.

Wang, Jianjun, and John Staver. 1995. "An Empirical Study about China: Gender Equity in Science Education." Paper presented at the Annual Meeting of American Educational Research Association, 19–22 April. San Francisco, CA.

Wang, Ying. 2014. "35 Years' Collaboration on Marine-Earth Sciences of Nanjing University with Canadian Universities." Paper presented to the conference on "Transforming Canada-China Educational Cooperation: Significant Legacies and Future Challenges," Tsinghua University, 9–10 May. http://www.oise.utoronto.ca/cidec/UserFiles/File/Research/CIDEC_Projects/Conference2014/WANG_Ying_paper.pdf.

Wang, Ying, and Charles Schafer. 1992. *Island Environment and Coast Development*. Nanjing: Nanjing University Press.

Wang, Zhenmin. 2002. "Legal Education in Contemporary China." *The International Lawyer* 36: 1203–12.

Watson, David. 2007. "Chinese Universities in the Service of Society: A Report on the China-England Study of National Policy on Higher Education Management." *Higher Education Funding Council for England*. British Council.

References

White, Rodney R., ed. 1991. *GIS-Based Erosion Management Outreach Program (SEMGIS II) for China: Consolidation and Training, 1996–2001*. Toronto: Institute for Environmental Studies, University of Toronto.

Whitney, Joseph B., and Chen Yongzong, eds. 1992. *Soil Erosion Geographical Information System (SEMGIS) in the Wangjiagou Experimental Basin Lishi, Shanxi Province, North China; Final Report*. Toronto: University of Toronto, Institute of Environmental Studies and Shanxi Province: Chinese Academy of Sciences and Ministry of Soil and Water Conservation.

Wilson, Jennifer. 2001. "A History of CIDA's China Program." Report prepared for the China Program, Asia Branch, Canadian International Development Agency.

Woo, Margaret Y. K. 2001. "Reflections on International Legal Education and Exchanges." *Journal of Legal Education* 51: 449–56.

Xun, Yuan. 2012. "Reflections on the Social Role of Chinese Universities in the Reform Era." *Frontiers of Education in China* 7(3): 232–52.

Yang, Zhong. 2006. "Globalisation and Higher Education Reform in China." *The Australian Association for Research in Education*. Accessed 5 June 2010. http://www.aare.edu.au/05pap/zh005780.pdf.

Zeng, Xianyi. 2002. "Legal Education in China." *South Texas Law Review* 43: 707–16.

Zha, Qiang. 2010. "Canadian-Chinese Educational Relationship: Looking Back, Around, and Beyond." *Academic Matters: The Journal of Higher Education*, 14 December. http://www.academicmatters.ca/2010/12/canadian-chinese-educational-relationship-looking-back-around-and-beyond/.

– 2011a. "Canadian-Chinese Education Collaborations: From Unilateral to Bilateral Exchanges." In *The China Challenge: Sino-Canadian relations in the 21st Century*, edited by Huhua Cao and Vivienne Poy, 100–19. Ottawa, Ontario: University of Ottawa Press.

– 2011b. "China's Move to Mass Higher Education in a Comparative Perspective." *Compare: A Journal of Comparative and International Education* 41(6): 751–68.

– 2012. "Transnational Higher Education: Towards a Critical Culturalist Research Agenda." In *Education and Global Cultural Dialogue: A Tribute to Ruth Hayhoe*, edited by Karen Mundy and Qiang Zha, 125–38. New York: Palgrave MacMillan.

– 2013. "China's Confucius Institutes – More Academic and Integrative." In *International Higher Education* 71: 15–17.

Zhao, Jun, and Ming Hu. 2012. "A Comparative Study of the Legal Education System in the United States and China and the Reform of Legal Education in China." *Suffolk Transnational Law Review* 35: 329–61.

Zhao, Shansheng. 2000. "In-School Educational Administrators' Understandings and Perceptions of Gender Equity in Education and the Implications to Educational Administrative Training in Jilin Province, People's Republic of China." Unpublished MEd thesis, University of Regina.

Zheng, Yongnian. 2014. *Contemporary China: A History since 1978*. Hoboken, NJ: Wiley-Blackwell.

Zhou, Yongming, and Fu Tingdong. 2014. "A Review of 25 Years of Educational Cooperation and Exchanges between Huazhong Agricultural University and Canadian Institutions." Paper presented to the conference on "Transforming Canada-China Educational Cooperation: Significant Legacies and Future Challenges," Tsinghua University, 9–10 May. [Paper was prepared by the Department of International Cooperation and Exchanges, Huazhong Agricultural University and presented by Professor Zhou Yongming.] http://www.oise.utoronto.ca/cidec/UserFiles/File/Research/CIDEC_Projects/Conference2014/FU_ZHOU_paper.pdf.

Zhū, Xī. *Lún yǔ jí zhù* 6(28). Online edition at: http://www.chineseclassic.com/content/42.

Zou, Keyuan. 2003. "Professionalising Legal Education in the People's Republic of China." *Singapore Journal of International and Comparative Law* 7: 159–82.

Contributors

PAUL BEAMISH holds the Canada Research Chair in International Business at the Ivey Business School at Western University, London, Canada. He is a past editor of the *Journal of International Business Studies* and is a Fellow of the Royal Society of Canada, the Academy of International Business, and the Asia Pacific Foundation of Canada. Beamish has responsibility for Ivey Publishing (IP), the world's second largest producer and distributor of business case studies. He has personally authored 120 case studies (thirty-four of which focus on China) and been the editor for six series of case books (totalling sixty-two volumes) for the China market. He has been visiting China every year for over thirty years.

FRED BILD currently serves as an adjunct professor at the Centre of East Asian Studies, Université de Montréal. He has held diplomatic appointments in Japan, in Korea at the International Control Commission in Indochina, and in France. From 1979 to 1983, he served as Canadian Ambassador to Thailand, with concurrent appointments to Laos and Vietnam. From 1987 to 1990, he was the assistant deputy minister for international and security affairs in the Department of Foreign Affairs, Ottawa. From 1990 to 1994, he served as Canadian Ambassador to the People's Republic of China and to Mongolia.

JING M. CHEN is a professor and Canada Research Chair in the Department of Geography at the University of Toronto and a Fellow of the Royal Society of Canada. He previously worked as a researcher in the Canada Centre for Remote Sensing in Ottawa. His research interests are in biogeochemical cycle modelling, remote sensing, climate change, micrometeorology, hydrology, geographic information systems, and isotope modelling. He served as project director for the University of Toronto's Tier One project in Confronting Global Warming: Enhancing China's Capacity for Carbon Sequestration (2002–06). He currently serves as a high-level consultant to China's Ministry of Science and Technology, advising on key national research programs.

PAUL EVANS is a professor and former director of the Institute of Asian Research, University of British Columbia. He has directed research centres and programs at UBC, Harvard University, York University, and the University of Toronto, and from 2005 to 2008 served as co-CEO of the Asia Pacific Foundation of Canada. An advocate and generalist in support of Asia Pacific institution building, his writings have focused on Canada-China relations and regional security processes. In 2011–12, he chaired a university committee developing a new China strategy for UBC. His most recent book, *Engaging China: Myth, Aspiration and Strategy in Canadian Policy from Trudeau to Harper*, was published by the University of Toronto Press in 2014.

FAN ZHIMIN is director of breast surgery at the No. 1 Hospital of Jilin University in Changchun. He is a full professor and top medical specialist who supervises master's and doctoral degree students in the field. He is a member of the standing committee of the Breast Cancer Training Centre and a member of China's national committee on cancer treatment. He is also a member of China's national committee on disease prevention and its subcommittee on breast cancer treatment. He serves as a member of the standing committee of Jilin Province's Medical Association and Surgery Committee and is the vice chair of surgery for Jilin's Cancer Prevention Society, as well as holding other committee memberships. He is a member of the editorial committees of two journals, *Zhonghua zhongliu yufang zazhi* (The China Tumour Prevention Journal) and *Zhongguo yiyuan yongyao pingjia* (The China Journal of Evaluation of Hospital Drug Use).

DILANTHA FERNANDO is a professor in the Department of Plant Science at the University of Manitoba. He is an internationally recognized plant scientist who has contributed to managing diseases through environmentally friendly methods around the world. His research has impacted the world with reduction of pesticide use and poverty alleviation, especially in China, India, and Sri Lanka. He has contributed to the development of thirty-two canola/rapeseed cultivars that are grown in Canada. He has been recognized numerous times through awards, invitations by many countries for keynote addresses at international conferences, and invitations to numerous boards. He currently serves as editor-in-chief and editor of two prestigious international journals. In addition, he has trained over seventy graduate, post-doctoral, and visiting scientists. The training of high-quality personnel in his lab has contributed to science in a major way, with many firsts and discoveries that have been published in high-impact peer-reviewed journals, bringing recognition to Canada.

FU TINGDONG is an academician of the Chinese Academy of Engineering and professor of agricultural science of the Huazhong Agricultural University. He has made outstanding contributions to the discovery and study of Pol cytoplasmic male sterility (CMS) and to the development and utilization of hybrid cultivars in rapeseed. He has bred thirteen varieties, with a total accumulative area of over seven million hectares. Recently, he found a new type of CMS. His group has provided the linkage map construction and cloning of genic male sterility genes in this plant. His suggestion of sowing rapeseed as forage during the vacant period after the wheat harvest in northwestern China has provided economic benefits to poor farmers. Professor Fu is the recipient of: the Superior Scientist Award of the International Consultative Research Group on Rapeseed (GCIRC), Paris; the Third World Academy of Sciences Prize (agriculture sciences, 2003); the Memorial Lifetime Achievement Award, Mustard Research and Promotion Consortium (MRPC), New Delhi; and the National Technology Specialized Talent Prize of China.

CHRISTY HAYHOE is an academic and educational editor and writer in Toronto, Ontario. She is the language editor of an international academic journal sponsored by the Chinese Academy of Engineering. Hayhoe has co-authored and edited many scientific textbooks and other materials published by prominent Canadian and American publishers. A graduate of the University of Toronto, Hayhoe obtained her Hon. BSC in chemistry (with high distinction) and several awards, including the Women's Centenary Silver Medal and the Lash Millar Award in Chemistry, in 1997.

RUTH HAYHOE is a professor of comparative higher education at the Ontario Institute for Studies in Education of the University of Toronto. Her professional engagements in Asia have spanned thirty years, including foreign expert at Fudan University in Shanghai (1980–82), head of the Cultural Section of the Canadian Embassy in Beijing (1989–91), and director of the Hong Kong Institute of Education (1997–2002). She has authored or edited more than a dozen books and published about eighty journal articles. Her recent books include *Portraits of 21st Century Chinese Universities: In the Move to Mass Higher Education*, co-authored with Jun Li, Jing Lin, and Qiang Zha (2011) and *Portraits of Influential Chinese Educators* (2006). She is an honorary fellow of the University of London Institute of Education (1998) and the Comparative and International Education Society (2011). In 2002, she received the Silver Bauhinia Star of the Hong Kong SAR Government and was made Commandeur dans l'ordre des Palmes Académiques by the Government of France.

PING-CHUN HSIUNG is a professor of sociology at the University of Toronto. Her research areas include gender roles and family relations in Chinese societies, feminist methodologies and epistemologies, and practices and the development of critical qualitative research in the Global South. Her writings on these topics have been published in English and Chinese. Recently, her work has been translated into German. Over the past decades, she has collaborated with Chinese feminist scholars to establish curricula and women's studies programs in key Chinese universities. She has also worked with women's NGOs in China.

GUY LEFEBVRE served as the dean of the Faculty of Law of the Université de Montréal from April 2012 to October 2014, when he was appointed vice-rector, International Relations and à la Francophonie. He is the author of numerous publications in French, English, Chinese, and Portuguese. Lefebvre teaches at several universities, including the China University of Political Science and Law (CUPL), the East China University of Political Science and Law, and the University of Macau. In 1997, he founded the Centre for the Law of Business and International Commerce of his faculty and in 2006, he created the first master of laws program in Canada designed exclusively for foreign students. Lefebvre has received several distinctions during his career, including the Canadian Bar Association's Paul-André-Crépeau Medal and the Medal of Merit from CUPL. He is also fellow of the Centre for Public Law at the Chinese Academy of Social Sciences.

LI CHONGAN served as vice-chairman of the China Democratic League (2003–12). He has also served as a member of the Standing Committee of the National People's Congress (NPC), deputy director of the NPC's Law Committee, and vice-president of China's National Association of Vocational Education. Prior to moving to Beijing in 2003, Professor Li served as a professor and vice-president of the Lanzhou Railway Institute (1973–96), Deputy Director of the Provincial Education Commission of Gansu Province (1996–98), and vice-governor of the Gansu Provincial Government (1998–2003). He was also president of the Association of Science and Technology of Gansu Province. Professor Li studied in the Department of Mathematics and Mechanics, Peking University (1962–68), and served as a research associate in mechanics of composite materials at Drexel University (1981–83).

LI HUAIZU is a professor in the School of Management at Xi'an Jiaotong University. As coordinator of the University of Alberta-Xi'an Jiaotong University Linkage, he took part in the whole process of initiating and implementing the collaborative program of Xi'an Jiaotong University and University of Alberta as well as its sister universities supported by the Canadian International Development Agency.

LÜ SHUNJING is director of the Division of International Relations of the Guangzhou Daily Press Group. Mr Lü was formerly the director of the Foreign Affairs Office of Lanzhou Railway Institute (LRI, Lanzhou Jiaotong University today). He got his MA in English and American literature at Lanzhou University as well as a TESL diploma from the University of Wellington, and was formerly an associate professor in English at LRI. Mr Lü has been responsible for setting up and leading the Division of International Relations of the Guangzhou Daily Press Group, mainly looking after the work of international exchange and cooperation between the GZ Daily Group and other media agencies and teaching and research institutions as well as professional associations overseas, in such areas as cooperative training, personnel, and technical exchanges.

ROLF MIRUS is CN-Professor of Trade Policy (Emeritus) at the School of Business, University of Alberta. He obtained his bachelor's degree (equivalent) from the Free University of Berlin, and his MA and PhD (Economics) from the University of Minnesota. He has held appointments at the University of Alberta's School of Business since 1971. Dr Mirus specializes in commercial policy and international finance, contributing thirty articles to refereed academic journals, as well as numerous book chapters and conference papers. He co-authored a (bilingual) textbook for MBAs in China, served on the editorial boards of *The Journal for International Business Studies* and *Management International Review*, and held visiting scholar/professor positions at the University of Michigan,

Christian Albrechts University in Kiel, Lahore University of Management Sciences, Wirtschafts-Universitaet Wien, University of Nairobi, Xi'an Jiaotong University, Jiangxi University of Finance and Economics, as well as at the Indian Institute of Management (Bangalore). From 1984–2002, Dr Mirus served as China Project Director of the Alberta School of Business. His awards include the Eric Geddes Senior Faculty Fellowship and MBA Teacher of the Year (1995). Prior to his retirement in 2006, Dr Mirus acted as vice-provost and associate vice-president (international) of the University of Alberta.

NI JIE is a postgraduate student of organizational management and decision analysis at Xi'an Jiaotong University. His research interests include leadership, organizational change, and strategic management.

JULIA PAN is an associate member of the School of Graduate Studies at the University of Toronto and a research associate in the Ontario Institute for Studies in Education of the University of Toronto. Julia's academic interests include international academic relations, knowledge transfer across cultures, and the role of universities in international development. Over the last two decades, Julia has directed and managed Canadian government-sponsored Canada-China University Linkage Programs in the areas of higher education and environmental studies, collaborating with many Chinese leading universities and CAS research institutions nationwide. She fervently believes such higher education and research cooperation can make a significant contribution to environmental science and social development in both nations.

QIANG HAIYAN is a professor of comparative education at the South China Normal University (SCNU) in Guangzhou, China. She has had rich overseas experience as a graduate student in the University of Massachusetts, a visiting scholar at the Ontario Institute for Studies in Education (OISE), University of Toronto, and a visiting academic fellow at the Institute of Education at the University of London. Prior to her appointment at SCNU, she served as associate dean for academic affairs at Shaanxi Normal University and directed a major project on women and minorities as educational change agents as part of a CIDA-supported university linkage with OISE. She has published widely on gender and education, bilingual education, and comparative school management, and has also initiated a network of English-immersion schools in various parts of China.

MARIE-CLAUDE RIGAUD is an assistant professor in the Faculty of Law, Université de Montréal, where she currently serves as associate dean, external affairs and communications. She is also the current director of the Business Law in a Global Context LLM Program. She teaches and conducts research in the areas of alternative dispute resolution, legal ethics, and professionalism. After many years in practice in the areas of litigation and domestic and international commercial arbitration in Toronto, Zurich, and Montreal, she received her doctor of laws degree (with highest distinction) from Université Paris XII for her thesis entitled "Transnational Arbitral Procedure." Rigaud is also a graduate of McGill University, where she obtained her BCL and LLB in 1992. She is a member of the Quebec Bar and of the Law Society of Upper Canada.

ELIZABETH STEYN is a doctoral candidate at the Université de Montréal's Faculty of Law, where she holds the prestigious Jacques Frémont Scholarship and a doctoral scholarship from the Fonds de recherche du Québec (FRQSC). Originally from South Africa, she completed her bachelor of laws degree (cum laude) at the University of Johannesburg and her master of laws degree (cum laude) at the University of South Africa (UNISA). In addition, she holds a certificate in advanced corporate law and securities law (cum laude) from UNISA. She has received several distinctions, including academic colours from the University of Johannesburg, as well as the UNISA Council Award. She is admitted as an advocate of the High Court of South Africa and has served on the University of Johannesburg's Faculty of Law as a lecturer for eight years. Her private practice experience spans a decade and comprises the areas of commercial law, corporate law, and energy law.

JAN W. WALLS is professor emeritus and founding director of the David Lam Centre for International Communication at Simon Fraser University, and is also founding director of the Asia-Canada Program in the Faculty of Arts. He has taught Chinese language and culture courses and contributed to Asia-focused program development at the University of British Columbia (1970–78), University of Victoria (1978–85), and Simon Fraser University (1987–2006). From 1981 to 1983, he served as first secretary for cultural and scientific affairs in the Canadian Embassy in Beijing, and from 1985 to 1987 he was senior vice-president of the newly established Asia Pacific Foundation of Canada, where he developed their first programs in cultural and educational affairs.

WANG JIAYI is director of the Education Department of the Gansu Provincial Government and professor of education at Northwest Normal University. He is also a member of the National Education Association of China, the National Committee of Curriculum and Teaching, and the Education Research Association of Gansu Province. His research covers educational development in western China, curriculum and teaching for rural areas, educational research methods, and the education of minority students. Current projects include education development strategies for western China during the eleventh five-year plan, compulsory education in minority regions, the quality of compulsory education in poverty-stricken regions in western China, and resource allocation in higher-education institutions in developing regions. Wang Jiayi obtained his BA in psychology in 1988, his MA in education in 1991, and his PhD in 1994, all at Northwest Normal University.

WANG YING is an academician of the Chinese Academy of Sciences and professor of coastal and ocean science at Nanjing University. She holds an assistant doctorate degree from Peking University's Geography and Geology Departments (1961) and an honourary doctorate in environmental science from the University of Waterloo in Canada (2001). From 1979 to 1982, she was a research fellow in marine geology at the Department of Geology, Dalhousie University and a visiting scholar of the Bedford Institute of Oceanography of Canada. At Nanjing University, she has served as dean of the College of Geosciences and director of the National Pilot Laboratory of Coast and Island Development. She has been conferred a number of significant awards in recognition of her research on coastal evolution and river-sea systems.

JOSEPH WHITNEY is professor emeritus at the University of Toronto and Fellow of the Royal Geographical Society. He was born in England and educated at Cambridge University, and obtained his doctorate from the University of Chicago. He was a Fulbright Fellow from 1968 to 1969 and taught at the University of Toronto from 1969–94 in the Department of Geography and Planning and at the Centre for the Environment. From 1976 to 1978, he was director of the Joint Centre on Asia-Pacific Studies, York University/University of Toronto. He was chair of geography, 1989–94. He has taught environmental courses at Hong Kong University, Waseda University, Japan, the Asian Institute of Technology in Bangkok, and the University of Khartoum. He directed and participated in several major environmental research projects in China and Vietnam and has written extensively on environmental problems in Africa, China, and Southeast Asia. He is a registered professional planner.

XI YOUMIN is executive president of Xi'an Jiaotong-Liverpool University, a Sino-British joint venture established in 2006. He is also pro-vice-chancellor of the University of Liverpool, and professor of the School of Management, Xi'an Jiaotong University. In 1987, he was awarded the first PhD degree in management engineering in mainland China, and in 1992 he was promoted to full professor of management. As a visiting professor, he has conducted joint research projects and lectures in universities in Canada, USA, Singapore, and Japan as well as Hong Kong, Macao, and Taiwan. Professor Xi participated in the collaboration program of Xi'an Jiaotong University and University of Alberta as well as its sister universities, supported by the Canadian International Development Agency in 1992 and 1995. In 1996, he became the dean of the school and was in charge of the program until 2000. Professor Xi's research and teaching areas cover strategic management and policy analysis, decision-making and decision support system, management behaviour and leadership, etc. He established harmony theory in 1987 and developed it into the *He Xie* (harmonious) management theory. He is chief editor of *Management Scientists* and a member of the editorial board of several Chinese academic journals. He is also member of many national science committees and professional research committees and societies.

YAO LING obtained an MSC degree in human geography at Fujian Normal University in 2011. She then took up the role of editor for *Education and Vocation*, a highly influential Chinese journal founded in 1917 by Mr Huang Yanpei, one of China's best-known leaders in vocational education. Ms Yao is responsible for primary checking of papers and editing papers for a column in *Education Management*, as well as participation in academic meetings related to higher vocational education with authors and experts.

QIANG ZHA is an associate professor at York University. He has published widely on Chinese and East Asian higher education and internationalization of higher education in journals such as *Compare, Higher Education, Higher Education in Europe*, and *Harvard China Review*. His most recent books include a co-authored book (with Ruth Hayhoe et al.), *Portraits of 21st Century Chinese Universities: In the Move to Mass Higher Education* (Comparative Education Research Centre, University of Hong Kong and Springer 2011), and two edited volumes, *Education and Global Cultural Dialogue* (co-edited with Karen Mundy, Palgrave Macmillan 2012) and *Education in China: Educational History, Models, and Initiatives* (Berkshire Publishing 2013). He is currently working on a new book titled *Massification and Diversification of Higher Education in China: An Exploration of State, Market and Institutional Forces*, which is to be published by Routledge.

ZHANG XIAOFENG is a PhD candidate in organizational management and decision analysis at Xi'an Jiaotong University. His research interests include leadership science and decision analysis.

ZHANG XIAOJUN is a lecturer in the Institute of Leadership & Education Advanced Development (ILEAD), Xi'an Jiaotong-Liverpool University. His research focuses on indigenous leadership and institutional change, as well as on the impact of cultural factors on leadership effectiveness. He has published dozens of papers in various international journals such as *Leadership Quarterly* and *Chinese Management Studies*. He has also conducted policy research for the Chinese Ministry of Education and published policy suggestions about higher education reform. Dr Zhang currently serves as the deputy director of ILEAD, which is a research institute that focuses on research on future universities and that provides training programs for higher education practitioners (senior managers, teaching staff, and administrative staff at universities).

ZHOU YONGMING is director of the Laboratory of Rapeseed Genetics and Breeding of Huazhong Agricultural University and a professor in the College of Plant Science and Technology. He was a research fellow at the University of Saskatchewan from 1999 to 2004. Dr Zhou has been working on genetics and metabolism engineering of canola seeds and functional studies of important genes for canola seed development and quality. He has published over sixty refereed papers and is the principal inventor of five patents. He is currently the director of the Laboratory of Rapeseed Genetics and Breeding administered by China's Ministry of Agriculture, and a member of the International Consultative Group on Rapeseed.

Index

1985 Decision, 215, 216
1993 Outline, 215
2020 Vision: China's Environmental and Development Task Force, 167

activism and activists in China, 281, 292, 293, 294
administrative development in China. *See* institutional management development in China
agents for change, developing in China, 256, 258, 279–81, 284, 285. *See also* Women and Minorities as Educational Change Agents
Agric-Food Canada, 300
agriculture, Canada-China collaboration in, 16–17, 22–3, 299–302. *See also* canola oil
Alberta Business School. *See* U of A: School of Business
All China Women's Federation. *See* China Women's Federation
Altbach, Philip, 6, 252
America. *See* US
American assistance to Chinese universities. *See* US
AMI (Asian Management Institute), 136

Appeal Court, Canadian, 257
Arnold, Mary Lou, 248
Asia Pacific Foundation of Canada (APFC): linkage with Ivey, 136; opinion polls produced by, 53n14; senior representatives from, 3
Asian Management Institute (AMI), 136
Association of Universities and Colleges of Canada. *See* AUCC
Atwood, Silveira et al., 270n26
AUCC (Association of Universities and Colleges of Canada): conference hosted by, 81; coordination of CCULP and SULCP by, 16, 191; funding by, 189n12; orientation program arranged by, 147
Australian support of China, 11

Bai Qiu En. *See* Bethune, Norman
Bamo Ayi, 201
Baoying, China, 181–6
Baraban, Cynthia Losure, 274n58
Beamish, Paul W., 30, 86, 125–37
Beihang University. *See* Beijing University of Aeronautics and Astronautics
Beijing Normal University. *See* BNU

Beijing University of Aeronautics and Astronautics (Beihang University), 149
Beijing University, 91, 267n4
Beijing, collaborative work in, 12, 172; events held in, 3, 18, 26, 27, 260; Fred Bild's time in, 30, 54, 57, 72; as a major or political centre, 13, 38, 61, 195; visits to, 95; water management in the region of, 178–80; workshops in, 286
benefits to Canada from collaboration with China: to Canadian students, 188; from CCMEP, 95–6; in experience abroad, 25; in exposure to different legal cultures, 265; in gaining access to data, 69; in learning from China, 90, 95–6, 218, 242; in learning to manage international projects, 14, 110; in networking, 23, 26; to Ryerson Polytechnic Institute, 21
Bennion, A., 106–7
Bethune, Norman, 54, 59–61, 144, 302, 304
Bethune-Laval Oncology Unit (BLOU), 21, 22, 60–1, 302–3
Biddulph, Sarah, 256, 267n5
Bild, Fred: as author of chapter 3, 54–76, 305, 306, 310; experiences in and reflections on China, 30, 126; regarding inspection of the LRI project by, 164n3; market economy, 39; regarding sustained contacts in research, 51
bilingual education in China, 218, 237
Bissell, Claude, 36
BLOU. See Bethune-Laval Oncology Unit

BNU (Beijing Normal University), 17, 19, 181, 230, 264
Bolden, Richard, et al., 105, 106
Bonnycastle, Geoffrey, 95
Boyd, Dwight, 248
brain drain: affecting China, 247; affecting peripheral universities, 23, 233, 238; in CCMEP, 13, 40, 85, 104; from China to Canada, 69–71, 309; commented on by Chinese officials, 56–7; compared to brain train, 273n55; not a hindrance, 265; as researched by Philip Altbach, 6; strategies against, 272n48
Burawoy, M., 295
Bureau of Soil and Water Conservation, 175
Business Law in a Global Context, master's of laws (LLM) at UdeM, 262–4
business management in China. See China, business management in; institutional management development in China; management education

CAE (Chinese Academy of Engineering), 149, 154
Cai Qiangguo, 175, 178
Canada: behaviour of students in, 116, 118, 120; business pedagogy in, 89, 113, 116, 118; engineering schools in, 70; flaws in the constitutional system of, 55; government objectives in international education, 259; international graduate students in, 259; as provider of raw materials and energy, 71; public perception of China in, 51, 53n14;

purposes in collaborating with China, 109; reasons for encouraging brain drain, 70; research methods and conditions in, 118; training Chinese students in, 71; warm reception of Chinese visitors, 147
Canada China Business Council (CCBC), 137
Canada Scholarship Council Doctoral Scholarship Program, 264
Canada-China academic relations. *See under individual development areas*; Canada-China collaboration.
Canada-China collaboration: academic relations within, 38–45, 51, 58, 64; attitudes of project leaders during, 14, 43; bilateral agreements and strategic partnerships within, 37, 38, 42, 54; common experiences in, 307; history of, 36–43; individual analysis / stories of, 195–201, 218–19, 283; as a learning process, 244–5; multisectoral, 49–50, 73, 97; overview of, 4, 5, 11; in research, 67, 151, 152, 170, 179, 192; strengths of, 134, 146, 187–8, 232, 308; in support of developing countries, 16, 27; timeliness of, 217–26, 236, 241, 259, 304–5. *See also under individual development areas*; benefits to Canada from collaboration with China; current Canada-China collaboration; future Canada-China collaboration; graduate programs, Canada-China joint
Canada-China cooperation. *See* Canada-China collaboration
Canada-China diplomatic relations: establishment and history of, 36–42, 144–5, 167; restoration of, 4; after the Tiananmen event, 5, 13, 40, 57–8; universities as part of, 25; university linkages from the perspective of, 54–76
Canada-China Higher-Education Program. *See* CCHEP
Canada-China Human Development Training Program, 39
Canada-China Joint Doctoral Programs in Education: main programs, 17–20, 230–1, 235–7; spin-off projects from, 19
Canada-China Language and Cultural Program, 39
Canada-China Language Training and Testing Centre. *See* CCLTTC
Canada-China Management Education Program. *See* CCMEP
Canada-China University Linkage Program. *See* CCULP
Canada-China University-Industry Partnership Program. *See* CCUIPP
Canada's International Education Strategy, 259
Canadian Association of Graduate Management Schools, 15
Canadian educational assistance to China. *See* Canada-China collaboration
Canadian Embassy in Beijing: creation of sinologist-in-residence position at, 37; first three Canadian ambassadors, 36; parties at, 188; senior representatives from, 3, 32n2. *See also* Bild, Fred; St Jacques, Guy
Canadian Federation of Deans of Management and Administrative Studies. *See* CFDMAS

Canadian Institute for the Administration of Justice, 268n10
Canadian International Development Agency. See CIDA
Canadian teaching methods. See Canada: business pedagogy used in
Canadian Treasury Board, 81
cancer care, Canada-China collaboration in, 59–61, 302
canola oil: commercial success in China of, 22–3, 299–302; most important cash crop in Canada, 300
carbon sequestration in China, 180–6
Carroll, Jude, 270n29, 273n56
CAS (Chinese Academy of Sciences), 23, 25, 175
case method. See case-study method
case-study method: in Canada, 112; Chinese application of, 113; introduction of to China, 11, 89, 110, 125–37. See also CCMEP; Ivey Business School
case-writing training, 130–2
CASS (Chinese Academy of Social Sciences), 92, 262, 286
CCBC (Canada China Business Council), 137
CCHEP (Canada-China Higher-Education Program), 88, 96, 109, 178, 298
CCICED (China Council for International Cooperation on Environment and Development): establishment of, 25, 41, 167; funding of, 25, 42
CCLTTC (Canada-China Language Training and Testing Centre), 17, 83, 94
CCMEP (Canada-China Management Education Program): academic publications from, 86, 114, 127, 128–30, 136; brain drain during, 13; budget of, 4, 9; challenges in, 89–90, 96, 115–16, 120, 134; description of, 4, 79–100, 109, 161, 164n4; legacy of, 91–100, 122; phase I, 81–4, 88–91; phase II, 84–8; results of, 10–16, 107–24, 133–5, 306; start of, 15, 16; strengths of, 134; Vancouver conference (1994), 87

CCP. See Chinese Communist Party
CCUIPP (Canada-China University-Industry Partnership Program), 15
CCULP (Canada-China University Linkage Program): in agriculture, 22–3, 299–302; benefits and challenges of, 23–4, 147, 151, 161–2, 244–5; budget of, 4; in cooperative education, 152–3; in education, 17–20, 211–29, 230–1; in engineering and transport, 20–1, 68–9, 141–66; general description of, 4, 9, 16–17, 23–4, 57; impact and legacy of, 150, 152, 154–63, 175; in marine-earth sciences, 298; in medicine and health, 21–2, 60, 150, 302–3; in minorities development, 190–3, 218; in soil erosion management, 172–5; suggested re-evaluation of, 56; sustaining collaborative relations after, 17–18. See also Canada-China Joint Doctoral Programs in Education
CDGDC (China Academic Degrees and Graduate Education Development Centre), 132
CEIBS (China Europe International Business School), 132
Central China University, 264
Central Committee of the Chinese Communist Party, 255

Central Institute of Nationalities. *See* Minzu University
central planning in higher education, 223
centres. *See* dependency theory: centres and peripheries
CFDMAS (Canadian Federation of Deans of Management and Administrative Studies), 87
challenges in Canada-China collaboration, 23–4, 115–16, 161–2, 187–8, 244–5. *See also* CCMEP: challenges in; CCULP: benefits and challenges in; SULCP: downsides and upsides
Chan, Luke, 86
Changbaishan, China, 181–6
Changchun: international conference on cancer in (1993), 60
change agents. *See* agents for change, developing in China
Chen Xiaoyue, 129, 130
Chen Yongzong, 172–5
Chen, Jing M., 30, 167–89, 306
Chen, Liang-Hsuan, 259
Cheng Yu Tung Management Institute, 136
Chesterman, Simon, 273n52
chief of protocol at the Chinese Foreign Ministry, 56
China Academic Degrees and Graduate Education Development Centre (CDGDC), 132
China Council for International Cooperation on Environment and Development. *See* CCICED
China Democratic League, 30
China Europe International Business School (CEIBS), 132
China Investment Corporation, 100
China Machine Press (Huazhang Graphic), 128
China Management Case-Sharing Centre (CMCC), 132
China National MBA Education Supervisory Committee (CNMESC), 132
China Project. *See* Ivey Business School: China Project at
China Scholarship Council. *See* CSC
China Teaching Project (CTP), 135
China University of Political Science and Law. *See* CUPL
China Women's Federation, 280, 282, 283, 286
China Women's University, 301
China, People's Republic of (PRC): areas of concern / development in, 28, 88, 235; behaviour of students in, 113, 116, 120, 130; business management in, 102; curricular change in, 211, 220, 236–7, 240–1; democratic development in, 8, 63, 99, 134, 168; economic reform in, 38, 40, 62, 214; economic rise of, 15, 27, 55, 72–3, 214, 308; educational reform in, 213–16, 218, 222, 232, 236–7; environmental training in, 298; founding of the PRC, 213, 216; health and social policy in, 28; human rights development in, 8, 43, 51, 62–5, 168; industrialization in, 144, 145, 156–7, 161, 178; legal reform in, 255–6, 269n24; legal training in, 255–6; minorities in, 190; moral education in, 218–22, 232, 237–9, 241, 242; multicultural education in, 219, 240; public perception of Canada, 144; reform and opening up of, 54, 80, 102–3, 142; rule of law in, 267n2; social justice in, 134; striving for world-class university

standing, 7, 45; technological development in, 146, 148, 156–7; university faculty development in, 15, 230–53; urbanization in, 178. *See also under individual development areas*
China-Canada cooperation. *See* Canada-China collaboration
Chinese Academy of Engineering. *See* CAE
Chinese Academy of Government, 95
Chinese Academy of Sciences. *See* CAS
Chinese Academy of Social Sciences. *See* CASS
Chinese Commission of Development and Reform, 185
Chinese Communist Party (CCP), 255, 282
Chinese Journal of Moral Education, 248
Chinese Ministry of Railways, 68
Chinese Ministry of Water Resources, 177, 178
Chinese National Forestry Administration, 183, 185
Chinese People's Association for Friendship with Foreign Countries, 56
Chinese Queer (*Tongzhi*) Group, 292
Chinese Society for Women's Studies, 292
Chinese studies at Canadian universities, 49, 53n13. *See also under* McGill University; UBC; Chinese studies at; UT,
Chinese University of Hong Kong, 168
Chinese Women Organizing. *See* Workshop on Chinese Women Organizing
Chinese women's movement, 293, 305

Chongqing Architectural Engineering Institute: linkage with McGill University, 149–50. *See also* Chongqing University
Chongqing Graduate School of Business, 91
Chongqing University, 92, 150
Chrétien, Jean, former prime minister of Canada, 256
CIDA (Canadian International Development Agency): additional funding, 189n5, 189n7, 189n12, 189n20; assistance with this study, 32n5; establishment of its Chinese program, 54, 62, 167; funding of the Canada-China Human Development Training Program, 39; funding of the Canada-China Language and Cultural Program, 39; funding of the CCICED, 25, 167; funding of the CCLTTC, 83; funding of the CCMEP, 4, 39, 79, 88, 94; funding of the CCULP, 4, 39, 191, 217, 234; funding of Chinese legal programs, 269n19; funding of the Judges Training Project by, 256; funding of the SULCP, 41,.217, 234; Gender and Development (GAD) program of, 275; gender equity policies, 31, 175, 183, 229n11, 276–7; goals and objectives in China of, 17, 41, 83, 167–8, 217; Human Research Development Program, 235; ICDS of, 81, 83; new China Country Development Policy Framework by, 5, 24, 41, 167, 168; possible role in China's economic rise, 6, 27; relationship with the MoE, 14, 80, 102, 108; reports to, 88; review of its

Chinese program, 64; spending on higher education, 5, 39, 42, 217, 227; study on China involvement by, 8. *See also* Massé, Marcel

CIDA management education program. *See* CCMEP

Clark, Joe, former Canadian foreign minister, 40, 57

classrooms: environments, 19, 221, 239; organization of, 20, 221; silencing in, 288

Climate Change Office, 185

climate change: collaborative research in, 25; research in China on, 25. *See also* global warming

CMCC (China Management Case-Sharing Centre), 132

CNMESC (China National MBA Education Supervisory Committee), 132

cognition improvement. *See* CCMEP: results of

Cold War: CIDA university partnerships before and after, 6; during, 65; economic globalization after, 7; engagement as an alternative to, 36; struggles of colonial and developing societies after, 6

collaboration: collaborative research, 28; importance of, 20, 64; results of, 74. *See also* Canada-China collaboration; international cooperative programs

commonalities and legacies of CIDA projects, 303–7

Communist Party of China, 84

computers and other new technology: at Chinese universities, 20, 94, 156; provided by university linkages, 148, 172–8, 191, 222, 306; transformation of Chinese system management due to, 20–1

Comtois, Claude, 68, 75n13

Concordia University: case-study method at, 12; Chinese scholars visiting, 12; linkage with SEU, 154; other university linkage involvement, 69

Conference at Tsinghua University (May 2014): description of, 3–4, 297; discussion at, 55; hosts of and planning of, 31n1; invitations to, 5; speakers at, 4, 101n4, 227; website of, 5, 32n3, 310n1

Confronting Global Warming: Enhancing China's Capacity for Carbon Sequestration, 25

Confucius: ideas from, 258, 278; Institutes, 28, 44, 50; philosophical heritage from, 7, 29, 204, 224–5, 245; quotes from, 29, 203

Consolidation of the Management Training Project: Educational Policy Implementation and Gender Equity in Human-Resource Development. *See* EPGEP

Consortium for Global Governance and International Legal Order, 266

Cooperation Agreement Concerning Candidates at the Doctoral Level, 264

cooperation as a learning process, 244–5

cooperative education. *See* CCULP (Canada-China University Linkage Program): in cooperative education

Couture, Jean, 59, 60, 302, 303

cross-cultural international collaborations. *See under specific areas of collaboration*; Canada-China

collaboration; international cooperative programs
cross-cultural theories, 104
Crowston, Wallace, 87, 96, 101n3
CSC (China Scholarship Council), 26, 44
Cultural Revolution: Canadian assistance to Chinese universities after, 3; effect on educational system of, 79, 80, 211, 213; harm done to medical services by, 61; situation after, 70, 156, 214, 216, 220
culture: differences in Canadian and Chinese, 107, 113, 120, 160, 244–5; exploration of differences in Canadian and Chinese, 257; sensitivity to in university linkages, 265
CUPL (China University of Political Science and Law): linkage with UdeM, 26–7, 254–72; Sino-Canadian Law Research Centre at, 261
current Canada-China collaboration, 44; between Ivey Business School and Chinese institutes, 135, 137; between NBUMS and Laval, 22; between UdeM, CUPL, and ECUPL, 27, 31; between UM and HAU, 23

Dai Chengping, 197
Dalhousie University: linkage with Xiamen University, 12, 82
Dalian University, 85, 128, 132
Dalian University of Technology, 299
Dashan. See Rowswell, Mark
Day, Chad, 196, 199
DEA (Canadian Department of External Affairs), 37, 62
Decision on the Reform of the Education System, 215, 216

Decision Support System (DSS), 173, 183
deforestation, 186
democratic development in China. See China: democratic development in
democratic governance development in China, 99, 168
Deng Xiaoping, former paramount leader of the PRC: advocation of China learning from advanced foreign countries by, 304; *First Liberation of Thought* by, 80; *The Four Transformations* by, 80; reform and opening up (*Gaige Kaifang*) by, 58, 102, 108, 214, 216. See also Open Door policy
Denzin, Norman K., 286; 296n2
Department of Foreign Affairs Trade and Development, Canadian, 84
dependency theory: regarding Canada-China collaboration, 230–53; centres and peripheries, 6, 27, 146, 163, 230–53; as a framework, 6, 189. See also Altbach, Philip
Deqing area, 169–72
Deqing County Government, 168
Deschenes, Luc, 303
Development and Education of Female University Students in China, 219
development cooperation. See under individual development areas; Canada-China collaboration.
DFAIT. See DEA
DFATD. See DEA
Dipchand, Cecil, 86, 100n1
Doctoral Scholarship for Chinese Students Program, 264–5
doing of feminist collaboration, 275–96

Douville, Yvan, 303
Du Fangqin, 28

East China Normal University. See
  ECNU
East China University of Political
  Science and Law. See ECUPL
East Meets West Feminist Translation
  Group, 292
Eckstein, Max, 251
ECNU (East China Normal
  University): university linkages
  with, 228n3, 228n4, 230, 244
economic reform in China. See China:
  economic reform in
economic rise of China. See China:
  rapid economic rise in
Economy, Culture and the Environment,
  195
Eco-planning and Environmental
  Management in Coastal
  Communities, 299
ECUPL (East China University of
  Political Science and Law): cooper-
  ation with UdeM, 27, 260, 262,
  263, 266; as an example of impact
  of Cultural Revolution, 267n5
Education Management Training
  Centre in Changchun, 224, 225
Education Management Training
  Program, 225
educational administration training,
  Canada-China collaboration in,
  224, 225, 231, 237
educational development, Canada-
  China collaboration in, 17–20,
  211–29, 230–53. *See also under individual development areas*
educational management in China,
  236–7

Educational Policy and Gender
  Equity Program. See EPGEP
educational reform in China. See
  China, educational reform in
Educational Sociology, 240
educational system in China: centralized, 213, 214, 216; decentralization of, 215, 216, 222, 225;
  depoliticization of, 214, 215, 220
Eichler, Margrit, 287
EMBA (executive MBA program) at
  Ivey Business School, 136
engineering education and transportation, Canada-China collaboration
  in, 16–17, 20–1, 68–9, 141–66,
  306. *See also* CCULP: engineering
  and transport; SULCP: engineering
Environment Canada, 42, 181
environmental economics, 88, 99
environmental research, Canada-
  China collaboration in, 24–6, 167–
  89, 191, 194, 298–9
EPGEP (Educational Policy and
  Gender Equity Program), 224, 225
ÉRI. *See* UdeM: Industrial Relations at
Europe: assistance to China, 32n6
Evans, Paul, 35–53, 163, 227, 306, 309
Everbright Bank, 91
executive MBA program (EMBA) at
  Ivey Business School, 136

failure analysis in China, 149
Fan Zhimin, 302
Fang Junming, 250
Federal Court, Canadian, 257
feminism: collaboration in, 31;
  education in, 219, 240–1, 275–96;
  literature in China on, 18; research
  methods in, 241. *See also* gender
  issues education and equity

feminist collaboration, 275–96
feminist epistemology, 279, 282–4, 286
feminist pedagogy, 287–91
Feminist Pedagogy (CD-ROM), 291
feminist praxes, 290, 292
Fernando, Dilantha, 299–302
Final Assessment: Women and Minorities as Educational Change Agents, 253
Five Constant Virtues, 188, 203, 204, 309
Ford Foundation, 219, 278, 287
Foreign Affairs Office of the Hailar District in Inner Mongolia, 193
foreign market entry, 126
Fourth World Conference on Women in Beijing (1995), 18, 277
France, 12, 32n6
Francis, June, 198, 199
Frontiers of Education in China, 32n11
Fu Tingdong, 300
Fudan University, 85
future Canada-China collaboration: in arctic research, 69; in education, 252, 253; with minority nationalities, 202–3; reasons for, 71–4; requirements for, 50–1, 227

GAD (Gender and Development program), 275, 294–5, 305
Gaige Kaifang. *See* Open Door policy
Galtung, Johan, 243
Gansu Province, 30, 69, 232, 246
Gansu Provincial Department of Education, 31. *See also* Wang Jiayi
Gao Xiaoxian, 293–4
gap in development: between Canadian and Chinese systems, 114–19, 121, 122, 124; between Chinese and world universities, 236, 252; between periphery and centre, 247–8
Gender and Women's Development, 219
gender discrepancies, 225
gender issues education and equity, Canada-China collaboration in: among minorities, 194–5; in higher education, 218–19, 224–6, 231–2, 237–8, 275–96. *See also* gender studies in China
gender studies in China, 18, 219, 240–1, 248, 278–87
General Agreement on Development Cooperation, 4, 167
Germany: assistance to China, 32n6, 228; comparison to China, 72
Gibbins, Michael, 86
GIS (geographic information systems), 24, 25, 172–8
Global Change Key Program of the Chinese Ministry of Science and Technology, 186
global governance, China's emerging role in, 28
global issues, 7
global knowledge economy: characteristics of, 28, 163; as a CIDA goal, 39; as a theme in this book, 7; universities as knowledge institutions, 7, 43, 49, 212, 299
global knowledge society: as a CIDA goal, 39; networks in, 226, 227; as a result of university linkages, 43, 121; as a theme in this book, 7
Global Teaching Project (GTP), 136
global warming, Canada-China collaboration in, 180–6
Gordon, Myron, 86, 100n1
governance according to law in China, 255

government of Quebec, 303
graduate programs, Canada-China joint: in agriculture, 300; in education, 17–20, 218, 230–1, 249; in engineering, 154; in law, 262; in management education, 109; by Tsinghua University and the UWO, 85; by UBC, 49; by XJTU and the U of A, 98
gratitude: from Chinese participants in university linkages, 147, 307
Great Leap Forward, 280, 286
grounded theory, 108, 111
Guangdong Province, 168–72
Guangxi, China, 190, 194, 195, 201
Guangzhou Institute of Geography, 168, 170, 171
Guangzhou Province, 69, 135
guanxi, 129
Guiyang, China, 286

Habermas, Juergen, 7, 28
Hainan, 190, 194, 195, 298
Hainan Province, 299
Hainan Research Academy of Environmental Sciences, 299
Hangzhou, China, 286
Harper, Stephen, former Canadian prime minister, 42
Hatch, James, 131
HAU (Huazhong Agricultural University): linkage with UM, 23, 299–302
Hayhoe, Christy, 297–310
Hayhoe, Ruth: as co-author of chapter 1, 3–32, 187, 194, 232, 251; as co-author of chapter 10, 211–29; as co-author of chapter 14, 297–310; as CIDA program director, 287; as a factor in project success, 246; in other works, 80, 163, 190, 243
He Weifang, 267n4
health and social policy in China. *See* China: health and social policy in
HEC (École des Hautes Études Commerciales de Montréal), 82
Heihe, China, 181–6
Heinonen, Tuula, 301
Helwig, Charles, 248
Herbart, Johann, 17
Higher Education Research Institute, 31n1
Hill, Martha N., 274n59
Hole, Lois, 88
Hong Kong, programs in, 136
Hsiung, Ping-chun, 31, 227, 241, 248, 275–96
Hu Jintao, former Chinese president, 42
Hu Yaobang, 80
Hu, Ming, 267n4
Huang Jin, 260
Huazhong University of Science and Technology. *See* HUST
Hubei Province, 232
human capital, 7. *See also* global knowledge economy
human needs. *See* human well-being
Human Research Development (HRD) program, 235
human resources: collaborative project on, 222–4; focus on by CIDA, 17, 83, 144, 217, 305–6; focus on in China by Canada, 24, 67, 96, 155, 191; needed in China, 163, 216
human rights in China. *See* China: human rights development in
Human Settlement Institute, 150
human well-being, 16, 163, 194

HUST (Huazhong University of Science and Technology), 82, 85, 228n4, 231, 243

IBJ (Ivey Business Journal), 131
ICBC (Industrial and Commercial Bank of China), 97
ICDS (Institutional Cooperation and Development Support Division), 81
identity, academic, 107
IDRC (Canadian International Development Research Centre), 24, 39, 41, 62, 168
IGSNRR (Institute of Geographic Science and Natural Resources Research), 24–6, 168–78, 180–6
Ih Ju League, 175
impacts of Canada-China collaboration. *See* impacts of university linkages
impacts of university linkages: on cancer research and treatment in China, 60–1, 303; on Chinese farmers, 167–80, 301; on Chinese universities, 194, 217, 235, 154–61, 305; on course development, 222, 240, 296; on curriculum development, 217–22, 225, 237, 240–1, 250; on engineering education, 148, 151, 162–3; on gender studies, 284–7; in Hainan, 298; on industry, politics, and society, 171–2, 177–8, 185–6, 194, 200–1; on management education, 91–100, 133–5; on pedagogy, 217, 219, 240, 244; on politics, 306; on students and scholars, 107–24, 242, 248, 250, 291; on teachers and administrators, 231
in land use, Canada-China collaboration in, 152, 167–89

Industrial and Commercial Bank of China. *See* ICBC
industrial development in China. *See* China: industrialization in
industrialization in China. *See* China: industrialization in
industry connections: with management programs, 114, 121; with engineering universities, 154
Inner Mongolia, 24, 175, 190, 194, 303
Institute of Crop Genetics and Breeding, 301
Institute of Geographic Science and Natural Resources Research. *See* IGSNRR
Institute of Geography (INSGR) at the CAS. *See* IGSNRR
institutional leadership, strengthening of in China, 222–4
institutional management development in China, 20, 80, 102, 224. *See also* management education
institutional memory, 42, 55, 59, 135
international capital theory, 103, 104
international cooperative programs: individual-level analysis of, 103–4, 106, 108, 112, 123–4; process-level analysis of 105, 108, 117–21, 123, 124; research on, 103–8, 121, 122, 123, 124; *See also under individual development areas*; Canada-China collaboration
International Law Review, 260
International Sedimentation Centre, 170
international women's movement, 277
Investigative Research (IR) by Mao Zedong, 279, 286

Ivey Business Journal (IBJ), 131
Ivey Business School: Asian Management Institute with, 136; case-study method at, 89; Case Writing Workshops by, 127, 130–1; Cheng Yu Tung Management Institute with, 136; China Project at, 125–8; China Teaching Project at, 135; developing Chinese case studies, 12, 86, 125–33; executive MBA program, 136; Global Teaching Project at, 136; Ivey-Tsinghua Casebook Series, 128–30, 134; Joint Case Training Development Project at, 132; linkage with Tsinghua University, 125–31; overview of work in China by, 125–37. *See also* Beamish, Paul; case-study method
Ivey Casebooks. *See* Ivey Business School: Ivey-Tsinghua Casebook Series
Ivey Publishing, 129, 131
Ivey School of Business. *See* Ivey Business School

Jaccard, Mark, 199
Jackson, Edward T., 22, 28, 74
Japan: breaking out of a dependent mode in, 6; collaboration with Chinese universities, 24, 154; comparison to China, 72; universities assistance to China, 32n6
Jaschok, Maria, 292
Ji Yongqiang, 199–200
Jiang Yen, 283
Jiang Zemin, former president of the PRC, 255
Jiangsu Province, 232, 299
Jie, Jiao, 260

Jilin Education Institute. *See* Jilin Institute of Education
Jilin Education Press, 220
Jilin Institute of Education, 211, 224–6
Jilin Province, 59, 60, 224, 225, 232
Jilin University, 21, 267n4, 302
Jinan University, 135
Johanson, Jan, 126
Johnson, David, governor general of Canada, 299
Joint Case Training Development Project (JCTDP), 132
joint graduate programs. *See* Canada-China Joint Doctoral Programs in Education; graduate programs, Canada-China joint
Journal of Environmental Management, 184, 185, 186, 187
Judges Training Project, Canada-China Senior, 254, 255, 256–8
judges, training of in China. *See* China: law and good governance development in; Judges Training Project, Canada-China Senior

Kairov, Ivan, 17, 236
King, K., 16, 20, 28
knowledge economy. *See* global knowledge economy
knowledge networks, 226, 227
Korea, 6
Kunming, China, 286
Kyoto Agreement, 185. *See also* Kyoto Climate Change Accord
Kyoto Climate Change Accord: China's commitment to, 25, 187

La Revue juridique Thémis de l'Université de Montréal, 261

Labelle, Huguette, 167
Lanzhou Cold and Arid Regions Environmental and Engineering Research Institute of CAS, 181–6
Lanzhou Jiaotong University (LJU). See LRI
Lao Tzu, 254
Laurentian University. See LU
law and education, Canada-China collaboration in, 26–7, 66, 254–74
leadership cohort in Chinese Education, development of, 230–53
Lefebvre, Guy, 31, 66, 73, 76n17, 254–74
legal education in China. See China: legal training in
Li Chongan: as co-author of chapter 7, 30, 141–66, 306; as former vice-governor of Gansu Province, 30; quotes from, 304, 305, 306, 310; as vice-chairman of the China Democratic League, 30
Li Huaizu, 96, 100n1, 102–24
Li Peng, former premier of the PRC, 256
libraries: open access to in Chinese universities, 20
light rail transit. See LRT
Lincoln, Yvonna S., 286
Liping, China, 181–6
Lishi, 172–5
Liu Gaohuan, 178
Liu Guojin, 59, 60, 302
Liu Jiyuan, 180
Liu Yuming, 196–7
Liu Zongyuan, 186
Locke, E.A., 106–7
Loess Plateau, 172–5
London, 7

Longlin County, 200–1
LRI (Lanzhou Railway Institute): linkage with Ryerson Polytechnic Institute, 148–9, 161, 306; transformation of during CCULP, 21, 148–9, 157, 306
LRT (light rail transit), 68
LU (Laurentian University), 150–1, 308
Lü Shunjing, 141–66
Luk, Shiu-hung, 168, 174

Macau University. See University of Macau
Management College at Xiamen University. See under Xiada
management education, Canada-China collaboration in, 10–16, 79–101, 102–24, 125–37
management engineering. See management education
Management Program in Urumqi, 91
Management Research Methodology, 114, 119
Management School of Shanghai Jiaotong University. See under Shanghai Jiaotong University
manufacturing technology, Canada-China collaboration in, 154
Mao Zedong, 279
Marginson, S., 105
marine-earth sciences, Canada-China collaboration in, 298–9
market economy in China: building, 39; CIDA's policy to create, 168; creating a need for leadership in engineering universities, 144; creating a need for management education, 10, 147, 161, 236; creating a need for moral education, 19;

creating a need for public administration training, 12; development of 214–6; observing in Canada, 133
marketization of education, 216
Martin, Paul, former Canadian prime minister, 42
Massé, Marcel, 39, 43
MBA programs. *See* graduate programs, Canada-China joint
McGill University: Chinese studies at, 36; linkage with Chongqing Architectural Engineering Institute, 149–50; linkage with Renmin University, 82; other university linkages with, 69, 178–80, 268n10
McLean, Martin, 250, 251
McMaster University, 85, 159, 168
medicine and health: Canada-China collaboration in, 21–2, 59–61, 67–8, 301–2
Memorandums of Understanding. *See* MOUS
Mencius, 278
Middle Way, 188, 203, 204
Milwertz, Cecilia, 292
mini-BLOU. *See* Bethune-Laval Oncology Unit
Minister of External Affairs, 80
Ministry of Building Materials Industry (Bureau of Building Materials), 150
Ministry of Economic Relations and Trade. *See* MOFERT
Ministry of Education of China. *See* MOE of China
Ministry of Foreign Trade and Economic Cooperation. *See* MOFTEC
Ministry of Justice, 255

Ministry of Railways, 148
Ministry of Science and Technology, 25
minorities development, Canada-China collaboration in, 30, 156, 190–207, 218, 231–2, 237–8
Minority Area Development Research Project, 191, 193
Minzu University: linkage with SFU, 190–207
Mirus, Rolf, 30, 79–101, 304, 305
missionaries in China, 36, 79, 87
Mo, John, 26
MOE (Ministry of Education) of China: current projects funded by, 27; Department of Minority Education of, 240; and educational reform, 215; International Cooperation Department of, 155; involvement in CCULP and SULCP, 16, 147, 195; involvement in engineering education, 142, 146, 153; involvement in management education, 11, 87, 108–9, 132; relationship with CIDA, 14, 80, 102, 108; response to brain drain, 13–14; senior representatives from, 3, 10
MOFERT (Chinese Ministry of Economic Relations and Trade, now the Ministry of Commerce), 62, 80, 87
MOFTEC (Ministry of Foreign Trade and Economic Cooperation), 108, 146
Montreal Heart Institute, 67–8
Montreal: events held in, 26, 27
moral education in China. *See* China: moral education in
Moral Education: Action Research in Secondary Schools, 220

Morgan, Katherine, 289
MOUS (Memorandums of Understanding): involving CIDA, 80; involving CUPL, 263; involving Ivey, 132; involving UBC, 46–7; involving UdeM, 263; involving U of A, 97
Mu, Fengli, 131
Mulroney, Brian, former prime minister of Canada, 57
multicultural education in China, 219, 240
multiculturalism: research in Canada, 18
Murray, Victor, 95

NAEA (National Academy of Educational Administration), 211, 222–4
Nanjing Agriculture University, 181
Nanjing Forestry University (NFU), 181
Nanjing Institute of Soil Science, 181–6
Nanjing Institute of Technology (Southeast University), 85, 128
Nanjing Normal University. See NNU
Nanjing University: collaboration in global warming, 181; School of Geographic and Ocean Sciences at, 298; Sino-Canadian College at, 299
Nanjing, China, 286
Nankai University: joint PhD programs at, 85; linkage with York University, 82; other university linkages, 178–80, 266
Nankivell, Jeff, 84, 101n4
Nanning, China, 286
National Academy of Educational Administration. See NAEA

National Accounting Institute in Xiamen, 13
National Coordinating Office. See NCO
National Curriculum Reform for Basic Education in China, 242
National Judges College, 26, 268n10
National Magistrates College of China, 66
National Outline for Medium- and Long-Term Educational Reform and Development, 222
National People's Congress, 255
Natural Resources Canada, 181
Natural Sciences and Engineering Research Council of Canada. See NSERC
Natural Sciences Foundation of China, 93
NBUMS (Norman Bethune University of Medical Sciences): First Teaching Hospital of, 302; linkage with Université Laval, 21–2; 59–61, 302–3, 309
NCO (National Coordinating Office), 87, 88, 96
NENU (Northeast Normal University): rural education at, 250; School of Education at, 247; university linkages with, 228n3, 228n4, 230, 243
neocolonialism, 230, 233, 234, 235, 251
new teaching methods. See CCMEP, results of
Ni Jie, 102–24
NIES (National Institute of Education Science in China), 19, 221
Ningxia University, 199, 200
Ningxia, China, 190, 194, 195

NNU (Nanjing Normal University): Institute of Moral Education at, 248, 250; university linkages with, 228n3, 228n4, 231, 243
Noah, Harold, 251
Norman Bethune University of Medical Sciences. See NBUMS
Northeast Normal University. See NENU
Northwest Normal University. See NWNU
NPC (National People's Congress), 255
NSERC (Natural Sciences and Engineering Research Council of Canada), 39, 41
NWNU (Northwest Normal University): minority education at, 250; university linkages with, 228n3, 228n4, 243
NW-Polytechnic University, 91

OECD (Organization for Economic Cooperation and Development), 5
OISE (Ontario Institute for Studies in Education): and Canada-China Joint Doctoral Programs in Education, 17, 18; in university linkages, 212, 217–18, 230–2, 244; visiting scholar to, 243
"On Qualitative Research: Engendering Sociology from Feminist Perspectives," 286
"One Thousand Talent Plan," 103
Ontario Institute for Studies in Education. See OISE
Open Door policy, 38, 58, 133, 235
Organization Department of the Central Committee of the Communist Party of China, 103

Organization for Economic Cooperation and Development. See OECD
organized cooperation: in university linkages, 8
Outline for Educational Reform and Development in China, 215
Oxford University, 292

Pan Hui, 197–8
Pan, Julia, 3–32, 133, 167–89, 194, 246, 287
path dependence, 7, 27
pedagogy. See Canada: business pedagogy in; feminist pedagogy
Peking University, 178–80, 264
People's Republic of China (PRC). See China, People's Republic of (PRC)
peripheries. See dependency theory: centres and peripheries
Petroleum University, 91
PhD programs. See graduate programs, Canada-China joint
Policy on Women in Development and Gender Equity, 229n11
Postman, Neil, 202
poverty alleviation in China: by canola oil development, 22; by Pan Hui, 197–8, 306; by Yang Guangfu, 200–1
power in gender issues, 283, 284, 290, 294
PRC. See China, People's Republic of (PRC)
Provincial Court of Quebec, 257
public administration development in China, 12, 224

Qiang Haiyan, 30, 227, 230–53, 278, 309, 310

Qingdao, China, 303
Qinghai Province, 232
Qiongzhou University, 198
qualitative research (QR): in social science inquiry, 279–82, 285; in the United States, 286
Queen's University, 83

rapeseed. *See* canola oil
RBC (Royal Bank of Canada), 97, 98
remote sensing (RS), 173, 181, 183, 184, 185
Renmin University: linkage with McGill University, 82; linkage with UdeM, 264; School of Labour and Human Resources at, 67
research methodology of this book, 9
Rigaud, Marie-Claude, 254–74
Rowswell, Mark, 61, 303
Royal Bank of Canada. *See* RBC
Russia. *See* Soviet Union, the former
Ryan, Janette, 270n29, 273n56
Ryerson Institute of Technology. *See* Ryerson Polytechnic Institute
Ryerson Polytechnic Institute (Ryerson University), 20–1, 148–9, 161

sanctions imposed on China by Canada, 57–8
SARS outbreak (2003), 179, 180, 185
Sawir, E., 105
School of Economics and Management at Tsinghua University. *See* Tsinghua University
School of Labour Economics at the Capital University of Economics and Business, 67
School of Management at XJTU. *See* XJTU: School of Management at

Science and Technology University, 91
SCNU (South China Normal University), 31, 168. *See also* Qiang Haiyan
security and institution building in China, 41, 231
SEdC. *See* MOE
"Sedimentation Process of Tidal Embayments and Their Relationship to Deep Water Harbour Development along Hainan Island, China," 298
SEMGIS I. *See* GIS
SEMGIS II. *See* GIS
Senior Judges Training Project. *See* Judges Training Project
SEU (Southeast University): linkage with Concordia University, 153–4. *See* Nanjing Institute of Technology
SFU (Simon Fraser University): connection with the CCICED, 26; David Lam Centre at, 190, 191; linkage with Minzu University, 190–207; School of Resource and Environmental Management at, 196, 199. *See also* Walls, Jan W.
Shaanxi Association for Women and Family (SAWF), 293–4
Shaanxi Province, 232
Shanghai Administrative Institute, 95
Shanghai Institute of Mechanical Engineering, 151–2
Shanghai Jiaotong University: CCMEP at, 11; current collaboration with UdeM, 262; joint conference at, 85; linkage with UBC, 14, 15, 82; Management School of, 14; selection of joint PhD candidates by, 85
Shanghai University of Engineering Science, 152–3

Shanghai University of Science and Technology. *See* Shanghai Institute of Mechanical Engineering
Shanghai: global ranking system for universities led by, 7; institutes and offices located in, 13, 27, 50, 74, 152; as a major centre, 61; programs in, 15, 132, 135, 136, 232; Shanghai MBA Case Library, 132; sister-city relationship with Montreal, 68; visits to, 68, 95
Shanxi Institute of Soil and Water Conservation, 172
Shanxi Ministry of Water Conservancy, 175
Shanxi Ministry of Water Resources, 177
Shanxi Province, 24, 172–5, 178
Shen Youling, 206n1
Shenchong Experimental Basin, 169–72
Shenyang, China, 303
Shenzhen, China, 303
Shivnan, Jane C., 274n59
Shun, Kwong Loi, 291
Sichuan Institute of Building Materials. *See* SWIT
Siegel, Linda, 246, 249
silencing in the classroom. *See* classroom: silencing in
Simon Fraser University. *See* SFU
Simon, Herbert, 86
Singer, Martin, 38, 46
Sino-Canadian legal partnerships, 254–74
Sino-Foreign Cooperative in Running Universities, 103
Smith, Roger S., 81, 100n1
SNU (Shaanxi Normal University): collaboration in gender studies, 278–9; leadership of the Canada-China Joint Doctoral Programs in Education, 19, 247; linkage with OISE, 228n3, 230; linkage with UBC, 228n4; subsequent activities, 243
social norms. *See* intercultural understanding
Social Sciences and Humanities Research Council of Canada. *See* SSHRC
soft power, 65–6
soil conservation in China. *See* soil erosion management
soil erosion management, Canada-China collaboration in, 24, 167–78, 186. *See also* GIS
SOM (School of Management) at XJTU. *See* XJTU: School of Management at
Song Jian, 167
South China Normal University. *See* SCNU
Southeast University. *See* SEU
Southwest Institute of Technology. *See* SWIT
Southwest Normal University. *See* SWNU
Soviet Union, the former: influence in China from, 10, 79, 214, 218, 236
SPC (Supreme People's Court), 255
Special University Linkage Consolidation Program. *See* SULCP
SSHRC (Social Sciences and Humanities Research Council of Canada): application to, 4; this book funded by, 9; funding of programs with Chinese institutions by, 39, 41

St Jacques, Guy, 4
State Education Commission. *See* MOE
State Environmental Protection Administration in Beijing, 26
State Science and Technology Commission, 39
Steffansson, Baldur, 300
Steyn, Elizabeth, 254-74
strategic planning in higher education, 222, 223
subversion in qualitative research, 285
SULCP (Special University Linkage Consolidation Program): in agriculture 22-3, 299-302; budget of, 5; description of, 4-5, 9, 16-17, 23-4, 41; downsides and upsides, 23-4, 243; in education, 17-20, 212-29, 231-2, 235; in engineering, 20-1, 141-2, 153-5; in gender equity and training women in higher education, 225, 231-2, 237-8, 305; impact of, 154-61, 177-8, 199; in marine-earth sciences, 298; in medicine and health, 21-2, 60, 302-3; in minorities education, 190, 193-5, 231-2, 237-8; in soil erosion management, 22-3, 175-8
Summer Institute on Feminist Pedagogy and Curriculum Development, 278, 287-91, 294, 296
Sun Jianxuan, 173
Sun Lizhe, 128, 129, 130
Superior Court, Canadian, 257
Supreme People's Court, 255
sustainable water management. *See* water management
SWIT (Southwest Institute of Technology), 150-1, 158, 308
Switzerland, 154

SWNU (Southwest Normal University), 228n3, 230

Taiwan, 6, 279, 282, 286, 295
Technical University of Nova Scotia (TUNS), 157
technological advances from university linkages. *See* computers and other new technology
technological development in China. *See* China, technological development in
Three Gorges Dam, 55
"Three Sustainables" project, 194, 201-3
Tiananmen event (June 1989): Canada-China relations after, 57, 104, 174; concerns for future caused by, 62; maintaining linkages after, 61, 87, 108, 308-9; non-return of Chinese students in Canada after, 23, 86, 134; reconsideration after, 5, 8, 171. *See also* Canada-China diplomatic relations, after the Tiananmen event
Tianjin, China, 61, 178-80, 286
Tianjin University, 82, 85
Tibetan Culture Reading Book, 240
timeliness. *See* Canada-China collaboration: timeliness of
Tongji University, 80
tourism development in China, 195, 198, 199, 202-3, 299
"Transformation, Subversion, and Feminist Activism: Report on the Workshops of a Developmental Project, Xi'an, China," 285-6
Transitional Year Program (TYP), 289
Trudeau, Gilles, 260

Trudeau, Pierre, former Canadian prime minister, 36, 37
Tsinghua University: assembly hall of, 3; brain drain from, 13; case-study method at, 12; CCMEP at, 11; conference at, 3; feedback from scholars at, 11–14; Institute of Education at, 31n1; Ivey-Tsinghua Casebook Series, 128–30; linkage with Ivey, 125–31, 135; linkage with McMaster University, 85; linkage with UWO, 31n1, 82, 84–5; other university linkages, 178–80, 264; School of Economics and Management at, 12, 32n1, 128
tumour registry in China, 60, 302

U of A (University of Alberta): after CCMEP, 96–8; linkage with NAEA, 211, 222–4; linkage with XJTU, 14–15, 81–5, 88, 91, 110; program in business at, 95; School of Business at, 14. *See also* Mirus, Rolf
UBC (University of British Columbia): as a case study of Canadian-Chinese academic relations, 46–50; Centre for Chinese Research at, 48; China Strategy Working Group at, 47, 52n11; Chinese studies at, 36; Faculty of Medicine at, 48; Institute of Asian Research at, 48, 204; linkage with Shanghai Jiaotong University, 14, 15, 82; other university linkages, 178–80, 228n4, 231, 244; Sauder School at, 14
UdeM (Université de Montréal): agreement with the CSC and Chinese institutions, 264; agreement with Renmin University, 264; current collaboration with China, 74; faculty of law at, 26; Industrial Relations (ÉRI) at, 67; internationalization strategy at, 258; International Research Centre on Globalization and Labour at, 67; linkage with CUPL, 26–7, 254–72; linkage with ECUPL, 260, 262, 266; linkage with the National Magistrates College of China, 63, 66, 73; linkage with Shanghai Institute of Mechanical Engineering, 151–2; sister-city relationship with Shanghai, 68. *See also* Lefebvre, Guy; Judges Training Project
UK (United Kingdom), 12
UM (University of Manitoba): Chinese experience during CCMEP, 83; Department of Plant Science at, 299, 300, 301; linkage with Beihang, 149; linkage with HAU, 23, 299–302; partnership with China Women's University, 301; partnership with the West China School of Public Health at Sichuan University, 301
UN (United Nations), 42
UNESCO, 170
United Nations Development Program (UNDP), 256
Université de Montréal. *See* UdeM
Université de Sherbrooke, 83
Université du Québec à Montréal. *See* UQAM
Université Laval: in CCMEP, 86, 101n2; partnership with NBUMS, 21–2; 59–61, 302–3, 309;
universities: cultural role of, 212; social roles of, 212;

university linkages. *See under institution names*
University of Alberta. *See* U of A
University of British Columbia. *See* UBC
University of Calgary, 83
University of Carleton, 83
University of Guelph, 298, 300
University of Helsinki, 266
University of International Business and Economics of China, 266
University of Macau, 260, 262
University of Manitoba. *See* UM
University of New South Wales, 266
University of Regina, 83, 211, 224–6
University of Saskatchewan, 81, 83, 300
University of Science and Technology Beijing (USTB), 159
University of Toronto Scarborough. *See* UTSC
University of Victoria, 69
University of Waterloo: linkage with Shanghai University of Engineering Science, 152–3; other university linkages with, 83, 85, 128, 298, 299
University of Western Ontario. *See* UWO
UQAM (Université du Québec à Montréal), 69, 82
US: assistance to China, 32n6; cooperation between American and Chinese universities, 12, 24, 50, 249; participation in case-study method conference, 12; refusal of assistance to Chinese management education, 11
UT (University of Toronto): Chinese studies at, 36; Institute of Women's Studies and Gender Studies at, 288–90; later collaborative projects, 25; linkage with Huazhong University of Science and Technology, 82; mentioned 17, 168; other university linkages, 178–80; partnership with the Guangzhou Institute of Geography, 168–72; partnership with the IGSNRR, 24–6, 168–78, 180–6. *See also* Hsiung, Ping-chun; Transitional Year Program (TYP); UTSC
UTSC (University of Toronto Scarborough): in Canada-China collaboration, 287; Sexual Harassment Office (SHO) at, 290. *See also* UT
UWO (University of Western Ontario), 12, 31n1, 82

Vahlne, Jan-Erik, 126
values: academic, 50, 105, 107; Canadian cultural, 29, 37, 42, 50; Chinese cultural, 18, 50; conflicting, 50, 220; dialogue regarding, 27, 50

Waincymer, Jeff, 259
Walls, Jan W., 30, 188, 190–207
Wang Guiping, 178
Wang Jiayi, 30, 230–53, 309, 310
Wang Ying, 298–9
Wang Yingluo, 81, 92, 93, 96, 100n1
Wangjiagou Experimental Basin, 172–8
water conservation, Canada-China collaboration in, 24, 178–80, 186
West China School of Public Health at Sichuan University, 301
White, Rodney, 175
Whitney, Joseph, 168, 172, 167–89

Wilfrid Laurier University, 298
Williams, Peter, 198, 199
Women and Development: The Role of Women and Their Contributions to Social, Economic and Environmental Development, 195
women and higher education in China and Canada, 279. *See also* gender studies in China
Women and Minorities as Educational Change Agents, 218, 231–2, 237–8, 278–9
Women and Social Development, 241
women entrepreneurship, 88, 99
women's NGOs in China, 282, 286, 296. *See also* Shaanxi Association for Women and Family (SAWF)
women's organizing, 293, 294
women's studies program development, Canada-China collaboration in, 287–91
Wong, Edy, 92
Wong, Renita, 287
Woo, Margaret Y. K., 268n15, 270n27
Workshop on Chinese Women Organizing, 278, 291–4, 295
World Bank: effect on China by, 27, 42; loans to Chinese universities from, 24; projects by, 17, 64, 180; support of Chinese Universities after the Tiananmen event by, 5
Wu Kangning, 240
Wuhan University, 86, 262, 264, 266

Xi Youmin, 30, 102–24, 110, 115, 130
Xi'an Jiaotong University. *See* XJTU
Xi'an Jiaotong-Liverpool University in Suzhou, 15, 30, 91
Xi'an Workshop, 278–87, 294, 296

Xiada (Xiamen University): brain drain from, 13; CCMEP at, 11, 12; early MBA at, 12; feedback from scholars at, 11–14; linkage with Dalhousie University, 12, 13, 82; linkage with UdeM, 266; Management College at, 12, 13
Xiamen Institute. *See* National Accounting Institute in Xiamen
Xiamen University. *See* Xiada
Xiang Bing, 110, 115
Xingguo, China, 181–6
XJTU (Xi'an Jiaotong University): after/during CCMEP, 86; during CCHEP, 88; linkage with U of A, 14–15, 81–5, 88, 98, 110; ranking in China, 15, 92, 305; School of Management at, 82, 92, 93, 110, 114, 120; selection of joint PhD candidates by, 85; visits to, 96

Yang Guangfu, 200–1
Yao Ling, 141–66
Yao Qingyin, 168
Yinnan Prefecture in Ningxia, 193
York University, 14, 82
Yuan Guilin, 250
Yunnan Province, 190, 193, 194

Zha Qiang, 66, 3–32, 133, 193, 211–29
Zhang Dongsheng, 185
Zhang Xiaofeng, 102–24
Zhang Xiaojun, 102–24
Zhao Chunjun, 130
Zhao Jun, 267n4
Zhao Ziyang, 80
Zhejiang University, 157
Zheng Xinrong, 241, 248, 250
Zhongnan University of Economics and Law, 260, 262

Zhou Enlai, former premier of the PRC, 37
Zhou Yongming, 300
Zhu Haibing, 198–9
Zhuhai, China, 303
Zou Keyuan, 256, 267n6, 268n9